To Have and to Hit

• the role of extended family (mainly mothers- & daughter in-laws)

• stigmas of divorce

• stereotypes of men & women

• preference for sons; the burdens of daughters (financial, sexual control)

TO HAVE AND TO HIT

Cultural Perspectives on Wife Beating

SECOND EDITION

Edited by
Dorothy Ayers Counts,
Judith K. Brown,
and Jacquelyn C. Campbell

UNIVERSITY OF ILLINOIS PRESS
URBANA AND CHICAGO

To Beatrice B. Whiting,
with admiration, gratitude, and friendship,
and to those women around the world
who are being beaten and those trying to help them

This book is printed on acid-free paper.

The first edition of this book was published by Westview Press in 1992
as *Sanctions and Sanctuary: Cultural Perspectives on the Beating of Wives.*

Library of Congress Cataloging-in-Publication Data
To have and to hit : cultural perspectives on wife beating / edited by Dorothy Ayers Counts,
Judith K. Brown, and Jacquelyn C. Campbell. — 2nd ed.
p. cm.
Includes bibliographical references and index.
ISBN 0-252-02481-8 (cloth)
ISBN 0-252-06797-5 (pbk.)
1. Wife abuse—Developing countries—Cross-cultural studies.
I. Campbell, Jacquelyn.
II. Counts, Dorothy Ayers.
III. Sanctions and sanctuary.
IV. Brown, Judith K.
HV6626.23.D44T6 1999
362.82'92—dc21 98-58070
CIP

1 2 3 4 5 C P 5 4 3 2 1

CONTENTS

FOREWORD TO THE SECOND EDITION

Harriet D. Lyons

When the first edition of this book appeared in 1992, it was a daring volume to publish. It still is. Anthropologists who wish to study maltreatment of women cross-culturally are stuck between the proverbial rock and its corresponding hard place. To state the facts risks violating anthropology's hard-won tradition of cultural relativism; to minimize the problem may be a betrayal of legions of abused women. This may well help to explain why this book has had few, if any, imitators. Because of its distinctive strengths, the volume remains the benchmark work in its field. The attention to relative frequency of a given behavior is an important aspect of comparative research, one that we would have missed if the editors had not had the courage to take on this project.

Reading the essays in this collection, one is struck by two things: the wealth of ethnographic detail and the skill with which each author integrates the data on wife abuse into a total cultural setting. This is important for two reasons: the cultural embeddedness goes a long way toward avoiding ethnocentrism, and the links between wife abuse and other social facts suggest patterns that may have major import for our global understanding of a worldwide social problem. These features are enhanced by the inclusion of essays that offer explanations for the infrequency or absence of wife beating in certain societies, including some where wife beating is officially accepted (see the essays by William E. Mitchell, Jill Nash, Virginia Kerns, Lauris McKee, and Michael Lambek). This variation is important because otherwise the wide distribution of wife beating, and of ideology supporting it, might lead one to think we are dealing with a more or less unchangeable fact of human nature, particularly as this book includes an excellent essay by Karen Keljo Tracy and Charles B. Crawford on the possible evolutionary significance of violence in primate mating situations.

A number of themes occur in the various societies described with sufficient consistency to consider them as cross-culturally valid patterns. Perhaps the most salient of these, emphasized by Judith K. Brown in her introduction, which also provides a useful review of the theoretical literature on wife beating, is the tendency for wife abuse to be absent or lessened in severity when a woman has close kin living nearby. Where this is a usual situation there may be lessened violence toward women; where it is infrequent, wife beating may be general, sometimes with serious injuries as a result. In some cases, even relatives who do not live nearby may be sought out as a refuge or be called to come to a kinswoman's home to intervene. Neighbors may, in some cases, stand in for kin until they can be summoned. This is significant for a number of reasons. As Brown indicates, it has been noted in European and North American studies of domestic violence that isolation is a major predictive factor in determining risk for spousal violence; the studies in this volume make it clear that this is the case in many other societies as well. It is important, in considering this pattern, to maintain a culturally sensitive approach. For example, in several of the studies, women achieve and sustain the support of their kin by acting as "proper" wives and mothers: kin or neighbors may not come to the aid of an adulteress or someone perceived to be lazy or too much of a scold. Furthermore, in many cases relatives or bystanders will not intervene to stop or prevent violence per se but only violence that they perceive as going beyond culturally approved bounds. Dorothy Ayers Counts's essay on wife beating in Kaliai, Papua New Guinea, pays attention to the complexity of factors that may be involved in separating accepted from unacceptable violence and the multiple techniques employed to prevent the latter. This essay and Nancy McDowell's on household violence in a Yuat River Village are particularly concerned to demonstrate the multiplicity of cultural norms implicated in domestic violence, though virtually all the essays stress this to some degree.

Because of the frequency of this pattern, the volume makes a distinction between wife beating and wife battering, with battering defined as a beating that is sufficiently severe to cause injury or death. In a summary essay, Jacquelyn C. Campbell explains this distinction in anticipation of likely objections to it. Although wife beating is not a cultural universal, it is much more common, at both the individual and societal level, than wife battering. Cultures that accept, and even advocate, wife beating may be strongly opposed to wife battering. The sanctions against husbands and the sanctuary for wives, to which the title of the first edition of this book referred, are much more likely to be available in cases of battering than in instances where beating is not sufficiently severe to maim or kill. Campbell assures readers that the distinction is not meant to imply that wife beating is more acceptable to the authors than battering but rather that the difference is sufficient that battering can be treated as a theoretically useful variable. Wife beating, by contrast, is much closer to being a constant and is therefore resistant to correlations with other factors.

Many feminists will find *any* level of violence against women intolerable and will be unimpressed by careful attempts to determine what is and is not accepted in another culture. Indeed, this position of nontolerance of wife abuse is slowly coming to be the official legal position even in countries like Papua New Guinea, where wife beating has been an accepted practice among many cultural groups. It is widely recognized, however, that official positions and enforcement are very different things, especially where policemen and judges beat their own wives or expect that such behavior will be a normal part of the marital relationship. Nonetheless, to refuse to engage with the topic of acceptable and unacceptable domestic assault is to neglect information that may be important in understanding how women may be protected from serious injury or death.

Intervention is made more likely by the open living patterns in many of the societies discussed in this volume, where violence cannot be hidden readily behind closed doors. Again, we have evidence that isolation is one of the most significant factors putting women at risk. Another significant element in assessing the cross-cultural status of women is that docile or subordinate behavior may be a consciously employed strategy to ensure support from one's kin in time of need. On the one hand, this may be viewed as an instance of women being intimidated into subservience; on the other, it indicates that women do employ conscious strategies to protect themselves, even in the most male-dominated cultures. It might also be added that several essays refer to situations in which women use violence against men with some cultural tolerance, though this appears to be much less frequent than male violence against women, particularly as an approved method of control. Where legal protection is available, women do attempt to access it under some circumstances, though they may be reluctant to do so for a number of reasons: fear of losing the income of a husband in jail; the desire not to provoke anger that will eventually lead to further abuse; fear of loss of support from relatives if the family is shamed; and, finally, the perception that the local legal system cannot or will not do much to help them. As these considerations figure into use of the legal system by abused women in countries where wife abuse has been the subject of extensive attention by social scientists, this cross-cultural data may corroborate claims that, though the law may sometimes be useful, it is not generally organized in a manner helpful to women in distress. Jean Zorn's essay on international law and the culture of domestic violence, which is new to this second edition, discusses changes in international law as a factor in changing cultural norms regarding spouse abuse. Zorn argues that relativism should not blind us to the fact that all cultures are subject to change and that legal change can facilitate changes in custom that are favorable to women.

One factor that emerges as relevant to the incidence and severity of wife beating in many cultures will undoubtedly appear quite foreign to readers in North America and Europe: namely, the role played by perceived supernatural influence. Supernatural forces enter into domestic conflict in several ways, according to some of the essays in this volume. Men or women may threaten their spouses with sorcery or other supernatural vengeance. This may act as a check on the incidence and violence of physical assault or be employed as a substitute mechanism of control. Where women are believed to be polluting—for example, during menstruation—they may use men's fear of such contamination as a barrier against spousal violence. All of these supernatural components are relevant to wife beating in Kaliai, according to Counts.

The role played by the supernatural taxes relativism in several ways. For instance, while some of the essays mention that women may be protected where men will resort to curses or spells rather than fists, it is important to remember that the supernatural threat is real enough in cultures that find it credible and that a person receiving such a threat may perceive herself to be truly assaulted. By contrast, women also use, or are believed to use, supernatural forces against men or other women, particularly co-wives or in-laws. Laurence Marshall Carucci, in his essay on displays of disfranchisement on Ujelang Atoll, sees female use of malevolent magic as a substitute for masculine physical strength. In some cases supernatural powers may give women a weapon against violence; in other instances, some of them familiar from European history, suspicion of malign supernatural power may itself provoke violence against women. In one case my husband and I observed during our fieldwork in Benin City, Nigeria, a woman showed us bruises she said she had received because her husband and his kin suspected her, unjustly, of witchcraft. The fear of female pollution is also double-edged: its use as a mechanism to keep violent husbands at a safe distance is dependent on a view of women as dangerous and unclean, which may serve as an important element in ideologies justifying men's right to discipline and control such threatening beings. In any event, the complex relationship these essays reveal between belief systems and domestic violence indicates that changes in beliefs, which are inevitable in modernizing communities, may have unpredictable effects on women's safety. The findings should also serve as a cautionary tale for reformers who assume that eliminating negative beliefs about women will necessarily improve the conditions under which women live.

Other effects of modernization may also worsen women's risk of serious abuse. Western-style settlements typically offer more privacy than traditional living arrangements. Patricia Draper, in her essay on !Kung women, notes that two of the four instances of wife beating she recorded during her fieldwork took place in comparatively modern settings: in one instance, bystanders claimed that the noise and crowding at a tavern diminished their ability to hear and observe the beating. Draper also provides us with an exception to a general rule (discussed below) that older women are less likely to be badly beaten than younger women, though her example underscores the role of kin in protecting women from serious injury. Two of the incidents she reports involved older women who, she says, were vulnerable because they had no living parents to protect them and lacked the adult sons who would normally replace parents in this role.

The tendency for the extended family to give way to increased nucleation may reduce the support women can count on, and labor migration and other changes in patterns of employment will alter not only the relationship between husbands and wives but also between women and the families on whom they often rely for protection. Among the Wape of New Guinea, as they are described in the essay by Mitchell, one can imagine that desirable improvements in adult and juvenile health would actually result in increased violence: the author suggests that lassitude resulting from poor nutrition may be a factor in the generally low level of violence in the society, not only between men and women, but between parents and children and among children themselves.

As has been suggested, the extended kin groups that protect women can themselves be a source of both empowerment and abuse. In some societies, like those described in this volume for Indo-Fijians, as well as in India, Taiwan, and the Middle East, women are much less likely to suffer abuse in the later stages of marriage. In such cases, as Brown's introduction and the essays by Mary Elaine Hegland, Barbara Diane Miller, Shireen Lateef, and Rita S. Gallin make clear, significant abuse suffered by young women may be meted out not by men but by senior women, generally mothers-in-law, who are often charged with maintaining family discipline and honor in cultures that place a high value on female chastity and modesty. (The tendency toward the relative empowerment of women in later life is documented more extensively in *In Her Prime* [Kerns and Brown 1992], a collection of essays on menopausal women in which several of the contributors to this volume were also involved.) The fact that this newfound power is often executed over younger women, sometimes violently, to "keep them in line" may make it seem to be a divisive rather than a solidary factor so far as women as a group are concerned, but *To Have and to Hit* makes it clear that older women also use their power, quite regularly, to protect young wives from severe battering. Lateef mentions one mother-in-law who, though she may have incited her son to beat his wife, intervened when she felt he had gone too far.

Another difficult issue raised in this volume is the question of female suicide as a response to abuse. Counts notes that among the Kaliai suicide is sometimes a tragic outcome of wife beating but that suicide threats or attempts can deter a husband from further violence or mobilize a woman's kin to act on her behalf. By contrast, Lateef suggests that Indo-Fijian women commit suicide when they can no longer endure abuse, achieving only escape and some posthumous sympathy.

Alcohol is a factor in wife abuse whose significance is much debated in the North American literature. Several of the essays in this volume mention drunkenness as a precipitating factor in specific incidents of domestic violence, but they also point out that the total social and personal context in which abuse takes place, especially ideology concerning the proper behavior of men and women, to some degree construct the responses of individuals to inebriation. Victoria Burbank's essay on interpersonal aggression in an Aboriginal community sets alcohol and abuse in a broader context, as does Lateef's essay.

Both Burbank's and Lateef's essays also contain the interesting assertion that women sometimes find a beating to be a regrettable but acceptable price for not capitulating to male wishes, though Lateef stresses that this is a likely equation only in situations where women are not economically dependent on their husbands or in-laws. Counts speaks of enduring an expected beating as a conscious strategy a woman in Kaliai may employ to gain more freedom from male control.

One essay new to this volume first appeared in a special issue of *Pacific Studies* on the topic of domestic violence in Oceania (Counts 1990). Richard Scaglion provides detailed case histories of several family relationships—both marital and kin—in Abelam society that involve violence. The Abelam appear to accept that women require occasional physical punishment from husbands, older brothers, or uncles to discipline them, particularly for sexual misbehavior. Violence against women by male kin appears not to be very severe, and marriages are likely to break up if the violence is greater than the woman or her kin perceive to be just. Scaglion makes the interesting observation that while the Abelam accept levels of violence against women that would be regarded as abusive in North America, they would be deeply disapproving of the degree of physical punishment of children accepted as appropriate by most residents of Canada or the United States. The Abelam, like most of the other societies discussed in the book, recognize that some men are prone to repeated and severe violence against women, a phenomenon familiar to North Americans and Europeans. Abelam women are encouraged by their kin to leave such men, a pattern that is relatively recent and by no means universal in the West.

In her introduction Brown expresses the contributors' hope that this volume's "new information and enlarged perspective will call attention to the worldwide plight of battered wives, promote their cause, and further the efforts of those working to eliminate the abuse of women." There can be little doubt that *Sanctions and Sanctuary* did just that. We can expect, with every confidence that this new edition will continue to aid in this worthy objective.

REFERENCES CITED

Counts, Dorothy Ayers, ed. 1990. *Domestic Violence in Oceania.* Special issue of *Pacific Studies* 13 (3).

Kerns, Virgnia, and Judith K. Brown, eds. 1992. *In Her Prime: New Views of Middle-Aged Women.* 2d ed. Urbana: University of Illinois Press.

FOREWORD TO THE FIRST EDITION

David Levinson

When Jacquelyn C. Campbell asked me to write this foreword, my first thought was, "I wish this collection had been published two years earlier." My wish for earlier publication was selfish, as in 1988 I was churning through the ethnographic literature looking for information about spousal violence and detailed descriptions of wife-beating events in non-Western societies. Although I eventually found enough information to survey violence between spouses in ninety societies, it was obvious that spousal violence is a topic that is often ignored or given only passing attention by ethnographers. *Sanctions and Sanctuary* is a significant step in filling this gap in the ethnographic record. Fourteen of the seventeen chapters provide overviews of wife battering (see chapter 1 for the editors' distinction between wife beating and battering) in fourteen different societies and detailed descriptions of wife-battering events and their social context in those societies with battering. While the emphasis is on societies in Melanesia, groups from Central America, South America, Taiwan, the Middle East, and Africa are also covered. But the value of this volume is not in a probability sampling of the world's societies; rather, it is in the rich ethnographic descriptions that indicate the range and diversity of wife battering and its contexts around the world. Thus, societies with frequent, less frequent, infrequent, and no wife battering are included, as are societies in which wife battering is linked to female suicide (a phenomenon largely ignored in Western-based research on family violence) and where women have alternatives that allow them to escape batterings. Reading these chapters gives one a real sense of what might strike some as the surprising variation in the types and frequency of wife battering around the world. They provide information that places wife battering in the political, economic, and social contexts in which it occurs. This is important, since cross-cultural research consistently shows that individual behavior must be interpreted and explained within its broader cultural context. To go one step further, the descriptions here also support, though in an ancedotal way, previous cross-cultural findings on the relationship between battering and economic and political inequalities between men and women.

While the detailed ethnographies are the major strength and contribution of this collection, it is far more than just a compendium of descriptions. The three more-analytical chapters (1, 2, and 18) provide conceptual and theoretical contexts that place the description in more general frameworks including prior cross-cultural research, evolutionary biology, and Western-based research. Additionally, because the authors followed the same general outline in organizing their ethnographic information, the chapters tend to flow and complement one another, no mean achievement in an edited volume.

Beyond informing, this collection also stimulates the reader to think about and study topics and issues perhaps ignored in earlier cross-cultural and single-culture studies of family violence. These include the aftermath of family violence: the feelings and responses of the victims, the perpetrators, and the community; the distinction between socially acceptable and unacceptable violence in the family context; the role of social change over time and place; and the emotion of "anger" from a cross-cultural perspective.

To sum up, this collection adds valuable information to the growing cross-cultural literature on family violence. These descriptions of wife battering in fifteen cultures need to be considered by any serious student of family violence, whether his or her interests are descriptive, conceptual, theoretical, or applied. The book also serves as a model for other such collections on other topics, through the consistency in coverage from chapter to chapter and the integration of the data into broader perspectives.

PREFACE

Dorothy Ayers Counts

The conversations and symposia resulting in both editions of this book began in 1985 when I returned from Papua New Guinea newly aware of the problem of wife beating in that country. In an effort to learn how other anthropologists had dealt with incidents of wife abuse and domestic violence in the societies they had studied, I looked for books and articles on the topic. When I found almost no anthropological discussion of wife beating or battering, I called on Judith K. Brown for help. Because of her long interest and considerable expertise in women's issues, I knew that if anyone would be familiar with the anthropological literature on wife beating and battering it would be Judy. Intrigued with the problem, she did her own search of the literature. Her research results were similar to mine; clearly, anthropologists had ignored or had glossed over with throwaway one-liners a topic of great importance to women. In an effort to bring the problem to the attention of other anthropologists, we called on our colleagues who had data on wife beating and battering in societies where they had worked to share their experiences and insights with us. To this end, Judy and I coorganized a session on wife beating at the 1987 meetings of the American Anthropological Association, and I organized a series of sessions and a symposium at the Association for Social Anthropology in Oceania meetings in 1986, 1987, and 1988. Many, but not all, of the chapters in this volume were presented at one or more of these sessions. Jacquelyn C. Campbell, who published one of the first cross-cultural studies on wife beating and who has conducted research on and had practical experience with shelters for battered women, participated in the American Anthropological Association meetings, after which she joined us as a coeditor.

The reactions of some of our colleagues when we began to discuss wife beating and battering as a cross-cultural problem give us insight into why anthropologists have until very recently either ignored domestic violence or given it only summary treatment. Some argued that we should not exploit our hosts' hospitality by exposing a dark side of their culture; others said that they would talk about the problem but they would not publish on it because they feared such publication would result in their being denied permission to return to the field. Some were concerned that their informants might be punished if it were known that they had discussed the subject with an outsider. One woman told me that she was publishing, as fiction and under a pseudonym, a collection of accounts of wife beating from the African society where she had worked for many years. She was publishing in this way because she believed that if she wrote under her own name her informants could be identified, and she feared for their lives. Others argued that if we raised the topic we would be imposing our political agenda on other societies with results that might be harmful to them. One colleague—an indigenous member of one of the societies being discussed—argued that the topic of domestic violence should not be examined. He feared that if women were encouraged to protest traditional gender roles in marriage—including the right of husbands to beat their wives—the institution of marriage would be destabilized and family life in his society would suffer.

These concerns point up a dilemma faced by anthropologists. On the one hand, the people of other cultures may use standards that are very different from ours to define what constitutes acceptable—or unacceptable—behavior. By the standards of some societies there may be no category of illegitimate wife beating, and the people of that society—women as well as men—may reason that the stability of their society rests on the continuation of long-accepted practices grounded in the teachings of their ancestors or in religious doctrine. As anthropologists we must concede this, and most of us try not to judge other people by the values of our society or to suggest that they should conform to ideals that arise from our culture—ideals that we preach but may not practice. We respect the right of other peoples to hold values different from our own, and it is not our place to criticize them for behavior that is acceptable in their society but is unacceptable and the subject of political agendas in our own. On the other hand, we are uncomfortable with analyses that are restricted to describing and explaining violence toward women and with explanations that seem almost to justify practices that we personally find abhorrent—practices that may result in the suffering, maiming, suicide, or murder of women who have befriended us and whom we care for and respect. We are caught between our own ethnocentrism, on the one hand, and the sterile aloofness of extreme relativism, on the other.

There is no easy solution to this dilemma. However, it is appropriate to note that while we must not apply our own values to and pass judgment on behavior that is not seen as deviant or abusive by the majority of the people of a community, many of the people—men as well as women—in the societies where anthropologists work do perceive domestic violence in general and wife beating and battering in particular to be a problem. Leaders in these societies welcome discussion, for solutions to such problems can be found only after those problems are publicly admitted and a dialogue begun. In Papua New Guinea, for example, the national government is aware of the personal, social, and economic costs of wife beating and battering. Consequently, it has supported efforts by the Women and Law Committee, the Law Reform Commission of Papua New Guinea, and concerned private citizens to educate men and children about alternatives to violence and to make women aware of their rights if they are beaten. It is our hope that this volume will contribute in some small way to a search for successful sanctions against wife beating and battering and the establishment of sanctuaries for abused women in our own societies and in the communities that have been our hosts.

We wish to express our thanks to all our colleagues who participated in the symposium on wife beating at the American Anthropological Association meetings and in the Association for Social Anthropology in Oceania sessions on domestic violence. Dale Robertson, editor of *Pacific Studies,* generously gave permission for us to include in this volume essays by Laurence Marshall Carucci, Shireen Lateef, Nancy McDowell, Jill Nash, William E. Mitchell, and Richard Scaglion that previously appeared in 1990 in a special issue of that journal (vol. 13, no. 3). We greatly appreciate his cooperation and his willingness to do whatever was necessary to help this edition toward publication.

The editors are indebted to George Preisinger for making changes to the map he drafted for the first edition. He was courteous and prompt: a pleasure to work with. We also wish to thank Elizabeth Dulany, our editor at the University of Illinois Press. Without her support, encouragement, and patience this edition would never have seen the light.

To Have and to Hit

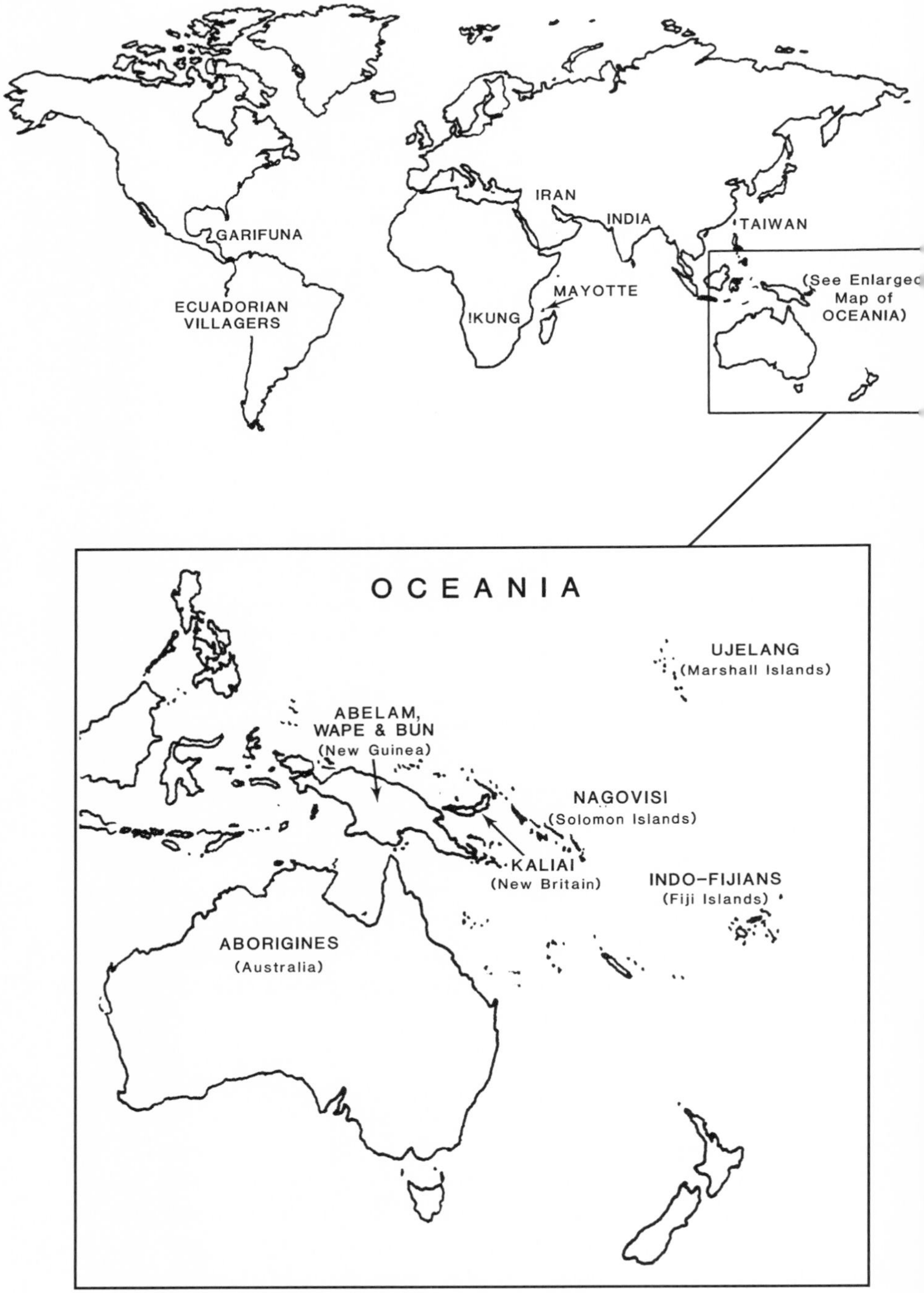
GARIFUNA
ECUADORIAN VILLAGERS
IRAN
INDIA
TAIWAN
MAYOTTE
!KUNG
(See Enlarged Map of OCEANIA)
OCEANIA
UJELANG
(Marshall Islands)
ABELAM, WAPE & BUN
(New Guinea)
NAGOVISI
(Solomon Islands)
KALIAI
(New Britain)
INDO-FIJIANS
(Fiji Islands)
ABORIGINES
(Australia)

ONE

Introduction: Definitions, Assumptions, Themes, and Issues

Judith K. Brown

Our purpose in putting together this collection of essays is to provide a unique and innovative perspective on wife beating, a complex problem that has only in the last two decades generated public concern in Euro-American society. These ethnographic explorations (largely firsthand) present an overview of customs in a variety of cultures and are supplemented by evidence for analogous behavior among nonhuman primates. Descriptive information is drawn from societies that vary in the prevalence and severity of reported wife beating, are located in widely scattered geographic areas, and range in complexity from hunter-gatherer to horticultural (with special emphasis on Melanesia, a culture area in which wife beating has been widely reported) to industrializing. All of those who have contributed to this volume hope that this information and enlarged perspective will call attention to the worldwide plight of battered wives, promote their cause, and further the efforts of those working to eliminate the abuse of women.

This introduction begins by providing some definitions and assumptions shared by the contributors. Next, a brief review of previous cross-cultural studies is presented and other promising areas of research are suggested. The chapters are then introduced, and a final section identifies the themes and issues raised by the contributors.

Definitions and Assumptions

Most earlier cross-cultural studies have dealt with more than one type of family violence. The subject of this volume is restricted to wife beating, which will be defined as a man intentionally inflicting pain on a woman, within a nontransient, male-female relationship, whether or not the partners are officially married. The subject is further restricted to physical aggression, because it can be identified unambiguously. Psychological abuse, verbal assault, threats, intimidation, calumny, humiliating ridicule, emotional blackmail, and extortion are no doubt as pervasive and may be as injurious as a physical attack. However, nonphysical aggression is not as readily amenable to observation by an outsider, particularly by an ethnographer from another society.

Care must be exercised to distinguish between wife beating and wife battering.[1] This is an important difference, although an unfamiliar one in U.S. society, where almost all of what is labeled as wife beating is actually wife battering. The distinction had its beginning in an exchange between Erchak (1984) and Gibbs (1984), the first dialogue on husband-to-wife aggression to appear in a major anthropological journal. (For further elaboration of the difference, see Counts 1992a.)

In many nonindustrial societies, husbands beat their wives in what Beatrice Whiting (personal communication 1986) refers to as a "physical reprimand." Where such behavior is customary, it is viewed as unremarkable. The distinction between wife beating and wife battering is necessary to accommodate data from these societies, where men who beat their wives are not "abnormal" or "deviant" but merely behaving in a culturally expected manner. The women in these societies are not meek and accepting. They are compelled to tolerate such treatment but would decidedly prefer husbands who do not beat them (Counts this volume). Wife battering, by contrast, is something extraordinary, possibly resulting in severe injury, incapacitation, or even death. In most instances, such behavior is not viewed as usual or acceptable by members of the society and elicits intervention by a third party or parties. The distinction does not depend entirely on the response of others to the assault but also on the extent of the aggression, since in some instances even the murder of wives provokes no reaction (see below).

A full explanation of aggression against wives must include not only sociocultural but also psychological variables. It must indicate whether the individual's behavior is the result of psychophysical factors—such as alcoholism (Leonard and Jacob 1988) or neurological disorders (Elliott 1988)—or of a particular life history. Psychological reasons for wife beating and wife battering are largely independent of cultural variables. Thus, even societies in which wife beating and wife battering are reported as virtually absent and as strongly disapproved are not immune to the presence of the occasional brutal individual who ill treats his wife for idiosyncratic reasons. (The analysis of psychological variables is beyond the scope of this volume.) It is therefore assumed that wife beating is universal, but its incidence in any particular society can range from being an extremely rare, individual matter to being a frequent and regular occurrence; and the severity can range from mild to actual murder. Frequency and severity of wife beating vary independently (Kerns this volume).

In U.S. society there is supposed disapproval of both wife beating and wife battering. However, this is no deterrent, since American men seem to perceive the sanctions as neither certain nor severe, according to a chilling study by Carmody and Williams (1987). Some societies share our disapproval of wife beating and wife battering and negatively sanction both. Other societies condone wife beating and may even view it as necessary, but wife battering is disapproved, rare, or self-defeating. (This pattern is particularly appropriate for a society in which women make a major contribution to subsistence.[2] Husbands physically chastise women for poor work performance and other shortcomings, but a woman's injury or incapacitation would work a hardship on her kin, including her husband, whose physical survival depends on her productivity.) The third pattern is one in which neither wife beating nor wife battering is disapproved, and even the murder of a wife may go unpunished, as in the murders of wives in Brazil (*60 Minutes* transcript 1988) and the dowry murders in India (Claiborne 1984; Bordewich 1986; Miller this volume). In a number of these societies, mothers-in-law instigate and take part in the aggression against young wives (see below). Women contribute little to subsistence in such societies, but their vulnerability is not the result of economic factors alone. Wifely behavior that elicits a beating or battering can vary from the inadequate performance of duties, such as a late or poorly prepared meal, to practicing sorcery; from immodesty, suspected infidelity, and actual adultery to the ill treatment of a child, a co-wife, or the children of a co-wife; from insolence toward affines to disobedience and insubordination (Counts 1990a, 1992a; Lateef this volume.) The latter two wifely offenses are widely viewed as egregious and are punished with the extreme severity typical of righteous indignation (Mushanga 1977–78). Surprisingly, disproportionate vehemence and violent rage are seen as justified because of the firm belief that the entire social fabric would unravel if such wifely behavior were countenanced. A wife's assertiveness or her flirtations with autonomy are viewed as equivalent to insurrection and as a threat against the sacred social order.

Some Previous Cross-Cultural Studies: A Brief Review

For a variety of reasons, anthropologists typically strive to paint "their" village in a favorable light (Counts 1990a, 1990b). The result is that the ethnographic literature provides scant data on unlovable behavior such as wife beating (an imbalance this volume attempts to rectify). Nevertheless, a number of cross-cultural studies have made use of the relative frequency of wife beating as a variable in testing hypotheses using a sample of nonindustrial societies. (Cross-national studies dealing with Euro-American industrialized societies will not be reviewed here.) The validity of the conclusions of cross-cultural studies depends on the statistical significance of the findings, the appropriateness of the test statistic, the size and selection of the sample societies, and ultimately the quality of the ethnographic data reported for those societies on the variables under consideration. It is the latter factor most especially that is open to question in the studies to be reviewed below. This note of caution concerning possible variation in the validity of the original data should be kept in mind.

Early Correlational Studies Using a Worldwide Sample

As early as 1962, John W. M. Whiting and his co-workers at Harvard University's Palfrey House had devised a set of codes for wife beating, based on data for seventy-one societies described in the Human Relations Area Files. Slater and Slater (1965) and Lester (1980) utilize these ratings. For Slater and Slater, frequency of wife beating is one of a series of variables that are positively and significantly correlated with "narcissism," the subject of their research. Lester's article is one of several that seeks to find a relationship between the presence of wife beating and other indices of aggression at the societal level. He also examines the relationship of "the oppression of women" and the frequency of divorce to wife beating and concludes that wife beating is more prevalent where the divorce rate is high, where women's status is inferior, and where cruelty and aggression are not uncommon occurrences. His article is extremely brief and reports only the significance of various correlations. The sources of the codes of the antecedent variables are not always given, nor is there information on the size and composition of the samples for each of the reported correlations. Like Lester, Masumura (1979) examines the relationship of wife beating to other forms of aggressive behavior such as homicide and personal crime. A much fuller account than Lester's, Masumura's article nevertheless does not identify his eighty-six sample societies. Masumura concludes that the significant correlation between wife abuse and other forms of aggression may be due to underlying factors such as sexual jealousy and the possibility that certain societies are violence prone. For two other early cross-cultural studies, Naroll (1969) and Schlegel (1972), wife beating is not a central focus but one of many variables in research concerned with aspects of methodology and with "the sick society," in the case of Naroll, and "female autonomy," in the case of Schlegel. Whiting and Whiting (1975) allude to the Palfrey House ratings in their study of intimacy and aloofness in marriage. These characteristics of marriage are unrelated to wife beating. However, the Whitings suggest a relationship between wife beating and the degree of isolation of the married pair. They note that "there is safety in numbers," an important observation to be discussed below and confirmed in several of the chapters that follow.

Using a subsample of forty-six societies from the Human Relations Area Files Probability Sample Files, Levinson (1981) examines the correlation between wife beating and the use of physical punishment to discipline children, testing one portion of the hypothesis suggested by Straus: "violence in one family role is associated with violence in other family roles" (1977:721). Levinson's findings, though statistically significant, only partially support the hypothesis. Although both forms of intrafamilial violence tend to be rare in some societies, the predicted relationship between frequent use of physical punishment and frequent wife beating is not borne out. Most societies that scored "common" or "frequent" on wife beating scored "rare" or "infrequent" on physical punishment of children.

The last of the earlier cross-cultural studies using a worldwide sample coded for wife beating was conducted by Broude and Greene (1983). Using Murdock and White's Standard Cross-Cultural Sample of 186 societies plus 15 alternate societies, the authors were able to find information on wife beating for only seventy-one cases, and in fifty-seven wife beating was coded as "present." They created seventeen scales to measure nonsexual aspects of the relationship between husbands and wives, such as how marriages are arranged, customs pertaining to newlyweds, attitudes toward and ease of divorce. Of all these variables, only one—remarrying widows having their husbands chosen for them—was significantly related to wife beating. This single finding could be the result of chance and suggests that wife beating in many societies may have little to do with the nonsexual relationship between husbands and wives (as is suggested below).

Previous Studies Using Anecdotal Cross-Cultural Evidence

Several earlier studies have used cross-cultural evidence concerning wife beating in a less-quantified and less-systematic way. For example, Mushanga (1977–78) provides a descriptive study (considered more fully below) that presents data only from sub-Sahara Africa. Straus (1977) uses anecdotal anthropological evidence in support of his hypotheses concerning intrafamilial violence. (As noted above, Levinson (1981) tests one of these cross-culturally.) Straus suggests "near universality" for intrafamilial violence (which includes wife beating) but cautions that its actual prevalence is not fully known. His basic conclusion is that "the level of physical aggression in the conjugal relationship tends to be isomorphic with the level of physical aggression in nonfamily spheres of life" (1977:724). He also argues that the level of violence in the husband-wife relationship is "isomorphic" with the level of violence in the parent-child relationship. Straus's use of the ethnographic literature seems somewhat haphazard. He does not explain the basis for his choice of tribal examples or why he uses particular sources (e.g., citing information on the !Kung from Irenäus Eibl-Eibesfeldt rather than from the classic works by Lorna Marshall, Patricia Draper, or Richard Lee). The ethnographic literature, vast and somewhat uncharted for the nonanthropologist, contains more- and less-reliable sources. Ethnographic examples are convincing only when their choice is explained and when sources are evaluated.

Steinmetz (1981) conducted a study using questionnaires on individuals from a sample of six societies, examining among other variables the frequency and severity of marital abuse. The questionnaire is described as "structured," and her brief article does not include examples of the questions. The sample size for each society varies, and there is no information on the conditions under which the tests were administered, how the subjects were chosen, or how the protocols were scored. No tests of significance appear in the tables that accompany the article. Steinmetz rightly concludes that the study raises more questions than it answers. A three-way comparison among India, Ireland, and the United States, conducted by Tellis-Nayak and Donoghue (1982), attempts to relate marital violence to the structuring of decision-making authority. The research design, the quality of the data, and the method of analysis are such as to render any of the conclusions tentative at best.

Other Cross-Cultural Studies

Campbell's (1985) important exploratory research differs from all other cross-cultural studies of wife beating because she restricts her sample to societies described by female ethnographers working with female informants. The sample is small, the number of variables examined is extensive, and the results are more suggestive than conclusive. Yet the study is significant for the care with which ethnographic sources were selected and hence for the validity of the data.

Two works by Levinson (1988, 1989) are ambitious cross-cultural studies of various forms of family violence. The first is an anthropological chapter in a major comprehensive handbook on family violence (Van Hasslet et al. 1988) and provides an informed overview for the nonanthropologist. The second, Levinson's more technical, book-length cross-cultural study, is also based on his ongoing, long-range holocultural research. Two elaborate appendexes provide information on methodology and coding. His sample of ninety societies, whose accounts are drawn from the Human Relations Area Files, are identified and the scales on which they were rated are reported. Some of his conclusions: wife beating is more likely in societies in which men control the family wealth, in which conflicts are solved by means of physical violence, and in which women do not have an equal right to obtain a divorce. One finding that invites further investigation: societies characterized by female work groups tend to have infrequent incidences of wife beating. Is there a third variable responsible for this correlation? Are these work groups associated with matrilocal residence, or are they the result of female domination of subsistence activities? Are there other manifestations of women's coalitions and solidarity that may serve as a deterrent to wife beating?

Other Lines of Evidence

Anthropological and cross-cultural data provide only one of several approaches to the phenomenon of wife beating. (The need to consider psychological variables was noted above.) There are three other promising areas of research, one or more of which have influenced several of the chapters that follow. The first is concerned with the psychophysiological aspect of male sexual arousal and response. In their pioneering cross-cultural study of sexual behavior, Ford and Beach (1951) suggest that male sexual excitement may actually be enhanced by aggression (see Miller this volume). Further research on the relation of sexual arousal and aggression, provided by Tannenbaum and Zillmann (1975), and Zillmann (1984, 1986), suggests that there is a neurological reason for the connection between male sexual pleasure and aggression. (Alternatively, both sex and violence provide control over women, and this basically similar motivation may underlie both behaviors, whether or not there is a neurological explanation.) Zillmann's findings are troubling and unwelcome but cannot be ignored. They call attention to the interrelatedness of wife beating, sexual activity, and male sexual performance, a promising area for further research.

The possible relationship between male sexual behavior and wife beating has been overlooked by anthropological research, with one exception: the study by Mushanga (1977–78) dealing with wife "victimization" (which appears to include the murder of wives) in sub-Sahara Africa. The beaten and murdered spouses were not only being insubordinate and untraditional but had been derogatory of their husbands' sexual performance. Mushanga seems to suggest that the women deserved what happened to them.

A second area of promising related research is evolutionary biology. In a complex and wide-ranging chapter, Burgess and Draper (1989) consider a number of variables pertaining to family violence and interpret these in terms of "inclusive fitness," "parental investment," and "paternal certainty." Among mammals, humans are unusual in combining an exclusive sexual partnership with life in heterosexual social groups, rendering paternal certainty problematic. The widespread cultural solutions are: the separation of the sexes in daily life, patriarchal rule (with men also controlling most forms of wealth), and patrilocal residence. In the nonindustrial world, the latter two are far more usual than alternative arrangements. The authors note that in human social groups there is pervasive stress on patriarchal values and the sexual double standard, but Burgess and Draper do not regard these as inevitable, simply because they are in the service of paternal certainty. Although the authors regard marital violence as predictable from the point of view of evolutionary biology, they nevertheless take account of the modifying influence of culture, of social circumstances, and of individual differences.

Daly and Wilson, who have also applied evolutionary biology to the data on wife beating and the murder of wives (Daly et al. 1982; Daly and Wilson 1988a, 1988b), focus on male sexual jealousy, which in their view serves human adaptation by augmenting paternal certainty. They suggest that this explains why there is a qualitative difference between male and female jealousy, why male sexual jealousy is the predominant motive in violence against women, and why male sexual jealousy is a cross-cultural universal. In support of the latter assertion, the authors re-examine previous cross-cultural studies dealing with sexual behavior and explain contradictory evidence as misinterpretations on the part of comparativists. Daly and Wilson did not engage in an independent search for ethnographic data; if they had, they would have discovered negative evidence from South America in Carneiro (1958) and from West Africa in Muller (1969), Netting (1969), and Smedley (1974). Male sexual jealousy appears not to be universal and does not provide the motive for a phenomenon like the notorious dowry murders (Claiborne 1984; Bordewich 1986; Miller this volume).[3] This is not to deny that, in explaining violence against women, male sexual jealousy is indeed an important variable and may very well have originated in the service of human adaptation. However, the expression of male sexual jealousy is molded by culture, by social circumstances, and by personal inclination. Foster's (1972) anthropological study of the related subject of envy suggests some of the complexities in the cross-cultural study of human motives. Daly and Wilson provide an intriguing hypothesis that invites some modifications.

A third area of promising related research is the investigation of aggression against females among nonhuman primates. Both observational studies in the wild (Tracy and Crawford this volume) and laboratory studies give evidence of primate behavior analogous to wife abuse among humans (Nadler 1988; Turkington 1987). Nadler reports that among the great apes mating behavior in the wild follows three distinct patterns, none of which typically includes sexual aggression. However, in a laboratory situation that gave the great ape males free access to a female, sexual behavior did not follow the pattern seen in the wild but took the form of pronounced sexual aggression. In a "limited access test" situation in which the laboratory female was provided with the option of escaping from the males, sexual activity became more like that displayed in the wild and male sexual aggression was obviated. (Apparently, in the wild the female's smaller size gives her an advantage in speed and also makes possible her escape via loftier branches that will not hold the heavier male.) Data from nonhuman primates, even species related as closely to humans as the great apes, must be interpreted with caution, particularly when behavior is artificially induced in a laboratory setting. Nevertheless, the importance of the option to escape from the male is pertinent to the practical need for sheltering among human victims of male violence.

The evidence from studies of nonhuman primate male aggression, the alleged evolutionary significance of marital violence and of male "proprietary jealousy," and the possible neurological connection between male aggression and enhanced male sexual pleasure all raise troubling issues but are not presented here to make aggression against women appear so deep-seated as to be inevitable and unalterable. The purpose is not to provide an apologia for violence against women but rather to underscore the urgency of the worldwide problem of wife beating and wife battering and to suggest that future research may have to encompass more than the traditional social sciences.

Introductory Comments

Drawing on anthropological and ethological data, the ensuing chapters present descriptions of primate behavior as well as ethnographic information from societies that vary in the incidence and severity of wife beating and wife battering. The collection begins with a chapter by Karen Keljo Tracy and Charles B. Crawford that reports observations of male to female aggression among nonhuman primates in the wild. These data in many instances appear strikingly analogous to human behavior. The remaining chapters are arranged according to societal complexity, beginning with hunter-gatherers, moving to horticulturalists, and ending with industrializing societies.

The chapters dealing with rapidly changing hunter-gatherer societies focus on Australian Aborigines (Victoria K. Burbank) and the !Kung of southern Africa (Patricia Draper). The horticultural societies include five from Melanesia: the Lusi speakers of Kaliai (Dorothy Ayers Counts), the villagers of Bun on the Yuat River (Nancy McDowell), the Abelam (Richard Scaglion), the Wape (William E. Mitchell), and the Nagovisi (Jill Nash). This overrepresentation of Melanesia is intentional in order to afford the reader an opportunity for an intraregion comparison between two negative cases, the Nagovisi and the Wape, and three more typical Melanesian cases, the Bun, the Abelam, and the Kaliai, in which wife beating is prevalent.[4] Other horticultural societies represented in this collection include the Marshall Islanders of Micronesia (Laurence Marshall Carucci)[5], the Garífuna of Belize (Virginia Kerns), the mestizo villagers of Ecuador (Lauris McKee), and the Malagasy speakers of Mayotte, an island off the coast of East Africa (Michael Lambek). Somewhat greater societal complexity is represented by the industrializing societies: India (Barbara Diane Miller) and its provincial counterpart among Indo-Fijians (Shireen Lateef) and the villagers of Iran (Mary Elaine Hegland) and Taiwan (Rita S. Gallin).

A summary chapter by Jacquelyn C. Campbell relates the ethological and ethnographic material provided throughout this collection to circumstances in U.S. society and notes implications for action as well as for further research. The final chapter, by Jean G. Zorn, examines the relationship between international law and culture and reports on the effort to broaden international law to include within the concept of human rights the right of women not to be subjected to domestic violence.

Themes and Issues

In U.S. society, the ordinary citizen regards wife beating as evidence that a marital relationship has gone deplorably awry and views the husband's behavior as brutal and unacceptable. But as the following chapters demonstrate, and as suggested above, the perspective provided by ethology and anthropology suggests that matters are far more complicated and involve more than the relationship between spouses and the individual proclivities of the husband. (These two variables are not without importance and bear examination, but as psychological variables they are beyond the scope of this volume.)

Draper (this volume) suggests that a potential for wife beating inheres in the dimorphism of the sexes in humans, a potential that is modified by various cultural factors. Collier (1988) inquires into the nature of inequality and suggests that the right to beat a wife differentiates a woman's relationship to her husband from her relationship to her brother and to her lover. Both authors use very different types of anthropological evidence to imply that the ubiquity of wife beating should be regarded as less remarkable than its infrequency or near absence in some societies. What emerges from the material about to be presented suggests that the prevalence or relative absence of wife beating in any particular society is predictable when certain factors are known. These can be categorized as dealing with aspects of womanhood, the relationship of men to men and women to women, the isolation of wives, and sanctions and sanctuary. Of these, the latter are the most important determinants of the frequency and severity of wife beating and wife battering.

Aspects of Womanhood

In every society, the treatment women receive depends in large part on their age, their economic role, and their acknowledged or denied adulthood. First, older wives, although not immune from ill treatment (Draper this volume), are less likely to be beaten than younger wives (Kerns this volume; McKee this volume).[6] In part this is the result of the greater extradomestic support an older woman can muster: she will have established coalitions within her community, even if she was once an outsider, having moved there as a young bride; and she is likely to have grown children, particularly sons, who will come to her aid. In addition, an older woman's old or middle-aged husband, with lessened energies at his disposal, will be preoccupied with other matters, such as arranging marriages, dealing in politics, accumulating wealth, and gaining supernatural power (Counts 1992b). Second, societies in which women have an important economic role may approve physical reprimand but will not condone the abusive treatment permitted in those societies in which women are viewed as more expendable. Third, women are less likely to be beaten in societies in which they are regarded as autonomous adults (Kerns this volume; Lambek this volume).

Relationships of Women to Women and Men to Men

In many societies the prevalence of wife beating has less to do with the relationship between the partners than with the relationship among a society's women or the position of the husband in the dominance hierarchy of the male peer group or the standing of the husband's kinship group in the community. On the one hand, the relationship among women can exert a positive influence on how wives are treated. Research as diverse as Levinson's (1989) cross-cultural study, the nonhuman primate evidence reported by Tracy and Crawford (this volume), and Mitchell's study of the Wape (this volume) suggests that the presence of coalitions of females can reduce male to female aggression. Furthermore, in some societies older women have the role of peacemakers and are expected to intervene in marital disputes and to prevent serious injury (Kerns this volume).

On the other hand, elder women in their roles as senior wives (Counts this volume) or as mothers-in-law (Miller this volume; Lateef this volume; Gallin this volume) may actually instigate or participate in the ill treatment of young wives. Is it possible to predict which of these opposite roles older women will fulfill in any particular society? Elsewhere I suggest that postmarital residence, descent, and the contribution women make to subsistence determine the relationship between a society's matrons and their younger female kin (Brown 1992). Taking a Marxist feminist view, Sacks (1992) suggests that antagonism between mothers-in-law and brides, particularly among agrarian peasantries, functions to preserve patriarchal power. She reports that if the antagonism did not exist and if mothers-in-law and brides were in a position to collude, their "enormous economically destructive potential" would seriously threaten patriarchal power (1992:5).

In some societies a man may feel compelled to beat his wife in order to establish and assure his position within the male peer group. The beating has little to do with the husband-wife relationship but a great deal to do with a man's avoidance of ridicule and his position as "a man among men." Thus, in the well-known case of the Yanomamo, a man must appear fierce and can do so convincingly by beating his wife (Chagnon 1968; see also Gelber 1986; Counts 1990a; Draper this volume; McKee this volume). Or a man may assert physical control over "his" womenfolk to ensure the standing of his kin group within the community. In many societies, particularly those in the circum-Mediterranean region, the respectability accorded a household is proportional to the imposed virtue and modesty of its women (Papanek 1979; Lateef this volume). This, in turn, has economic implications for the group and explains in part the ready willingness of the older, more integrated women of the household to help chaperon, chastise, and confine the younger female members.

There's Safety in Numbers

In U.S. society, a number of notorious wife abuse cases reported in the media have called attention to the remarkable physical and psychological isolation imposed on women by their abusive partners.[7] Tracy and Crawford (this volume) note analogous behavior for nonhuman primates. Several other chapters (e.g., those by Burbank, Mitchell, and Kerns) stress the importance of community intervention in preventing serious harm and note the potential danger for isolated wives.

In many societies the isolation of a wife, particularly a young wife, is the result of the rules for postmarital residence. The crucial factor is not which spouse moves at marriage but the proximity of the wife's kin to the newly established household. A wife has the support of her kin not only in matrilocal societies (Nash this volume), which are few in number worldwide, but in all societies that do not practice community exogamy. As a rule, when a woman's kin are nearby, their presence provides a deterrent against wife battering. But if her behavior is viewed as truly infuriating, her brothers (McDowell this volume) and her father (Gallin this volume) may actually join her husband in beating her. However, a wife is in a much more vulnerable position, and there is a far greater likelihood that she will be ill treated if she is isolated from her family by rules for postmarital residence that compel her to move to her husband's distant community.[8]

The isolation of a wife is also determined by the degree of privacy a society traditionally assigns to the domestic sphere. In general, when domestic activities take place almost entirely out of doors and in full view of the rest of the community, or when domestic activity is audible through thin house walls, it is less likely that women will be battered because others will step in (Burbank this volume; Draper this volume). There is greater danger that wives will be abused when the domestic sphere is veiled in privacy. This is more typical of complex societies, where some protection may be afforded through a wife's recourse to law enforcement agencies and the courts. In some societies, women's access to these institutions is made very difficult (Counts 1992a), or it may be illegal for any agency to intervene in domestic matters (Zorn this volume). Such circumstances serve to isolate women and to place them in great jeopardy. In addition, as Counts (1992a), among others, has pointed out for Melanesia, when the authorities themselves beat their wives, they are unlikely to prosecute other men for doing so.

Sanctions and Sanctuary

Not only is there cross-cultural variation from society to society in the amount, frequency, and severity of aggression against women and in what is condoned or disapproved but also in the sanctions that apply and in the availability of sanctuary for beaten wives. In U.S. society, the question frequently asked about a battered wife is "Why does she stay?" rather than "Where does she go?" The answer is that she stays because she is terrified, because leaving will mean separation from her children, because she does not have the resources to manage without her partner, and, above all, because our society provides no easy solutions to the immediate problem of where to go (see also Draper this volume; Kerns this volume). Effective sanctuary must provide the guarantee of safety to the woman (without imposing the penalty of separation from her children), as well as to those who offer her refuge. It must provide the wife with the possibility of prolonged support, whether by her own labors or by the generosity of others. And it must be available at the very moment when it is needed, no matter what hour of the day or night. Generally, in those societies in which a married woman remains in or near the community of her own family, such sanctuary is readily available. But there are exceptions (Hegland this volume), such as when the family lacks the socially recognized authority or the resources to take her in. In some instances sanctuary may be provided by neighbors, elders, community leaders, and, in complex societies, by specialized shelters. As Kerns (this volume) points out for the Garífuna, because women are able to leave partners who beat them, they are never battered. However, in other societies sanctuary is as problematical as in the United States, and women are often compelled to remain with their abusive spouses (Lateef this volume).

Sanctions imposed by society may be informal or formal, negative or positive. Informal negative sanctions include gossip about a wife beater or expressions of open disdain by his family and neighbors. Formal negative sanctions can take the form of court-ordered punishment. The incidence of wife beating is reduced whenever sanctions are certain, immediate, and severe, regardless of whether they take the form of wrath and retribution from the spirits of her ancestors (Mitchell this volume) or of retaliation from her living kin or result in incarceration and fines imposed by a law enforcement agency.

Society may also provide inducements of a positive kind to encourage alternatives to wife beating. Informal positive sanctions include the community's admiration for a man who can keep peace among his wives without the use of force, whose wife performs her duties willingly, or who commands domestic respect without having to impose it. Formal positive sanctions include the political power that derives from the support of a wife's kin. But perhaps the greatest reward is a harmonious marriage, which appears to be a universal ideal.

Evening the Score

The extent of wife beating in any particular society can be predicted in large part from the certainty, immediacy, and severity of the sanctions that apply and from the sanctuary that is available to wives, both of which, in turn, depend to a large degree on the customary postmarital residential arrangements. Of course, matters are never quite this simple, and there are other factors that must be taken into account, as noted above. There is, however, one additional deterrent to wife beating: the means at a woman's disposal for getting even. Some wives may strike back using a weapon of some sort (McDowell this volume; Scaglion this volume). Others may leave their partners and return to their kin. Still others may resort to shaming abusive husbands publicly and noisily or else attempting suicide. Invoking supernatural revenge (Carucci this volume) or poisoning her husband's food are other ways a wife can get even. She may also mobilize public opinion against her husband and cause problems in his relationship with her kin group (a particularly troublesome matter where marriages are arranged by an exchange of sisters) or allow gardening or cooking or child care to lapse below standard. Wives may also shamelessly flaunt their relationships with lovers or assert their autonomy by pointedly engaging in other types of interdicted behavior. However, any one of these countermeasures may result in a Pyrrhic victory, as when the suicide attempt succeeds (Counts 1992a; Mitchell this volume), when leaving a husband means giving up one's children (Counts 1992a), or when a husband retaliates with even greater violence and brutality (Counts 1992a). Nevertheless, the ethnographic record suggests that women in nonindustrial societies have found a great many ways to even the score.

Postscript

Wife beating in U.S. society has hardly declined since the appearance of *Sanctions and Sanctuary*, the first edition of this volume, in 1992. Because the staggering social, psychological, and economic costs, the severity, and the extent (see, e.g., Peterson 1997) of wife abuse were formerly not acknowledged, it may appear to be a new and contemporary phenomenon or perhaps a special problem of complex postindustrial societies. Neither is the case. Indeed, the Beijing Declaration and Platform for Action, adopted in 1995 by the Fourth World Conference on Women, identifies violence against women, including violence within the family, as one of twelve areas of critical concern worldwide.[9]

Sanctions and Sanctuary was the first cross-cultural collection devoted exclusively to field data on wife beating. Although the anthropological research on the subject remains part of a much-needed "natural history stage," some tentative conclusions are possible. First, wife beating is virtually universal, with analogous behavior occuring among nonhuman primates (Smuts 1996; Tracy and Crawford this volume). Wife beating is reported as extremely rare or absent in only a small number of societies, and it is important to note that when an ethnographer fails to mention wife beating, we cannot assume that it does not actually occur (see Counts 1990b). Second, the data suggest a continuum from the few societies in which wife beating is rare or nearly absent (Lambeck this volume; Mitchell this volume; Nash this volume) to those societies in which wife abuse is frequent and violent, even to the point where wives are murdered or driven to suicide (Hegland this volume; Miller this volume). Many societies fall between the two extremes, such as those in which wife beating is frequent but wife battering is virtually absent (Burbank this volume; Kerns this volume).

The first edition of this book was also unique in reporting exclusively on wife beating and wife battering, setting these apart from other forms of violence against women, such as sexual, psychological, and economic abuse, and from other types of violence within the family, such as child abuse and elder abuse (cf. Sev'er 1997a, 1977b). This single focus, which was dictated by the nature and the limitations of the ethnographic data, made it possible for this volume to avoid involvement in the heated controversy over what constitutes the proper context for wife-beating research. Any review of recent studies of wife beating must take account of this dispute, as noted below. It is our hope that the primate and ethnographic data presented in this volume without preconceptions as to context may provide information that will lead to the resolution of these sharp disagreements.

The first context is that advocated by authors such as Levinson (1988, 1989) and Straus and Gelles (1990), which places research on wife abuse clearly within the context of family violence, suggesting, for example, that there is actually "spouse abuse" rather than wife abuse and that wife beating is related to other types of family violence such as aggression by parents against their children. A second context is suggested by authors such as Dobash and Dobash (1979), who insist that all research on wife abuse begins with the premise that the ill treatment of women is yet another manifestation of patriarchal violence and exploitation. The controversy created by these conflicting views has been described by Brush (1993), Kelly (1997), Kurz (1989), Propper (1997), Renzetti (1994), and Sev'er (1997b).

One possible solution to this dilemma, as it applies to wife-beating research in the United States, has been suggested by Johnson (1995), who identifies two distinguishable phenomena: "common couple violence" and "patriarchal terrorism." Feminist studies have dealt with the latter, while family violence researchers have focused on the former. Johnson notes that this difference in subject matter, as well as differences in method, have caused the two research communities to talk past each other in their "often rancorous debates" (1995:284) but that a reconciliation between the two approaches should be possible. Since the distinctions he suggests have not yet been applied by ethnographers, it remains to be seen if the two categories also pertain in societies other than our own.

A third context focuses on the culturally embedded nature of the concepts utilized in the study of wife abuse. Harvey and Gow (1994a), in their introduction to *Sex and Violence: Issues in Representation and Experience*, raise the possibility that we are imposing our own culture's categories and definitions on "violence" and "sexuality" and are disregarding possible alternative meanings found in other societies (see also Counts's preface in this volume; Zorn this volume).

A fourth context for the study of wife abuse is to view such behavior in its many forms as one item among many in large-sample cross-cultural surveys of violence. Ember and Ember (1993) provide an overview of this research. Erchak and Rosenberg (1994), building on the study by Levinson (1989) and using a sample of seventy societies, identify wife beating as one aspect of "generalized patterns of violence in a society" (1994:113).

A fifth context combines the study of wife beating with other forms of violence that specifically target women, such as sexual assault. This is the approach taken in the interdisciplinary volumes edited by Sev'er (1997c) and Buss and Malamuth (1996). The latter collection is remarkable because it represents an attempt to bridge two previously opposing points of view: the feminist and the evolutionary.[10]

Although the formulation of hypotheses appeared premature, the introductory chapter in *Sanctions and Sanctuary* identified certain cultural factors that appeared to influence the prevalence and severity of wife-beating in any given society. One such factor was the culturally dictated isolation of the wife. Although, as previously noted, a wife's isolation (especially from her own kin and from supportive other women) creates vulnerability for abuse, there is some contradictory ethnographic evidence. Stølen (1996) describes a rural community in Argentina in which women are extremely isolated in their homes on farmsteads located at great distances from each other, yet only one member of the community beat his wife and his behavior was strongly disapproved by everyone. By contrast, among the Nandi of East Africa, where women not only marry men within their own community but have the option of woman-woman marriage, Oboler (1985) reports that wife beating is frequent and expected and that even the female husband, though she may be less abusive, nevertheless has the right to beat her wife (a right that is not shared by the wife's male consort). As the Whitings suggested in 1975, there tends to be safety in numbers. However, the relationship between a wife's culturally dictated isolation and her vulnerability to abuse appears to be complicated (Brown 1997b).

The second factor, the relationship among female kin (which, in turn, is the result of aspects of a society's social structure, such as postmarital residence, and the culturally expected role of women in subsistence), has major significance for the prevalence and severity of wife beating and battering. On the one hand, older female relatives can be supportive of younger women and protect them from abuse by husbands; but on the other hand, older female kin can instigate the ill treatment of young wives and even participate in the abuse (Brown et al. 1998). For the few societies in which married women continue to live in their mothers' households, the ill treatment of young wives appears to be minimized. Here, older women support young wives and may steer them away from behaviors that anger their husbands. By contrast, in those societies where the young bride is compelled to marry outside her community and lacks the support of her older female kin, she is typically treated harshly and is beaten by her husband as well as by her mother-in-law, who is expected to encourage the abuse inflicted by her son on his young wife.[11]

Smuts (1996) provides a fuller consideration for yet a third factor: the relationship of men to men. One of several of her hypotheses suggests that male aggression (of various forms) toward women is more common in societies where alliances among men are "particularly important and well developed" (1996:243). In such societies men are less concerned with their marital relationships and with supporting their female kin (should these women be the victims of wife abuse) than they are with maintaining their loyalty to other men.

Sanctions and Sanctuary, now updated and expanded—and retitled *To Have and to Hit*—joins other recent publications (Harvey and Gow 1994b; Sev'er 1997c) in calling attention to the worldwide problem of the abuse of women by their partners. What Sev'er has noted in regard to the collection of essays in her volume also applies here: "What binds all these efforts together is looking at wife abuse from a perspective that centres on women and their right to live their lives without being victimized" (1997a:v).

NOTES

An earlier version of this chapter was read at the 1987 meeting of the American Anthropological Association. My thanks to all who participated in the original symposium and to those who have contributed chapters to this book. This chapter has benefited from discussions I have had with Beatrice B. Whiting and from suggestions and comments by many of the contributors to this volume, particularly Victoria Burbank, Charles Crawford, Patricia Draper, Virginia Kerns, Lauris McKee, and Karen Tracy, as well as by my colleagues Peter Bertocci, Pauline Kolenda, Denise Schmandt-Besserat, and Sylvia Yanagisako. Above all I am indebted to Jacquelyn Campbell and Dorothy Counts for sharing insights and ideas and for their patience, grace, and good humor.

1. Beatrice Whiting first alerted me to the importance of this distinction.

2. The fact that the abuse by a husband may be limited to injuries that do not interfere with a woman's subsistence activities and child-bearing capacities was first suggested to me by Patricia Draper.

3. Pauline Kolenda (personal communication 1971) has pointed out that these murders are an urban phenomenon in India.

4. Data compiled by Gelber (1986) for the New Guinea Highlands suggest that physical violence against women is widespread.

5. The Marshall Islanders are reluctant cultivators who gather and fish.

6. Older wives are also less likely to be the victims of spousal homicide in Euro-American society, according to Daly and Wilson (1988a, 1988b).

7. The Hedda Nussbaum case in New York City comes to mind.

8. See Burgess and Draper (1989) and Counts (1990a) for an examination of the relationship among various forms of social structure and marital violence.

9. For recent data from other parts of the world, see Bunch et al. (1998); Dobash et al. (1997); Faison (1996); Fernandez (1997); Handwerker (1997); Hanmer et al. (1989); Human Rights Watch Women's Rights Project (1995); Koman (1996); Nzomo (1998); Schuler (1992); and Tiffany (1998).

10. For other recent examples of an evolutionary approach to the subject of wife beating, see Figueredo and McCloskey (1993) and Wrangham and Peterson (1996).

11. I have noted elsewhere the geographic distribution of the abusive mother-in-law (Brown 1997a). The "Great Mother-in-Law-Belt" stretches across the Old World from western North Africa to the Mediterranean to Western Asia to South Asia and on to the Orient.

REFERENCES CITED

Bordewich, Fergus M. 1986. "Dowry Murders," *Atlantic Monthly* 250 (1): 21–27.

Broude, Gwen J., and Sarah J. Greene. 1983. "Cross-Cultural Codes on Husband-Wife Relationships," *Ethnology* 22:263–80.

Brown, Judith K. 1992. "Lives of Middle-Aged Women." In *In Her Prime: New Views of Middle-Aged Women.* 2d ed. Ed. Virginia Kern and Judith K. Brown. 17–30 (includes "Addendum to the Second Edition," 23–27). Urbana: University of Illinois Press.

———. 1997a. "Agitators and Peace-Makers: Cross-Cultural Perspectives on Older Women and the Abuse of Young Wives." In *A Cross-Cultural Exploration of Wife Abuse: Problems and Prospects.* Ed. Aysan Sev'er. 79–99. Queenston, Ont.: Edwin Mellen Press.

———. 1997b. "Is There Safety in Numbers: Women's Coalitions and Wife Beating." Paper presented at the American Anthropological Association meetings. Washington, D.C.

Brown, Judith K., Perla Subbaiah, and Therese Sarah. 1998. "Being in Charge: Older Women and Their Younger Female Kin." In *Women among Women: Anthropological Perspectives on Female Age Hierarchies.* Ed. Jeanette Dickerson-Putman and Judith K. Brown. 100–123. Urbana: University of Illinois Press.

Brush, Lisa D. 1993. "Violent Acts and Injurious Outcomes in Married Couples: Methodological Issues in the National Survey of Families and Households." In *Violence against Women: The Bloody Footprint.* Ed. Pauline Bart and Eileen Geil Moran. 240–51. Newbury Park, Calif.: Sage.

Bunch, Charlotte, Roxanna Carrillo, and Rima Shore. 1998. "Violence against Women." In *Women in the Third World: An Encyclopedia of Contemporary Issues.* Ed. Nelly Stromquist. 59–68. New York: Garland.

Burgess, Robert L., and Patricia Draper. 1989. "The Explanation of Family Violence: The Role of Biological, Behavioral, and Cultural Selection." In *Family Violence.* Ed. Lloyd Ohlin and Michael Tonry. 59–116. Chicago: University of Chicago Press.

Buss, David, and Neil Malamuth, eds. 1996. *Sex, Power, Conflict: Evolutionary and Feminist Perspectives.* New York: Oxford University Press.

Campbell, Jacquelyn. 1985. "Beating of Wives: A Cross-Cultural Perspective." *Victimology: An International Journal* 10 (1–4): 174–85.

Carmody, Dianne C., and Kirk R. Williams. 1987. "Wife Assault and Perception of Sanctions." *Violence and Victims* 2 (1): 25–38.

Carneiro, Robert L. 1958. "Extra-Marital Freedom among the Kuikuru Indians of Mato Grosso." *Revista do Museu Paulista* N.S. 10:135–42.

Chagnon, Napoleon. 1968. *Yanomamo: The Fierce People.* New York: Holt, Rinehart and Winston.

Claiborne, William. 1984. "Dowry Killings Show Social Stress in India." *Washington Post,* 22 September, 1–3.

Collier, Jane F. 1988. *Marriage and Inequality in Classless Societies.* Stanford, Calif.: Stanford University Press.

Counts, Dorothy Ayers. 1990a. "Domestic Violence in the Pacific: Conclusion." In *Domestic Violence in Oceania.* Ed. Dorothy Ayers. Counts. 225–54. Special issue of *Pacific Studies* 13 (3).

———. 1990b. "Domestic Violence in the Pacific: Introduction." In *Domestic Vio-*

lence in Oceania. Ed. Dorothy Ayers. Counts. 1–6. Special issue of *Pacific Studies* 13 (3).

———. 1992a. "The Fist, the Stick, and the Bottle of Bleach: Wife Bashing and Female Suicide in a Papua New Guinea Society." In *Contemporary Pacific Societies: Studies in Development and Change.* Ed. V. Lockwood, T. Hardy, and B. Wallace. 249–59. New York: Prentice Hall.

———. 1992b. "*Tamparonga:* 'The Big Women' of Kaliai (Papua New Guinea)." In *In Her Prime: New Views of Middle-Aged Women.* 2d ed. Ed. Virginia Kerns and Judith K. Brown. 61–74. Urbana: University of Illinois Press.

Daly, Martin, and Margo Wilson. 1988a. "Evolutionary Social Psychology and Family Homicide." *Science* 242:519–24.

———. 1988b. *Homicide.* New York: Aldine De Gruyter.

Daly, Martin, Margo Wilson, and Suzanne J. Weghorst. 1982. "Male Sexual Jealousy." *Ethology and Sociobiology* 3:11–27.

Dobash, Rebecca E., and Russell Dobash. 1979. *Violence against Wives: A Case against the Patriarchy.* New York: Free Press.

Dobash, Russell, R. Emerson Dobash, Kate Cavanagh, and Ruth Lewis. 1997. "Criminal Justice Programs for Batterers: Can They Contribute to the Efforts to End Violence against Women." In *A Cross-Cultural Exploration of Wife Abuse: Problems and Perspectives.* Ed. Aysan Sev'er. 201–51. Queenston, Ont.: Edwin Mellen Press.

Elliott, Frank A. 1988. "Neurological Factors." In *Handbook of Family Violence.* Ed. Vincent Van Hasselt, Randall L. Morrison, Alan S. Bellack, and Michel Hersen. 359–82. New York: Plenum.

Ember, Carol, and Melvin Ember. 1993. "Issues in Cross-Cultural Large Survey Research on Violence." *Violence and Victims* 8 (3): 217–33.

Erchak, Gerald M. 1984. "Cultural Anthropology and Spouse Abuse." *Current Anthropology* 25 (3): 331–32.

Erchak, Gerald, and Richard Rosenfeld. 1994. "Societal Isolation, Violent Norms, and Gender Relations: A Reexamination and Extension of Levinson's Model of Wife Beating." *Cross-Cultural Research* 28 (2): 111–33.

Faison, Seth. 1996. "In Sign of Times, Shanghai Aids Battered Women." *New York Times,* 2 May.

Fernandez, Marilyn. 1997. "Domestic Violence by Extended Family Members in India: Interplay of Gender and Generation." *Journal of Interpersonal Violence* 12 (3): 433–55.

Figueredo, Aurelio José, and Laura Ann McCloskey. 1993. "Sex, Money, and Paternity: The Evolutionary Psychology of Domestic Violence." *Ethology and Sociobiology* 14:353–79.

Ford, Clellan S., and Frank A. Beach. 1951. *Patterns of Sexual Behavior.* New York: Harper and Row.

Foster, George M. 1972. "The Anatomy of Envy: A Study in Symbolic Behavior." *Current Anthropology* 13 (2): 165–202.

Gelber, Marilyn G. 1986. *Gender and Society in the New Guinea Highlands: An Anthropological Perspective on Antagonism toward Women.* Boulder, Colo.: Westview.

Gibbs, James L. 1984. "On Cultural Anthropology and Spouse Abuse." *Current Anthropology* 25 (4): 533.

Handwerker, W. Penn. 1997. "Power and Gender: Violence and Affection Experienced by Children in Barbados, W.I." *Medical Anthropology* 17 (2): 101–28.

Hanmer, Jalna, Jill Radford, and Elizabeth A. Stanko, eds. 1989. *Women, Policing, and Male Violence: International Perspectives.* New York: Routledge.

Harvey, Penelope, and Peter Gow. 1994a. "Introduction." In *Sex and Violence: Issues in Representation and Experience.* Ed. Penelope Harvey and Peter Gow. 1–17. New York: Routledge.

———, eds. 1994b. *Sex and Violence: Issues in Representation and Experience.* New York: Routledge.

Human Rights Watch Women's Rights Project. 1995. *The Human Rights Watch Global Report on Women's Human Rights.* New York.

Johnson, Michael. 1995. "Patriarchal Terrorism and Common Couple Violence: Two Forms of Violence against Women." *Journal of Marriage and the Family* 57:283–94.

Kelly, Katharine. 1997. "The Family and Woman Abuse Debate: Reviewing the Literature, Posing Alternatives." In *A Cross-Cultural Exploration of Wife Abuse.* Ed. Aysan Sev'er. 27–50. Queenston, Ontario: Edwin Mellen Press.

Koman, Kathleen. 1996. "India's Burning Brides." *Harvard Magazine* 98 (3): 18–19.

Kurz, Demie. 1989. "Social Science Perspectives on Wife Abuse." *Gender and Society* 3 (4): 489–505.

Leonard, Kenneth E., and Theodore Jacob. 1988. "Alcohol, Alcoholism, and Family Violence." In *Handbook of Family Violence.* Ed. Vincent Van Hasselt, Randall L. Morrison, Alan S. Bellack, and Michel Hersen. 383–406. New York: Plenum.

Lester, David. 1980. "A Cross-Cultural Study of Wife-Abuse." *Aggressive Behavior* 6:361–64.

Levinson, David. 1981. "Physical Punishment of Children and Wifebeating in Cross-Cultural Perspective." *Child Abuse and Neglect* 5:193–95.

———. 1988. "Family Violence in Cross-Cultural Perspective." In *Handbook of Family Violence.* Ed. Vincent Van Hasselt, Randall L. Morrison, Alan S. Bellack, and Michel Hersen. 435–55. New York: Plenum.

———. 1989. *Family Violence in Cross-Cultural Perspective.* Newbury Park, Calif.: Sage.

Masumura, Wilfred T. 1979. "Wife Abuse and Other Forms of Aggression." *Victimology: An International Journal* 4 (1):46–59.

Muller, Jean-Claude. 1969. "Preferential Marriage among the Rukuba of Benue-Plateau State, Nigeria." *American Anthropologist* 71 (6): 1057–61.

Mushanga, Tibamanya Mwene. 1977–78. "Wife Victimization in East and Central Africa." *Victomology: An International Journal* 2 (3–4): 479–85.

Nadler, Ronald. 1988. "Sexual Aggression in the Great Apes." In *Human Sexual Ag-*

gression: Current Perspectives. Ed. Robert A. Prentky and Vernon L. Quinsey. 154–62. New York: New York Academy of Sciences.

Naroll, Raoul. 1969. "Cultural Determinants and the Concept of the Sick Society." In *Changing Perspectives in Mental Illness.* Ed. S. C. Plog and R. G. Edgerton. 128–55. New York: Holt, Rinehart and Winston.

Netting, Robert McC. 1969. "Women's Weapons: The Politics of Domesticity among the Kofyar." *American Anthropologist* 71 (6): 1037–46.

Nzomo, Maria. 1998. "Women in East Africa." In *Women in the Third World: An Encyclopedia of Contemporary Issues.* Ed. Nelly Stromquist. 543–52. New York: Garland.

Oboler, Regina. 1985. *Women, Power, and Economic Change: The Nandi of Kenya.* Stanford, Calif.: Stanford University Press.

Papanek, Hanna. 1979. "Family Status Production: The 'Work' and 'Non-Work' of Women." *Signs* 4 (4): 775–81.

Peterson, Karen. 1997. "White-Collar Wife-Beaters: Some Executives Take Home Need for Power and Control." *USA Today,* 16 December, D-1, D-2.

Propper, Alice M. 1997. "Measuring Wife Assault by Surveys: Some Conceptual and Methodological Problems." In *A Cross-Cultural Exploration of Wife Abuse: Problems and Perspectives.* Ed. Aysan Sev'er. 51–77. Queenston, Ont.: Edwin Mellen Press.

Renzetti, Claire M. 1994. "On Dancing with a Bear: Reflections on Some of the Current Debates among Domestic Violence Theorists." *Violence and Victims* 9 (2): 195–200.

Sacks, Karen Brodkin. 1992. "Introduction: New Views of Middle-Aged Women." In *In Her Prime: New Views of Middle-Aged Women.* 2d ed. Ed. Virginia Kerns and Judith K. Brown. 1–6. Urbana: University of Illinois Press.

Schlegel, Alice. 1972. *Male Dominance and Female Autonomy.* New Haven, Conn.: HRAF Press.

Schuler, Margaret, ed. 1992. *Freedom from Violence: Women's Strategies from Around the World.* New York: United Nations Development Fund for Women.

Sev'er, Aysan. 1997a. "Foreword." In *A Cross-Cultural Exploration of Wife Abuse: Problems and Perspectives.* Ed. Aysan Sev'er. v–vii. Queenston, Ontario: Edwin Mellen Press.

———. 1997b. "Introduction." In *A Cross-Cultural Exploration of Wife Abuse: Problems and Perspectives.* Ed. Aysan Sev'er. 1–26. Queenston, Ont.: Edwin Mellen Press.

———, ed. 1997c. *A Cross-Cultural Exploration of Wife Abuse: Problems and Perspectives.* Queenston, Ont.: Edwin Mellen Press.

60 Minutes transcript. 1988. "Machismo: Wife Murder in Brazil." Produced by John Tiffin. 21 February. *CBS News* 20 (23): 2–5.

Slater, Philip, and Dori A. Slater. 1965. "Maternal Ambivalence and Narcissism: A Cross-Cultural Study." *Merrill-Palmer Quarterly* 11 (3): 241–59.

Smedley, Audrey. 1974. "Women of Udu: Survival in a Harsh Land." In *Many Sisters:*

Women in Cross-Cultural Perspective. Ed. Carolyn Matthiasson. 205–28. New York: Free Press.

Smuts, Barbara. 1996[1992]. "Male Aggression against Women: An Evolutionary Perspective." In *Sex, Power, Conflict: Evolutionary and Feminist Perspectives.* Ed. David Buss and Neil Malamuth. 231–98. New York: Oxford University Press.

Steinmetz, Suzanne. 1981. "A Cross-Cultural Comparison of Marital Abuse." *Journal of Sociology and Social Welfare* 8 (2): 404–14.

Stølen, Kristi Anne. 1996. *The Decency of Inequality: Gender, Power, and Social Change on the Argentine Prairie.* Oslo: Scandinavian University Press.

Straus, Murray A. 1977. "Societal Morphogenesis and Intrafamily Violence in Cross-Cultural Perspective." In *Issues in Cross-Cultural Research.* Ed. Leonore L. Adler. 717–30. New York: New York Academy of Sciences.

Straus, Murray, and Richard Gelles, eds. 1990. *Physical Violence in American Families.* New Brunswick, N.J.: Transaction Press.

Tannenbaum, Percy, and Dolf Zillmann. 1975. "Emotional Arousal in the Facilitation of Aggression through Communication." In *Advances in Experimental Social Psychology,* vol. 8. Ed. Leonard Berkowitz. 149–92. New York: Academic Press.

Tellis-Nayak, V., and Gearoid O. Donoghue. 1982. "Conjugal Egalitarianism and Violence across Cultures." *Journal of Comparative Family Studies* 13 (3): 277–89.

Tiffany, Sharon. 1998. "Women in Oceania." In *Women in the Third World: An Encyclopedia of Contemporary Issues.* Ed. Nelly Stromquist. 637–45. New York: Garland.

Turkington, Carol. 1987. "Male Apes Show Aggressive Mating Behavior." *Monitor of the American Psychological Association* 18 (3): 16.

Van Hasselt, Vincent, Randall L. Morrison, Alan S. Bellack, and Michel Hersen, eds. 1988. *Handbook of Family Violence.* New York: Plenum.

Whiting, John W. M., and Beatrice B. Whiting. 1975. "Aloofness and Intimacy of Husbands and Wives: A Cross-Cultural Study." *Ethos* 3 (2): 183–207.

Wrangham, Richard, and Dale Peterson. 1996. *Demonic Males: Apes and the Origins of Human Violence.* New York: Houghton Mifflin.

Zillman, Dolf. 1984. *Connections between Sex and Aggression.* Hillsdale, N.J.: Lawrence Erlbaum.

———. 1986. "Sex-Aggression Linkages." Paper presented at the Invited Symposium in Social Psychophysiology, 94th Annual Meeting of the American Psychological Association. Washington, D.C.

TWO

Wife Abuse: Does It Have an Evolutionary Origin?

Karen Keljo Tracy and Charles B. Crawford

Wife beating is a form of male violence toward women that has received much attention in American social science literature in the last two decades. Although the literature has been very useful in bringing the issue to public awareness and in generating legislation to make wife beating a criminal matter, it has not been very effective in theory building. It has been described largely in terms of social and psychological pathology, as a "dysfunctional behavior," a rather bizarre occurrence outside of normal human experience. As Katha Pollitt has observed, "We need to stop thinking of male violence as some kind of freak of nature, like a tornado. Because the thing about tornadoes is, you can't do anything about them" (1989:20).

The ubiquity of wife abuse, both within and across cultures, suggests that it could have its origin in our evolutionary past. Evidence presented since 1982 (Emery and Billings 1998:121), including much of the data reported in other chapters in this book, indicates that wife beating may be a cross-cultural behavioral universal, despite its wide variety in terms of frequency and severity across cultures. As such, it may indicate underlying biological predispositions congruent with, but not necessarily proving, the mechanism of natural selection (Barash 1978:276–308). Darwin's theory of evolution through natural selection is that living organisms have been formed over long periods of time by a continuous process involving differential survival and reproduction. It should be mentioned here that in the usage of modern evolutionary theory, natural selection pertains to individuals, not groups or species. It favors those who optimize the number of surviving offspring.

From an evolutionary perspective a behavior is the result of an adaptation, a behavior that was shaped by differential reproduction in an ancestral population. Some of these behaviors were beneficial in ancestral populations but not today, and vice versa. For example, a "beneficial effect" is a behavior that currently contributes to fitness but did not contribute to fitness in an ancestral population and therefore was not shaped by natural selection, such as adoption and the rearing of non–biological kin. Another behavior, "pseudopathology," is adaptive in an ancestral population but no longer contributes to biological fitness, such as excessive male jealousy. In essence, adaptations have evolved to help animals deal with the contingencies of their environments and favor those individuals that optimize their number of surviving offspring (Crawford 1998:23–25).

Behavioral traits are only adaptive for a specific environment in a particular context. Since less than 1 percent of human ancestral heritage has occurred outside the context of hunting and gathering bands (Symons 1981: 35), most of our current behavioral predispositions evolved to suit the conditions in that particular environment. However, genetic predispositions that were functional in that environment may not be suitable for other environmental conditions. Therefore, in this chapter wife abuse will be discussed in an evolutionary psychological context: Is it a beneficial effect or a pseudopathology?

Since adaptations evolved to help ancestral organisms deal with environmental conditions, it may well be that by altering certain aspects of the environment, abusive behaviors can be decreased or eliminated. However, it is important to understand the evolutionary basis for such behavior in order to know what types of environmental changes would be the most effective. Because we can only speculate about spouse abuse in human ancestral history, we have chosen to focus on "wife abuse–like" behavior that has been observed in nonhuman primates; however, let it be noted that such behaviors are prevalent in a large number of species and are not by any means the exclusive domain of the primate order. Although we are fully aware that these cases can only serve as analogues to the human case, we believe that studying the behaviors of those species that most resemble our own could be useful in understanding the dynamics involved in the human situation.

In studying the primate literature, we have selected three areas that relate to an evolutionary psychological view on wife abuse. The first involves sexual dimorphism between male and female of a given species and incorporates Darwin's theory of sexual selection. The second comprises the arena of mate retention, which includes such behaviors as mate guarding, sexual jealousy, and sequestration. The third area comprises social interactions between male and female partners in which real or perceived nonreciprocation can generate aggressive responses.

Ultimate Causation and Wife Beating

According to modern evolutionary theorists, the ultimate goal of an animal's behavior is to perpetuate its own individual genes; this goal is referred to as "reproductive fitness." The assumption is not that the organism is driven to produce lots of offspring. It is rather that natural selection has shaped behavioral mechanisms, motives, cognitive biases, and so on, that resulted in ancestral organisms producing more offspring than those who did not have these behaviors. The behavior of a given individual is thus ultimately self-interested by nature. Let it be emphasized, however, that this goal is not a conscious one; neither humans nor animals behave in a volitional, deliberate way in order to maximize their reproductive fitness.

In evolutionary terminology, trying to interpret behavior from an "ultimate" causal perspective is to understand why a given individual behaves in a particular way—specifically, how behavior enhances reproductive fitness. "Proximate" causal analysis, by contrast, focuses on how an individual acquires and displays certain behaviors. To this point, most of the social science literature on wife beating has centered on proximate rather than ultimate causes of the behavior. Research centering on proximate causes is indeed useful to behavioral science. However, if we do not also understand the ultimate cause of this behavior, we have no solid theoretical base from which to work.

Evolutionary psychology focuses on ultimate cause. It is concerned with (a) the conditions in ancestral populations that rendered some behaviors adaptive and others maladaptive; (b) the mechanisms that evolved to produce adaptive behaviors; and (c) the way the mechanisms that evolved to produce the adaptive behaviors function in contemporary environments. Thus, evolutionary psychology provides a paradigm for understanding how variations in environmental conditions can lead to conflict, violence, and pathological behaviors, perhaps eventually leading to an understanding of how environmental conditions can be modified to change troublesome behaviors.

For an individual of any primate species, including *Homo sapiens,* the most direct path to this ultimate goal of "reproductive fitness" requires mating with an animal of the opposite sex and generating offspring, which must be protected and tended until they are capable of surviving and mating on their own. However, it would also include behaviors (labeled "inclusive fitness") designed to ensure the survival of blood kin, who share the individual's genes. If this theory is correct, then one would expect little violence, especially of a life-threatening kind, toward kin. Indeed, a vast body of literature has been built and continues to expand in support of this idea of nonviolence toward blood relatives throughout the animal kingdom (Symons 1981:51–58; Trivers 1985:118–21; Wilson 1980:55–63). Thus, it is posited that some sorts of innate mechanisms exist to inhibit violence between individuals related by blood.

Because of incest avoidance in mating behaviors in most primates, mates are generally not related by blood. Thus, a possible mechanism that would inhibit violence between blood relations will not obtain in this specific situation. Indeed, Daly and Wilson (1987:302–3; 1998:121) have demonstrated that in human populations, domestic violence culminating in death significantly more often involves non-blood-related kin than blood relatives.

Because mates are necessary to produce progeny and provide resources to rear them, they have a high value for an animal's reproductive fitness. All primate species have had to develop mechanisms to attract and mate with typically nonrelated opposite-sexed individuals. Although most of these mechanisms involve consensual, cooperative behaviors, some rely on coercion and aggression. Because of the high valence attached to a mate, behaviors directed toward that mate are often highly emotionally charged. Since mating relationships are so vital for reproductive fitness, any indication of disruption of that relationship can evoke a powerful emotional and behavioral response in the animal.

While Darwin's concept of natural selection involves the relative capability of organisms to adapt to their surroundings, Darwin posited another construct, which he called "sexual selection," to describe males' and females' differential ability to attract sexual partners and pursue their goal of reproductive fitness. Sexual selection involves both intersexual selection and intrasexual selection (Kevles 1986:4–14; Symons 1981:22; Trivers 1985:15). Intersexual selection is founded on the choice of mate by the sex making the higher minimal parental investment (usually females). Intrasexual selection involves competition between the members of the sex making the lower minimal parental investment (usually males) for access and control of the sex making the greater minimal parental investment (usually females). It results in sexual dimorphism in size, physical aggressiveness, and the production of organs of threat. Reproductive strategies differ between males and females; thus, some authors believe that some amount of conflict is inherent in male-female relationships. Catton and Gray summarize these differences in strategies as follows: "In the battle of the sexes the males have most of the weapons, and whenever they can avoid looking after the young they will use every possible means to try and fertilize more females. In the females' armoury there is often only one defence against the male onslaught, but its effect is devastating. Females can say no" (1985:152). It is clear that female consent delimits the male's ability to reproduce. In order to win this consent, the male employs many strategies, which may include fighting off competing males, preventing females from mating with other males, and providing resources that the female can use in maintaining herself and caring for her young. The female, who must bear and generally also provide most of the rearing of the young, uses the strategy of choosing the male who can best provide her and her progeny with resources, such as food, protection, and assistance in rearing her young. Although animal data is not always pertinent to the human case, David Buss (1989:735–36), who studies human mate retention, believes that differential means of reproduction lead men and women to pursue different strategies in securing and retaining mates. Whenever these strategies clash, conflict should be anticipated.

Sexual Dimorphism

One of the results of sexual selection is sexual dimorphism. In most primate species, as well as our own, males are bigger in size and musculature than are females; in many species males also have bigger canines than females and thus are more likely to inflict serious injury than are females. Although the size and strength difference may have evolved primarily due to intrasexual competition among males, this difference may also have had the "beneficial effect" of allowing the males dominance over the females in many species. In general, the greater the sexual dimorphism, the more the male is apt to be clearly dominant over the female, the more likely the mating pattern is to be polygamous, and the less the male is apt to be involved in parental care of the young.

Although there is not currently much data regarding male-female violence in the wild, what evidence there is points to more male-female violence in sexually dimorphic species than in those in which male and female are physically similar in strength and size. For example, in Hamadryas baboons, in which the male is twice as large as the female, a male holds a harem of females. If a female should stray, he threatens her or bites her neck until she stays close to him (Kummer 1985:374–75). Similarly, when an unfamiliar human approaches a group of mountain gorillas, the male cuffs the females in his harem, succeeding in getting them to flee with him; again, the male is twice the size of the female (Nichols 1989:83). Fossey reports an incident in which a male, apparently unprovoked, attacked a female and beat her to death, returning again and again to savage the body even after she was dead (1981:508–11). This act would be classified as "pseudopathology."

Goodall has also recorded many acts of male-to-female violence among common chimpanzees, in which the female weighs about 75 percent as much as the male (Hrdy 1983:175), in the wild. She observed that a male would attack a female in several different kinds of situations. Some of the more common situations involved a female's refusal to mate with a male, the refusal of a female to accompany a male on a "consortship" journey (Wrangham and Peterson 1996:144–46), the approach of another male when a more dominant male was dominating a female during her fertile period, the approach of an unfamiliar female, and a "spillover effect" of aggression from a male who had engaged in fighting other males. Since the first three situations relate to mate retention, they will be discussed in that section. The "spillover effect" seems to be purely a function of the size and power advantage of the male over the female (Goodall 1986:313–41).

Goodall reports that females tended to flee with their infants whenever male-male violence erupted, as the loser(s) would often attack a female or her infant after such a battle, with no provocation whatsoever on the part of the victim (1986:482). De Waal (1989:150, 248) reports similar unprovoked aggression of males toward females in several sexually dimorphic species of primates. Both Goodall and de Waal emphasize, however, that male violence severe enough to cause injury to a female was exceedingly rare (Goodall 1986: 313; de Waal 1989:77), in part due to the female's efforts at peacemaking when males became angry and, when appropriate, to female avoidance of angered males. Incidents resulting in severe injury to the females tended to erupt only when the male dominance hierarchy was in flux, thus causing much intrasexual aggression, which then spilled over on the females. Despite the rarity of severe male aggression toward females, minor aggression and threats were commonplace. However, a lone adult female attacked an adult male only in one specific type of situation—that is, when that male was threatening her young.

Evidence from laboratory studies reported by Nadler (1988:160) suggests that the female's smaller size may allow her to avoid male aggression by being able to evade the larger male, particularly in arboreal species. Thus, the female's smaller size may be a "beneficial effect" for her in that she can more easily escape injury or forcible copulation by a substantially larger male, thereby enhancing her ability to exercise mating choice. In orangutans, when an adult male and an adult female animal were placed in a zoo cage and allowed free access to each other, the male immediately chased and caught the female, wrestled her down to the floor, and copulated with her. Although she struggled at first, he was able, by his greater size and strength, to subdue her and engage in forcible copulation. However, if the cage was modified so that the female could escape through a door that was too small to accommodate the male, the male soon changed his behavior, performing a display for the female and waiting immobile until she initiated copulation. Recent evidence from field research, however, indicates that females actively seek sex with large males. Most rapes are committed by small adult males and juveniles who can successfully chase and capture females in the course of their escape attempt through the treetops (Wrangham and Peterson 1996:135–36).

There is almost no intersexual violence in species for which little sexual dimorphism exists, such as the tamarin and the gibbon. When such violence erupts, there is no sex difference regarding the initiation of the fight. The male and the female tend to form monogamous pair bonds, with no clear dominance pattern of one above the other, and they share the care-giving chores of their offspring. Of course, biology is not destiny entirely when it comes to primates. In some species with little dimorphism, such as spider monkeys, males tend to dominate and aggress against females. There is no species with substantial sexual dimorphism, however, in which females display equal or greater aggression toward the males than the males display toward the females. Goodall (1986:482) suggests that this is due in part to the healthy respect given males by females, as females will necessarily lose to males of superior size and strength. Thus, females tend to prevent aggressive incidents by deferring to dominant males and, in addition, acting as peacemakers to reduce male-male aggression (1986:585–86), in order to diminish the possibility of its overflowing onto themselves and their offspring. However, in three decades of observation of the sexually dimorphous bonobo, no violence to females has been seen (Wrangham and Peterson 1996:200–215). Possible reasons include sexual codominance, lifelong bonds between mothers and sons, concealed ovulation, and powerful female coalitions.

What of the human case? Humans are judged to be mildly sexually dimorphic, with males about 5–12 percent taller (Hrdy 1983:175) and 20–30 percent heavier (Mitchell 1981:10) than females (males also have significantly greater upper-body strength). Reviewing wife beating in the United States, Saunders (1986:49) states that while battering husbands tend to be average in height and weight, their battered wives tend to be below the norm in both. However, unlike other animals, humans have access to lethal weapons; and the use of weapons such as guns can exacerbate or override differences in size and strength.

De Waal and others believe that wife beating in human societies is an ever-present danger given the average superiority in strength of the husband: "Nonhuman primates are endowed with particularly highly developed checks on escalated fighting. Some of these are innate, other seem publicly enforced. Severe attacks by young adult males on females, for example, are often stopped by other members of the group. Older males have learned to control their aggression against females. . . . In human social life . . . male aggression may tip over into violent crime if the appropriate balancing mechanisms and social controls are lacking" (de Waal 1989:11). Although the appropriate balancing mechanisms and social controls to check the aggression of husbands toward their wives may have been present in the tightly knit context of the ancestral hunting and gathering band, they are apt to be less reliably present in the context of modern urban societies. There the anomic conditions of large cities and fluctuating populations may result in individuals living hundreds of miles from their extended families. De Waal considers the lack of respect for women by men a dangerous situation (pseudopathology) in modern times and sees the education and social example set for young boys as the key to preventing wife beating.

Mate Guarding

As was mentioned earlier, the reproductive interests of males are not necessarily congruent with those of females. It is unlikely that wife abuse has ever been in the reproductive interest of women. However, it might in some cases have been advantageous for men in ancestral populations in that wife abuse may have represented one tactic used by a man to control the reproductive behavior of his wife.

Sexual reproduction necessitates locating and retaining a mate, for at least as long as it takes a male to copulate with a female. Money and Tucker write: "When it comes down to the biological imperatives that are laid down for all men and women, there are only four: Only a man can impregnate; only a woman can menstruate, gestate, and lactate" (1975:38). These differences have implications for optimal reproductive strategies for each sex. Since men need only inseminate in order to reproduce, the use of deviousness and coercion in attracting and retaining a mate might have made sense in an ancestral population. Since women invest not only in fertilization but also in pregnancy and lactation, it would have behooved them to exercise careful choice before permitting sexual intercourse.

For primates, females bear the young and have no doubt as to the maternity of their infants. Since the female invests more directly in offspring, it is to her advantage to exercise choice in her selection of mate, selecting a male who is physically healthy with sound genes and other resources to invest in mate and offspring. After she has been impregnated and has garnered whatever resources she can from one male, it might benefit her to attract several other males in order to amass resources for rearing her offspring and to ensure male protection from predators and other males for herself and her young.

Male primates, however, have no guarantee of paternity and are not necessarily involved in the rearing of offspring. Males of many species, therefore, have developed strategies for enticing females to mate with them and for guarding against cuckolding. Mate-retention behaviors aimed at ensuring exclusive sexual access include several different tactics. One such tactic is "mate guarding," exemplified in behaviors such as "herding" in the Hamadryas baboon (Cosmides and Tooby 1989:64–65). If a female in the harem of the male Hamadryas strays too far from him, he threatens and, if necessary, bites her. This action will cause the female Hamadryas baboon to stay close to him. Interestingly, however, if a male Hamadryas should try the same technique on a female Savannah baboon, which is physiologically very similar to the Hamadryas baboon, she will flee him and not allow him to approach her in the future.

Another male mate-retention tactic is exemplified by the "consortship journeys" (Goodall 1986:457–65) undertaken by male common chimps in which a female is singled out from the troop and coaxed into accompanying the male—alone—to a spot in the forest that is well isolated from the other chimps. If she tries to call out to alert others of her whereabouts or tries to flee, the male will forcibly cover her mouth or strike and bite her to bring her into compliance. On this journey, the male has exclusive sexual access to the female and sometimes is successful in impregnating her.

While "consortships" are sometimes successful in perpetuating an individual male's genes, they are riskier than staying with the troop and claiming exclusive rights to a fertile female. Thus, the most dominant male in a troop will instead monopolize the sexual access to a female during her four fertile days (Goodall 1986:450–53). Because this male has already established dominance, most of the time other males will not even approach his consort. If another male does approach, however, the dominant male will typically attack the female. This strategy is more beneficial for him than attacking the other male for many reasons:

1. While the dominant male is fighting the intruder, a third male could slip in and copulate with the fertile female.
2. The dominant male is unlikely to receive any injury from attacking the female but is at risk from another male.
3. By attacking the female, the dominant males discourages her from accepting the advances of other males in the future.

Although rape is rare in common chimps, Goodall (1986:466–69) did witness female chimps refusing the sexual advances of a son or a brother. In such cases, the male often beat the female severely and forcibly copulated with her. Also, Goodall sometimes saw a situation in which a male tried to initiate copulation with a female only to have her refuse to get into a copulatory crouch position. The male was then observed to whip the female with a branch. Such incidents were rare, as females typically readily complied with requests for copulation. Nadler cites an example in which male chimps were observed trapping females in trees from which escape was impossible and forcibly copulating with them. He concludes that "some degree of male aggressivity is inherent in the species-typical mating pattern of chimpanzees" (1988:158). Nadler argues that female compliance in copulatory activities initiated by the male does not necessarily imply receptivity but rather reflects an attempt to appease a potentially hostile male to avoid injury to herself.

Some authors believe that human wife beating stems from sexual jealousy and the need for mate retention. Some of the jealousy is appropriate: 9–13 percent of human children have "putative fathers [who] are not their genetic fathers" (Buunk et al. 1996:359). However, there is no significant correlation between actual female cheating and wife beating. Carlson (1987:19) reports that the best predictor of male-female violence in dating couples was sexual involvement. Daly and Wilson write that "intensive studies . . . are unanimous in suggesting that male sexual proprietariness constitutes the dangerous issue in marriage" (1988:200). These authors cite studies from several different cultures (although their literature reviews are not exhaustive) demonstrating that husbands who killed their wives generally did so for one of three reasons, all having to do with their retention of and sexual control over their wives:

1. their wives had left them or threatened to end the relationship;
2. they suspected or knew that their wives were being unfaithful;
3. their wives had refused their sexual advances.

Daly and Wilson conclude, "Men . . . strive to control women. . . . women struggle to resist coercion and to maintain their choices" (1988:205).

Daly and Wilson (1998:438–40) state that male jealousy far outweighs any other cause for spouse abuse. Without citing any empirical support for their position, they maintain that for each woman killed (which they agree is usually dysfunctional), the hundreds of beatings and lethal threats given to wives are evolutionarily beneficial for the husbands. They affirm that "a credible threat of violent death is a valuable social tool, and credibility may only be attainable at the cost of some sincere willingness to accept costs in order to punish transgressors" (1998:449). By contrast, Crawford asserts that much male jealousy is excessive; he classifies it as a "pseudopathology," adaptive in ancestral times but, "because of changes in the environment in recent times, [it] has become maladaptive, unethical, or otherwise harmful" (1998:24).

Reciprocity

Most primates, including humans, are social animals; it is to their advantage to cooperate and live together harmoniously in order to survive and reproduce. One type of cooperation feasible between two individuals, such as a mating pair, is "reciprocal altruism," defined as "the trading of altruistic acts in which benefit is larger than cost so that over a period of time both enjoy a net gain" (Trivers 1985:361). The problem with this system is that one of the individuals may not reciprocate, thus leaving the other with a net loss rather than a net gain. An unwary altruist, therefore, would ultimately lose in reproductive fitness. In primate literature, there is evidence that failure to reciprocate engenders fiercer attacks than other types of irritating behaviors. Trivers (1985:377) uses anthropomorphic language to describe such intense reactions in common chimps; he terms it "moralistic aggression." Researchers such as Cosmides and Tooby (1989:86–92) present evidence that the human brain is preprogrammed with a propensity to "detect cheaters" (nonreciprocators). It must be emphasized here that what is important is the perception of nonreciprocation by a particular individual in a given relationship, not what an impartial judge might decide is a fair amount of give and take. While norms of reciprocity between husband and wife may have been relatively simple and clear to both spouses in the context of the ancestral hunter-gatherer band, these norms are not always clear in more modern settings. In cultures such as those in current technological societies, cultural diversity is so great and cultural change is so rapid that individual husbands and wives may frequently hold very different expectations as to what behaviors are appropriate for themselves and their partners to maintain an equitable situation within a marriage.

Reciprocal systems involve a rather delicate balance; if there is a power disparity in a relationship, the possibilities of altruistic exchanges are diminished. Several authors indicate that in North America a status inconsistency between partners is associated with a higher risk of wife beating (Gelles and Cornell 1985:75; Shields et al. 1988:94; Tavris and Wade 1984:288). Although many do not specify the direction of this inconsistency, Walker (1984:11) has found that a sample of battered American women had significantly higher educational levels and higher social class backgrounds than their husbands as compared to nonviolent control couples. The same pattern was found by Browne (1987:20–21) in her sample of battered American women who ultimately killed their husbands. In a similar vein, Okun (1986:48–49) concludes from his search of North American wife-beating literature that there is a consistent tendency for wife abuse to be higher in couples in which the wife had a higher educational or occupational level than did the husband, which would constitute a pseudopathology. Anderson (1997:665) reports the same results for income/occupational level but found that wives with either higher or lower levels of education were more at risk. Thus, such a husband may feel "one down" in the relationship and believe that he is at risk for being cheated in some way by his wife. He may thus resort to violence in order to tip the scales in his favor. Saunders writes that "one episode of violence of any intensity may shift the power balance in the relationship by making the woman more passive" (1986:48). Once this power has shifted, it may be increasingly easier for the husband to obtain what he wants by violent means, and increasingly harder for the wife to resist.

Reconciliation

More powerful than the need to dominate and aggress among social primates is the need to maintain harmonious social relationships. Researchers studying the common chimp (de Waal 1989:48; Goodall 1986:357–61; Trivers 1985: 377) believe that these animals may consider interruptions in relationships more potentially threatening than the physical harm done by aggression. De Waal cites an example of a female who, after being severely bitten by a male, reconciled and chose to sleep close to him for the night (1989:48). Goodall (1986:361) reports that after a male has severely attacked a female he will often attempt an immediate reconciliation, hugging and patting her. More commonly, the female will seek postfight reassurance from the male.

Conclusion

Recent observational studies of primate behavior demonstrate that wife-abuse-like behavior is found in a number of species close to *Homo sapiens* on the phylogenetic scale. The variety of situations evoking male aggression toward females is great, and the responses of individual animals to this aggression is also diverse. We need a much broader research base before we can begin to understand the causes and solutions for wife beating. One strategy used by female primates to combat male aggression is to form a coalition with another female or a male animal (de Waal 1989; Goodall 1986:573; Mitchell

1981:105). Unfortunately, among most human societies, competition for attracting and retaining the "best" men tends to break up female coalitions (Wrangham and Peterson 1996:206–7). Another strategy is to flee, a technique facilitated by the female's smaller size and mobility. Still another is for the female to appease a male before he becomes aggressive or for her to initiate reconciliation immediately following a fight. Goodall (1986:571) has observed females actively taking a peacemaking role as a preventive measure after a fight between males, since males more frequently attack females after fighting with other males.

Solutions to wife beating are not simple, and perhaps wife beating will never totally be eliminated on a worldwide basis, but it can certainly be reduced and its severity alleviated. Although wives also beat husbands, they tend to do so in self-defense and typically do much less physical damage than do males (Browne 1987:6–9). Emery and Laumann-Billings (1998:122) report that in 1995, according to the Federal Bureau of Investigation, one-third of female homicides were committed by male intimates. Data from the same source lists wife battering as the most common cause of injury for females aged fifteen to forty-four. Gelles and Straus (1988:19) believe that "human beings are less fearful of violence and injury than the violation of social order." Thus, perhaps on both an individual and a societal level, spouse abuse, which is a potential threat to such order, is hushed up, glossed over. Those individuals who violate societal norms to the extent that they bring such abuse to the attention of society are often stigmatized. Such abuse, once it comes to the attention of the public, is seen as "unnatural" and "sick"; therapists view it as a pathology rather than a pseudopathology, as posited by Crawford (1998:23–25). But as long as wife beating is viewed as a bizarre event, with blame cast on both batterer and victim—rather than as a remnant of our ancestral past, when it was "beneficial"—it will continue to occur. Effective remedies cannot be undertaken at the individual level unless societies choose to censure wife beating.

The evidence we have cited from the area of sexual dimorphism suggests that there is a sufficient strength advantage of the average male over the average female that physical means to control wives will tend to be used unless a society exacts penalties for wife beating. As Gelles and Straus (1988:32) note, wife beating results in the quick reward of working off anger, seeing immediate compliance in the victim, and having an increased amount of control over the victim. Once begun, it tends to be habit-forming. A popular misconception is that the wife must have provoked the beating and thus should be held accountable for her own abuse. The primate literature on male attacks on females tends to support Angela Browne's observation on the immediate antecedents of an attack: "In most cases, although the violence may have been preceded by verbal abuse or other signs of difficulty, the actual assault was triggered by a seemingly minor occurrence or seemed to have no trigger at all" (1987:51). One way to combat wife beating is therefore to condemn interpersonal violence in general.

One principle that is evident from the literature we have cited under the topic of mate guarding is that the commonsense notion of simply leaving a battering spouse is misguided. The act of leaving or of threatening to leave may put the wife and, in some cases, her children at greater jeopardy than any other act. This danger is especially acute in the time immediately following a woman's flight in which emotions are high and tend to cloud her judgment. Therefore, the availability of a safe place to which a woman may flee with her children during volatile episodes, which was not an option in most ancestral environments, enhances her ability to escape continued violence. Over the past two decades in North America, battered women's shelters have been formally established to serve this vital function and to provide guidance for such families to halt future violence.

The concept of social reciprocity is useful in explaining why habitual abusers feel justified in beating their wives. Many report that their wives deserved to be battered. Browne suggests: "Most strong emotions, particularly unpleasant ones, become translated into anger and then externalized as somebody's 'fault.' The 'offender' is labeled and punished, and the abusive man becomes the victim and, therefore, is 'justified' in his aggression" (1987:83). Once a husband has thus cognitively justified his uses of force against his wife, a cycle is set up whereby any behavior by a wife that is "disobedient" by the husband's subjective standards is seen as justification for a beating. Such incidents seem to arouse an emotion akin to what Trivers (1985:377) calls "moralistic aggression" in primates, cases in which the aggression appears to be vastly disproportionate to the "offense" that was committed.

A common fallacy is to assume that what is natural is necessarily good. Even if it were proven unequivocally that wife beating is a "natural tendency," that does not mean it is either good or else uncontrollable. Daly and Wilson (1998:499), in calling violence "valuable as a social tool" with respect to jealous males' behavior toward their wives, provide a good example of this fallacy. Wife beating can be prevented to a large extent by laws (Catton and Gray 1985:212–13) where appropriate social controls do not exist, such as in major cities of the world today. In addition, as de Waal (1989:11) suggests, young boys need to be educated both at home and in social institutions to respect women and refrain from using force as a means of conflict resolution. Although our biological nature may set broad limits and some predispositions on our behavior, it cannot determine how we are capable of acting, nor does it address the moral issue of how we should act.

REFERENCES CITED

Anderson, Kristin L. 1997. "Gender, Status, and Domestic Violence: An Integration of Feminist and Family Violence Approaches." *Journal of Marriage and the Family* 59:656–69.

Barash, David P. 1978. *Sociobiology and Behavior.* New York: Elsevier.

Browne, Angela. 1987. *When Battered Women Kill.* New York: Free Press.

Buss, David. 1989. "Conflict between the Sexes: Strategic Interference and the Evocation of Anger and Upset." *Journal of Personality and Social Psychology* 56 (5): 735–47.

Buunk, Bram P., Alois Angleitner, Viktor Oubaid, and David M. Buss. 1996. "Sex Differences in Jealousy in Evolutionary and Cultural Perspective: Tests from the Netherlands, Germany, and the United States." *Psychological Science* 7:359–63.

Carlson, Bonnie E. 1987. "Dating Violence: A Research Review and Comparison with Spouse Abuse." *Social Casework* 68 (1): 16–23.

Catton, Chris, and James Gray. 1985. *Sex in Nature.* New York: Facts on File Publications.

Cosmides, Lena, and John Tooby. 1989. "Evolutionary Psychology and the Generation of Culture, Part II." *Ethology and Sociobiology* 10:51–97.

Crawford, Charles. 1998. "The Theory of Evolution in the Study of Human Behavior: An Introduction and Overview." In *Handbook of Evolutionary Psychology: Ideas, Issues, and Applications.* Ed. Charles Crawford and Dennis Krebs. 3–42. Mahwah, N.J.: Lawrence Erlbaum Associates.

Daly, Martin, and Margo Wilson. 1987. "Evolutionary Psychology and Family Violence." In *Sociobiology and Psychology.* Ed. Charles Crawford, M. Smith, and D. Krebs. 293–309. Hillsdale, N.J.: Lawrence Erlbaum Associates.

———. 1988. *Homicide.* New York: Aldine de Gruyter.

———. 1998. "The Evolutionary Social Psychology of Family Violence." In *Handbook of Evolutionary Psychology: Ideas, Issues, and Applications.* Ed. Charles Crawford and D. Krebs. 431–56. Mahway, N.J.: Lawrence Erlbaum Associates.

de Waal, Frans. 1989. *Peacemaking among Primates.* Cambridge, Mass.: Harvard University Press.

Emery, Robert E., and Lisa Laumann-Billings. 1998. "An Overview of the Nature, Causes, and Consequences of Abusive Family Relationships." *American Psychologist* 53 (2): 121–35.

Fossey, Dian. 1981. "The Imperiled Mountain Gorilla." *National Geographic* 159 (4): 500–523.

Gelles, Richard J., and C. P. Cornell. 1985. *Intimate Violence in Families.* Beverly Hills, Calif.: Sage.

Gelles, Richard J., and Murray A. Straus. 1988. *Intimate Violence.* New York: Simon and Schuster.

Goodall, Jane. 1986. *The Chimpanzees of Gombe.* Cambridge, Mass.: Belknap Press of Harvard University Press.

Hrdy, Sarah Blaffer. 1983. *The Woman That Never Evolved.* Cambridge, Mass.: Harvard University Press.

Kevles, Bettyann. 1986. *Females of the Species.* Cambridge, Mass.: Harvard University Press.

Kummer, Hans. 1985. "A Male-Dominated Society." In *The Encyclopedia of Mammals.* Ed. David Whyte and David Macdonald. 374–75. New York: Facts on File Publications.

Mitchell, G. 1981. *Human Sex Differences.* New York: Van Nostrand Reinhold.

Money, John, and Patricia Tucker. 1975. *Sexual Signatures.* Boston: Little, Brown.

Nadler, Ronald D. 1988. "Sexual Aggression in the Great Apes." In *Human Sexual Aggression: Current Perspectives.* Ed. Robert A. Prentky and Vernon L. Quinsey. 154–62. *Annals of the New York Academy of Sciences* 528.

Nichols, M. 1989. *Gorilla: A Struggle for Survival in the Virungas.* New York: Aperture Foundation.

Okun, Lewis. 1986. *Woman Abuse: Facts Replacing Myths.* Albany: SUNY Press.

Pollitt, Katha. 1989. "Hers." *New York Times Magazine,* 18 June, 18–20.

Saunders, D. G. 1986. "When Battered Women Use Violence: Husband-Abuse or Self-Defense." *Violence and Victims* 1 (1): 47–60.

Shields, Nancy, George McCall, and Christine Hanneke. 1988. "Patterns of Family and Nonfamily Violence: Violent Husbands and Violent Men." *Violence and Victims* 3 (2): 83–97.

Symons, Donald. 1981. *The Evolution of Human Sexuality.* New York: Oxford University Press.

Tavris, Carol, and Carole Wade. 1984. *The Longest War.* New York: Harcourt Brace Jovanovich.

Trivers, Roger. 1985. *Social Evolution.* Menlo Park, Calif.: Benjamin Cummings.

Walker, Lenore E. 1984. *The Battered Woman Syndrome.* New York: Springer.

Wilson, Edward O. 1980. *Sociobiology.* Abridged ed. Cambridge, Mass.: Belknap Press of Harvard University Press.

Wrangham, Richard, and Dale Peterson. 1996. *Demonic Males: Apes and the Origins of Human Violence.* Boston: Houghton Mifflin.

THREE

Fight! Fight!: Men, Women, and Interpersonal Aggression in an Australian Aboriginal Community

Victoria K. Burbank

Addressing the question of how male aggression affects relations between men and women, this discussion of fighting between men and women in the Australian Aboriginal community of Mangrove[1] develops the theme that the manifestation of male aggression does not inevitably lead to asymmetries in gender relations.

Mangrove was established in the early 1950s. Situated on an approximate half square mile of coast in southeast Arnhem Land, this settlement was the home of about 400 Aboriginal people in 1977. By 1988 the population had grown to about 575. During these years the people of Mangrove lived in the midst of houses, trucks, pots and pans, processed food, toilets, showers, clothes, laundry detergent, tape recorders, playing cards, and videos. They were, to varying degrees, engaged in and dependent on such introduced institutions as Western-styled forms of education, medicine, government, religion, a money economy, and wage labor. Still, much of their behavior was informed by distinctively Aboriginal models of etiquette, religion, kinship, and marriage.[2] It is difficult, if not impossible, to ascertain whether the amount of aggression present on the settlement represents levels that might have been present in nomadic times (see Burbank 1994).

Between 1977 and 1988 I visited this southeast Arnhem Land community on three occasions; for eighteen months in 1977 and 1978, for nine months in 1981, and for seven months in 1988. On each trip I recorded cases of aggressive behavior; some of these I observed, many more were recounted by Aboriginal people, usually women. Although I cannot know for sure, the public nature of aggression on the settlement and the interest that people demonstrate in talking and hearing about it suggest that I may have been able to record the majority of acts of physical aggression that occurred during my visits.

Elsewhere I present a detailed quantitative analysis of these cases (Burbank 1994). Here, let it suffice to say that aggressive interactions between men and women are not uncommon. For example, of the 101 fights recorded for a 19.5-month period in 1977 and 1978,[3] 58 were between men and women. Women were not merely the recipients of male aggression. In the case of 37 fights it was possible to ascertain who initiated the physical aggression of the encounter—that is, the first person reported to have picked up a weapon, destroyed an object, or physically attacked an opponent.[4] Women initiated physical aggression in 17 cases; men initiated physical aggression in 20 cases. However, male aggression appears to have been more injurious. Men reportedly struck or injured women more than twice as often as women struck or injured men. For the most part, these were battles between members of the immediate family, often husbands and wives. In general, these were fights precipitated by family issues such as sexual jealousy or the infidelity of a spouse, use of household resources, or sometimes a man's intoxication (Burbank 1980a, 1980b). As such, these fights might be compared with what police and social agencies in the United States call incidents of "domestic violence." However, it should be noted that the distinction between "domestic" and "political" issues in Mangrove is not always clear-cut (Burbank 1994; see also Collier 1974 and Lamphere 1974).

Physical aggression hurts. It can incapacitate or kill. When its use parallels conflicting desires or interests, it can be seen as an attempt to coerce, intimidate, or dominate. It is in this guise that male aggression has been nominated as a foundation stone of gender asymmetry (e.g., Maccoby and Jacklin 1974; Mukhopadhyay and Higgins 1988; Quinn 1977; Rosaldo 1980). The proposition that a male potential for aggressive behavior may limit female power or autonomy does not require that male aggression be manifested toward women. It is necessary, however, to demonstrate that women not only perceive the potential for such aggression but perceive it as a danger to be avoided.

The women of Mangrove are certainly aware of the possibility that a man may attack a woman. They see or hear of these attacks even if they do not actually experience them. Indeed, when they speak about women and aggression they often speak about male attack. For example, in 1988 I asked six women to visualize a fight in which an adolescent girl was being beaten. When I asked who they thought might be doing this, three of the women answered that it would be a "young boy" (i.e., adolescent boy), a lover, or a "boyfriend." I also asked these six women if they could tell me about any fights they might have been in. Two chose to tell me about fights with their husbands. A third woman, the only one who said she had never been in a fight, attributed this to, among other things, the fact that she had followed the advice of the "European" minister who married her. This is her account of what he said: "Love your husband, take care of your husband; if your husband says anything to you, do it. And don't go running around with anyone, mind your husband as long as you live."

The following account of an Aboriginal practice at one time current for the people of Mangrove indicates that at least some women anticipate a greater potential for aggressive male behavior:

> Emu and bush turkey have strong power. If you eat them and somebody is fighting, the spear will come to you. They make you deaf and you fight. Younger boys can eat and women can always eat, but when a man is young neither he nor his mother will eat things like emu, turkey or fat from the dugong and turtle. . . . If he does eat emu, when somebody throws a spear he won't run away. He will throw back and kill that man. When a man becomes old, gets gray hair or has children, then he can eat.
>
> The women do this because this is the Law; they help the boy. If a boy eats, he will be cranky and fighting. If his mother eats, she won't get cranky, but he will.

At least some women also see male aggression as more dangerous than female aggression. For example, I asked four women who would be "really hurt" in a fight between men and women. "The woman," answered all four. It is not clear, however, that all women see men as more aggressive than women. In 1978 I asked women if they thought men or women were more "cheeky" (i.e., aggressive). Six women responded that men are more "cheeky." For example:

> Men are more cheeky than women, because men get spears and want to kill men. Women only get sticks and pull each other's hair. Women never murder their husbands, only men murder their wives.

> Men get more angry than women. They have lots of muscle, they are stronger than women. They get spears, [metal spears, and spear throwers].

One group of at least five women said that "some women are cheeky, just like men." Three other women also thought that men and women were both "cheeky." The first woman quoted above told me in 1988, when I asked the same question again, that women are more "cheeky" because they start fights. In the intervening years she had changed her mind or was now thinking of "cheeky" in a different way.

Short of death or permanent incapacitation, the power of aggressive behavior to intimidate, coerce, or dominate depends on how it is experienced by its target. A man may literally try to beat a woman into submission, but submission is not an inevitable response to aggression. In this regard, bruises and wounds need be viewed as no more than a potential cost of a chosen course of action.

How do the women of Mangrove experience male aggression? Some women talk about male aggression as though it were a means of dominating them. For example: "Some women are frightened of cheeky men. When women are married to a cheeky man they know they had better be careful." And: "George's wife is running off to another man, I don't know why, her husband is a young man. She keeps running around because he doesn't hit her. If he did, she would stop."

While women may experience male aggression as a form of attempted domination, at least some women may also see male aggression as a rather ineffective means of trying to dominate them. For example, one woman told me about a married woman who had a boyfriend and ran off with him on a number of occasions; the woman's husband would bring her back and beat her, but after a trip to the clinic she would run off again. Pursuing this theme in women's discourse, in 1988 I asked six women the following question: "A married woman got a hiding from her husband because he heard she has a friend [lover]. Should she go meet her friend again?" Only two answered that she should not. Two of the remaining four urged caution. For example, one woman said that she should wait until her husband left the settlement and another suggested that she should wait a few months before resuming her affair. But none of the four thought that a "hiding" would deter a woman from meeting her lover.

Women make many statements about male aggression as a response to women's behavior. For example: "A woman sleeps with her husband. If she didn't he would chase her with a [metal] spear." And: "Those men don't drink, fight, steal for nothing. They want women. Mothers might even get speared by them if they don't give their daughters in marriage."

It is clear that women say that men may act aggressively when women frustrate their desires. It is not clear that these speakers see dominance as the motive behind male aggression. On the basis of these statements alone, one could just as easily say that male aggression is seen only as an expression of anger (see also Myers 1986:161–62).

I suggest that at Mangrove male aggression is relatively ineffectual in changing women's attitudes and behavior because women do not see that as its primary goal. Rather, they see male agression largely as a means by which men display and express their anger—not because the men of Mangrove do not attempt to dominate women through aggression (though I don't know that they do), but because of a cultural emphasis on aggression as an expression of anger (Burbank 1980a, 1989).

That women of Mangrove are not intimidated by male aggression is suggested by the apparent willingness with which women attack men, thus inviting male attack: "Last night Hetty and her husband had a fight over Brenda. He has been running around with her. Hetty was very angry and got a [metal spear] and speared her husband in the leg. Then he took the spear and speared her in the hand."

The women of Mangrove see men as stronger than themselves and if not more aggressive then at least more dangerous. These perceptions are undoubtedly created and reinforced by the greater amount of injury that they suffer at the hands of men. Why, then, do they fight with men?

I suggest that women at Mangrove initiate aggression against men because the norms of their community permit and encourage such behavior. Women, like men, have learned that anger is appropriately expressed through aggressive behavior (see also Straus 1980). They know that women are sometimes hurt or even killed by men, but they perceive that they themselves are unlikely to be seriously injured. Hence, when they get angry at men, they attack them.

Fighting at Mangrove is a structured activity, largely predicted and patterned by cultural rules (see also Fox 1968). Although what follows is a case in which a man attacked a woman, it illustrates the sociocultural context in which Mangrove women dare to attack men.

Sunny was in her early thirties in 1988. She was married, had three children, and, like many of the women of Mangrove today, lived with her mother and married sisters and brothers. The incident described is somewhat atypical insofar as it took place when Sunny was living away from Mangrove, her husband was drinking (if not intoxicated), and her injury was more severe than the injuries usually inflicted on such occasions, though she is not the first Mangrove woman to be stabbed.[5]

> When I was married, not to this husband, to the other one, when he was drunk, he always fought and argued with me. One day, Sunday afternoon, we went to the beach. He was drinking. We went crabbing and fishing and got a lot of fish. After we went out fishing, we came back home and we went down to the river and we were swimming but he was still drunk. I was carrying my son Timmy. My husband went and asked one of his cousins for a car, a white Falcon. And they gave him the key and then we went down to the top crossing and I didn't know he had a beer. He was hiding it. And then we got off and he told me, "I've got beer." "Well," I told him, "Don't drink,

you might hit me and Timmy." He had a gun but that gun didn't have any bullets. "I'll hit you," he said to me. "No."

"I'll hit you."

"No."

And we ran away and we were walking down by the side of the river, and he was following us with the car, but he didn't walk down by the riverside. He was driving on the road, looking for our tracks but he didn't find us.

He got home first and we came last. The door was wide open and we went inside. I was carrying Timmy and I put him on the bed. Timmy was crying and my husband woke up and shut the door and he said, "I'll stab you with the knife." He was coming closer and closer and I was shouting and screaming and I opened the door and took Timmy outside and my husband's cousin's son heard us and went and got Timmy and said, "I'll take Timmy to my father's house. I'll take him." "OK," I said. "He's full drunk, he might hit him." After I gave Timmy to his cousin's son, I went back inside. My husband told me to shut the door. I wouldn't shut it so he did. I sat down on the bed. He started arguing more and got a knife and stabbed me. [Here Sunny shows me six scars on her arms and two on her legs.] And I was crying and I started to bleed, blood was all over the floor, bed, I was jumping, screaming, crying. My blood was on the wall. I ran outside now screaming and crying and his cousin's wife saw me.

"What's wrong?"

"He stabbed me with the knife."

And he was fighting with his [other] cousin now and her husband. And they started arguing about me and I was running and I saw him chasing me with that same knife. His cousin was there and she asked her husband, "What's wrong?" They looked down the road and they saw him chasing me. I ran to my uncle's house. I saw my uncle there. He said, "You stand behind my back" and he said to my husband, "You come close, I'll hit you." But my husband didn't listen. He came forward and punched me and when he punched me I bled more. My uncle told his eldest sister, my sister-in-law, "Take her to the hospital" and she did. First he told her to wash me and she washed me, but the blood was still running and after that we went. And he had a fight, my uncle hit my husband from the step, and my husband fell down and he was bleeding then and my uncle's two wives talked for their cousin, growled at my uncle, but my uncle said, "He is wrong, he stabbed her."

I was in hospital and we rang the police and the police came there and checked up. They didn't fix me at the mission, they fixed me at the town. My sister-in-law and I were in the front of the police car and my husband was in the back of the same car and we went to the hospital and the [nursing] sister fixed me and did the stitches. The police took me to the police station to put the statement and I put the statement and I didn't go to court. He went to trial for stabbing me and they gave him one more chance.[6]

Closing the door was clearly an act of significance in the attack on Sunny. Fights are public events in the village of Mangrove. Everyone knows when a fight is taking place. Adults and children stop whatever they are doing and turn in the direction of the altercation. Cries of "Fight! Fight!" can be heard, as can the raised voices of participants and the barking of excited dogs. Life at Mangrove is spent outside; most activities are performed in public. Even the enclosed Western-style houses of the settlement do not interfere with open-air living, for they are used primarily for sleeping and storage. Cooking, eating, work, and play take place out-of-doors, within view and earshot of other people. So too fighting is largely a public event and thus easily monitored by neighbors and kin.

Mangrove women recognize that the public nature of fighting provides an important safeguard (see also Burgess and Draper 1989; Draper 1975; Erchak 1984). As knowledge of its occurrence is almost instantaneous, steps can be taken to minimize the effects of aggressive behavior. Comparing wife beating in America and Mangrove, one woman pointed out that, on the settlement where people fight "outside," there is always somebody to stop a fight. When a woman in a nearby community was fatally stabbed by her husband, another woman explained how this was possible: "That man and woman were fighting in front of everybody on Monday and she was alright. But yesterday when they were alone, he stabbed her. He locked the door of the house and then stabbed her with a spear."

A third woman, recounting her husband's aggressive displays of jealousy, was advised by her neighbor not to "go bush" with him: "By and by he'll strike you." This advisor explained further that a man who wishes to give his wife a beating without interference may attempt to isolate her. One means of doing so is on the pretext of a hunting or fishing trip.

It is probably not just Sunny's good fortune that so many people protected her from the worst effects of her husband's aggression. Like the people of Mangrove, they undoubtedly recognized rules that specify appropriate behavior for assisting or otherwise intervening in fights, and they acted accordingly.[7] One such rule may be stated as follows: If a member of my kindred is attacked, I should come to his or her assistance. This rule may be modified by the reason attributed to the attack. If, for example, it is understood that a man is beating his wife for her infidelity, her kin will refrain from interfering, but only to a certain point. If they perceive that injury is imminent, they will come to her assistance, regardless of the reason for the attack: "If her husband is too rough, marking her, making her sick, making her dead, then we take partner [i.e., intervene]."

Similarly, rules that specify that attackers should be stopped are also recognized. The general rule may be stated as follows: I should stop a member of my kindred if he or she is about to seriously injure someone in a fight. It is in the interest of members of a kindred to see that an aggressive act on the part of a family member does not result in the serious injury or death of another person, male or female, for it is said that aggression provoked by aggression can travel from one member of a kindred to another: "When a man [kills or injures] somebody [trouble] will come to his family, everybody, father, mother, mother's sister, mother's brother, mother's father, everybody, the family. At [a nearby settlement] a man killed a woman. His father, sisters, uncles, his two old mothers were taken away to keep them from the trouble."

Even Sunny's husband may have acted to protect her. According to her account, he was alone with her in a house with a closed door, he had a knife, and he was drunk. Yet he did not stab her in a vital spot; he chose instead to strike at her arms and legs, areas of the body that are prescribed targets according to the rules of fighting (Burbank 1980a, 1994). Even though he had been drinking and had no one to remind or restrain him, Sunny's husband followed the rules.

Mangrove is a community like any other insofar as it is made up of diverse individuals with their own motives, needs, strengths, weaknesses, and powers of understanding. Some women, at least during some periods in their lives, may be more intimidated by male aggression than others. But the willingness of at least some of the women of Mangrove to attack men on occasion indicates that some of the women in this community are willing to risk male attack. This brief examination of rules surrounding fighting suggests that this willingness is based on women's realistic evaluation of their social circumstances. Men have killed women and the women of Mangrove know this. But the frequent help and protection that women see or receive from neighbors and kin is likely to have more salience than two deaths that occurred many years ago. These experiences remind them that people will attempt to prevent serious injury to a woman who is fighting with a man. Male aggression is seen as potentially dangerous but rarely is in actuality. It is not an experience to be avoided at any cost:

> I used to have fights with my husband, before we had our children. He used to think about other men staring at me and he used to see them and get jealous and we used to fight inside the house. He used to hit me and I used to grab him by the hair or sometimes scratch his face, sometimes hit him with a stick, not a [woman's fighting stick], but just any stick. He used to lock me up in the house, tell me not to come out. These days I have free time and go out with other girls, talk, tell stories. Before he used to never let me go with other girls.

When I asked why her husband wasn't locking her up, she answered: "Maybe he's giving up. He knows I know how to fight back. When I get a stick I just go ahead, I don't pull back, I just let go." If the women of Mangrove do not always do what they want, it is likely for reasons other than a fear of physical aggression.

NOTES

Funds for research and analysis of data presented in this chapter were provided by the Australian Institute of Aboriginal Studies, the Harry Frank Guggenheim Foundation, and the National Institute of Mental Health. An earlier version of this essay was presented at the Second International Conference on Hunting and Gathering Societies, held in Quebec in 1980. I wish to thank Lila Abu-Lughod, Patricia Draper, and Beatrice Whiting for their very helpful comments. I also want to thank Judith Brown and James Chisholm for help and encouragement while I was writing this essay .

1. This is a pseudonym, as are all personal names used in this chapter.

2. For a detailed discussion of Mangrove and the changes it represents for Aboriginal people in the area, see Burbank 1988.

3. I include here the eighteen months of fieldwork and a six-week break taken during 1977 and 1978, as at least some fights occurring during the latter period were reported.

4. It is, of course, quite possible that some actions were left out of these accounts. In the telling, a man's more dramatic attack on a woman might eclipse her milder attack on him, and vice versa.

5. In 1988 I asked Sunny, along with seven other women, to respond to a series of questions about aggressive behavior in Mangrove. I explained to each woman that I wanted this information for a book that I was writing about "fighting" in the settlement, that I would not use her name in the book, and that she could refuse to answer any of my questions. While I attempted to write down their answers verbatim, it should be noted that the statements presented here have been translated and edited. Although I tried to remember word for word any comments made in casual conversation, I usually did not record them until later; thus, these comments can be regarded only as approximations of what people said.

6. Unlike the "European" police, Sunny's relatives did not give her husband "one more chance." The day after the incident, two of her classificatory "fathers" sent a chartered plane to bring Sunny and her son back to Mangrove. Once she was back in the settlement, they advised her not to return to her husband.

7. At the time of the stabbing, Sunny was residing in a neighboring settlement. People from that settlement and Mangrove often move back and forth between the two. Some of the people living around Sunny and her husband might well have been people who normally resided in Mangrove; their response to her need suggests that at the very least they recognized rules similar to those recognized in Mangrove.

REFERENCES CITED

Burbank, Victoria K. 1980a. "Expression of Anger and Aggression in an Australian Aboriginal Community." Ph.D. diss., Rutgers University.

———. 1980b. "Male Aggression and Female Autonomy: A Case from Aboriginal Australia." Paper presented at the Second International Conference on Hunting and Gathering Societies, Quebec.

———. 1988. *Aboriginal Adolescence: Maidenhood in an Australian Community.* New Brunswick, N.J.: Rutgers University Press.

———. 1994. *Fighting Women: Anger and Aggression in Aboriginal Australia.* Berkeley: University of California Press.

Burgess, Robert, and Patricia Draper. 1989. "The Explanation of Family Violence: The Role of Biological, Behavioral, and Cultural Selection." In *Crime and Justice: An Annual Review of Research.* Vol. 11. Ed. Michael Tonry and Norval Morris. 59–116. Chicago: University of Chicago Press.

Collier, Jane F. 1974. "Women in Politics." In *Woman, Culture, and Society.* Ed. Michelle Z. Rosaldo and Louise Lamphere. 89–96. Stanford, Calif.: Stanford University Press.

Draper, Patricia. 1975. "!Kung Women: Contrasts in Sexual Egalitarianism in Foraging and Sedentary Contexts." In *Towards an Anthropology of Women.* Ed. Rayna Reiter. 77–109. New York: Monthly Review Press.

Erchak, Gerald M. 1984. "Cultural Anthropology and Spouse Abuse." *Current Anthropology* 25:331–32.

Fox, Robin. 1968. *Encounter with Anthropology.* New York: Harcourt and Brace.

Lamphere, Louise. 1974. "Strategies, Cooperation, and Conflict Among Women in Domestic Groups." In *Woman, Culture, and Society.* Ed. Michelle Z. Rosaldo and Louise Lamphere. 97–112. Stanford, Calif.: Stanford University Press.

Maccoby, Eleanor, and Carol Jacklin. 1974. *The Psychology of Sex Differences.* Stanford, Calif.: Stanford University Press.

Mukhopadhyay, Carol, and Patricia Higgins. 1988. "Anthropological Studies of Women's Status Revisited." *Annual Review of Anthropology* 17:461–95.

Myers, Fred. 1986. *Pintupi Country, Pintupi Self: Sentiment, Place, and Politics among Western Desert Aborigines.* Washington, D.C.: Smithsonian Institution Press.

Quinn, Naomi. 1977. "Anthropological Studies on Women's Status." *Annual Review of Anthropology* 61:181–225.

Rosaldo, Michelle Z. 1980. "The Use and Abuse of Anthropology: Feminism and Cross-Cultural Understanding." *Signs* 5:389–417.

Straus, Murray. 1980. "Victims and Aggressors in Marital Violence." *American Behavioral Scientist* 23:681–704.

FOUR

Room to Maneuver: !Kung Women Cope with Men

Patricia Draper

Among the !Kung San of Botswana, women are sometimes beaten by their husbands and coerced by other men, particularly their fathers. The factors that contribute to this form of aggression are various and are changing over time as a consequence of new economic and residential practices now seen among the !Kung as they have transformed themselves from mobile foragers to primarily sedentary food producers. The responses of women and their supporters to incidents of wife abuse are also changing. In this essay several episodes of wife beating that came to my attention during recent fieldwork among the !Kung will be reported and discussed in terms of the cultural values relevant to their former nomadic life and in terms of the realities of life-styles in the 1980s.[1] In a concluding section, the prospects for future patterns in wife abuse will be discussed. Before proceeding, a few words are in order regarding the general phenomenon of wife beating in society and regarding the particular subject of wife beating among the !Kung.

The Biosocial Background of Sexual Asymmetry

The reality is that in human societies all women must face at least the prospect of being beaten by their husbands. This unhappy circumstance is not simply a matter of social or political inequality (Burgess and Draper 1989). The human male is larger and more aggressive than the female; around the world positions of authority are almost exclusively monopolized by men (Martin and Voorhies 1975). The tools of force are overwhelmingly the province of male interest and training, a situation that exacerbates the inequality between the sexes. The fact that sometimes individual women, by virtue of their kinship position or inherited power, come to stand in positions of power normally allocated only to males does not discredit the empirical association between male physiological sex and masculine gender role, on the one hand, and the use of force, whether legitimately conferred by the group or illegitimately seized by the individual, on the other hand.

The size difference between men and women is observed generally among mammals (with a few interesting exceptions) and is an outcome of mammalian reproductive physiology (Alexander et al. 1979). The "reasons" why dimorphisms of size and behavior run deep in our phylogeny have to with the reproductive specializations of the sexes. Many eons ago, when our primitive reptilian ancestors developed the capacity to retain fertilized eggs, the stage was set for the reproductive asymmetry now seen in mammals, one that is carried out in extreme form among the primates. This transformation required a long time to reach its current stage of elaboration and involved not only retained fertilized eggs but also lengthy internal gestation, postnatal nourishment, and prolonged maternal care. In this way, some populations of organisms developed an alternate means of reproducing, one in which the sexes contributed unequally to the nurturing of the young.

Once a female developmental specialization in reproduction and parenting was established, the way was opened for males to become more specialized in directing effort toward finding access to mates and toward somatic developments that would favor successful competition with other males also seeking mating opportunity with the reproductive monopolists—namely, females (Clutton-Brock et al. 1981; Trivers 1972). In nonsocial species in which males play no parental role in provisioning the mother or in defending the young, the reproductive specialization of the sexes and the dimorphism in size has no necessary implications for the ability of one sex to coerce the other. However, in humans and in the few other mammalian species in which the male parental role is critical to survival of the young, the "price" that females pay for gaining the economic cooperation of their mates is male sexual jealousy (Daly and Wilson 1988).

Humans carry the mammalian specialization to an extreme by producing only a few offspring who mature slowly and require large amounts of parental care in order to survive. Women are committed to a disproportionate amount of this parental work since, unlike males, they cannot recoup one or a few infant or child deaths by finding another mate (Lancaster 1985). A woman who loses a child has lost not only that individual with whom she has personal ties but irreplaceable reproductive time. A man who loses all his children may experience an acute sense of personal loss, but he can replace them by establishing one or more additional mating relationships with other women. The reproductive inequality between the sexes gives rise, of course, to the behavioral and somatic dimorphisms between the sexes and to the differing reproductive potentials of the sexes (cf. Leacock 1978; Maccoby and Jacklin 1974:368–69; Mukhopadhyay and Higgins 1988:469).

There are at least three elements to consider in understanding the unique encumberment of the human female. These elements play a central role in her victimization.

First, because of the extremely dependent state in which young are born, and because of their slow development, any roles that conflict with a woman's reproductive roles are generally avoided by her as an individual or denied her by other interested parties, especially her kin and her mates.

Second, unlike other primate females who terminate care of the next oldest offspring when a new infant is born, a woman maintains not one but several dependent offspring, albeit at different stages of dependence (Lancaster 1985). With each new child she adds to her encumberment and goes further and further into "debt" in the sense that her dependents multiply but her own physical reservoir of energies remains the same.

Third, in order to rear offspring a woman must have help. Some aid comes from her kin, but nearly all human groups attempt to regulate access to the reproductive capabilities of women by designating a mate (husband) and making him share in the work of rearing or defending the children.

Unlike most nonhuman social species, humans live in groups that include numerous other individuals who are eligible as mates. As a result, the sexual contract (paternity certainty in exchange for protection and economic resources) has consequences for other male-female relationships besides marital ones. For example, daughters and sisters of men have a vested interest in maintaining alliances with their male consanguines, not only because they benefit from men's labor, but because these men protect them from other men. A woman's mate, if she has children by him, is also more likely to benefit her and her children than are foreign, unrelated men. It is probably true that in past environments of evolutionary adaptation in which human social, psychological, and sexual behavior have been molded by natural selection, a woman has had few degrees of freedom. The fitness penalties for a woman's error in judging economic or social support have been too severe. This fundamental and rather dismal picture (from the point of view of modern individualistic and humanitarian values) should be kept in mind by those who claim not to understand why so many women remain for so long in abusive environments.

An extremely interesting aspect of cultural variability is the extent to which the underlying reproductive asymmetry of men and women is institutionalized. Any circumstance in which fertility is low and monogamy is imposed, either as a result of ecological constraints or social conventions, is a good place to look for restraints on the ability of males to coerce females. The reason is that in this situation the reproductive interests of the sexes are the same (Alexander et al. 1979:256–59; Alexander 1987:71–73) or more nearly identical than in other human groups (as, for example, among the !Kung; see below). In technologically more advanced societies that have surpluses in the form of stored grains or herds of domestic animals, the fitness interests of the sexes are not the same. Men can advance their own fitness at the expense of other men by competing for access to more than one mate. Under the ecological conditions in which most (but not all) recent hunter-gatherers have lived, the requirements for male labor are sufficiently high that most men can only support one mate and her children at a time. Where resources are potentially abundant and can be disproportionately controlled by a single man or alliances of men, male-male competition has direct consequences for male fitness (Dickemann 1979). In such social systems the variance in male reproductive success is high.

The Case of the !Kung Bushmen: Ethnographic Background

The !Kung of the Kalahari Desert in Namibia and Botswana, some of whom until the 1960s lived primarily as hunter-gatherers,[2] have been well described in the anthropological literature by the numerous field researchers who have lived among them (e.g., Howell 1979; Lee and DeVore 1976; Marshall 1976). The !Kung are a particularly valuable cultural group for anyone interested in the study the relationships among ecological factors, mating behavior, and male-female dynamics.

By the late 1980s, when my most recent field research was carried out, all the !Kung of western Botswana were settled about sources of permanent water. They were no longer full-time hunter-gatherers; instead, they lived in villages ranging in size from fifteen to thirty people. They kept small stock, a few cattle, and tended gardens while continuing to obtain a portion of their livelihood from the bush, supplemented by a periodic government dole of maize meal and cooking oil.[3]

Hunter-Gatherer Days: Prospects for the Coercion of Women

In the past, there were undoubtedly times when !Kung women were physically compelled and beaten by their husbands and others (Howell 1979; Lee 1982:44, 1979; Marshall 1976:282; Shostak 1981:231–33). Yet there would have been many economic and practical restraints on the intimidations of women. Because of the arid and harsh environment in which they lived, their simple technology, and probably also competition from numerous other predatory species in the environment, the ability of men to compete with other men was limited. Resources in the form of game and wild vegetable food were widely scattered and unpredictable in a terrain only sparsely inhabited. Regular and more or less daily work by a husband and wife was necessary to support their children. Further, more efficient forms of labor organization (involving larger, cooperative groups) were apparently not feasible because during most times of the year local food and water supplies would not support large aggregates of people. In this sense there were strong ecological inhibitions on various forms of more hierarchical social relations and more highly rationalized forms of economy.

Polygyny was rare, chiefly because both men and women had to work regularly to provide enough food for themselves and the numbers of old and young who also lived in the bands. Polygyny remains common elsewhere in Africa in agricultural and pastoral communities largely because of the disproportionate subsistence load carried by women (Boserup 1970; Burton and White 1984; White et al. 1981). In such cases, given the agricultural technology, women can work to feed themselves and their children without compromising the welfare of their children. Men, especially middle-aged and older men, are relieved of the necessity of producing food (Draper 1989) and can turn their attention to acquiring multiple wives, whose labor underwrites their high levels of leisure.

In subsistence-level societies women are valuable not only for their economic labor but for their reproductive labor. !Kung women, when living in hunting and gathering groups, were no exception. However, it appears that women were shielded from exploitation by a number of factors. The work of women was sufficiently taxing and incompatible with child care that increased work by women was harmful to their children (Blurton Jones and Sibly 1978) and therefore harmful to the fitness interests of women's husbands. For example, the gathering work required that women travel far from base camp, and at these distances it was not practical to carry children as well as, on the return trip, the gathered food (Draper 1978; Draper and Cashdan 1988). As a consequence, all but nursing infants and toddlers were left at the base camp, under the care of other women and men. Hierarchical relations did not appear among !Kung men, apparently because the continuous economic need for cooperation undermined the expression of most forms of male-male competition. Kinship was bilateral, and reports by various scholars confirm a long tradition of bilateral postmarital residence practices (Harpending and Wandsnider 1982:42; Lee 1982:43). The availability of kin, together with the small size of the foraging groups, meant there were few if any occasions when women were outside the ubiquitous, if informal, influence of public surveillance (Draper 1975).

Perhaps one of the most important safeguards against the physical harm of women came from the pervasive !Kung value condemning aggression. The !Kung strongly discouraged physical aggression as well as milder forms of interpersonal dominance. !Kung values opposed physical punishment for children and, indeed, any form of harsh treatment more severe than an occasional scolding (Draper 1976, 1978; Konner 1976). Husbands had no social entitlement to physically chastise wives; when spouses fought, it was looked on as shameful and stopped as quickly as possible.

During my 1987–88 fieldwork, I talked to elderly !Kung in the context of collecting life history narratives. In the men's narratives, the theme of masculine anger, and particularly the poorly controlled anger of young men, was mentioned frequently.

> Gau, a man in his late 60s, while deploring an episode of recent wife beating by a young man in a nearby village said, "These young men have too much anger. They don't know how to hold themselves back. In the old days, young men like this one [the wife beater] would never have been given a wife. In those days there were no Bantu and no police. When a man beat a woman her kinsmen would jump up and go at him with spears. They would even come from far away. People knew about this and were afraid of the anger and fighting that would follow. They wouldn't give a woman to such men."

While in former times women enjoyed the protection of their kin from abuses by husbands, it is interesting to note that many elderly women's recollections of their girlhood stressed the trauma they felt at their first marriages. In the past, when !Kung spent months at a time in the bush and had no regular contact with cattle people, !Kung parents arranged for their daughters to marry at early ages, sometimes before the age of menarche. Parents believed it was essential for a daughter to have a husband who would hunt and provide meat for her and her kin. Girls typically married men about ten years older than themselves (Howell 1979).

By being married at a young age and to older men, and placed in circumstances in which the elders were making the decisions for them, !Kung women began their marital careers with little power in their relationships. Given the physical mobility of bands in the hunting and gathering days, together with the frequent movement of families in and out of bands, young brides could expect to be separated from their parents and siblings at least some of the time. Of the eight elderly women interviewed, half indicated that one of their parents had already died by the time they had married. These women stated that the death of one parent was used by their remaining elders as a reason for hastening marriage negotiations.

Many elderly women depicted their early years of marriage as stressful and coercive, more often blaming their parents than their husbands. Women stated that their fathers were severe and sometimes physically coercive in insisting that women stay with their husbands (Shostak 1981). Women claimed that as girls they were afraid of their husbands, whom they regarded as foreign, unwelcome interlopers. Not all women recall being physically beaten by their husbands or fathers, but their recollections emphasize their insecurity, their fearfulness and dread of being separated from their families. The intensity of these emotions about separation from their parents is somewhat surprising, given that the !Kung custom of groom service meant that !Kung husbands often joined their brides as live-in sons-in-law.

> N!uhka, aged fifty-five, and old enough herself to have grown up living near Bantu, remembered from her childhood the terrible ordeal of her older sister whom their father insisted should marry a Bantu man. The father (without support from his wife, the mother of the girl) forced the girl to stay in the Bantu village with her mother-in-law and, according to the informant, beat her when she returned to her mother. One night the girl ran away, intending to find sanctuary in a distant village. The next morning she was discovered missing and a search party was launched. In this case, as she had been staying at a cattle post, her tracks were destroyed by the hooves of domestic stock as they left the kraals in the morning. Though search parties sought her for days she was never found. N!uhka flatly stated that her sister must have been eaten by wild animals.

This story clearly illustrates coercion of young !Kung women, in this case not by the husband but by the wife's kin on behalf of the husband. N≠isa, a woman in her fifties, remembers her marriage to her husband (fifteen years her senior) with a story that is both humorous and stark.

> My mother and father wanted me to marry Bo [her present husband]. But I refused all talk of this marriage. The trouble went on for months and months. My parents insisted that I was married to him and that I must stay at the hut I had with my husband. I couldn't bear it. I kept coming back to where my mother and father lived but they drove me back. I wouldn't do anything for my husband! I didn't look at him, I didn't cook for him. When he brought me food I wouldn't eat it. If he gave me food, I just threw it around in the dirt. I sneaked away at night and slept in the bush. Even though I was so scared

> I wouldn't stay with that man. I searched in the bush for guinea fowl eggs and smeared them all over my body to make myself ugly and so I would smell bad. But it had no effect. He became angry that I wouldn't live peacefully with him and wouldn't prepare food but he didn't give up. One day he grabbed me and pushed me in the hut and forced me to have intercourse with him.

The !Kung Transition to Settled Life and Food Producing

Since the 1960s, the !Kung of western Botswana have settled around sources of permanent water and are becoming food producers. This transformation is extremely interesting on a number of grounds but particularly for the opportunity it offers to study the dynamic between changes in resources and technology and the social and sexual relations between men and women.

Although economic practices have changed dramatically, and the continual reshuffling of people by interband mobility has ceased, in other ways the everyday tenor of social and emotional life of the !Kung does not seem drastically different. The local residential unit is a small village composed of about fifteen to thirty people related to each other by bilateral ties of kinship and marriage. Most !Kung are monogamous, and marriages tend to be durable once they are well established. Fertility remains low, although there is some indication that younger cohorts of women have somewhat higher fertility. Cohorts of women aged sixty years and over, forty-five to fifty-nine years, thirty to forty-four years and nineteen to twenty-nine years average 3.6, 4.9, 3.8, and 2.5 live births, respectively.[4]

These data suggest that whatever combination of nutritional, environmental, epidemiological, and hormonal influences may have operated in the past to keep !Kung fertility low, they are still influential for sedentary !Kung (Harpending and Draper 1990; Harpending and Wandsnider 1982; Konner and Worthman 1980).

One might predict that the position of !Kung women has worsened along with the shift to sendentariness and that they have become more vulnerable to domination by their husbands. This prediction would be based on other social-structural factors that are often associated with food-producing techniques such as increased material wealth (especially in the form of livestock), the increased division of labor by sex, and the increased tendency for production to be organized in multigenerational family units with authority vested in senior males. The economic practices of contemporary !Kung are modeled explicitly after those of nearby Bantu-speaking peoples (Tswana and Herero), and it would not be unusual to find that the !Kung have also adopted

Bantu cultural values, which stress patriarchal authority and give men explicit control over women. In fact, in the late 1980s it was not evident that economic changes had unambiguously worsened the position of women.

When a people experience cultural change, some customs change markedly, whereas others persist in the new setting. In the !Kung case, there are elements of their former life-style (such as availability of kin) that are preserved in the modern, sedentary setting and continue to offer a degree of protection for women from physical assaults by their husbands. Other practices, such as the early marriage of girls, are no longer followed so scrupulously. As a consequence, adolescent girls are less subject to manipulation by kin and husbands. On the negative side, other changes, such as consumption of alcoholic drinks and the ability of people to gather in social settings that are beyond the influence of close kin, lead to increased incidents of violence (Colson and Scudder 1988).

In spite of their changed economy, the !Kung have retained many of their former customs that gave women some immunity from husband coercion when they lived as hunter-gatherers. In other cultures wives can be particularly subject to mistreatment, not only from their husbands, but from their husband's kin, when women come as wives from outside their husband's community (Brown, this volume; Burgess and Draper 1989; Levinson 1989). In the late 1980s, the !Kung continued to stress bilateral ties in choosing with whom to reside and cooperate. !Kung adults showed no sex difference in coresidence with one or both parents. For example, 59 percent of !Kung women lived with a father, 52 percent with a mother. Of !Kung men, 54 percent lived with a father, 59 percent lived with a mother. These data, collected in 1987–88, replicate findings based on !Kung residence patterns in 1968 (Harpending and Wandsnider 1982).

The traditional practice whereby girls married in their early teens (or younger) is disappearing. Increasingly, girls in the fifteen-to-twenty-year age range remain unmarried and continue to live with their parents. They frequently have children, sometimes with Herero and Tswana men, but these are informal liaisons, not marriages. The interethnic children are reared by the mother and her kin (Draper and Kranichfeld 1990; Draper and Buchanan 1992). Whereas women aged sixty years and over report only 6 percent of their children were fathered by Bantu, the percentages of ethnically mixed children are higher for younger cohorts of women: 18 percent for those aged forty-five to fifty-nine years; 16 percent for those aged thirty to forty-four years; and 27 percent for those aged nineteen to twenty-nine years.

The delayed age of marriage and increased numbers of outmatings are related to at least two new conditions of modern life. First, the value of young men as hunters is much reduced due to the scarcity of game. These youths, who earlier would have been sought as sons-in-law, are now less essential. Many men of the twenty-five-to-thirty-five-year age range are unmarried and without good prospects for finding wives. Some of these men are a concern for their elders as they get into fights and drink excessively. Second, young women marry later and spend more of their adult years as free agents. In the new settled economy, parents do not believe that early marriages for daughters are essential; they do not seem to think that sons-in-law are critical sources of labor.

Especially if the parents or grandparents of young women have cattle and goats, they willingly keep the young women at home. Their labor is useful in the settled villages where labor is more intensive than among the foragers. Their children are also welcomed. Many middle-aged !Kung parents appear to find daughters and grandchildren more readily incorporated into the new economy than sons-in-law. Of course, the sedentary economy requires work from men: watering stock from deep wells, driving cattle to distant grazing, cutting thorn brush for stock enclosures, and hunting are key masculine tasks. However, it appears that for routine purposes these activities can be done relatively efficiently by a few conscientious men. Even though women's time is more or less co-opted by child care, forcing them to combine gardening, milking, and water and fuel collecting with their maternal roles, some young men do not make similar accommodation to the new subsistence routines. They are idle and restless and a source of substantial resentment by older, harder-working men. In this transitional setting it is easy to understand how the marriage age of girls is delayed, how unmarried daughters and their children are readily absorbed into what is becoming a residentially localized, multigenerational, extended family, and how increasingly these young women form informal unions not with young men of their own age and ethnic group but with Tswana or Herero men whose superior social status and wealth give them an advantage over !Kung youths. In sum, and at this particular point in the !Kung transition to a sedentary, food-producing economy, young !Kung women appear to be free of coercion at the hands of parents who formerly insisted on early marriages of daughters to men in their twenties. Those girls who remain unmarried in the settled villages are likewise not subject to potential mistreatment by inexperienced husbands who lack self-control.

In an earlier essay based on research in the late 1960s among those !Kung who were already sedentary, I describe trends that I predicted would lead to decreased autonomy for !Kung women (Draper 1975). At that time my fieldwork included two populations of !Kung, some who hunted and gathered and others who were settled. I was struck by a number of contrasting practices in the two groups. In comparison with the villages of foraging !Kung, sedentary villages were smaller and less heterogeneous in their groupings of kin. !Kung in the settled villages accumulated more material wealth in the form of stock, larger and more durable houses, and more clothing and household implements. In comparison with the women of the mobile groups, who were frequently out of camp, ranging far on their own in their gathering expeditions, settled women appeared home-bound, concerned only with local domestic tasks and more deferential to men. In terms of settlement pattern and architectural features, it seemed that a number of steps were being taken in the settled villages (erecting fences around homesteads and visual barriers around individual houses; more distant spacing of houses) that, when combined, would lead to women spending more time alone, isolated from potential supporters and unable to protect themselves from abusive husbands. In other respects, the egalitarian style of interaction between the sexes that was seen in the foraging groups appeared to be on the wane among the settled !Kung. Men were named as household heads; men, not women, learned Bantu languages and entered into contractual relations with Bantu cattle owners. Whereas in the bush setting men and women exchanged tasks normally associated with one or the other sex, the sedentary people had a narrower tolerance for crossing gender roles. In particular, women's tasks, such as collecting water and cutting thatching grasses, were scorned by men.

When I returned to the field in 1987–88, I noted that these tendencies had not coalesced in ways that promoted violence against women. I learned of episodes of violence against women living in the settled groups (as there were undoubtedly among the foraging !Kung), which are detailed below. The precipitating circumstances and the social settings of violence had changed somewhat, as had the types of responses women and their supporters made.

In their new life-style, the !Kung continued to live in small villages in which individual household buildings associated with different families were situated close together. While the placement of individual huts was no longer as close as has been reported for !Kung living in mobile camps (Draper 1973), the various structures were within easy sight and sound of the residents. Further, the !Kung continued their habit of living primarily out of doors in the full view of other village residents and visitors. True, the !Kung no longer lived in temporary grass shelters; instead they had built the more typical southern African mud hut or rondavel. However, few !Kung structures matched those of the neighboring Herero. Their mudded rondavels were comparatively insubstantial and had poorly fitted doors that could not be locked or barred from the inside. This meant that a violent man could not isolate his wife and beat her while keeping outside those people who would help her. The lack of visual privacy, coupled with the physical proximity of others, meant that an attack on a woman by her husband would be observed and stopped.

Four Case Histories: Wife Beating in the Modern Setting

Four episodes of wife beating came to my attention during 1987–88. While I did not observe any of these events personally, I was able to interview close kin of the victims in the days following the events and discern some common patterns. The episodes differ in such factors as the setting of the violence, the ages and childbearing histories of the victims, the decisions by the wives whether to remain with the husbands, and the role of the wives' kin as interveners following the attacks.

Two of the beatings took place at !Angwa, the administrative center of western Ngamiland, rather than at the domestic, residential compounds of the principals. !Angwa, a village of about 180 people, is unusual for having several discrete "neighborhoods." Other villages in !Kung territory are not only much smaller in total area but more homogeneous, being essentially the linked compounds of closely related families. At the center of !Angwa are several small government-built structures, a clinic, a small store, a police station, and the headman's office. Nearby are several compounds where beer is brewed and sold for about $.05 per cup. Radiating out in various directions from !Angwa center, at a distance of one-half to one kilometer, are separate compounds where Tswana, Herero, and !Kung live in family groupings.

> In the first case, N/ahka, a middle-aged woman, was attacked by her husband, resulting in injuries to the face, head and lips. The husband accused her of sleeping with another man, in this case a Tswana. N/ahka and her husband had been married for many years but had no children together. Her only child was a girl of about fourteen years whose father was a Herero, and to whom N/ahka had not been married. The father had never contributed to the child's support and for many years the child had been reared by N/ahka's parents who lived at a different village. When N/ahka's parents heard about the beating, they made plans to lodge a formal complaint with the headman at !Angwa against their son-in-law. Other people, not close relatives of N/ahka or her husband, claimed that the couple had a long history of discord, allegedly because the wife liked to sleep with Bantu men.
>
> In another case, also at !Angwa, Kwoba, a woman of about forty-five years, was beaten by her husband. Kwoba and her husband had a home village else-

where but had come to !Angwa to visit relatives who lived there. One evening the husband and wife were drinking at one of the open-air taverns. On the way home they began to argue and the husband beat Kwoba with his fists and a walking cane. People said later they had heard screaming, but they claimed that because the crowds at the tavern were often raucous, no one paid attention. I saw Kwoba two days following the beating. Both her eyes were blackened and swollen nearly shut; her lips were raised with scabs; her upper arm bore long, linear bruises, presumably from being struck by the husband with his cane.

The beatings of N/ahka and Kwoba occurred at locations that, compared to other villages, were comparatively free of the restraints of kin and long-term village mates. Informal social controls are also weakened at !Angwa due to the ethnic heterogeneity of the population and the availability of alcohol. Another factor undoubtedly exacerbates sexual tensions at !Angwa and that is the attractions, described above, that !Kung women find in Tswana and Herero men. When !Kung men and women mix with the other ethnic groups in the context of the disinhibiting effects of alcohol, flirtations between !Kung women and Bantu men are resented by !Kung men who have a claim on a particular woman. Being not only physically smaller but judged socially inferior to Bantu as well, !Kung men faced with direct sexual competition by Bantu men and "emboldened" by alcohol probably retaliate violently against a woman they perceive to be straying, rather than attacking her Bantu suitor.

After being beaten, neither N/ahka nor Kwoba left her husband, an outcome related, perhaps, to the fact that neither of these middle-aged women had adult children who maintained independent households. Although N/ahka's parents threatened to take their son-in-law to the headman and to lodge formal charges against him, they spoke of winning damage payments from the husband, not of ending the marriage. N/ahka did not try to join her parents following the beating, though they lived less than a day's walk from !Angwa. Her parents were among the more impoverished !Kung of the area and were already supporting her daughter and N/ahka's aged and decrepit grandmother.

When I saw the second victim, Kwoba, two days after her beating, she was sitting at her home village in an apparently harmonious family grouping composed of her husband, her co-wife, and her co-wife's children and grandchildren. Kwoba herself had no surviving children. More than twenty years earlier her only child had died as an infant. Both of Kwoba's parents were dead. Her adult half-siblings lived in the same village and so could not (or did not) give her sanctuary in the usual sense of the term. Like N/ahka, Kwoba was middle-aged and without grown children to whom she might turn. It is likely that N/ahka's and Kwoba's decisions to remain with their husbands were influenced by the fact that they had nowhere else to go.

The two remaining cases of wife beating concern young women, both in their late teens.

> Kxaru, about sixteen years, had been married for two years to a man, Kumsa, about thirty-three years old. As yet Kxaru had no children. Her husband, Kumsa, had a reputation for being sullen and angry and given to drink. The second time he beat his young wife while in a drunken state, he bruised her face and split her lip, making a scar still visible many months later. At that time Kxaru had been living with her husband and his family, whereas her own parents and adult siblings lived about 50 kilometers away. Kxaru's maternal grandparents, however, lived in a nearby village and were well acquainted with her husband and his kin. Upon hearing about the attack, the grandmother went to Kxaru's hut and led her away, keeping Kxaru at her own village until she recovered, later sending her back to her parents. Kxaru's parents were economically better off than many !Kung. They owned cattle of their own and also herded cattle belonging to a wealthy Herero family. As such they had a better and more predictable supply of milk than many !Kung. Even months later, the grandmother and grandfather were visibly indignant about the beating of Kxaru and declared that they personally had annulled the marriage. The union, in fact, appeared to be over; Kxaru remained living with her parents and was being sought by another suitor. Kumsa continued to live at home with his parents, sleeping frequently during the daytime and generally behaving like a lout.
>
> /Asa, aged nineteen, had been living at Chum!kwe, Namibia, a regional administrative center about 70 kilometers from where her parents lived in Botswana. Her husband was a man about twenty-seven years old and who was unusual among !Kung men for being literate and having a regular wage-earning job at Chum!kwe. /Asa's husband beat her, striking her on the head and laying open her scalp. Fortunately for /Asa, there was a medical clinic at Chum!kwe where the laceration was stitched together. I saw the wound several weeks later; the scar was about three inches long across the top of her head. /Asa's father arranged for his nephew (also living at Chum!kwe) to bring /Asa and her year-old child back to her parents' village. They declared the marriage ended and helped her build a permanent mud hut in their own village. The father said he expected her to stay with them. He pointed to the nearby huts of his other grown children and the kraals that held the family's goats and few cattle as evidence of material wealth and kin support sufficient to incorporate his returned daughter.

The cases of Kxaru and /Asa (but not the cases of N/ahka and Kwoba) illustrate the continued power of a woman's kin group and the willingness of people to unilaterally intervene on behalf of the injured wife. Whereas in former times assaults on women reputedly led to counterviolence directed at the husband or someone in his kin group, no such action was taken in the case of any of the four victimized women. The !Kung know that the old days of self-help and blood feud are over, since the Tswana have imposed their own system of law on the area.

Implicit in the contrast between the first and second pair of cases are the ages of the wives. Both Kxaru and /Asa were young and had their full reproductive careers ahead of them. Their youth benefited them in several ways. Because they were young, they stood a better probability of having two living parents and living siblings to act on their behalf. In addition, their parents were prosperous enough to take them back.

In the cases of the two older abuse victims, several factors appear to be implicated in the lack of action being taken by the victims themselves: their age, the number of children, their ability to call on their parents, and the economic resources available to their kin. N/ahka and Kwoba were at least twenty-five years older than Kxaru and /Asa. As such, their reproductive value to their husbands and to their kin was diminished. Further, both were of low proven fertility (both had one child in the young adult years but no other births in the last fifteen years). Not only did they have no grown children to act on their behalf, but they had no support group of descendant kin whose existence as tacit symbols of support might discourage aggression by their husbands. Although N/ahka had two younger adult brothers of marriageable age, neither had found wives, nor were they living in independent households, both circumstances a testament to the family's poor prospects. Kwoba, as stated above, had adult half-siblings, but they were already living in her village. Presumably, had she been beaten by her husband while in her own compound, they would have intervened.

Finally, as older women, the probability was small that either N/ahka or Kwoba had living parents who could take their part. Kwoba's parents were long dead; N/ahka's parents were alive but in such poor economic straits that they were apparently unable to act. Among the !Kung, generally, mortality rates are high, with the result that as adults age there is a steep decline in the probability a person will have a living parent. For example, in 1987–88 the percentages of adults of varying cohorts whose fathers and mothers were alive are:

Age (years)	Father Living	Mother Living
60 and older	2%	5%
45–59	13	25
30–44	41	47
19–29	73	72

A sample of four cases is insufficient to speak to the issue of wife beating in !Kung society, but these few case histories do suggest that future, more ambitious studies of violence against wives should pay close attention to the woman's age and reproductive status, the number, ages, and availability of her kin, and the economic resources of her potential supporters.

Conclusion

In this chapter I have described the social and economic conditions that influenced the coercion of women by husbands in !Kung society. Past and contemporary life-styles of the !Kung have been contrasted. The transition from a foraging and hunting economy to a subsistence economy based on settled food producing has not led, in any simple fashion, to increased physical coercion of women. The cultural changes the !Kung experienced between the 1960s and the late 1980s did not transform all areas of life equally. Economic practices and former patterns of spatial mobility changed drastically, as did marriage customs that favored early marriages for girls. By contrast, bilateral residence arrangements, the physical and social intimacy of everyday village life, and the strong ties maintained between a woman and her kin group have been brought from the bush and installed in the permanent settlements with little if any change.

The fact that the !Kung not only changed their subsistence base but entered into regular association with other ethnic groups of Botswana must also be taken into account. The accumulation of external stresses are known in other cultural settings to promote pathological behaviors within families. Bantu-speaking peoples constitute an economic threat as they and their domestic stock move in increasing numbers into an area of western Botswana that was previously occupied primarily by the !Kung. Many !Kung are inexperienced with the demands of a more complex economy and are struggling simultaneously to make a livelihood and to win political recognition of their claims to land and water rights in what they conceive to be their traditional territory.

An added irritant to fundamental conflicts of interest that affect !Kung men and women in the modern setting is the increased frequency with which Bushmen women make informal unions with non-!Kung men. A consequence has been an increased number of half-Bantu children born to !Kung mothers. It appears that the children themselves are not disadvantaged, but each half-Bantu child represents a lost mating opportunity for a !Kung man. Perhaps young !Kung men who succeed in finding wives will be less willing to invest in women who already have children by other men (particularly by

Bantu men) and in women whose behavior suggests poor certainty of paternity. It will be ironic if the temporary gains realized by women (delayed age of marriage and reduced dependence on husbands) turn out to be the flip side of family disorganization and increasingly hostile relations between the sexes.

In future decades, if the !Kung succeed in increasing their ownership of stock, they may adopt more patriarchal values and patrilocal forms of residence, as is common among the neighboring Bantu groups of Botswana. These developments could undermine women's autonomy and make them more vulnerable to coercion by men. In the meantime, the !Kung retain many customs that in the mobile economy promoted the welfare of wives. At this point in their transition to stable food production, there are numerous possible outcomes and many suggestions that their cultural transformation will carry the strong stamp of their former traditions.

NOTES

1. I have done fieldwork with the !Kung in 1968–69, 1975, 1978, and 1987–88. My last research trip was supported by National Institute of Aging Grant No. P01AG03110. Case histories presented in this chapter are from my field notes.

2. See Yellen (1977), contrasted with Denbow and Wilmsen (1986) and Wilmsen (1989), on !Kung culture history.

3. In 1984, in response to a severe drought that lasted until 1987, the Botswana government began a food distribution program directed at poor people living in remote areas.

4. Data throughout this chapter, unless otherwise noted, derive from reproductive interviews with more than three hundred !Kung collected in 1987 and 1988.

REFERENCES CITED

Alexander, Richard D. 1987. *The Biology of Moral Systems.* New York: Aldine de Gruyter.

Alexander, Richard D., R. D. Hoogland, K. M. Howard, and P. W. Sherman. 1979. "Sexual Dimorphisms and Breeding Systems in Pinnipeds, Ungulates, Primates, and Humans." In *Evolutionary Biology and Human Social Behavior: An Anthropological Perspective.* Ed. Napoleon Chagnon and W. G. Irons. 902–35. North Scituate, Mass.: Duxbury Press.

Blurton Jones, Nicholas G., and R. M. Sibly. 1978. "Testing Adaptiveness of Culturally Determined Behavior: Do Bushmen Women Maximize Their Reproductive Success by Spacing Births Widely and Foraging Seldom?" In *Human Behavior and*

Adaptation. Ed. Nicholas G. Blurton Jones and V. Reynolds. 135–57. Society for the Study of Human Biology, Symposium No. 18. London: Taylor and Francis.

Boserup, Esther. 1970. *Woman's Role in Economic Development.* London: Allen and Unwin.

Burgess, Robert, and Patricia Draper. 1989. "The Explanation of Family Violence: The Role of Biological, Behavioral, and Cultural Selection." In *Crime and Justice: An Annual Review of Research.* Vol. 11. Ed. Michael Tonry and Norval Morris. 59–116. Chicago: University of Chicago Press.

Burton, M. L., and Douglas R. White. 1984. "Sexual Division of Labor in Agriculture." *American Anthropologist* 86:568–83.

Colson, Elizabeth, and Thayer Scudder. 1988. *For Prayer and Profit: The Ritual, Economic, and Social Importance of Beer in Gwembe District, Zambia, 1950–1982.* Stanford, Calif.: Standford University Press.

Clutton-Brock, T. H., S. D. Albon, and F. E. Guiness. 1981. "Parental Investment in Male and Female Mammals." *Nature* 289:487–89.

Daly, Martin, and Margo Wilson. 1988. "Evolutionary Social Psychology and Family Homicide." *Science* 242:519–24.

Denbow, J., and Edwin Wilmsen. 1986. "The Advent and Course of Pastoralism in the Kalahari." *Science* 234:1509–15.

Dickemann, M. 1979. "The Reproductive Structure of Stratified Societies: A Preliminary Model." In *Evolutionary Biology and Human Social Behavior: An Anthropological Perspective.* Ed. Napoleon A. Chagnon and W. Irons. 331–67. North Scituate, Mass.: Duxbury Press.

Draper, Patricia. 1973. "Crowding among Hunter Gatherers: The !Kung Bushmen." *Science* 182:301–3.

———. 1975. "!Kung Women: Contrasts in Sexual Egalitarianism in Foraging and Sedentary Contexts." In *Toward an Anthropology of Women.* Ed. Rayna Reiter. 77–109. New York: Monthly Review Press.

———. 1976. "Social and Economic Constraints on !Kung Childhood." In *Kalahari Hunter-Gatherers.* Ed. R. B. Lee and I. DeVore. 200–217. Cambridge, Mass.: Harvard University Press.

———. 1978. "The Learning Environment for Aggression and Anti-Social Behavior among the !Kung." In *Learning Non-Aggression.* Ed. Ashley Montagu. 31–53. New York: Oxford University Press.

———. 1989. "African Marriage Systems: Perspectives from Evolutionary Ecology." *Ethology and Sociobiology* 10 (1): 145–69.

Draper, Patricia, and Anne Buchanan. 1992. "If You Have a Child You Have a Life: Demographic and Cultural Perspectives on Fathering in Old Age in !Kung Society." In *Father-Child Relations: Cultural and Biosocial Contexts.* Ed. Barry Hewlett. 131–52. New York: Aldine de Gruyter.

Draper, Patricia, and Elizabeth Cashdan. 1988. "Technological Change and Child Behavior among the !Kung." *Ethnology* 27 (4): 339–65.

Draper, Patricia, and M. Kranichfeld. 1990. "Coming in from the Bush: Settled Life by the !Kung and Their Accommodation to Bantu Neighbors." *Human Ecology* 18 (4): 363–84.

Harpending, Henry, and Patricia Draper. 1990. "Estimating Parity of Parents: An Application to the History of Infertility among the !Kung of Southern Africa." *Human Biology* 62 (2): 195–203.

Harpending, Henry, and L. Wandsnider. 1982. "Population Structures of Ghanzi and Hgamiland !Kung." In *Current Developments in Anthropological Genetics.* Vol. 2. Ed. Michael Crawford. 29–49. New York: Plenum Press.

Howell, Nancy. 1979. *Demography of the Dobe Area !Kung.* New York: Academic Press.

Konner, M. J. 1976. "Maternal Care, Infant Behavior, and Development among the !Kung." In *Kalahari Hunter-Gatherers.* Ed. R. B. Lee and I. DeVore. 218–45. Cambridge, Mass.: Harvard University Press.

Konner, M. J., and C. Worthman. 1980. "Nursing Frequency, Gonadal Function, and Birth Spacing among !Kung Hunter-Gatherers." *Science* 207:788–91.

Lancaster, Jane B. 1985. "Evolutionary Perspectives on Sex Differences in the Higher Primates." In *Gender and the Life Course.* Ed. Alice S. Rossi. 3–28. New York: Aldine.

Leacock, Eleanor. 1978. "Women's Status in Egalitarian Society: Implications for Social Evolution." *Current Anthropology* 19:247–55.

Lee, Richard B. 1979. *The !Kung San: Men, Women and Work in a Foraging Society.* Cambridge: Cambridge University Press.

———. 1982. "Politics, Sexual and Nonsexual, in an Egalitarian Society: The !Kung San." In *Politics and History in Band Societies.* Ed. Eleanor Leacock and Richard Lee. 37–59. Cambridge: Cambridge University Press.

Lee, Richard, and I. DeVore, eds. 1976. *Kalahari Hunter-Gatherers.* Cambridge, Mass.: Harvard University Press.

Levinson, David. 1989. *Family Violence in Cross-Cultural Perspective.* Newbury Park, Calif.: Sage.

Maccoby, Eleanor, and Carol Jacklin. 1974. *The Psychology of Sex Differences.* Palo Alto, Calif.: Stanford University Press.

Marshall, Lorna. 1976. *The !Kung of Nyae Nyae.* Cambridge, Mass.: Harvard University Press.

Martin, M. Kay, and Barbara Voorhies. 1975. *The Female of the Species.* New York: Columbia University Press.

Mukhopadhyay, Carol C., and Patricia J. Higgins. 1988. "Anthropological Studies of Women's Status Revisited, 1977–1987." *Annual Review of Anthropology* 17:161–95.

Shostak, Marjorie. 1981. *Nisa: The Life and Words of a !Kung Woman.* New York: Vintage.

Trivers, Roger. 1972. "Parental Investment and Sexual Election." In *Sexual Selection and the Descent of Man, 1871–1971.* Ed. Bernard Campbell. 136–79. Chicago: Aldine.

White, Douglas R., M. L. Burton, and M. M. Dow. 1981. "Sexual Division of Labor in

African Agriculture: A Network Autocorrelation Analysis." *American Anthropologist* 83:824–49.
Wilmsen, Edwin. 1989. *Land Filled with Flies.* Chicago: University of Chicago Press.
Yellen, John. 1977. *Archaeological Approaches to the Present.* Orlando, Fla.: Academic Press.

FIVE

"All Men Do It": *Wife Beating in Kaliai, Papua New Guinea*

Dorothy Ayers Counts

Look, gentlemen, we've all done it. . . . But I will not stand for it any longer. We've got to stop beating our wives.

—Police commissioner David Tasion to a gathering of provincial police commanders, Port Moresby, Papua New Guinea ("The Island Press" 1987:48)

The Lusi-Kaliai people of coastal West New Britain Province, Papua New Guinea, tell a story about an aggressive (and ugly) woman named Silimala who harasses and forces herself on a young man, Akono, until he marries her. In an attempt to discourage her attentions, Akono beats Silimala to death. But this being a folk tale (and a comedy at that), Silimala is not daunted. She persists until he agrees to marry her, and she accompanies Akono home as his second wife. There she behaves obnoxiously. She is lazy, she takes over the house that is occupied by Akono's first wife, Galiki, and tosses Galiki and her belongings out the door, and she burns, strikes, and otherwise torments Galiki, who endures the abuse passively, as a good woman should. Akono, she explains, must have desired this woman or he would not have brought her home. It is, therefore, her lot to accept whatever Silimala does, for it is Akono's will. Finally, shamed by Silimala's treatment of Galiki, Akono conspires with Galiki and her mother to trick Silimala into committing suicide.

When I have heard this story told I have been impressed by several things.

—Silimala is an assertive, aggressive, stubborn woman who persists, despite violent punishment, until she has what she wants.

—Galiki's passive behavior allows her to overcome adversity and eventually to win the struggle with the support of her husband.

—Co-wife violence is taken for granted as an aspect of polygynous marriage, although the usual pattern of co-wife violence is reversed in this story. Commonly, the second, new spouse is the one cherished by the husband and is attacked by the jealous first wife.

—Everybody loathes Silimala. She deserves to be beaten. She even deserves to die. Both women and men laugh with approval when Silimala is fooled into killing herself. Furthermore, it is not unusual for a male member of the audience—overcome by his anger at Silimala's intransigence—to break into the narration and urge Akono to "hit her again."

The story of Silimala and the audience's response to the tale express a number of the assumptions and stereotypes that underlie domestic violence in Kaliai: the male should be the master in male-female interactions; a woman should not push herself on a man, and if she is rejected she should withdraw quietly; an assertive, aggressive, lazy woman who insists on having her way despite obvious male displeasure is an object of contempt and rage; it is correct for a man to do physical violence to such a woman.

Violence does not dominate family relationships or community life in Kaliai. Personal interactions are marked more by laughter, helpfulness, and cooperation than by anger and hostility. Ordinarily, a Kaliai village is a cheerful and pleasant place to live, both for its residents and for a visiting anthropologist. Nevertheless, violence is a component of Lusi-Kaliai family life. Adults laugh approvingly when toddlers hit older children, and children are expected to fight with one another. Wife beating is common, and village women say that nearly all women can expect to be beaten by their husbands sometime during their marriage. Women strike their children, fight with their co-wives, and hit their sexual partners. The co-wife relationship is a particularly stressful one and has the potential for attempted murder or suicide, either by the first wife or by the husband, who is shamed by his inability to control his wives. I am aware of four unsuccessful suicide or homicide attempts (three by women and one by a man) and two successful suicides (both by men) arising directly from the strife in a polygynous marriage.

The Lusi-Kaliai are not unusual, for domestic violence is common in Papua New Guinea. Nearly 75 percent of the women murdered in the country are killed by their husbands (Law Reform Commission 1987:4). The national government has recognized that domestic violence is a serious problem. Consequently, the Law Reform Commission of Papua New Guinea (LRC) has initiated a program of research to understand the causes of domestic violence and to design and implement reforms to reduce it (Toft 1985, 1986; Toft and Bonnell 1985). Among its findings is that violence is so embedded in the marital relationship that people often do not see it as a problem unless it exceeds the society's norms of acceptability or unless it becomes the basis of conflict between men (Law Reform Commission 1987).

The LRC does not distinguish between acceptable and unacceptable violence, nor does it emphasize the alternatives that are available to women in isolated rural areas. In this chapter on wife beating in Kaliai I will focus on these topics. I also raise the question, implicit in Silimala's story, of why Lusi-Kaliai women sometimes behave in ways that they know will result in their being beaten. What does their behavior, in the face of violent retribution, suggest about male-female relationships and gender roles in Kaliai?

Domestic Violence in Kaliai

The Lusi-Kaliai live in five villages located along the northwest coast of West New Britain. They are slash-and-burn horticulturalists who earn most of their cash income by producing copra, the primary commercial crop of the area. Their social organization is patrilineal and ideally virilocal. In the past, most marriages have been between people of the same or neighboring villages, so that wives usually reside no more than two or three hours away from their natal families. Nowadays, this pattern is often broken by educated young people who choose mates from among friends in high school or another town. In these cases, young wives may live many hours, or even days, away from their families.

Authority in both household and community affairs is based on sex and age. There is a political ideal of equality for males, and of the right of men to hold authority over women and younger men, but this right may be overridden by the force of an individual's personality. Although it is not the rule, a strong-willed and intelligent woman may boss her younger relatives and achieve a reputation as a skilled manipulator of the exchange system. These women are called *tamine ra tamone* (manly women); although they are respected by both women and men, they do not become political leaders.

Political leaders, or *maroni,* achieve their position by the conspicuous distribution of wealth items that include shell money, pigs, and pandanus mats made by women. These distributions occur when children are acknowledged as members of their fathers' lineages, when people marry, and during mortuary celebrations. Marriages are formalized by bridewealth, and divorce is not difficult, but when a marriage ends, custody of the children usually remains with their father. This creates an emotional hardship for the mother if her natal home is far from her ex-husband's residence.

It is my impression that domestic violence is less prevalent among the Lusi-Kaliai than among some of their neighbors, where it is reported to be "particularly common and severe" (Chowning 1985:72). It is difficult to estimate accurately how often wife beating occurs in rural communities for, as one of my consultants observed, most of it occurs at night or when the couple is alone in their gardens and unobserved by others. It is almost never a daily occurrence in any one family because the relatives of a woman whose husband beat her every day or several times a week would soon interfere to stop the violence. Nevertheless, it is not uncommon in village life. During the four months of my research in 1985, there were, in the community of about 350 people where I lived, two episodes of wife beating severe enough to lead others to interfere, as well as a number of others that did not merit outside intervention. Incidents of domestic violence do not usually result in serious physical injury or bloodshed, for onlookers readily intervene to prevent these. While it is rare, a woman may attack her husband if she believes he is having an affair or is planning to take a second wife. A woman who explodes in violent anger for these reasons generally has the sympathy of onlookers. If she leaves him, however, she may lose public support, and she jeopardizes her rights to her children, who belong to their father and his kin group.

It is much more common for husbands to strike their wives. My consultants, female as well as male, generalize that "all" men hit their wives at one time or another, but this is a normative rather than a statistical statement for, in fact, some do not. Women from the community where I did research name a half-dozen men (out of approximately eighty male householders) who either never strike their wives or who have not done so in many years and an equal number who "don't just slap, they hit to 'kill,'" that is, to inflict real pain or injury. Women who are married to gentle men say their husbands are exceptional and they consider themselves fortunate.

Just as public opinion supports the violent anger (but not the desertion) of a woman whose husband has taken a new sexual partner, both women and men uphold the right of a husband to hit his wife for cause. The justifications for wife beating in Kaliai are similar to those discussed by the Law Reform Commission of Papua New Guinea (Toft 1985). A husband has the right (even the duty) to strike his wife if she flirts with other men or commits adultery; if she draws blood in punishing their children; if she fails to meet her domestic obligations, such as preparing meals, caring for their children, keeping their house and its grounds clean and tidy, or working in the gardens; if she behaves in a way that publicly shames or insults her husband or his kin; if she fails to assist her husband in meeting his ceremonial obligations; if she fights with her co-wives or abuses his children by another woman. I have heard women comment critically that a male relative who failed to punish his wife for carelessness in her domestic chores was himself responsible for the disheveled state of their household because he did not discipline her for neglecting her duties.

Although both women and men accept wife beating in principle, and there is a strong feeling that others should not interfere in marital conflict, there is a point beyond which violence ceases to be acceptable and becomes abusive. Lusi-Kaliai willingly offer opinions as to whether a woman's behavior in a specific case merited a beating and whether the punishment she received was too severe. Nevertheless, abuse is situationally defined in each case according to the perceived offense of the wife, the degree of punishment given by the husband, the circumstances in which the beating took place, and the willingness of her kin to support her. The response to a beating—by the woman herself, by her relatives, or by witnesses not related to her—provides the best indication of when an "acceptable" level of punishment becomes abuse.

Abuse has occurred when the wife's kin support her effort to take the matter outside the domestic realm for redress or when others (usually, but not always, her relatives) interfere on her behalf. A woman's relatives will usually intervene if the beating is prolonged or if her husband publicly exposes her genitals, kicks her as though she were a dog, draws blood, or strikes her with a weapon larger than a small stick. Others, even the husband's relatives, may try to stop the beating if they fear that it is life-threatening or if it seems likely that the victim will be maimed or her bones broken. If a woman's natal family lives far away, a person of high standing in the community will likely intervene to stop the abuse because the reputation of the group will suffer when others learn that community members stood by while a woman was injured or unjustly beaten. Furthermore, the husband's group will be required to pay compensation when the wife's relatives learn of her mistreatment.

Regardless of the severity of the punishment, a major factor in the decision to interfere in a beating is whether others consider the wife to be guilty of the offense for which she is being beaten. Although I know of no instance in which an offending woman's kin helped her husband beat her for her misbehavior, they may refuse to help her escape from a violent husband, even one who is dangerously violent. In one instance, for example, the relatives of a woman whose husband attempted to kill her for suspected adultery agreed with his assessment of her behavior. Consequently, they not only failed to interfere on her behalf but refused her requests for help in leaving the community and her violent husband.

Strategies Available to Beaten Women

When a woman considers herself to have been beaten unjustly or excessively, a number of strategies are available. Many require the support of her family and all have serious limitations.

First, she may fight back. This option is sometimes chosen by women in other Papua New Guinea societies. In fact, when Papua New Guinea women commit murder, their victims are almost always their husbands, whom they kill in retaliation for long term abuse ("The Island Press" 1987:48). Lusi-Kaliai women do not often fight back because they fear more severe punishment or public shaming in return. If a woman who is severely or unjustly beaten passively accepts abuse, her kin may feel anger or pity for her plight, as did Galiki's husband, in which case they can be expected to do as Akono did and either attack or shame their kinswoman's tormentor or demand compensation payment.

Second, if her relatives do not intervene on her behalf, a women may leave her husband and return to her own kin. This option has two shortcomings: her relatives may be unwilling to accept her back, either because they are reluctant to return the bridewealth or because they fear retribution by her husband; and she will probably lose custody of her children, a cost that many women are unwilling to bear.

Third, a woman may expose her husband to *mali* (menstrual blood contamination) in order to cause respiratory illness and/or death, or she may collect his hair, cigarette butts, or other "dirty" possessions to use in sorcery. Although women attributed a number of illnesses and deaths to either menstrual contamination or sorcery, none of them admitted to using either option.

Fourth, she may take the dispute to the public arena and charge her husband before village or provincial court authorities. This option requires the support of a woman's male kin for a number of reasons, the principal one being that if the woman's action is successful, her husband will be fined and/or jailed and she will face his angry retribution. Also, his punishment costs his family scarce cash resources and deprives them of his labor while he is in jail. If a woman lacks her relatives' support in accusing her husband, she and her children may suffer real hardship.

There are problems with the use of the imposed legal system and its norms as a source of sanctuary for beaten women. The LRC and the Women and Law Committee (WLC) have concluded that although wife beating is against the law the majority of rural people (women as well as men) seem to be in favor of it and most rural husbands practice it (Bradley 1998:2). This has implications for the enforcement of laws against wife beating for, as Chowning has observed, "local government councillors and other village officials almost all strike their own wives and so are reluctant to prosecute other men except when exceptional brutality is involved" (1985:88). Recognizing this problem, the LRC made a number of recommendations (Law

Reform Commission 1987). Among these were remedial measures designed to improve the way rural village courts handle cases of domestic violence.

Although village courts have the power to punish assault and to issue Preventive Orders prohibiting further violence, in the past most magistrates did not realize that these powers applied to cases of wife beating. Consequently, village courts usually followed local custom, which in much of Papua New Guinea as in Kaliai meant that a husband was allowed to beat his wife within certain limits (Bradley 1998:6). The LRC suggested measures to educate village magistrates about their responsibilities in cases of wife bashing, while the WLC took steps to make village women aware of their legal rights. The WLC distributed leaflets explaining the law and giving step-by-step instructions on how a person could take a case through the courts. At the same time, the Village Courts Secretariat sent out leaflets to village magistrates informing them of what had happened in government courts. The leaflets seem to be effective. When village magistrates are made familiar with government law they are more likely to issue judgments consistent with national legal principles rather than local tradition (Bradley personal communication 1987; Fitzpatrick personal communication 1987). This encouraging trend suggests that Scaglion and Whittingham are correct when they say that village courts seem to be the most favorable forum presently available to women for managing domestic disputes (1985:132).

Fifth, a woman may leave her husband and take a lover or second husband. This option should be chosen only if all the other alternatives have been unsuccessful, for if a woman enters into an adulterous relationship without her kin group's consent, they are likely to withdraw support and leave her to her fate.

Sixth, an abused woman may commit suicide. Lusi-Kaliai consider this to be an honorable alternative, especially if the woman feels that her husband's act has been unjust. I have argued elsewhere that suicide is one way in which powerless, shamed Kaliai women can get revenge and that the majority of suicide attempts (two of three) and a high proportion of completed suicides (five of twelve) have occurred shortly after the woman was beaten by her husband (Counts 1980, 1987). A similar relationship between wife abuse and suicide is also reported for North America, where research by Campbell (1989:23) confirms the conclusion of Stark and Flitcraft that battering may be "the single most important precipitant for female suicide yet identified" (1985:22).

The factors influencing a woman's decision to kill herself are complex. Sometimes the way in which a woman is beaten results in suicide. One consultant observed that a woman who is beaten unjustly will have *ailolo sasi* (literally, "bad insides"; idiomatically, "self pity"), a mixture of anger, shame, and despair that may cause her to kill herself. Sometimes the beating is only one aspect of a situation in which the woman kills herself because she is shamed. Occasionally, villagers suspect that a death alleged to have been suicide is in fact due to injuries suffered as a result of marital violence. Sometimes two or more of these elements are present in a suicide case.

The Fate of Assertive Women

Occasionally a Lusi-Kaliai woman feels so strongly about achieving a goal or asserting her rights that she persists in behavior even though she knows she will be beaten as a result. Silimala provides the prototype for this kind of behavior, but there are other examples of forceful women in Kaliai myths and folk tales. The fate of these fictitious women—and the delight of audiences when they are killed—demonstrates that aggressive and assertive behavior by women is censured. Still, it does happen. I have seen women determinedly stick with a course of action in spite of warnings—from female and male kin or affines as well as husbands—that they will be beaten. For instance, one woman refused to marry the man her father chose for her; another insisted that her husband must not use family resources on behalf of the children of another wife; another refused to surrender her rights in a cash crop claimed by her maternal kin. All of these women were threatened with violence if they persisted, and two were beaten for their intransigence. Puri, the woman who defied her maternal kin, threatened to take her case to court and was supported in her claims by her husband. His backing and her willingness to take the dispute into the government arena discouraged her relatives from attacking her physically, although they did advance on her, clenched fists raised, during a public meeting where the dispute was aired (for more details of this case see Counts and Counts 1974:141–49).

The example of Mary is also instructive. In spite of her husband's angry warnings, Mary (who was a first wife) frequently attacked her co-wife. When her husband beat her, she fought back. When he knocked her unconscious and publicly shamed her in an attempt to control her belligerence, she attempted suicide. Bested, her husband no longer interferes when Mary fights with her co-wife. The cost was high, but Mary won. Are the actions of Mary, Silimala, and other stubborn and determined women aberrant? Or is this a pattern that scholars who attempt to understand domestic violence should note?

This latter possibility is suggested by the African sociologist Timbamanya

M. Mushanga. Using data from Bohannan's (1960) edited collection on homicide and suicide in African societies, Mushanga argues that African wives sometimes "provoke" their husbands into beating them to death (1977–78:482–83). This is most likely to happen, Mushanga says, among people who are employed in the traditional sector of the economy because they are the ones with orthodox views about the roles of women. In their view women should focus on child care and household and garden chores, and "above all" women should "remain subservient to their husbands" (484). These are the men who will not tolerate any "nonsense" about "equality" between women and men. Mushanga continues: "It would appear that the new ideas about women's liberation in communities that are generally traditional may create situations in which the wife may directly or indirectly bring about her own death. This may happen as a result of a woman's attempt to assert her own rights, which may conflict with cultural patterns of behavior and socially accepted responses of a wife towards her husband" (1977–78:484).

How do we evaluate Mushanga's argument? Is he providing an important indigenous insight into the complexity of marital relationships and family violence? Do women really intend to "provoke" their husbands into killing them? There is a profound difference in a woman's demanding her rights even though she expects to get a beating and a relationship that begins with a husband beating his assertive wife and deteriorates into a situation in which he repeatedly beats and finally kills her in an attempt to force her into submission. Mushanga's analysis, which appears to blame the victim for getting herself killed, does not account for this difference, nor does it attribute to the husband either responsibility for delivering the fatal beating(s) or culpability in his wife's death.

Although Mushanga's analysis is seriously flawed, he does raise an issue that must be addressed. We must recognize and understand the factors that motivate women to persevere in behavior that they know will result in violent retribution. One approach is suggested by Levinson's observation that social change is an ongoing and open-ended process that may affect patterns of domestic violence (1988:451). Mushanga attributes particularly virulent wife beating to specific kinds of social change. Other scholars also report an increase in domestic violence with modernization. For example, Scaglion (this volume) associates it with an increase in spousal violence among the Abelam of Papua New Guinea because educated, mobile young Abelam women are less tolerant of abuse, adultery, gambling, and neglect on the part of their husbands and more willing to fight back or even to strike the first blow than were women a generation ago. Similarly, Lateef (this volume) observes that modern working Indo-Fijian wives assert their rights and refuse to accept total male control unconditionally, even though they may be beaten as a result.

Au Doko, who is a member of the Law Reform Commission and the Women and Law Committee, also points out the relationship between change and wife beating. She observes that educated, employed women are independent and capable of speaking and thinking for themselves. This conflicts with the traditional notion that the husband is the head of the household and makes the decisions while the wife remains silent. In Au Doko's opinion, wife beating is an even more serious problem for educated urbanized Papua New Guinean women than it is for traditional women living in rural areas (South Pacific People's Federation 1989:3–5).

Some of my female informants insist that wife beating is increasing, especially among educated Lusi-Kaliai. There are a number of changes in West New Britain that have contributed to a new perception by women of their rights and therefore, at least indirectly, to their being beaten for insubordination. These include increased exposure to Western ideas about courtship and women's rights and the rejection—especially by educated women—of arranged marriage. One well-educated Kaliai woman who lived with a violent man for eight years insists that two factors relating to modernization—the availability of alcohol and the unwillingness of educated women to submit meekly—contribute to increased violence among educated Lusi-Kaliai. After listing a number of her kinswomen who had endured severe abuse and left their marriages after their husbands took second wives, she commented: "I used to think that there was something wrong with the women in my family. I looked at the marriages of the other village women, and I worried that it was our fault that we were beaten so badly and that our relationships were not stable. But now I realize that it isn't us. It's because we're educated, and we want to have an equal say in things. We want to have our rights. We fight like hell, and this enrages the men. So they look for other women who won't argue with them."

Changes in rights and authority that occur during the developmental cycle of the family also affect the level of violence between spouses. I have noted elsewhere that most wife beating in Kaliai occurs early in marriage (Counts 1992). This is when each spouse is attempting to assert his/her rights. By the time couples reach middle age, they have probably worked out a mutually acceptable relationship and are more likely to be united by common interests than divided by a struggle over rights and authority. Also, as other scholars have observed, by the time she is middle-aged a woman who is destined to achieve a position of respect and authority has probably done so (see, e.g., Keith 1980; Brown 1982). She may have the responsibility for supervising her daughters-in-law as well as her own children, and she is more likely to recommend (or practice) physical violence toward younger women than she is to be the victim of it (Brown 1982, 1992; ; see also Lateef, in this volume, for this pattern among Indo-Fijians).

Women may also assert themselves and attempt to achieve a measure of equality with their menfolk in order to become respected adult members of society. Being beaten may be the cost women must pay to achieve the status of adult person. This approach is suggested by McDowell (this volume), who attributes the determination of Bun women to assert their autonomy—and the violence of their male kin and husbands, who attempt to control them—to the ethos that requires an individual to maintain a balance between personal autonomy and social relatedness in order to achieve personhood. A shamed, controlled, nonassertive individual is a "rubbish person," not a human being, regardless of gender.

As McDowell reports for the Bun, Lusi-Kaliai women who defy their husbands and follow a course of action that they know will result in a beating may be following a strategy that permits them to assert their rights, increase their options, and expand their boundaries. They accept the beating as part of the cost of achieving a level of autonomy.

As is also true of many battered women in Canada, Lusi-Kaliai women who are beaten by their husbands may perceive themselves not as powerless victims but as stronger than the men who beat them and for whom they, ironically, feel pity (MacLeod 1987:41). When viewed in this way, beaten women—in Kaliai as well as in Canada—are not passive victims but coactors in an ongoing relationship. They are, at least to some extent, mistresses of their fate.

I must emphasize that the preceding paragraphs are *not* meant to suggest that a beaten woman deserves what she gets, nor does my discussion necessarily apply to all (or even to most) occasions of spousal violence. The scenario I describe is limited to those interactive situations in which a woman, in explicit defiance of male authority, asserts herself and is beaten in return. Although surely unnecessary, I will nonetheless state the obvious: that recognition of a pattern of interaction, or an examination of the complex factors contributing to spousal violence, does not imply justification for or approval of such violence.

Conclusion

While domestic violence and wife beating are part of family life in Kaliai, there are limits beyond which acceptable violence becomes abusive and outsiders will intervene to stop it. A severely beaten woman can sometimes motivate her relatives to intercede on her behalf by remaining passive. A woman who returns her husband's blows risks losing the sympathy of her kin and takes the chance of being even more severely beaten. Assertive, aggressive Lusi-Kaliai women who defy their husbands or other male relatives are often condemned for their behavior and risk being beaten for it. Nevertheless, women do challenge male authority and demand a voice in choosing a mate or deciding how to distribute family resources. They fight back when they perceive that they are being treated unfairly, and they insist on their rights of inheritance and self-determination. These women remind us that although Papua New Guinea women are often dominated by their menfolk, they are not necessarily passive, pathetic victims. Instead, many of them are determined to preserve their autonomy and maintain control over their lives, and they are willing to risk ill treatment to achieve their goals.

The avenues of relief available to beaten women, whether they are passive victims or persons insisting on their rights, are restricted in Papua New Guinea and may be of limited effectiveness or desirability. The most promising options seem to derive from the programs of public education and legal reform being instituted by the Law Reform Commission and the Women and Law Committee. There is emerging evidence that the efforts of these bodies are bringing about a change in attitudes toward marital violence and are helping to create a new climate for women. The courts provide women with sanctions against abuse and a forum where domestic disputes can be settled peaceably.

NOTE

The research on which this chapter is based was supported in 1966–67 by the National Science Foundation and Southern Illinois University; in 1971 by the University of Waterloo and the Wenner-Gren Foundation; in 1975–76 by the Canada Council and the University of Waterloo; and in 1981 and 1985 by the University of Waterloo and research grants from the Social Sciences and Humanities Research Council of Canada. I wish to thank David Counts, Judith Brown, Jacquelyn Campbell, and Ursula Kolkolo for reading and commenting on earlier versions of this chapter.

REFERENCES CITED

Bohannan, Paul. 1960. *African Homicide and Suicide.* Princeton, N.J.: Princeton University Press.

Bradley, Christine. 1998. "Should Human Rights Apply to Wives?: Wife-Beating and the Work of the Papua New Guinea Law Reform Commission." In *Modern Papua*

New Guinea Society. Ed. Laura Zimmer-Tamakoshi. 351–64. Kirksville, Mo.: Thomas Jefferson University Press.

Brown, Judith K. 1982. "Cross-Cultural Perspectives on Middle-Aged Women." *Current Anthropology* 23:143–56.

———. 1992. "Lives of Middle-Aged Women." In *In Her Prime: A New View of Middle-Aged Women.* 2d ed. Ed. Virginia Kerns and Judith K. Brown. 17–30. Urbana: University of Illinois Press.

Campbell, Jacquelyn C. 1989. "A Test of Two Explanatory Models of Women's Responses to Battering." *Nursing Research* 38:18–24.

Chowning, Ann. 1985. "Kove Women and Violence: The Context of Wife-Beating in a West New Britain Society." In *Domestic Violence in Papua New Guinea.* Ed. Susan Toft. 72–91. Papua New Guinea Law Reform Commission Monograph No. 3. Boroko.

Counts, D., and D. Counts. 1974. "The Kaliai Lupunga: Disputing in the Public Forum." In *Contention and Dispute: Aspects of Law and Social Control in Melanesia.* Ed. A. L. Epstein. 113–51. Canberra: Australian National University Press.

Counts, Dorothy Ayers. 1980. "Fighting Back Is Not the Way: Suicide and the Women of Kaliai." *American Ethnologist* 7:332–51.

———. 1987. "Female Suicide and Wife Abuse in Cross-Cultural Perspective." *Suicide and Life-Threatening Behavior* 17:194–204.

———. 1992. " *Tamparonga:* 'The Big Women' of Kaliai (Papua New Guinea)." In *In Her Prime: A New View of Middle-Aged Women.* 2d ed. Ed. Virginia Kerns and Judith K. Brown. 61–74. Urbana: University of Illinois Press.

Keith, Jennie. 1980. "The Best Is Yet to Be: Toward an Anthropology of Age." In *Annual Review of Anthropology.* Vol. 9. Ed. Bernard Siegal, Alan Beals, and Stephen Tyler. 339–66. Palo Alto, Calif.: Annual Reviews Inc.

Law Reform Commission of Papua New Guinea. 1987. *Interim Report on Domestic Violence.* Boroko.

Levinson, David. 1988. "Family Violence in Cross-Cultural Perspective." In *Handbook of Family Violence.* Ed. Vincent B. Van Hasselt, Randall L. Morrison, Alan S. Bellack, and Michel Hersen. 435–55. New York: Plenum Press.

MacLeod, Linda. 1987. *Battered but Not Beaten . . .: Preventing Wife Battering in Canada.* Ottawa: Canadian Advisory Council on the Status of Women.

Mushanga, Timbamanya M. 1977–78. "Wife Victimization in East and Central Africa." *Victimology* 2:479–85.

"The Island Press: From the Papua New Guinea *Post-Courier,* Port Moresby." 1987. *Pacific Islands Monthly* 58 (4): 48.

Scaglion, Richard, and Rose Whittingham. 1985. "Female Plaintiffs and Sex-Related Disputes in Rural Papua New Guinea." In *Domestic Violence in Papua New Guinea.* Ed. Susan Toft. 120–33. Papua New Guinea Law Reform Commission Monograph No. 3. Boroko.

South Pacific People's Federation. 1989. "Women's Development in Papua New Guinea." *Tok Blong South Pacific People's Federation* 29 (Oct.): 3–11.

Stark, Evan, and Ann H. Flitcraft. 1985. "Spouse Abuse." Working paper prepared for Surgeon General's Workshop on Violence and Public Health Source Book. Atlanta, Ga.: U.S. Public Health Service, Centers for Disease Control.

Toft, Susan. 1986. "Domestic Violence in Urban Papua New Guinea." Papua New Guinea Law Reform Occasional Paper No. 19. Boroko.

———, ed. 1985. *Domestic Violence in Papua New Guinea.* Papua New Guinea Law Reform Commission Monograph No. 3. Boroko.

Toft, Susan, and Susanne Bonnell. 1985. "Marriage and Domestic Violence in Rural Papua New Guinea." Papua New Guinea Law Reform Commission Occasional Paper No. 18. Boroko.

SIX

Household Violence in a Yuat River Village

Nancy McDowell

The people of Bun,[1] a small village on the Yuat River in the East Sepik Province of Papua New Guinea, are assertive and volatile, and violence among them is not infrequent. In order to understand violence within the household, it is necessary to examine a complex interaction of several factors and not search for any simple cause-effect relationship. For example, it is not that frustration generates aggression, or that increasing stress is displaced onto the nuclear family, or that warriors must be generally aggressive if the society is to survive—although all of these may be contributory, searching for one simple cause for a complex phenomenon is inadequate.

Nor is it possible to seek causes on only one analytical level: ideological, social, and affective factors are all relevant. Specifically, the meaning and incidence of household violence[2] cannot be understood without examining the indigenous conception of *person* (a cultural structuring), *ethos* and *affect* (psychological factors), and *social process* itself (kinship, power, and politics). The first section of this chapter describes Bun ethos and affect, emotional and psychological tendencies that relate directly to the production of violence. The second section describes Bun views of the world with a particular focus on the structuring of the person, for the process whereby one achieves personhood is seminal in the generation of violence. In the final section, the incidence of household violence is examined.

On Violence and Ethos

The Bun inhabit a single, small village (Bun) directly upriver from the people Mead (1963) described as the Mundugumor, and in many ways the two are very similar (see Mead 1963; McDowell 1976, 1977, 1978a, 1978b, 1980, 1984a, 1987, 1991). Perhaps the most striking similarity between the two is what

Bateson (1936) labeled *ethos:* the emotional tone and tenor of the society. Mead described both Mundugumor women and men as assertive, violent, volatile people. She noted that they also had a great capacity for joy and generosity as well as other traits Westerners might interpret as positive, but it was the violence, particularly in the context of childrearing, that she emphasized.

If one acknowledges the joyful side as well as the more aggressive one, then Bun ethos is very similar to that of their downriver neighbors. Both women and men tend to be assertive, volatile, and quick to defend themselves.[3] Strength is a major value and virtue, and one of the most obvious ways to demonstrate strength is through physical violence. There are other ways, such as sponsoring large and successful feasts, maintaining order in one's own orbit of influence, provisioning one's family well, demonstrating wisdom, and, traditionally, ritual power. However, physical violence plays an important role in self-assertion. It is a typical reaction to insult and frustration, an outgrowth of anger; it is a natural response to challenges to one's strength. Although there do exist some ritual challenges that allow one to demonstrate strength, to be called weak or inferior provokes anger, which often escalates from verbal abuse to physical violence.

The expression of anger through physical aggression is a theme in socialization. Children learn that violence is frequently the proper response when those in one's environment challenge or frustrate. Children's play groups are characterized by squabbling that often escalates to violence, and older siblings regularly hit younger siblings who are in their care. Parents often punish children by hitting them, throwing things at them, lashing out in various ways, almost always in anger.

On Person and Violence

Autonomy and control are issues faced by people everywhere, but they seem to be especially significant issues in Melanesia. Elsewhere (McDowell 1978a, 1980, 1984b) I have described how the need to assert one's autonomy is a central cultural and psychological issue in Bun: one must prove one's autonomy while simultaneously participating in social relations that always impair one's desired freedom. The Bun solve this dilemma by basing all internal relations on balanced and symmetrical exchange. One preserves one's autonomy by not allowing another to control or to be superior; one remains equal and unindebted. If one escapes being controlled by another, if one avenges insults and avoids shame and responds to challenges with self-assertion, then one achieves personhood.[4]

This concept of *personhood* is significantly different from the Western one, which stresses individualism and an acting or core and separate self. Several ethnographers (e.g., Clay 1986; Gewertz 1984; Read 1955) note that Melanesians are defined far more relationally and less individualistically than Westerners.[5] A Bun person is one who handles the delicate balance between autonomy and sociability by executing transactions that allow for both a relational and an autonomous self. There exists a slight gender difference in the attainment of personhood: although both women and men must strike a balance between autonomy and relatedness, men stress autonomy more than women (McDowell 1984a). Very few people fail completely to achieve personhood, but occasionally someone does. These are people who fall into the familiar category of "rubbish person." It is important to note that much of the process is relative—some people clearly achieve fuller personhood than others or are content to rest with a questionable achievement.

To accomplish personhood, one must first share with close kin (while, of course, expecting that they share back). In this domain, affect, closeness, and relational ties are emphasized. But to be a person, it is also necessary to transact in two exchange modes that are more formal. The first is that of *kamain*, a distant kin tie ritually transformed into an exchange relationship of both material and intangible goods. *Kamain* exchanges must be balanced and equal; if one fails to keep up, shame and a denial of personhood are inevitable. The second is participation in marital exchanges of people, that is, of siblings. The ideal is that all marriages occur by brother-sister exchange, a transaction in which equality and balance are guaranteed, and the vast majority of marriages are conceived as if they were between brother-sister pairs of classificatory cross-cousins. If a man does not have a sister, he is at a distinct disadvantage, but there are ways in which he can marry anyway (McDowell 1978b). A deeper problem confronts the man who has a sister but somehow loses her, either to his male kin (to execute their marriages) or to a husband who does not reciprocate with a wife for him. In these cases, the challenge to equity runs deep indeed.

Clearly, this process of asserting oneself, achieving personhood by remaining at least equal, maintaining one's autonomy and avoiding control by others (while simultaneously trying to control them) is a political process that is deeply intertwined with the acquisition of power. It played a significant role in the traditional political system in which individual men achieved status by maintaining their strength and controlling others in exchanging and feasting as well as in warfare and ritual. The arena in which one demonstrated one's strength was wider in traditional society, one that included warfare and intervillage raiding; today the arena in which it is manifested has shrunk. One can—indeed, one must—demonstrate one's ability to maintain equity in the context of the *kamain* relationship. Because formality and respect characterize the tie, it is not appropriate to win too much—the ideal is equity, and people who violate that ideal by trying to outdo their *kamain* are accused of trying to shame these relations, a serious breach of manners and a violation of appropriate kin behavior. The relationship between cross-cousins allows for somewhat more leeway; these relatives frequently provoke one another into a series of competitive feasts in which the goal is to provide so much that the others cannot possibly reciprocate (e.g., McDowell 1982). Business is providing a new means of asserting one's strength: if one proves one's strength by accumulating money to buy things (such as outboard motors), then one demonstrates strength superior to others. But by far the most significant contemporary arena for proving one's strength, and in which one's strength is most frequently challenged, is that concerning marital exchange.

On Social and Political Process

Ethos and personhood help to explain the prevalence of violence in Bun, but the pattern of violence must be understood in the sociopolitical context of marriage, for marriage provides the crucible out of which most interpersonal violence between adults emerges. It is within the process of attracting sexual partners and arranging marriages that much of the assertion of self takes place, and it is within this context that one is frequently frustrated and challenged by others.

Arranging these ideal marriages is enormously complex (McDowell 1978b) and requires detailed planning and a lot of luck. Rarely do plans work smoothly, for the simple reason that seldom are there classificatory cross-cousins of the appropriate age and sex who are *willing* to marry the partner indicated for them. Although both men and women phrase these exchanges as if brothers exchanged their passive and yielding sisters, the reality is that women rarely marry men they do not like. (Women and men both perceive that, like Collier's [1974] troublemakers, these are idiosyncratic actions of obstreperous women rather than a pattern of resistance to male authority [McDowell 1984a].) Women assert their autonomy by refusing to marry men to whom their brothers and fathers try to send them and frequently by insisting that they marry men of their own choosing. By contrast, men demonstrate their power by executing what they believe to be appropriate exchanges when they can. The process is made even more complex by the fact that men try to attract hopefully unreciprocated women. They foil other men's plans by trying to entice women who are not appropriate; and by so doing they assert their own power to attract and control. Maintaining a marriage and maintaining one's power over one's wife, or maintaining one's autonomy from one's husband, or choosing one's own husband are serious aspects of marriage that, when individuals' power and autonomy are threatened, can generate interpersonal violence.

Marriage exchanges are, then, essentially political processes: they involve ways of manifesting and demonstrating personal power. Disputes about these transactions are not located in either a domestic or a public sphere because the spheres, although they do exist (McDowell 1984a), are not clearly differentiated. In fact, it is precisely the process of arranging marriages that provides the most significant overlap of the public and domestic spheres. Marriages are the foundation of domestic life, but their arrangement involves a public and very political process. Violence in Bun, as elsewhere, is not random: it clusters around four related relationships within which power issues and assertions of self are deeply significant: (1) husband-wife; (2) co-wife–co-wife; (3) sister-brother; (4) affines or potential affines. The first two of these are relatively straightforward; understanding the dynamics of the second two is more problematic. Teasing these four out from the larger context in which they occur allows for more careful attention to each, but marriage is a process that involves all of these people who are embedded together in a single complex.

Physical violence between husbands and wives is commonplace. In just over fourteen months of fieldwork, I recorded thirty incidents of physical violence between spouses, and I am certain that there were many more cases that never came to my attention (the total population of the village during this time was approximately 220). Some couples did not fight physically at all during this period, but at least sixteen did. One couple accounts for six of the incidents, two couples fought four times, one couple fought three times, five couples fought twice, and seven couples fought physically only once during this period. The severity of the physical violence varied; in some instances, a person was only struck once and not physically harmed, but in other cases serious physical damage resulted. One woman's ribs were broken, another woman was badly battered, and in one case a man's collarbone was broken.

Although people say that a quarrel between husband and wife is their own business, bystanders and kin interfere for two reasons. One is simply that, although physical beatings are acceptable, there are limits—excessive damage to another person is not tolerated. Onlookers try to take weapons away to prevent permanent injury or death. The second reason people interfere in a quarrel between wife and husband serves to intensify and spread the physical violence rather than curtail it—namely, people use the occasion of their female relatives being beaten by their husbands to further quarrels with these men. For example, a man might hit his wife because she did not cook, but then her brother—angry at his brother-in-law because of the original marriage exchange or for an entirely different reason—would, under the pretext of helping his sister, attack his brother-in-law. In this way, seemingly constrained domestic quarrels ramify and become larger political events. In a case I did not witness, a man hit his wife because no food was ready. Her brother, who had opposed the marriage, decided to help his sister; he joined the fray to protect her and wound up hitting his brother-in-law. Later, the husband and his own brother went into the bush with the wife's brother and a tree fell on the wife's brother, killing him. No charges were ever brought, but many people speculated that anger had remained and that the man had been murdered by his brothers-in-law.

Although women usually end up the physical victims when they quarrel violently with men, in two cases it was the husbands who sustained serious injuries. Women do not always passively accept their husbands' beatings—sometimes, especially if they are very angry or feel that they have a chance to come out ahead, they fight back, and some women even initiate the physical aspects of a dispute. In one incident, people were pulling a canoe out of the forest to the shore when the rattan broke, and women who were helping all fell down. One husband made fun of his wife. She was angry about being ridiculed and insulted him and would not cook his dinner. When he tried to calm her down and attempted to ease her anger, she stuck a machete through his wrist. Another couple had very dramatic confrontations. In one incident, the husband began to beat his wife, but she grabbed an ax and was prevented from killing him by bystanders (informants believed that she would have killed him if she had not been stopped). On two occasions, this woman initiated the quarrel and hit her husband, even going after him with a spear. The Bun say that men beat their wives with their hands and feet and that women tend to make use of weapons to defend themselves and to harm their husbands. This rule seems to hold true, but in the case of this ax- and spear-wielding woman, the husband once became so exasperated that he grabbed a piece of oil palm and bashed her over the head with it.

The reasons wives and husbands quarrel are diverse, but all have to do with power issues—who controls whom in the relationship. This may be a truism for violence between all spouses at some level, but it is in the forefront in Bun. Women often resist new marriages by staying away from their husbands and refusing to behave in general as wives should, and men frequently respond by beating them. One man's marriage had been arranged years before my arrival, and his sister was firmly married to his future wife's brother; he was waiting for this marked bride to mature. He did not wait patiently, and before she was old enough to marry, he had an affair with her mother. They had an on-again/off-again relationship for about two years; it only ended as the bride gained maturity and the marriage seemed imminent. The bride's mother was disgruntled about the end of the affair and wanted to marry the man herself, despite the fact that he was a generation younger and her daughter's marked husband. The bride was young, shy, and easily influenced by her mother, who told her that he would not be a good husband for her and she should resist the plans that had been made for her marriage.

Soon after I arrived, the news broke that the bride-to-be had slept with an attractive and unattached young man. In the ensuing argument, she was badly beaten by her brothers, and her lover was slapped around as well. He paid compensation to her future husband and the affair ended; it was not clear whether the young man was not seriously interested in marriage to her or if she was not forceful enough to resist the marriage arranged for her. It was clear that she did not want to marry her marked husband. At her mother's urgings, she resisted passively for months. Because she would not behave as a wife—neither as a sexual nor a domestic partner—her husband became angry and frustrated. He beat his own mother, who insulted him about the issue, and tried to seduce his wife's sister but was caught and had to pay compensation. He was urged by various people to persist in his bond with the recalcitrant bride and did so, but at a high cost to her: I recorded four separate occasions on which he beat her for not behaving as she should. She had no support from relatives, other than her troublemaking mother, and eventually gave in. (Although I use this case to examine husband-wife violence, it could also serve as an example of brother-sister violence, adultery, and even mother–adult son violence.)

A man's stated reason for hitting his wife is frequently that she did not prepare food or did not work, the implication being that she was off doing what she wanted to do rather than what her husband thought she should be doing. In the case of the husband with the broken collarbone, the ostensible reason his wife hit him with a log was that he wanted to play cards while she wanted him to help her in the garden. On two occasions husbands complained that their wives were not adequately caring for children and therefore deserved to be beaten. Sexual and other sorts of jealousy, however, are probably the most frequent cause of violence between spouses. A husband's belief that his wife may be committing adultery often goads him into violence against her. Women get angry at and jealous of co-wives and potential co-wives (and their husbands' adulteries). When they do so, they insult their husbands and provoke, if not initiate, the violence. The woman who had broken ribs as the result of a kick from her husband had accused him in obscene and insulting terms of spending all of his money on women while he was away working; she knew that such an insult would provoke him—she only regretted that he acted so fast that she did not have a chance to defend herself. When a man indicates that he may be getting a co-wife (especially if he is having an affair with an eligible woman), wives complain, refuse to cooperate, and generally make their displeasure clear. They often initiate or provoke violence and make life so miserable for their husbands that the men give up their polygynous plans.

Another significant way in which women fight back against the potential acquisition of additional wives is by taking lovers of their own and causing such disruption that divorce is the only solution. They know that beatings will occur, but some seem to be willing to pay that price. The root of one complex case was a woman's unwillingness to accept a particular co-wife. She made her displeasure known, and her husband avoided the conflict by signing on as a coastal plantation worker for two years. When he returned, his new wife was still waiting for him, but his first wife was having an affair with another man and seemed fairly committed to him. The husband was furious and demanded that she return to him and that he be paid compensation. During the first of several village moots to discuss the case, the wife was severely beaten by her brothers for her behavior; one of these brothers had used her to execute his own marriage and feared that his sister's divorce would undo his marriage as well. The adultery-committing couple paid compensation, and it appeared that the wife had returned to her husband, but she was obviously dissatisfied with the outcome. The lovers continued to meet despite all attempts to keep them apart. The woman was beaten severely by her husband, while her lover was struck by the husband and his own maternal uncle. After the wife's pregnancy was announced, the husband beat the lover in front of the latter's relatives, who did nothing to protect him. The husband also tried to beat his wife again, muttering that he would kill her this time, but was prevented from doing so by bystanders. The participants recognized an impasse and took the case to the colonial court in Angoram.[6]

Women do not like to share husbands and do whatever they can to prevent their husbands from acquiring additional wives. One man was having an affair with an older woman, and he was clearly thinking about marrying her. His second wife, favored and beautiful, was deeply resentful and expressed her resentment frequently by insulting her husband, refusing to cook, and being obstinant in various ways (and was beaten by her husband for it; this is the couple who fought at least six times). After one particularly nasty beating, she became enraged and attacked her husband's lover with an ax, nearly fracturing her skull. The husband abandoned thoughts of acquiring a third wife.

Disputes between husband and wife and between co-wives are ethnographically commonplace. The pivotal importance of brother-sister exchange marriage and individuals' attempts to assert themselves within the context of such marriage exchanges generates two additional dyads in which violence is prevalent in Bun, that is, between brother and sister and between affines (or potential affines).

If executed properly, a brother-sister exchange marriage results in two married couples who are closely connected to one another. Ideally, such affines cooperate with each other and support one another in disputes. When the marriages are executed smoothly and with little acrimony, good relations usually are the rule. However, few marriages are arranged and carried out with no trouble; in fact, despite the public ideology that men arrange marriages for themselves and their sons and their sisters' sons, the reality is that these exchanges are, as often as not, conflict-ridden.

Because of these conflicts, the relations among the major participants are acrimonious and sometimes violent. The brother-sister tie is supposed to be a close one, and in general it is. The tie is especially close with the sibling with whom one participated in a marriage exchange. A woman gives food to such a brother—regularly and without question; a man provides meat to his marked sister, often over the protests of his wife. But brother-sister pairs often clash violently about arranging marriages. Most typically, the brother (with his senior male kin) works out a marriage road for himself and his sister without consulting her; when she hears of the plans and learns the identity of her intended husband, she balks and refuses to marry accordingly. She can make her intentions known simply by announcing her refusal. If her relatives ignore her wishes and go ahead with the marriages, she simply refuses to behave like a wife. Not infrequently she already has a lover she prefers to marry; if so, she makes this affair known publicly and thereby forces her relatives to deal with her desires in the public arena of a village moot. If she is strong enough, if she accepts the beatings given to her primarily by her brothers, then her will usually prevails.[7] Some women, however, are not strong enough and acquiesce to the demands of their relatives.

Brothers beat their sisters for other reasons, but most have to do with trouble concerning marriage. It is best to interpret violence associated with adultery in this context because adultery indicates a desire for divorce and a threat to the earlier arranged marriages; it is not just a violation or theft of rights of sexual access. Thus, some women who commit adultery are beaten by their brothers as well as their husbands. Of the six cases of brother-sister violence that occurred during the period of my fieldwork, four were concerned with arranging initial marriages and two with the threat of adultery to already existing marriages. Moots are held ostensibly to settle the dispute, but anger flares and violence erupts. I never saw a woman try to fight back in this context, but informants told me of other cases in which women did defend themselves. Men assert their desires and attempt to control their sisters; women resist control and assert their autonomy in choosing a spouse or terminating a marriage.

Men try to assert themselves in the marriage context in an additional way: they attempt to attract women without laying the necessary groundwork for an exchange. They engage in sexual affairs in the hope that they can acquire a wife (or additional wives), and sometimes they are successful in this. But they must pay the price for their attempted seductions of women: the woman's brothers resent what they perceive to be theft of their rights to the woman, and their resentment erupts in physical violence. Even if marriages are eventually arranged, conflict and animosity remain because seductions are interpreted as sister-stealing. Sisters are beaten, but so also are their lovers, despite the fact that lovers transform into affines with some regularity. It seems appropriate, then, to include in this discussion certain kinds of violence between affines or potential affines.

Most such violence occurs between men, as in cases of brothers beating their sisters' lovers. But sometimes women get involved in attempts to protect what they perceive to be their siblings' rights. Two brothers from another village married in Bun and brought sisters to exchange for their wives. One of these sisters ended up in an incorrect marriage, and, what was even worse, when her husband died she married her father-in-law. Her brothers were furious with her and especially with her second husband, but they were unable to do anything about it. They brought another sister to the village to replace the one who had gone astray, and her intended husband waited for her to mature. When it was discovered that she was having an affair with the son of the man who had stolen their other sister, her brothers were furious. They beat the young man, but he was defended by his own brothers; the conflict ramified through a larger network as others joined the fray to support various relatives. Women participated in this fight as well: both of the wives of the in-married brothers, who were in fact sisters, feared that their brother was going to be robbed of a wife by the same people who had cheated him before. One of them attacked the young man's mother for hiding him and his actions from public view; the other attacked the young woman, their brother's potential wife.

Summary

Violence among kin in Bun must be understood as a part of how the Bun define themselves and achieve personhood. It is when personhood is threatened, when autonomy is in jeopardy, or when accusations of inferiority and therefore inhumanity are made that one must assert oneself and thereby demonstrate one's humanity. Establishing and situating the self as person is culturally meaningful, but it is also the foundation of political process and the generation of power over others. Physical violence is directed at those who frustrate, who challenge, who evade, who attempt to control, and as such it is an inherent part of the political process as well. Because arranging and maintaining marriages are the central ways in which autonomy is achieved as well as threatened, more violence occurs in this context than in any other contemporary arena.

NOTES

I would like to thank the National Institute of Mental Health, the National Endowment for the Humanities, and Franklin and Marshall College for financial support during my fieldwork in Bun. This chapter is a revised, condensed version of "Person, Assertion, and Marriage: On the Nature of Household Violence in Bun," in *Pacific Studies* 13:3 (1990): 171–88. I would like to thank the journal for permission to use this material.

1. I conducted fieldwork in Bun for approximately thirteen months in 1972–73 and six weeks in 1977. I also made two brief visits there during 1981.

2. I use the phrase "household violence" to avoid the more common expression "domestic violence." In Bun, the domestic and public realms are not clearly delineated, and in fact this kind of violence straddles the line between these two potential domains. See the discussion below about arranging marriages for examples.

3. That there is little or no contrast in gender ethos or, to use Mead's (1963 [1935]) old terminology, "temperament," does not mean that there are no contrasts in gender ideology, nor does it imply that male and female roles are the same. See McDowell (1984a) for a discussion of gender in Bun that relates directly to some of the issues discussed here.

4. I failed to understand the entire process while in the field and cannot answer some signficant questions about it. For example, when does a growing child begin the process? Are children nonpersons or does another category, perhaps "yet-to-be person," exist? Parents begin exchanges in the names of their children . . . but what if they fail to do so? Many such questions remain.

5. For a description of the Western perspective, see Bellah et al. (1985); for a contrasting view, see Burridge (1979).

6. What happened there surprised even close participants, for when asked what he wanted to do, the husband replied that he did not want his first wife back—he only wanted compensation. His first and second wives, recognizing that they had a common goal in facilitating the first wife's divorce (the new co-wife did not want to be a co-wife to anyone), formed an alliance and together shamed the husband in front of a variety of people by asking him, "Why have you made all of this necessary? You're just sexually excited all the time—you only think of female genitals." The ensuing shame, the knowledge that he had little chance in the face of an alliance between the two, and the fear that in reality the colonial court usually favored the woman made him back down and relinquish his claims on his first wife. The divorce was executed and compensation paid to the husband, and the lovers were free to marry.

7. Fathers are also participants in this; father-daughter violence, however, seems less common and perhaps should be conceived as a subset here. Fathers bluster and shout at their daughters more than they seem to beat them.

REFERENCES CITED

Bateson, Gregory. 1936. *Naven.* Cambridge: Cambridge University Press.

Bellah, Robert N., Richard Madesen, William M. Sullivan, Ann Swidler, and Steven M. Tipton. 1985. *Habits of the Heart.* Berkeley: University of California Press.

Burridge, Kenelm. 1979. *Someone, No One: An Essay on Individuality.* Princeton, N.J.: Princeton University Press.

Clay, Brenda Johnson. 1986. *Mandak Realities: Person and Power in Central New Ireland.* New Brunswick, N.J.: Rutgers University Press.

Collier, Jane. 1974. "Women in Politics." In *Woman, Culture, and Society.* Ed. Michelle Z. Rosaldo and Louise Lamphere. 89–96. Stanford, Calif.: Stanford University Press.

Gewertz, Deborah. 1984. "The Chambri View of Persons: A Critique of Individualism in the Works of Mead and Chodorow." *American Anthropologist* 86:615–29.

McDowell, Nancy. 1976. "Kinship and Exchange: The Kamain Relationship in a Yuat River Village." *Oceania* 47:36–48.

———. 1977. "The Meaning of 'Rape' in a Yuat River Village." *Ethnology* 16:175–83.

———. 1978a. "The Struggle to Be Human: Exchange and Politics in Bun." *Anthropological Quarterly* 51:16–25.

———. 1978b. "The Flexibility of Sister Exchange: Case Studies." *Oceania* 48:207–31.

———. 1980. "It's Not Who You Are but How You Give That Counts: The Role of Exchange in a Melanesian Society." *American Ethnologist* 82:278–302.

———. 1982. "Strength, Autonomy, and Alcohol Use in Bun." In *Through a Glass Darkly: Beer and Modernization in Papua New Guinea.* Ed. M. Marshall. 257–70. Institute of Applied Social and Economic Research Monograph No. 18. Boroko.

———. 1984a. "Complementarity: The Relationship between Male and Female in the East Sepik Village of Bun, Papua New Guinea." In *Rethinking Women's Roles: Perspectives from the Pacific.* Ed. D. O'Brien and S. Tiffany. 32–52. Berkeley: University of California Press.

———. 1984b. "On Person, Reciprocity, and Change: Explorations of Burridge in Bun." Paper prepared for the Wenner-Gren Foundation Symposium No. 95, "Sepik Research Today," Basel, Switzerland, August 1984.

———. 1987. "Exchange and Systems of Competitive Equality in Melanesia." Paper read at the annual meeting of the Association for Social Anthropology in Oceania, Monterey, Calif.

———. 1991. *The Mundugumor: From the Field Notes of Margaret Mead and Reo Fortune.* Washington, D.C.: Smithsonian Institution Press.

Mead, Margaret. 1963 [1935]. *Sex and Temperament in Three Primitive Societies.* New York: William Morrow.

Read, Kenneth. 1955. "Morality and the Concept of Person among the Gahuku-Gama." *Oceania* 25:233–82.

SEVEN

Why Wape Men Don't Beat Their Wives: Constraints toward Domestic Tranquility in a New Guinea Society

William E. Mitchell

The West, as we know, is fascinated with violence. Western journalists, filmmakers, and anthropologists working in New Guinea have made the island famous with reports of head-hunting, cannibalism and male-female antagonism. The range of New Guinea societies, however, is great. While the gentler societies lack the riveting appeal of those that are more flamboyantly aggressive, they can be instructive nonetheless. The Wape of Papua New Guinea's Sandaun (formerly West Sepik) Province are a case in point. Like many other Melanesian peoples, the egalitarian Wape live in a mountainous tropical forest habitat in sedentary villages and are slash-and-burn horticulturalists. Marriage occurs through bridewealth payments, polygyny is allowed but rare, postmarital residence is generally virilocal, and patrilineal clans are ideally exogamous while patrilineages are strictly so.[1] But the Wape differ from a number of the societies with whom they share these customs: Wape men do not beat their wives. This does not mean that conjugal relations are always harmonious, but it is unusual for a man to slap his wife and I know of no instances where a woman suffered an injurious beating from her husband.

Because wife beating is an accepted custom in many parts of Papua New Guinea and considered by the government to be a serious public health problem (Toft 1985), in this chapter I identify some of the factors or constraints that help explain the comparative tranquility of Wape domestic life. These constraints—located on various but intersecting sociocultural, psychological, historical, ecological, and physiological levels of analysis—are inextricably bound together in a complex circular relationship. Our knowledge of this relationship does not warrant the postulating of constraints operating on one level as being more important than those on another, so the general tranquility of Wape domestic life cannot be explained by a simple "cause and effect" model favored by an experimental positivistic science. The explanatory model proposed here is an associational one, more descriptive than causal, whose very circularity is essential to the explanation.[2]

The data for this study, including a review of relevant court records, were collected during an eighteen-month field trip in 1970–72 and brief revisits in 1982 and 1989. Although I have visited many of the villages of the approximately 10,000 Wape during my three trips to Wapeland, my view of Wape society and culture is as seen from Taute village, my principal fieldwork site.

Correlates of Wape Domestic Tranquility

Ethos and Emotions

The ethos of Wape society is markedly pacific. Although the society is not without its points of stress and the people not without passion concerning their personal relationships, the overall affective thrust of social life is to keep emotions, especially those that might lead to violence, under control. Even before Western contact, when enemy villages engaged in payback killings, the attacks might be years apart. Some Wape villages, on learning that the invading whites had banned warfare, abandoned the custom even before government patrols could intervene. During my fieldwork, I never saw a physical fight between men, between women, or even between children. The preferred Wape response to potential violence is conciliatory, not confrontational.[3] When dissension in village life does occur, as it inevitably does, quarrels tend to be defused before culminating in physical violence; or, if someone does strike another, he or she does not strike back. As a stranger to Wapeland, I had the first of several personal lessons in their gentle interaction style a few days after I moved into Taute village. When I shouted at a group of children crowding onto the raised and rotting veranda of our temporary house to get off, a man who had befriended me said reprovingly, "Speak softly!" The Wape perceive expatriates, especially men, as unpredictable and potentially bellicose. To gain some control over expatriate emotions, villagers place magical ginger under the house ladder of a visiting patrol officer—and I imagine a visiting anthropologist as well—to soothe him as he climbs down into the village. Another time, when I rebuked a group of men during the building of our house for cutting down the ornamental shrubs that hid the outhouse, they simply turned and silently walked away.

Enculturating a resident anthropologist or Wape children is not always an easy task, but the methods are identical. Aggressive acts are met with disinterest. An enraged toddler is left alone to kick and scream on the ground reward systems.

until her or his reason returns. Children and anthropologists soon learn that public aggression is an embarrassing and nonrewarding activity. Consequently, the Wape restrain the expression of negative emotions toward others and are generally friendly in their everyday village activities. Antipathy toward another person is rarely expressed directly in public though it may be expressed privately to a confidant.

Still, there are times when adults feel so personally transgressed and furious that they must do something more drastic than confiding their anger to a friend. Several alternatives are available. An offended person may gossip openly to others about the offense or, as everyone knows some sorcery, privately execute a punitive ritual. If, for example, a man's dog attacks and cripples a woman's piglet and the man makes no attempt to correct the wrong, in desperation she might go to his house and, standing outside, deliver a self-righteous harangue heard by all the neighbors while the transgressor and his family sit silently within. If the problem escalates, a meeting of the entire village is called by one of the concerned parties and anyone remotely involved with the problem should attend; not to go is to compromise one's integrity or innocence. Gathered on the front verandas of the houses surrounding the central plaza, men, women, and even children have their say until finally, perhaps several hours later, a consensus is reached.

I have stressed here the pacific ethos of Wape culture as well as indicated some of the actions resorted to when an individual's emotions must be expressed outwardly, namely, gossiping, sorcery, haranguing, and public meetings. However, none of these actions—regardless of the degree of aggressive intent—usually involve direct physical violence. Later I will discuss two exceptions to this finding that document a darker side of Wape emotions.

The Gaze of the Ancestors

The Wape are not conciliatory solely because they have been socialized to believe that public anger is often unrewarding or humiliating. There is a powerful sanctioning agent that helps to keep their behavior in check: the spirits of their dead ancestors. As Hollan (1988:56) has similarly observed for the Toraja of Indonesia, "fear of supernatural retribution and social disintegration motivate the control of anger and aggression." The Wape believe that at death an adult's spirit returns to lineage lands in the forest. The spirit is also believed to be a frequent visitor to the village, where it looks after its descendants by sending illness and bad luck to family enemies. There is a high incidence of illness in Wapeland, testimony enough to ancestral power.

One night while visiting on a neighbor's veranda, I idly inquired about a slight, unidentifiable sound and learned that it was my host's dead father benevolently signaling his presence. Ancestral spirits are believed to see and hear all. This strongly discourages arguments among villagers because a spirit may avenge a descendant by negatively influencing an opponent's hunting, gardening, or personal health. For this reason also, individuals occasionally express their anger publicly in Tok Pisin, the region's lingua franca, so the older ancestors who never learned it cannot understand what is being said.

Frequent disagreements among family members or neighbors can jeopardize the welfare of the entire village. To appease the ancestors, a conciliatory ritual must be held where the opponents speak out to them, announcing that they are now friends and asking the spirits to desist in the punitive interventions.[4] A husband also knows that his wife's agnates as well as her classificatory mother's brothers are concerned about her welfare and, if he mistreats her, may resort to their ancestors or sorcery.

Gender Proximics

Another important factor pertaining to the absence of wife beating is that Wape society, while acknowledging male-female differences in terms of dress and division of labor, is organized not to polarize gender differences but to deemphasize them. Husbands and wives use the same paths and sleep together in the same house with their children. Village boys and girls, including teenagers, play at ease with one another. The lightly constructed houses are close together so that aural privacy is at a minimum; even a modestly raised voice is heard by all the neighbors, who are also relatives. Menstruating mothers and daughters are not secluded in menstrual huts but remain at home where husbands, if they are not going hunting, continue to eat their wives' food. At puberty, boys begin to sleep separately in a village bachelors' house, but they still interact daily with their parents and siblings and usually take their meals with them at home. Nor are boys or youths secluded from their mothers and sisters for initiation into manhood, as in some New Guinea societies, where, often brutally, they are cleansed of female contamination in preparation for a warrior's career.

Female Status and Strategies

This is also a society where women and girls do not provide all of the child care. My tape-recorded interviews with male informants are punctuated with a babysitting father's asides to his restless toddler or the hungry cries of his infant. Fathers, as well as sons, take an active part in the care of infants and toddlers, especially when the mother is in the forest processing sago or collecting firewood.

This brings us to another important factor to explain why Wape husbands do not beat their wives: Wape women produce most of the food eaten. A typical meal consists of sago jelly with boiled greens—both the result of women's labor—and, with luck, a scrap of meat. While hunting is of great ritual and social importance to men, the introduction of the shotgun has seriously, and in some areas ruinously, depleted wild game.[5] Pigs, of which there are few, are killed primarily for ceremonial exchanges among kin. As monogamy, both in the known past and present, is the Wape norm, a husband is dependent on a single wife to feed him.

Another point is that a young woman has considerable say in the choice of a husband, signaling a young man in whom she is interested by slipping him a small present of food or tobacco. If possible, women prefer to marry within their natal village and rarely marry into a village that is more than an hour or two by foot from their father and brothers. Throughout a wife's marriage—and divorce is unusual—she and her husband are in close contact with her agnatic kin through a continuing series of economic exchanges that necessitates back-and-forth visiting while her brothers hold special ritual sanctions over her children, members of her husband's lineage. By the same token, she is tied to her mother's lineage too, especially to her classificatory mother's brothers who, as already indicated, watch over her well-being and whose homes are available as a place of refuge. A woman who feels that her husband is abusing her does not hesitate to move in with relatives, where she may stay for a week or more until they return with her to her husband's house. In no case may a husband seek his wife's return. In the meantime, he becomes dependent on his agnates' wives to feed him, or else he must find his own food. Neither choice is a pleasant one.

The women of a hamlet, or at least the one in which I lived, develop strong solidarity bonds, something I only learned through observation. In the unlikely event that a couple becomes so angry during a quarrel that they begin to shout at each other, women of the hamlet, a few sometimes armed with large sticks, descend on the house and stand around it until the woman joins them outside.

A factor that relates to the interaction style of women is that they usually do not act in ways to further provoke or escalate a husband's anger toward them but are able to terminate his abuse with a very dangerous and ritualized action. While both Wape men and women are highly sensitive to personal shaming, when a wife is deeply humiliated or shamed by her husband's behavior toward her, she usually does not return the insult but instead attempts suicide. While female suicide attempts are not uncommon in Papua New Guinea, in most communities they appear to be more frequently precipitated by a husband's brutal beatings, as among the Gainj (Johnson 1981) and Kaliai (Counts 1980, this volume), than by his shaming words.

Three young wives of our small hamlet unsuccessfully attempted suicide while I lived there by drinking poison made from the root of the deadly derris vine. Interestingly, in each case the woman lived in a household with her husband and one of his parents. In two of the cases a precipitating event was criticism by her husband for not supplying enough food for the family.

There are no reliable suicide statistics for Wape society. But on the basis of my own data and that of Lynette Wark Murray (personal communication 1988), the experienced missionary physician who patrolled Wapeland during my initial fieldwork, suicide attempts by unhappy wives, although hushed up by the community, do occur and follow a definite cultural pattern.[6] Because an in-marrying wife's suicide is deeply stigmatizing to the husband's lineage, a woman who survives an attempted suicide finds herself the center of solicitous community attention. It is a desperate way to "get even" with an overly critical or abusive husband but, in the cases I observed, a most effective one, with the added compensation that it generated a favorable change in his domestic demeanor.

Although Wape men do not often commit suicide (I heard of only one inexplicable case), there is a corresponding dark side to men's behavior. While in the field I observed two instances (Mitchell 1987:197–203) and learned of several others where a man, said to be temporarily possessed by a wandering ghost, attempted to attack fellow villagers with his bow and arrows (see also Langness 1965). These amok attacks occur only among men and are episodic, often with long periods of lucidity between them. A man so possessed is considered "crazy" by other villagers and is not held completely responsible for his actions. Because the target of a man's attack is socially diffuse, he has the opportunity to direct part of his aggression toward his wife, but he never does so.

Diet and Drugs

While the use of drugs, including alcohol, alone cannot make wife beaters out of husbands, it should be noted that the Wape do not have easy access to alcohol, as is true in some parts of Papua New Guinea where wife beating is culturally accepted. The addictive substances that are available to the Wape, namely, tobacco and betel nut, are not gender differentiated: men and women alike are heavy users of both substances.

Severe protein and caloric deficiency are characteristic of the Wape diet and may, in a highly generalized way, be related to their pacific temperament and domestic tranquility. Sago is notoriously low in nutrients, and the mountain-dwelling Wape, unlike most sago eaters who live on the coast or along large rivers, cannot obtain adequate protein from fish. Wape soils are poor, and although sago is supplemented with seasonal garden produce, gardens are small, unfenced, and poorly cultivated. Medical growth and development studies indicate the birth weight of the Wape infant is one of the lowest reported in the world, and subsequent growth in height and weight is slow, with the onset of secondary sex characters correspondingly delayed (Wark and Malcolm 1969). For example, a girl's first menstrual period occurs at a mean age of 18.4 years. There also is a progressive and marked loss of weight with age in both male and female adults. Many villagers suffer from chronic upper respiratory infections, and malaria is holoendemic and uncontrolled. Several studies indicate that the health problems of the Wape were still severe as recently as the mid-1980s (e.g., Pumuye 1985; Division of Health, Department of West Sepik 1986). It is hardly surprising that Wape ceremonial life is centered on curing festivals (Mitchell 1990).

Christian Mores and Government Law

Finally, we must consider the influence of the Catholic and Protestant missionaries and local government officials in respect to the absence of wife beating in Wapeland. All Wape villages are under the influence of either Christian Brethren or Franciscan missionaries, and an indigenous fundamentalist church, New Guinea Revival, has also gathered considerable support. All of these churches are strong advocates of a harmonious family life and marital amity. The laws of the country further support these values, and government and health officials distribute literature and lecture to villagers about them. But, as we already have seen, "domestic peace" is not a new idea to the Wape people. The importance of the churches' and state's moral rhetoric and sanctions regarding domestic life is not one of innovation but of the reinforcement on another level of the contemporary Wape society's own tradition of domestic tranquility.

Conclusions

To answer the question of why Wape men do not beat their wives in a country where wife beating is a major public health problem, I have noted and discussed some of the implicated constraints. These can be summarized as follows:

—pacific and conciliatory cultural ethos supported by churches and the state;
—nonpolarization of gender differences;
—punitive intervention by watchful ancestral spirits;
—women instrumental in selecting their husbands;
—monogamy;
—married couples domiciled among watchful relatives;
—wives as principal food providers;
—near absence of alcohol;
—nutritionally deficient diet;
—solidarity bonds among hamlet women;
—threat of a wife's suicide if her husband shames her; and
—women's agnates and classificatory mother's brothers responsive to their welfare.

None of these constraints alone can explain the relatively tranquil nature of Wape domestic life. When viewed as an interrelated cluster, though, these constraints help us understand the absence of wife beating. If a society has very poor nutrition, a pacific conciliatory ethos, low access to alcohol, watchful and succoring neighbors and relatives, vengeful ancestors, husbands dependent on a single wife for sustenance, non polarization of the sexes, and the threat of a wife's suicide if shamed by her husband, it is difficult to conceive of a marital relationship progressing to a state where the husband will beat the wife.

However, this inquiry into the absence of Wape wife beating has uncovered another form of Wape domestic violence—attempted suicide by females—with a cultural scenario of its own. In desperation, wives humiliated by their husbands "beat up" on themselves and, indirectly, their spouses by attempting to poison themselves. The difference is that attempted suicide, unlike being beaten, is a self-empowering act of rectitude, an aggressive action against one's person that, if one survives, may reshape a damaged husband-wife relationship more equitably. To Wape men, the possibility of a wife's attempted suicide is a sobering symbol for the limits of oppression. To women, it is a desperate act fraught with peril, an act some know is worth the risk.

NOTES

Earlier versions of this chapter were presented at the session "Wife Beating and Wife Battering: Cross-Cultural Perspectives" at the 1987 American Anthropological Association meetings in Chicago and at the symposium on "Domestic Violence in Oceania" at the 1989 Association for Social Anthropology in Oceania meeting in San Antonio. An earlier version of this chapter also appeared in *Pacific Studies* 13:3 (July 1990): 141–50. I appreciate the journal's permission to include it in this volume. I am grateful to Dorothy Counts for suggesting that I prepare a "negative case" on domestic violence from my Wape data and for her subsequent comments. I also wish to thank Lynette Wark Murray for sharing with me her data on the Wape and Pauline Aucoin and Annette Weiner for their comments on my essay. Fieldwork was supported by a grant (#1 RO1 MH 18039 SSR) from the National Institutes of Health and a faculty research grant from the University of Vermont.

1. For a fuller account of Wape society, see Mitchell (1973, 1978a, 1978b, 1987, 1988a, 1988b, 1990).

2. I wish to emphasize that the explanation offered here is culture specific. For example, the domestic placidity documented for the Dugum Dani in West Irian by Heider (1979:78–84) or by Jill Nash (this volume) for the Nagovisi in the Solomon Islands cannot be explained by the same constraints discussed here. For an exploratory attempt to rank factors in a "multiple correlate" model on the reverse problem of wife beating and family violence, see Burgess and Draper (1989).

3. On the basis of my 1982 and 1989 observations, as well as information gleaned from villagers and from government officials and health workers who deal directly with the people, this conciliatory characteristic of Wape domestic life has not changed since my 1970–72 fieldwork.

4. Because the two shotguns in Taute village were owned collectively by hamlet members, poor hunting was usually explained in terms of ancestral revenge for village dissension. For a detailed discussion of the relationship among hunting, ancestral spirits, and village arguments, see Mitchell (1973, 1987:167–87).

5. During my 1989 visit I was told that wild game is gradually reappearing due to the prohibition against firearms because of disorder in other parts of the province.

6. See Mitchell (1987:204–8) for ethnographic details regarding the ritualized aspects of Wape wives' suicide attempts.

REFERENCES CITED

Burgess, Robert, and Patricia Draper. 1989. "The Explanation of Family Violence: The Role of Biological, Behavioral, and Cultural Selection." In *Crime and Justice: A Review of Research.* Vol. 11. Ed. Michael Tonry and Norval Morris. 59–116. Chicago: University of Chicago Press.

Counts, Dorothy Ayers. 1980. "Fighting Back Is Not the Way: Suicide and the Women of Kaliai." *American Ethnologist* 7:332–51.

Division of Health, Department of West Sepik. 1986. *Annual Report.* Wewak: Wirui Press.

Heider, Karl. 1979. *Grand Valley Dani: Peaceful Warriors.* New York: Holt, Rinehart and Winston.

Hollan, Douglas. 1988. "Staying 'Cool' in Toraja: Informal Strategies for the Management of Anger and Hostility in a Nonviolent Society." *Ethos* 16:52–72.

Johnson, Patricia Lyons. 1981. "When Dying Is Better Than Living: Female Suicide among the Gainj of Papua New Guinea." *Ethnology* 20:325–34.

Langness, L. L. 1965. "Hysterical Psychosis in the New Guinea Highlands: A Bena Bena Example." *Psychiatry* 28:258–77.

Mitchell, William E. 1973. "A New Weapon Stirs Up Old Ghosts." *Natural History* 82:74–84.

———. 1978a. *The Living, Dead, and Dying: Music of the New Guinea Wape.* Folkways Record Album No. FE 4269.

———. 1978b. "On Keeping Equal: Polity and Reciprocity among the New Guinea Wape." *Anthropological Quarterly* 51:5–15.

———. 1987. *The Bamboo Fire: Fieldwork with the New Guinea Wape.* 2d ed. Prospect Heights, Ill.: Waveland Press.

———. 1988a. "The Defeat of Hierarchy: Gambling as Exchange in a Sepik Society." *American Ethnologist* 15:638–57.

———. 1988b. *Magical Curing* (videocasette film). Prospect Heights, Ill.: Waveland Press.

———. 1990. "Therapeutic Systems of the Taute Wape." In *Sepik Heritage: Tradition and Change in Papua New Guinea.* Ed. Nancy Lutkehaus et al. 428–38. Durham: Carolina Academic Press.

Pumuye, Hilary. 1985. *The Assessment of Nutritional Status of Children in the Lumi District, West Sepik Province, Papua New Guinea.* Community Education for Disadvantaged Children Pilot Project Report. University Printery.

Toft, Susan. 1985. *Domestic Violence in Papua New Guinea.* Papua New Guinea Law Reform Commission Monograph No. 3. Boroko.

Wark, Lynette, and L. A. Malcolm. 1969. "Growth and Development of the Lumi Child in the Sepik District of New Guinea." *Medical Journal of Australia* 2:129–36.

EIGHT

Factors Relating to Infrequent Domestic Violence among the Nagovisi

Jill Nash

This chapter discusses the infrequency of physical violence between spouses among the Nagovisi of North Solomons Province (Bougainville), Papua New Guinea, who are matrilineal swidden farmers. A primarily ethnographic account is offered in discussing this situation. I also will make cross-cultural comparisons when possible. The largest number of studies on domestic violence deal with Western societies, especially the United States.

Sample Size and Estimated Incidence of Violence between Spouses

There are no figures available for a statistical survey, although I can provide estimates of the frequency of various kinds of disputes, especially violent ones. Domestic violence was not a subject in which I had much interest during my fieldwork (due perhaps in part to its infrequent occurrence); I was much concerned, however, with kinship, family life, and conflict resolution. My sample consisted of several villages whose total population numbered about 200. I heard news about an additional 300 or so people, whom I did not see regularly but whose genealogies I knew and most of whom I personally recognized. During the two and one half years during which I lived in Pomalate Village,[1] I recorded three episodes in which a husband assaulted his wife and one from a village just outside the study area.

My impression is that incidents of physical assault between spouses are rare. I never witnessed violence between a husband and wife. I did see a physical struggle between a brother and sister, between female relatives, and between men. I also heard children crying as a result of being hit by a parent (though I did not see the blow struck) or in the course of a tantrum that was part of the provocation for the parent to hit. I also saw a number of arguments that involved shouting or verbal insult. Informants told me news of the day, including any violent arguments in other villages. I also heard accounts of violent arguments that had taken place long ago. I no doubt missed hearing of some fights, but the Nagovisi take a great interest in conflict, and since most of it leads to court resolution, it is widely discussed. It is unlikely that any occurrence of domestic violence would remain a secret.

Forms and Causes of Arguments between Husbands and Wives

Arguments usually do not involve physical personal violence. Verbal insults are the primary form of disputing. A serious verbal insult requires litigation and usually a fine will be paid, as would be the case for an injury. Although the amounts asked for insults are less than for injury, in a sense insults and injuries are considered to be in the same legal category. Women can compete very well with men in verbal sparring, as opposed to physical conflict; in fact, I have argued that talk, in general, is the source of women's efficacy (Nash 1987). In the past, insults might have led the injured party to retaliate with deadly force, but this is no longer the case. Possible reasons for this are discussed below.

The following is an example of the sort of insult that may pass between a husband and wife: Bernadette[2] asked her husband, Francis, to clean up their toddler daughter's feces. He said he didn't have a shovel. She then said he should shovel it with his tongue. He got mad and went home to his sister. The sister demanded payment, which she received, for this insult. Bernadette was "dancing with anger" when she said this. Her husband was very lazy and many people felt that his behavior helped to cause the argument. Nevertheless, Bernadette was wrong to say such an insulting thing; consequently, it was appropriate for Francis's sister to ask for a fine.

A second form that arguments take involves property destruction. Informants claim that both men and women might destroy property during arguments, but my observations show this to be a particularly female expression of anger. The Nagovisi say that women destroy property because they cannot trounce their husbands, and that husbands destroy property because they do not want to kill their wives. For example: "Agnes chopped up her husband Simon's bag while we all watched. At the same time, she recited her grievances in a tense and angry voice. Because Simon had declared himself 'married' to his newly-widowed sister-in-law, Agnes claimed that Simon had only pretended to show sorrow for his brother and had been lusting after the dead man's wife for a long time. No one intervened."

I have stated elsewhere that the triggering causes of arguments between spouses often seem to be trivial. These causes include "surprise at the wife's having bought a new saucepan, the alleged withholding of tobacco from the husband, or nagging by the wife that her sick husband seek medical aid" (Nash 1974:65). Although male informants stated that "laziness" might be a reason for a man to hit his wife, failure to fulfill domestic duties did not appear to be a reason for any of the arguments I heard about. Some women who were a bit lazy were never hit or yelled at, and another, who was not at all lazy, was hit once by her husband, allegedly for not fixing his food as quickly as he wanted it. In some cases, the discovery of a spouse's adultery may cause an argument; in other cases, it is unacknowledged by husband and wife, even when it results in the conception of a child.[3] I do not recall any arguments between a husband and wife concerning bridewealth amounts or pig prices (such disputes would involve more than a married couple), nor regarding such matters as whether cocoa should be planted or not.

A look at my field notes shows that certain couples seem to go through difficult periods of nearly continual disagreement in which one or the other may resort to violence. Also, some individuals seem more ready to argue or to hit in the course of an argument. These people were fairly young, relatively recently married, and not accustomed to living with each other. One middle-aged man appeared to be having what I hesitantly call a midlife crisis. Thus, the biographies of individuals and the circumstances of a marriage seem to have more explanatory value regarding disputes, especially violent ones, than do more proximate causes; this observation fits with the absence among the Nagovisi of cultural patterns that use violence in arguments.

Cultural Factors Regarding the Consequences of Arguments and Their Resolution

The consequence of an argument between a husband and wife may involve any or all of the following: physical separation or withdrawal from part of domestic life, court hearing, assessment and payment of fine, and reconciliation. Background information on cultural and social practices is provided below to make these alternatives intelligible.

The Nagovisi are matrilineal (i.e., social groups are formed by recognizing kinship links between women and their children) and uxorilocal (i.e., a man moves to his wife's settlement at marriage). Descent groups include moieties, clans, and named and unnamed lineages. Villages are based on a core of matrilineally related women, usually comprising the female members of one or several named or unnamed lineages. Their imported husbands (and fathers) also are residents, as are unmarried males of the matrilineage. Households generally consist of a nuclear family, although it is not inappropriate for unattached relatives (but not the wife's mother) to be included.

The Nagovisi have become increasingly uxorilocal since the introduction of cocoa as a cash crop in the 1960s. Before that time, uxorilocality was the ideal, but other forms of residence were tolerated and practiced more frequently than in later years. My survey in 1969–70 showed 81 percent of all couples residing uxorilocally.

Due to the fact of uxorilocal residence, a man leaves his natal village at marriage to move into the village of his wife. Because most (71 percent) marriages are made between people whose natal villages are less than two miles apart, men find it convenient to visit the homes of their sisters and parents. It is here that a man will return in the event of serious marital discord. In the event of serious disagreements between a husband and wife, either may act. Sometimes, a wife will put her husband's belongings outside as a sign that he is to move back to his natal village. More often, a husband will leave of his own accord.[4] When this happens, negotiation begins, the result of which is usually that the wife's kin will pay valuables to the husband's kin. Then the husband returns. By leaving, the husband has raised the ante, so to speak, or registered the seriousness of whatever event occasioned his departure (e.g., in the example cited above, the directive to use one's tongue as a shovel). He has shown himself to be aggrieved and injured by the treatment of those who are supposed to treat him well.

Husbands can count on generally unqualified support and sympathy from their matrilineal kin. This is possible because most arguments between a husband and wife are not clear-cut cases of wrongdoing on the part of one individual only but situations in which shortcomings of both spouses have figured. Thus, the husband's kin may find it easy to stress the wrongful acts of the wife, ignoring his part in the affair. Another factor making for partisanship of the husband's kin has to do with the balances that should be maintained between affines (see below). Although uxorilocal residence may provide a solidarity group for women that protects them from spousal violence, there is an important advantage for men, too: by moving to his natal village, the man takes an escalating action that is not violent and is not seen as a defeat for himself but as a shaming of his wife. It dramatizes the intolerable state that a husband faces during this time of conflict. It is his way of saying that he cannot live with this impossible person.

If there is an argument, men may stay with their wives but cease to eat their wives' food. Usually, one food item (e.g., coconut) will be avoided until a fine has been paid to settle the dispute. The wife continues to cook her husband's food but is inconvenienced and daily reminded of the unresolved problem.

In the case of nearly any kind of argument, a favored method of resolution is to go to court. Wrongs can be righted through a system of fines, generally paid with a combination of cash and shell valuables. Three kinds of wrongs always require such compensation: insult, injury—especially drawing blood—and death (in precolonial times). Married couples do not give up their right to sue one another. In fact, the fines paid as a result of arguments are part of the continual adjustments—the evaluation of credits and debits—between a husband and wife that go on during the course of their marriage. These adjustments end with the payment (or decision that payment is not required) of death dues after the demise of one of the partners (see Nash 1974 for a lengthy discussion of these phenomena).

Other Kinds of Violence

Levinson has argued that "wife-beating is part of a broader cultural pattern of violent relationships between persons who reside in the same community" (1989:45). Below, I will review information concerning sexual violence toward women (rape and sexual assault) and physical violence toward children, between women, between men, and between brothers and sisters. In all of these areas, physical violence is minimal.

Rape

In the course of filling out a questionnaire for the Papua New Guinea Law Reform Commission in 1971, I made inquiries regarding the subject of rape. After much reflection, people recalled a single incident that had taken place ten miles away in the late 1940s. The rapist had been angry with a male relative of the victim. By and large, people could not quite imagine how rape would work: they said that the woman would cry out and people would come to her aid. Women do not "change their minds" about mutually agreeable fornication to later allege rape. To force a woman to copulate is not considered admirable in any sense but rather is disapproved or, more likely, considered ridiculous, given the probable consequences. A fieldwork incident illustrates this point: A young married woman from the study area was traveling alone to visit relatives in a village about ten miles away. A teenaged male from that village surprised her on the deserted track, indicating his intention to have sexual relations with her. The woman slashed the man's shirt with her garden knife, thus repelling him, and proceeded unmolested on her way.

This story was retold by men and women in my village with much amusement at the expense of the young man.

Parental Treatment of Children

Nagovisi children under the age of five are not usually subject to corporal punishment. With one exception of redirected aggression, in which a mentally unbalanced widow[5] hit her eighteen-month-old son when her boyfriend told her he would not marry her, any hitting or slapping was directed at older children. This may be for doing something dangerous (e.g., picking through the anthropologist's rubbish pit) as well as for disobedience. A struggle I witnessed between a teenaged girl and her mother seems different because the daughter was the same size as her mother. In this incident, slaps were exchanged when the girl delayed coming home from church by four hours and did not bring the bread she was supposed to have purchased. The girl's maternal uncle came to the assistance of his sister, pulled his niece away, and denounced her.

When older children (aged six to twelve) have tantrums or fight with younger siblings, parents may strike them with their hands or nudge them with their feet if the children are lying on the ground. I saw or heard the screaming of an angry child once or twice.

Physical Aggression by Children

Some kinds of physical aggression by children are ignored. For example, adults react only slightly to a toddler who beats them with a branch. The adult might move out of the way or duck while talking to someone else, but little attention is paid to the behavior. The child is not told to stop.

Children do not usually hit one another in play, even though they use knives and sticks as toys. Nor do I recall chasing and threats to hurt. Teasing and insults may cause damage to feelings, however: for example, one five-year-old burst into tears and went home after an older boy mentioned to the general amusement of a group of children that the five-year-old had had an erection on a previous occasion. The pattern of going home after an insult starts early.

Discipline by Parents

Parents complain about their children's behavior; frequently heard are the allegations that children are lazy and disobedient. Parents may lecture them on their shortcomings. Among the Nagovisi, younger children are frightened with warnings about ghosts, snakes, or white people to ensure obedience. Informants said that one villager, a former policeman, had employed the Papua New Guinea police punishment of *kalabus long san* (being tied up in the sun) to punish his son for truancy. The child was probably between seven and nine years of age when this happened, since he quit school after form 2. This is not an indigenous Nagovisi punishment, and all who spoke of it were disapproving.

Child Neglect?

Nagovisi parents are condemned (by gossip) for being bad parents when their children "do not grow"—that is, they are short, thin, or perhaps merely unprepossessing in some way (e.g., subject to insect bites, especially bad runny noses, or perhaps just shy). A child's growth may be stunted by withholding the appropriate ceremonies in his or her honor (especially for first-borns) or by not feeding them enough. Although this does not fit Western notions of abuse because of the magical concepts involved, it might come closest to a Nagovisi idea of serious and socially disapproved neglect of children. One young widow with four children ranging in age from one to twelve years appeared to be having trouble feeding her offspring. People would castigate her from time to time and suggest that she ought to remarry. Her very competent mother quite frequently fed and housed the two oldest children.

I should mention that the Nagovisi seemed proud of "good" children, even when the children are not their own. People commented favorably about children who were sturdy, straightforward in their manner, and mature for their age.

Fights between Women

Women sometimes had arguments with each other that involved name calling. Women would also challenge other women to competitive showings of shell valuables—an event that contained the potential for serious arguments. As mentioned above, a mother and teenaged daughter might fight physically. Most conflicts among women seemed to involve those of different named or unnamed lineages (*wetetenamo,* 'one grandmother'; see Nash 1974). I saw a fight between two women who are classificatory parallel cousins:

> Cecilia stabbed Helena in the head with a comb. The cause had to do with the alleged theft of the comb by Helena's children. Helena had also teased

Cecilia, saying she didn't have Cecilia's comb, but only had an old broken one. Helena's wound bled briskly for a while and there was much screaming and dramatic gesturing. This resulted in a long court hearing in which Cecilia was denounced. The first fine asked was large, and Cecilia's mother refused to pay, Cecilia herself having no money. Finally they settled on a smaller amount.

Fights between Men

The fights I saw between men were often intergenerational shouting matches, sometimes aggravated by alcohol. The latter type of argument is discussed separately below. Men were sometimes denounced by other men in angry voices, but they did not themselves get angry. The causes were varied. Young men at odds with their fathers might tell them to "get out of our village and go back to your own [natal] place." In one instance, a young man spit at his older sister's husband, but physical attacks were more apt to occur if alcohol had been consumed. Young men who had been drinking might attempt to assault their classificatory fathers, but their attempts were fairly ineffectual.

A Struggle between Brothers and Sisters

Brothers and sisters are not supposed to fight; in fact, they are responsible for one another's good behavior. Avoidance etiquette and uxorilocal residence makes the expression of strong emotions between brothers and sisters infrequent. Nevertheless, I witnessed one incident in which a widow and her uterine half-brother struggled publicly. The brother slapped her several times. She had been screaming in support of her lover and chopping holes in her house with a machete. An unrelated man also helped restrain this woman. Afterward, people said the brother had acted as he had because he was "embarrassed" by his sister's behavior. It was said to have been the right thing to do, and no one suggested that he pay any fine to her or she to him. It is important to stress that the struggle did not stem from a disagreement between the two.

Violence in the Past: Headhunting, Initiation

Like other Solomon Islanders, in the past the Nagovisi took trophy heads during feuding. This practice ended around 1925 with Australian pacification. Old people still remember the days of tribal fighting. Their memories are unromantic.

According to informants, the taking of heads might be facilitated by the ingestion of a certain kind of magical powder called *piko,* which was made out of human bone (and other things) at cremations. The effect of *piko* was to turn a man into an angry killer with red eyes and great strength, a *pikonara.* Certain children who showed unusual belligerence were considered likely to grow up to be *pikonaras.* Although valued in former times, according to my informants this type of person has disappeared.

An old man in the next village was represented to me as having been a *pikonara* in his youth. Many stories were told of his truculence as an adolescent, his numerous stormy marriages, and his bravery and treachery in World War II. In his old age there was no indication of anything pathological in his personality. On the contrary, he was one of the most intelligent and insightful people in the community. He managed his polygynous household peacefully. The Nagovisi explanation was that he had gotten old and was no longer a fighter.

Among the Nagovisi I studied there was no tradition of painful ordeals in adolescent initiation. A small feast might be held for young men after their first killing (or in preparation for it—informants were not clear on this subject), but this was optional. Piercing of the nasal septum was remembered by one informant as very painful; when I asked him whether or not he had cried, he said, "Did I ever!" No ritual significance was attached to this act; it was optional and evidently cosmetic. Girls' initiation, properly done for the first-born daughter on the occasion of her first menstruation, involved no painful acts.

Suicide

Suicide took place in the past among the Nagovisi and still occurs, sometimes in connection with unhappiness regarding the opposite sex. Protest suicide on the part of young women (usually a newlywed) formerly was directed not at cruel husbands but at parents for forcing a marriage (see Counts 1980). According to my informants, parents no longer seek to press unpopular candidates on their daughters. All local suicides and suicide attempts that I heard about were by men. Men might attempt suicide in reaction to adultery of their wives. Some people seem to have overreacted: one man killed himself from shame after he was discovered in an adulterous act. Another man killed himself because he believed erroneously that he had killed his child. Sometimes the reasons were obscure; no motive for suicide could be offered, other than what amounts to hereditary insanity (e.g., "his uncle was crazy, too").

Effects of Alcohol on Violence

It is not possible for me to state what part alcohol might play today (1998) in arguments. In the late 1960s and early 1970s, only men drank, and the bulk of alcohol was consumed at *pati* (all-night festivities with food and music). During my fieldwork, people thought that drinking made a man lose his strength and therefore fights were considered pointless or comic (cf. Nero 1990, in which the ability to consume large amounts of alcohol is seen as strength). A sober woman could always evade a drunken man, and women stood together when a drunk man was performing. Wives might shout ridicule at drunken husbands for their foolishness—for example, urinating in public, falling in the mud, dancing wildly, losing clothing, and so forth. Men did not appear to get angry at this. The only fighting was between men who were drunk; it was fairly ineffectual, except when bottles were used as weapons. When young men were drunk, they got angry at their fathers or other older men. Generally, drunken men did not seem to get angry at women or use their drunkenness as an excuse to act out prior anger toward women.

One instance of domestic assault did take place when the husband was intoxicated. The next morning, when he was sober, he joked about the whole thing—including his own behavior.

Comparison and Discussion

Nagovisi society is different from other societies in that physical violence between married people is neither common nor tacitly condoned. Behavior in the United States provides a marked contrast. According to Straus (1978), in America a marriage license is seen by some as a hitting license. Violence between persons who are not related is readily litigable in the United States, whereas many barriers stand in the way of a battered spouse who seeks legal redress—although, as Micklow (1988) points out, the situation is slowly changing. The contrast here is that the Nagovisi have legal recourse in cases of domestic violence.

Mushanga (1977–78) reports in an article on wife bashing in East African societies that "women ask for it." "Asking for it" consists of ridiculing men and talking back—thus causing the violence to escalate, sometimes to the point of murder. The Nagovisi do not believe that women or men wish to be hit. In fact, I do not recall anyone blaming the victim for having provoked the violence.

Also, fights in public or in houses with leaf walls draw the attention and intervention of others. People come to the aid of quarrelling couples: they feel that they should interfere. In town, isolation makes it easier to act on violent impulses and to carry them out without interference from concerned relatives or neighbors (Erchak 1984). I knew only one Nagovisi married couple living outside the home area; both were schoolteachers in Rigo, southeast of Port Moresby, and neither was violent. I heard secondhand of the suicide of a young Nagovisi woman married to a Siwai policeman domiciled in Port Moresby. The woman's uncle had complained to me about her irrational behavior years before this happened.

Two topics to which I have referred above—the influence of matriliny and its concomitants, and the subject of anger—require further discussion. I have described how matrilineally related social features of the Nagovisi, including uxorilocality, make it possible for men to separate themselves physically from their wives and thus reduce the possibility of assault. Furthermore, most marriages appear congenial. Friedl (1975) has reviewed a whole list of reasons why relationships between husbands and wives are not as tense in matrilineal societies as they are in patrilineal ones: ultimately, many of these have to do with the fact that the wife is not on trial in a matrilineal society, as she is in a patrilineal one. Nor does the husband in a matrilineal society assume the unenviable position of being a disloyal outsider. Rather, in a matrilineal society emotions are not so focused on the marriage tie but are diffused among numerous relatives. Furthermore, Melanesian matriliny has been profitably analyzed (Gregory 1982; Strathern 1984; Weiner 1976) as involving a life-long series of exchanges between affines in which balance is highly valued. Among the Nagovisi, the idea of reciprocity of actions and material items strongly permeates social behavior (Nash 1987). There is an awareness, from childhood on, that both positive and negative behavior must be repaid.

Although anthropologists have attempted studies of emotion (Lutz 1988; Rosaldo 1980), the understanding of anger still presents many difficulties. The Nagovisi once considered anger to be motivating and energizing; it had made possible men's great actions of warfare in pre-European times (Nash 1987). Anger in pre-European times was magically enhanced and the *pikonara* was recognized and valued, if also feared. In domestic relations as I observed them, however, anger was not much in evidence. Crying children were usually labeled "angry" rather than "sad" or "in pain," the crying in grief being considered a more adult behavior. Possibly, the expression of anger in outbursts has come to be seen as childish and inappropriate for adults. I saw a series of steps in the expression of anger, where insult and property destruction (and, for men, withdrawal to the natal village) were enacted first as signs of anger. Social factors do not favor hitting, and thus it is in a breakdown or loss of control that the occasional instances of domestic violence take place.

The Nagovisi seem to take pride in their ability to control the expression of their emotions. One informant counseled how important it was in court, for example, to keep one's self-control: "You can't win if you are angry," he said. People dread having their outbursts mocked as a form of gossipy entertainment, as one woman's cries in labor were, to take another example. Women should be stoic, and the anguished descriptions of perineal pain endured by a young primipara were repeated with amusement for weeks by her peers (Nash 1987). People often respond angrily, not to an offense itself, but after thinking about it for a while. Thus, angry displays may be rather controlled, like Agnes's performance, described above.

In summary, domestic violence is rare among the Nagovisi. I would argue that the incidence of domestic violence cannot be zero, however, because some couples will go through difficult times during the course of a marriage and some individuals, by virtue of temperament, are simply more given to physical violence than others are.

NOTES

Earlier versions of this chapter were presented at meetings of the American Anthropological Association in Chicago (1987) and the Association for Social Anthropology in Oceania in Savannah, Georgia (1988), and San Antonio, Texas (1989). I benefited from the presentations of other members of these sessions and especially from the comments of Dorothy Counts. An earlier version of this chapter also appeared in *Pacific Studies* 13:3 (July 1990): 127–40. I thank the journal for permission to include it in this volume.

1. I resided intermittently among the Nagovisi between 1969 and 1973. Support was provided by the National Institute of Mental Health and the Australian National University.

2. All names are pseudonyms. All quotations are from my field notes unless otherwise indicated.

3. I should perhaps note that people who are aware of some misbehavior on the part of a spouse may "save" their angry reaction until they themselves have caused trouble and then cite the previous offense as a distraction from or mitigation of their own actions.

4. In the rare event of virilocal residence, the wife leaves.

5. This woman figures into a number of my anecdotes involving physical violence.

REFERENCES CITED

Counts, Dorothy Ayers. 1980. "Fighting Back Is Not the Way: Suicide and the Women of Kaliai." *American Ethnologist* 7:332–51.

Erchak, Gerald M. 1984. "Cultural Anthropology and Spouse Abuse." *Current Anthropology* 25:331–32.

Friedl, Ernestine. 1975. *Women and Men: An Anthropologist's View.* New York: Holt, Rinehart and Winston.

Gregory, Chris A. 1982. *Gifts and Commodities.* New York: Academic Press.

Levinson, David. 1989. *Family Violence in Cross-Cultural Perspective.* Newbury Park, Calif.: Sage Publications.

Lutz, Catherine. 1988. *Unnatural Emotions.* Chicago: University of Chicago Press.

Micklow, Patricia L. 1988. "Domestic Abuse: The Pariah of the Legal System." In *Handbook of Family Violence.* Ed. Vincent B. Van Hasselt, Randall L. Morrison, Alan S. Bellack, and Michel Hersen. 407–34. New York: Plenum Press.

Mushanga, Timbamanya M. 1977–78. "Wife Victimization in East and Central Africa." *Victimology* 2:479–85.

Nash, Jill. 1974. *Matriliny and Modernization: The Nagovisi of South Bougainville.* New Guinea Research Bulletin No. 55. Port Moresby and Canberra: Australian National University Press.

———. 1987. "Gender Attributes and Equality: Men's Strength and Women's Talk among the Nagovisi." In *Dealing with Inequality.* Ed. Marilyn Strathern. 150–73. Cambridge: Cambridge University Press.

Nero, Karen. 1990. "The Hidden Pain: Drunkenness and Domestic Violence in Palau." In *Domestic Violence in Oceania.* Ed. Dorothy Ayers Counts. 63–92. Special issue of *Pacific Studies* 13 (3).

Rosaldo, Michelle Z. 1980. *Knowledge and Passion: Ilongot Notions of Self and Society.* Cambridge: Cambridge University Press.

Strathern, Marilyn. 1984. "Marriage Exchanges: A Melanesian Comment." *Annual Review of Anthropology* 13:41–73.

Straus, Murray A. 1978. "Wife Beating: How Common and Why?" *Victimology* 2:443–58.

Weiner, Annette B. 1976. *Women of Value, Men of Renown: New Perspectives in Trobriand Exchange.* Austin: University of Texas Press.

NINE

Nudging Her Harshly and Killing Him Softly: Displays of Disfranchisement on Ujelang Atoll

Laurence Marshall Carucci

In parts of the Pacific, the words "domestic violence" conjure up images of men strapping their wives into subservience. The Marshall Islands present a different scenario. Violence does occur there, but it is not necessarily initiated by males. It occurs between siblings and cousins, it is initiated by females as well as males, and its very presence so seriously threatens community and family solidarity that it is denied. Nevertheless, intrafamily and community violence are integral parts of daily life.

A knowledgeable Marshall Islands man of about sixty patiently explained to me that violence is not found in Ujelang families. It occurs only among foreigners. Ujelang people, he insisted, are considerate and loving. I had just witnessed a quarrel between a young couple and knew that physical violence did occur and that threats of abuse were common. Eventually I understood that he was subtly commenting about foreignness and about the causes of social disruption.

The two who had quarreled were cross-cousins of the same age. Their marriage was a sanctioned union. Naïvely, I took them to be very close—"one only," in local terms. Indeed, both were part of a large extended family and members of a small household attached to that larger whole. But these representations of unity did not exhaust their relationship. Because they were members of different clans, the young couple were also opposed, as male and female, as younger and older, as insider and outsider. Each of these opposed components counterbalanced their sameness with foreignness.

The knowledgeable man attempted to tell me how foreignness could be contextually manipulated to lend meaning to the apparent contradictions between what people said and how they acted. Affines, those of different gender and age, as well as people from other lands or other atolls, could be cast as "outsiders" when their actions violated the "codes for conduct" (Schneider

1968) that should be used by group members. As I learned of more instances of violence I began to understand that violence is indeed harmful to the maintenance of solidarity on this small atoll. I also learned how the concept of otherness might expand and contract in order to help maintain a perpetual balance between the necessity for social control and the requirement for close and continuous social alliances.

On Ujelang and Enewetak, the westernmost of the Marshall Islands, wives are seldom severely battered, yet talk about violence and threats of abuse are a communal preoccupation.[1] Indigenous terms of violence permeate daily discourse as mechanisms of social control: *mani* ("strike, beat, kill"), *kokurri* ("ruin, damage"), *kōmman joraan* ("create harm or damage"), even *maniman ñan mij* ("beat to death"). Though seldom enforced, threats of violence are the means older persons use to control younger siblings and children. Husbands also use threats to control their wives. Significantly, female-inflicted magical damage is discussed in similar terms. Violence has a physical form suited to young, warrior-like men and a magical form suited to old women. Both forms of aggression are dangerous and typify the actions of foreigners. In fact, family members rapidly contain young men's physical violence. Violence inflicted magically is more threatening because it is often lethal, and effective countermagic can be attempted only by a few outsiders who have sources of powerful foreign magic.

While violence on Ujelang and Enewetak is attributed to others, its roots are anchored in patterns of childrearing and socialization. Adults, particularly males, tease children into violence, and all boys and girls are taught to throw small paving stones. As boys mature, they replace pebble throwing with wrestling, fighting with fists and clubs, and throwing large rocks. These pursuits, suited to "real men," pose substantial threats that, in the past, were appropriate for young male warriors in training. Circumstances have changed, yet a warrior-like demeanor remains a critical component of masculine Micronesian identity (Marshall 1979; Carucci 1987a). Adolescent males risk ridicule if they continue childish acts like pebble throwing that fail to display real physical prowess. Indeed, Ujelang's first suicide (in 1980) is said to have resulted from a mother's public criticism of her son for actions she considered childlike.

Maturing females are, in contrast, associated with "caring for" and consideration: they epitomize rather than threaten sociality. Maturing females create extended families, transmit core elements of identity to their offspring, and maintain the integrity of other social forms. They are associated with the protected lagoon and with the inhabited village. Women continue to throw pebbles, usually to warn children of impending disapproval or, more aggressively, to respond to the embarrassing quips of suitors. Wrestling is used by older women, but mainly as a form of joking attack, and only the most masculine of Enewetak women fight with their fists. Hurling objects is a woman's mode of physical recourse. An irate wife may throw food, cookware, and a wide array of household items.

Adult women rely on their tongues to fight their battles. While men are said to be physically strong, women become *lej* ("acid-tongued"). Vociferous vocalization, of course, draws neighbors to the scene. The support of community members brings a physically abusive husband under society's control. As women age they also gain magical skills from their control of internal clan-contained force. Magical skills are often transferred from grandmother to granddaughter within a matriclan and are made efficacious by a mature woman's secret vocal incantations.[2] Evil magic is thought to cause the most violent forms of human suffering, and nearly all severe physical or psychological illnesses are magically induced. Magic is thought to be the most frequent cause of death; death from natural causes is almost an enigma. It is said that no Ujelang or Enewetak people control "bad magic," but magic is said to be a source of danger in all marriages and interactions with outsiders. Many people also modify their dealings with local islanders to avoid (supposedly nonexistent) sorcery.

Social and Cultural Contexts of Personal Abuse

Once holding independent status under their own chiefs, Enewetak and Ujelang now constitute the westernmost outliers of the Republic of the Marshall Islands, a group of atolls and coral pinnacles in the west-central Pacific Ocean. Formerly part of the U.S.-administered Trust Territory of the Pacific Islands, the Marshall Islands are now an independent state under a Compact of Free Association with the United States. During World War II, the population of Enewetak was reduced to about 140 (Carucci 1989), and in 1947 they faced further hardship when they were exiled on Ujelang Atoll to allow the United States to conduct nuclear testing and related experiments on Enewetak. Since 1980, most Enewetak people have returned to their home atoll. Considerable contact is maintained with Majuro and a few other locations in the Marshalls, and trust funds to compensate for nuclear-related damages have increased the rate at which outsiders marry into the community. In spite of rapid changes, the group still considers itself to be united by a strong sense of community.

Relations within the community have always been governed by egalitarian ideals, and decision making rests with the group, even though it is ruled by two chiefs. Statuses based on age and gender are not hierarchical, though an elder's position is respected by younger siblings and members of the younger generations. To the degree that overt control over political affairs is taken as a measure, males dominate females. Women have greater access to the magical potency of the clan line than do men, however, and important matters come under greater female control as people move through the life cycle and become ancestors (Carucci 1985).

During childhood, aggressive acts and words are common within the household. Most childrearing is performed by older siblings who seldom use positive reinforcement as a method of socialization. A mother's first warning phrase to deal with undesirable actions is "bad," followed by "I will beat you." Older siblings use the same phrases, but adults discourage them from physically punishing young children. Indeed, unless a child commits a serious offense, no punishment is forthcoming. Threats of serious violence are followed by inaction. When children chastise younger siblings with slaps or blows, adults reprimand the overseer, even if they do not condone the child's mischief. The same structural logic that unites grandparents and children in opposition to the authority of parents links adults with physically weaker and lower-ranked youngsters against the authority of their older siblings. The standards of how siblings treat one another are social in character rather than abstractly ethical and object oriented. Ujelang strategy teaches youngsters the solidarity of the sibling group (Radcliffe-Brown 1952:66–68) and about external causality. For Americans, events are shaped by individuals who get themselves into and out of situations. Ujelang people act as part of a group to deal with outside occurrences that happen to them. This has critical importance for an understanding of violence.

On Ujelang Atoll the unity of the whole gives people a way to deal with the unpredictability of the outside world (Lutz 1988). In the late 1970s, Ujelang residents constantly commented, "The people of Ujeland, we are all one family." Indeed, the location of the village in the center of the main islet allows everyone to participate in the affairs of others. From early childhood until death, a person's life is lived in this public arena. Caring for one another—a core requirement for members of a family—is important in the community.

Around puberty boys begin a period of unrestrained free license and exploration not unlike the *taure'are'a* time described by Levy for Tahiti (1973:190ff.). During this time the opposition between members of different clans becomes apparent. Young boys (both cross- and parallel-cousins) refer to one another with sibling terms, but young male cross-cousins develop animosities toward each other as a way to preserve close sibling ties with their own sisters who are members of their own clan. Female cross-cousins become similarly disenchanted with one another, though their disputes are less apt to be overt. The newly found antagonisms focus on tales of the sexual exploits of one's siblings. Sexual experimentation among children is coded as play. At puberty a new metaphor of war becomes equally prominent. These sexual battles (Carucci 1980:chaps. 2–3) typify the relationships between opposite clans, and youth who formerly interacted as siblings recognize their opposition as cross-cousins.

Disputes involving vocal and physical abuse quite commonly arise among same-sex youth from different clans. Females, who are culturally restrained from physical violence, vocally defend their brothers. Young men, who are supposed to be bold warriors, force confrontations with male cross-cousins. These confrontations begin with boasting and often escalate into physical violence. They occur in the village—usually in someone's household—but the parties to the disagreement seldom live together. Significantly, disputes between cross-cousins arise between youngsters who were once united by sibling ties as well as by sexual identity. Now faced with their opposition as members of different clans, they feel ambivalence toward their cross-cousins. These ambivalent feelings are expressed in contradictory moments that counterpose fights between cross-cousins with reconciliatory talk couched in terms of siblingship.

The perpetrators of physical violence are young males struggling with the opposing values that separate youth from mature men. Almost certainly seventeen to thirty-five years of age and often inebriated, these fellows are either married and wish they were not or unmarried and wish they were part of a union. They are, in other words, similar to the members of those categories to which they do not belong and to which they are opposed. The conditions for their symbolic displays of disaffection arise from this contradictory situation.

The ideal Marshallese male is a single warrior who travels around winning physical battles with outside males and sexual battles with females. The same term, *torinae* ("war, battle"), is commonly applied to both domains. The karate hero Bruce Lee was a modern-day analog of the mythic warrior (Carucci 1980, 1985). *Pojak* ("readiness") typifies a warrior's stance and irresistibility (a sort of macho-imbued charisma) characterizes his demeanor. During their life cycle, however, males give up these ideal characteristics and are "domesticated"—that is, brought within the female domains of village and household where the responsibilities of providing for a family predominate (Carucci 1985). When performed successfully, these duties help men become village leaders. Leadership positions are valued but limited in number. Though not without their own potency, village leaders, once "tamed," are less intriguing than are idealized war heroes.

A young married male, who still possesses the attitude and physical form of a warrior, seeks that which he has sacrificed through marriage. His warrior-like actions are often directed toward the person who represents his entrapment, namely, his wife. If he is inebriated, society forgives his behavior because alcohol caused him to revert to his naturally aggressive, socially recalcitrant warrior form (Marshall 1979; Carucci 1987a).

This is precisely the sort of performance embodied in the marital disagreement mentioned above. The pair were fighting over the husband's accusations that his attractive wife had slept with her recently pubescent cross-cousin. Indeed, she had joked with the young man, creating reason for jealousy, but there was no evidence of an affair. As the fight escalated, Lahren and Luela each accused the other of infidelity and each denied the accusations. Each insisted the other was crazy. Both were correct in that craziness connotes many asocial conditions where interpersonal relationships are out of balance.

Later on the day of the dispute, Luela's grandfather and an elder male from a neighboring land parcel came to visit me. They supported Luela's version of the story (as one would expect of close kin) but condemned her for joking with her cross-cousin. Lahren's actions, they claimed, were wrong because they would damage the marriage: "His thoughts are those of an adolescent male. He thinks he is very strong, a real man, but he does not know how to care for his own family. . . . He goes on and (gets) drunk for a while, walks around for a while, and then returns. And then, in his thoughts, he goes right ahead with his family."

This fight epitomizes the couple's ongoing attempt to define themselves as a legitimately married pair and yet retain the desirable attributes of being single. Luela and Lahren each manipulated one another by claiming the high ground of the adult and by accusing each other of typical adolescent actions. Luela's joking was appropriate for an unmarried woman but, in her husband's eyes, was evidence of adultery. She contended, however, that she was an ideal married woman while Lahren transformed himself into the irresponsible transient that he accused her of being. Both were trapped between their desire to be treated as adults and the attractions of being single. Alcohol also allowed Lahren to express his temporary rejection of the marriage, since it transformed his identity into that of an unmarried macho male.

Members of the community with irrevocable ties to both parties were also caught between the different versions of events and sought a new social balance. They warned Luela that adolescent joking is dangerous for married women. They contained Lahren's violence but did not severely sanction it, since severe sanctions might publicly announce that he had abused his marital privileges.[3]

Fights such as theirs are typical of couples in new marriages but also occur when a pair becomes disenchanted with one another. By 1989, when Luela and Lahren had four children, their union was stable and disagreements were infrequent.

Why do unmarried males, living instantiations of ideal men, have ambivalent feelings about themselves? One answer lies in the social contradictions that face maturing Marshallese males. Young pubescent males, fourteen to eighteen years of age, often practice their aggressive routines—boasting, competing for the largest catch or most copra, drinking, arguing, and, on occasion, fighting. They are, however, seldom seriously upset with anyone for very long because they are still learning how to portray themselves as young unmarried men. They do not yet face the ambivalence that occurs when they attempt to extend their position. As these young men become older, the disappearance of their cohorts in marriage reminds them of the limited social options that they face. Moreover, irresistibility, which is visible in physical skill and external characteristics (strength, smooth and shiny bronzed skin, jet-black "green-highlighted" hair), is difficult to maintain. As the population of single women in a young man's age bracket diminishes, it is harder for a man to manifest his attractiveness. Mature young women become increasingly interested in other qualities. They may, for example, favor a man with land over one who is physically enticing. Thus, a choice faces the young adult male: marry and sacrifice his claims to the masculine persona in favor of a future position in the community hierarchy, or remain single and gradually give up the means to maintain his claim to that ideal.

Most young males marry; yet, like Lahren, they take on the attributes of single young men when they become disenchanted with marriage. Disillusionment is almost inevitable because it takes years to become a respected elder in the community. In the interim, they have access to power only when they regress to the idealized behavior of the unmarried male warrior.

Single males are always drunk when they enter a household and begin to cause trouble. They may argue with anyone except the youngest and oldest members of the community. If disagreements escalate into fights, they never involve female relatives of the same generation. An opponent of the same generation will be another male, usually an older brother or cousin. Or a drunk may attack members of the "plus one" generation. Relatives with whom relationships are strictly governed by respect are apt to be attacked by an inebriated single male since this is the only way for men of low rank to publicly express feelings of disfranchisement. A man who is in this state of "mindless disinhibition" (MacAndrew and Edgerton 1969; Marshall 1983), or *kadek im bwebwe* ("crazy drunk"), is not held accountable since he expresses a potential social injustice. Moreover, his drunkenness allows the natural persona of uncontrolled male impulse to emerge in opposition to the unjust constraints of the social order (Carucci 1987a). Close kin help contain the fighting during these moments, and a man's "special mother" (his father's younger sister) will plead with him if the fight is serious. Her wails, like those at death, summon the well-socialized spirit of an inebriated young man and stabilize the situation by reuniting his spirit and body.

The condition of young males who have married into the community offers a special opportunity to view how the ambivalence of their situation interacts with definitions of group solidarity. Men from foreign locations have all of the symbolic weaknesses of newly married indigenous males. In addition, they lack a resident kin network for support and suffer the handicap of not being "really a person of this island." In such cases, the actions of the young male are redefined in terms that distinguish "insider" from "outsider." Outsider actions are always seen as malevolent.

The case of Paisen, a man of about thirty from Saipan, typifies the contradictory situation faced by nearly every in-married young male at some time during his life on the atoll. Paisen had lived on Ujelang for eight years. Originally a sailor, he was adopted by an Enewetak couple, married a local woman, and by 1978 had four children. Ujelang residents often praised Paisen for being a hard worker. Many wished he had married into their families.

In contrast, Paisen's wife, an attractive woman in her late twenties, was renowned on the islet for her sexual activity. On Ujelang these comments are neither derogatory nor malicious (Sahlins 1985). When Paisen returned to their cookhouse from a drinking circle to find his daughter left unattended by the cook fire, he accused his wife of attempting to kill the infant through neglect and of sleeping with other men.[4] She could not deny the charges, and others agreed.[5]

As the dispute escalated, Paisen, inebriated and upset, threw two large rocks at his wife. At least one of the rocks struck her shoulder, and as she ran away shrieking, her father began yelling at Paisen: "You are really crazy, are you? Leave this place. Just leave, for you are crazy. Are you thinking of killing my daughter? Do you not know the customs of this atoll? Go from this house. Return to your own island and do not think about coming back."

People assessed Paisen's actions differently than they had Lahren's. Paisen was now "very bad." True, his wife had been wrong, but "the people of this atoll do not 'murder' their spouses, they do not throw rocks. In a moment she would have died." When I suggested there were parallels between Paisen and Lahren, others disagreed. Although both had been drinking and both abused their wives, there were differences. Striking and throwing stones were not equivalent, and rock throwing—like the use of knives and guns—was associated with outsiders. In the best circumstances, Paisen was proudly accepted as "one of us." Just as easily, his actions transformed him into a foreigner very different from Ujelang people. He was radically dissociated from "people of this atoll [who] do not 'murder' their spouses."

Females and Violence

Ujelang people typically associate men with violent acts that are rooted in inherent qualities that tie "maleness" to men's warrior status. They associate females with love and reconciliation, seemingly the antithesis of violence (Carucci 1980). Nonetheless, women use physical force to discipline children, adolescent girls engage in aggressive sexual play, and aging women use supernatural force to control the acts of others.

Mead noted seven decades ago (1928) that child socialization in Samoa rests largely with children slightly older than their charges. On Ujelang, children carry babies slung across the hip at an age so young that they weave under the weight. As soon as weaning takes place, youngsters of both sexes take over a good deal of child care. Parents monitor the process, but their role shifts to maintaining harmony among siblings and among the play set, which includes relatives and agemates in the neighborhood.

By six or seven years of age, girls provide most of the child care, while boys are allowed to range far from home in an unconstrained fashion that continues into marriage. Children admonish younger siblings with phrases like "bad" or "do not [do] your sort of action." When undesired actions continue, scolding is repeated with added emphasis but no enforcement. Physical punishment is so slow in coming that I heard one American comment: "They do not learn how to obey because they go on and on without . . . ever *doing* something about it." Caretakers do move recalcitrant children away from mischief. When infants return to trouble, overseers throw small stones or continue scolding, but they do not take decisive action until damage has occurred. Youngsters are hit by parents and by other children, but battered children are unknown.

Mothers who are principal caregivers occasionally swat children, whether they are true offspring, classificatory children, or children through adoption (coparenthood). The most harsh-tempered mothers beat their children, ring their ears, or drag them by the hair. The latter acts are particularly demeaning since the head is the most highly ranked part of the body. From most women, however, children receive substantial verbal abuse and little physical punishment. This aligns with indigenous stereotypes that categorize outspoken and independent women as "disagreeable or mean-tempered," in possession of "sharp mouths [tongues]." In other words, females who are charged with maintaining the solidarity of the extended family and clan anchor their punishments in emotion-laden thought and talk instead of action. While these punishments, in their incipient form, are obviously less violent than the physical responses of males, they may be more volatile and dangerous when extended into the realm of magic. Indigenous terms equate malevolent magic and physical violence. Whereas the latter is characteristically associated with males in an ambivalent cultural situation, the former is controlled by females who are denied access to the use of physical force.

"The thoughts of that woman, so great is their damaged character, you could never weigh them." With these words a man warned me of the dangers of an Ujelang woman's magic. People generally say that malevolent magic, like other hostile behavior, is unknown on Ujelang Atoll. Bad magic is attributed to others, particularly to Marshall Islanders, Solomon Islanders, New Guinea residents, and outsiders to Enewetak and Ujelang. Nonetheless, I have records of many magically-influenced local events, and in most instances mature Ujelang women were involved.

Magic passes through matriclans and is often manipulated by women. A woman with strong magic either inherited the knowledge from clan elders or purchased it from a magical specialist in the Marshall Islands. Males may also purchase magical knowledge or even receive it from clan elders, but their magic also derives its strength from matrilineal sources.

Male magic is often restricted to curing. Young girls likewise use magical knowledge with positive intent, but as a woman ages "sometimes her thoughts are warped" and it is such women who use magic for manipulative purposes.[6] Men who use physical violence and women who practice malevolent magic are both upset with perceived social injustice. Women use love magic and potentially lethal magic to reimpose a morally just order to social relationships that they believe are out of balance.

On Ujelang, evil magic is never practiced openly since this act would contradict the contention that magic does not exist. However, women are said to be responsible for magical harm, and the discursive forms used to talk about male physical abuse are also used to describe damage from sorcery. While the blows and death threats of mature single men are dangerous, people fear older women's magic far more. Not only are the effects of magic more lethal than physical aggression, but because magic uses clan force that has a supernatural source, humans have a limited ability to assess the potential damage and to bring the situation back into control.

Conclusions

A cursory glance at interaction among Marshall Islanders might lead one to draw undue parallels with family violence in Western countries. Because physical aggression may well be directed against women by young men, one may infer that domestic violence is instigated by men and endured by women. A closer look, however, shows this interpretation to be simplistic and naïve.

First of all, violent activities on Ujelang are used to display feelings of disfranchisement and discontent. Children are never beaten for "wrongs against nature," and adults who use physical beatings or magic do so to communicate feelings of social injustice that must be brought into balance. The people of Ujelang are not empowered with a Western individuality or with the concomitant ability to shape events (Lutz 1988).

Second, violent acts occur because they are appropriate for certain role prototypes, not because they are inherent in persons. Young women usually construct their identities using ideal female attributes, but women with the "thoughts of men" may employ physical abuse to communicate their chosen social selves. Likewise, many men use physical force to communicate part of their warrior-like identity, but not all men adopt such aggressive personal styles. Identities, therefore, are actively constructed out of cultural signifiers that take on meaning in relation to prototypes of male and female discourse and practice (Carucci 1980, 1985, 1987b; Shore 1981; Strathern 1981, 1988).

Marshall Islands men and women use violence to point out domestic and village injustice. Restricted abuses may occur in interactions between members of adjacent generations or among siblings, but the most dangerous violence takes place between wives and husbands and among in-laws. Small acts of punishment among kin escalate into volatile forms of abuse among nonkin. Accordingly, men may physically "murder" (beat) their spouses, and women may "beat their husbands to death" with magic.

Solidarity, rooted in the ideology of bilateral extended families but also applied to the entire community, is the antithesis of violent interaction (Carucci 1980:chaps. 2–3). At an ideological level, Ujelang people see both magical and physical violence as typical of outsiders, and severe violent acts are consistently attributed to them. For example, residents of New Guinea or the Marshall Islands are said to use the most dangerous forms of magic, while people from Chuuk are particularly "murderous" since they fight with knives and machetes. Even within the community, the most violent actions are envisioned among spouses and in-laws—foreigners who have been brought into the domestic unit (Fortes 1943–44). The violent acts of Paisen are easily recast into those of a foreigner, while those of Lahren are attributed to a family that acts "unlike us."

Violent activities are also balanced throughout the life cycle. Ultimately, however, the overt, aggressive acts of young men are less threatening than the internal, potentially lethal magical aggression of aging women. Physical acts are contained by group members, who surround young men and restrain them, while magical acts remain threatening precisely because their parameters cannot be easily delimited and contained. Most important, both males and females have ways to express their discontent that line up with the shifting balance of power in the community.[7] The male ideal type, the single roaming warrior, is ultimately replaced by a sedentary male who is partly constrained by matrilines he does not control (Carucci 1985; Kahn 1986). His physical aggression, easily contained by the group, is a metonym of the ambivalent male position. In contrast, females—who initially lack the freedoms young men enjoy—gradually accumulate matrilineal power that expands with the successful transmission of female reproductive force. Their use of magical force—physically passive yet covert, supernaturally inspired, and difficult to control—increases with their own power and age.

To Ujelang residents, both physical and magical violence are inevitable expressions of the inherent capacities of men and women. While mortals may invert these natural forces for ritual purposes, in joking, or as an expression of personal style, they should not believe that in so doing they eliminate the distinctions. For earthly beings, there is only the hope of maintaining balance among them.

NOTES

My research on Ujelang was supported by a grant from the National Science Foundation, administered by the University of Chicago; the National Endowment for the Humanities provided funding for work on Enewetak. All interpretations are my responsibility, not those of the granting agencies or sponsoring institutions. An earlier version of this chapter, entitled "Negotiations of Violence in the Marshallese Household," appeared in *Pacific Studies* 13:3 (1990): 93–113. I would like to thank the editor for permission to include it in this volume.

1. My research was conducted on Ujelang Atoll between August 1976 and September 1978 and on Enewetak Atoll between May 1982 and May 1983. All quotations are from my field notes unless otherwise indicated.

2. As indicated below, men also may use magic, but it is primarily manipulated by women and derives its potency from matrilineal sources. As attributes of statuses, things like magical knowledge need not be used solely by females to be associated with them.

3. Lahren here lays claim to mission-inspired rules for adultery, even though he is not a church member. These stiff standards differ significantly from local practice, which permits a wider array of sexual relationships. Luela claims her husband has adhered to indigenous standards in his own conduct.

4. No one was in the cookhouse with Paisen and his wife. I summarize the controversy based on what I overheard from a nearby cookhouse. Only when the encounter became physically threatening did others rush to the scene.

5. Sleeping around could, by indigenous logic, introduce foreign substances into a woman's (white) milk from its connection with the white sperm of her paramours.

6. Thought here includes an emotive component, as Lutz (1988:93) notes of *nunuwan* on Ifaluk. It is the imbalance of thought/feeling that causes craziness (asocial interaction) for both men and women. The "paths" men and women follow to express their unsettled senses of self stretch along two different vectors.

7. Young women and old powerless men have least access to these modes of expression. Young women threatened by their husbands may take sanctuary with relatives, but old women do not magically kill spouses for them on request. People do fear magical retribution and "straighten" their actions to avoid sorcery. This is fear of the judgments of the magical specialist, however, since evil magic on Ujelang is neither purchased nor performed on behalf of others.

REFERENCES CITED

Carucci, Laurence Marshall. 1980. "The Renewal of Life: A Ritual Encounter in the Marshall Islands." Ph.D diss., University of Chicago.

———. 1985. "Conceptions of Maturing and Dying in the 'Middle of Heaven.'" In *Aging and Its Transformations: Moving toward Death in Pacific Society.* Ed. Dorothy Counts and David Counts. 107–29. Washington, D.C.: University Press of America.

———. 1987a. "Jekero: Symbolizing the Transition to Manhood in the Marshall Islands." *Micronesica* 20:1–17.

———. 1987b. "Ruwamwaijet im RiAnin: Outsiders Becoming Insiders." Paper delivered at the Annual Meetings of the Association for Social Anthropology in Oceania, Monterey, Calif.

———. 1989. "The Source of the Force in Marshallese Cosmology." In *The Pacific Theater: Island Representations of World War II.* Ed. Lamont Lindstrom and Geoffrey White. 73–96. Honolulu: University of Hawaii Press.

Fortes, Meyer. 1943–44. "The Significance of Descent in Tale Social Structure." *Africa* 14:362–84.

Kahn, Miriam. 1986. *Always Hungry, Never Greedy: Food and the Expression of Gender in a Melanesian Society.* Cambridge: Cambridge University Press.

Levy, Robert I. 1973. *Tahitians: Mind and Experience in the Society Islands.* Chicago: University of Chicago Press.

Lutz, Catherine A. 1988. *Unnatural Emotions: Everyday Sentiments on a Micronesian Atoll and Their Challenge to a Western Theory.* Chicago: University of Chicago Press.

MacAndrew, Craig, and Robert Edgerton. 1969. *Drunken Comportment: A Social Explanation.* Chicago: Aldine.

Marshall, Mac. 1979. *Weekend Warriors: Alcohol in a Micronesian Culture.* Palo Alto, Calif.: Mayfield.

———. 1983. "'Four Hundred Rabbits': An Anthropological View of Ethanol as a Disinhibitor." In *Alcohol and Disinhibition: Nature and Meaning of the Link.* Ed. R. Room and G. Collins. 186–237. Rockville, Md.: National Institute on Alcohol Abuse and Alcoholism.

Mead, Margaret. 1928. *Coming of Age in Samoa.* New York: Morrow.

Radcliffe-Brown, A. R. 1952. *Structure and Function in Primitive Society.* London: Cohen and West.

Sahlins, Marshall D. 1985. *Islands of History.* Chicago: University of Chicago Press.

Schneider, David M. 1968. *American Kinship: A Cultural Account.* Englewood Cliffs, N.J.: Prentice-Hall.

Shore, Bradd. 1981. "Sexuality and Gender in Samoa: Conceptions and Missed Conceptions." In *Sexual Meanings: The Cultural Construction of Gender and Sexuality.* Ed. Sherry Ortner and Harriet Whitehead. 192–215. Cambridge: Cambridge University Press.

Strathern, Marilyn. 1981. "Self-Interest and the Social Good: Some Implications of Hagen Gender Imagery." In *Sexual Meanings: The Cultural Construction of Gender and Sexuality.* Ed. Sherry Ortner and Harriet Whitehead. 166–91. Cambridge: Cambridge University Press.

———. 1988. *The Gender of the Gift: Problems with Women and Problems with Society in Melanesia.* Berkeley: University of California Press.

TEN

Spare the Rod and Spoil the Woman? Family Violence in Abelam Society

Richard Scaglion

This chapter addresses the question of differing cultural definitions of terms such as "violence" and "spouse abuse" by examining the nature of family "violence" in Abelam society. Among the Abelam, it is not uncommon for men to punish women physically. These men may be husbands, elder brothers, fathers, or other close relatives. When beatings are not too severe or too frequent, this behavior is socially approved by uninvolved persons of both sexes. Abelam men regard such physical punishment in much the same spirit as some Americans regard child discipline. They believe that occasional beatings are sometimes "necessary" in order to socialize women properly. Women tolerate occasional beatings, particularly when they admit fault. If they feel unjustly accused, however, women may defend themselves, sometimes employing counterviolence. Cases of pure "husband beating" are very rare, however. Nearly all Abelam family "violence" involves behavior that is considered to be discipline of wives by husbands or of sisters by elder brothers.

While American cultural standards seem to be changing, I believe it is still considered culturally appropriate by many Americans to discipline children with occasional physical punishment. A slap on the buttocks, following several verbal warnings, would probably not be considered "child abuse" by most Americans. Indeed, I have seen the public physical punishment of children in supermarkets, shopping malls, and so forth on numerous occasions. Only when such discipline becomes too severe or too frequent is it culturally defined as "abuse." By contrast, it is probably never considered "justified" in American society for a husband to strike his wife, and I believe all such incidents would be considered "abusive."

In Abelam society, these patterns seem to be almost reversed. I am sure that the Abelam would regard many Americans as being physically abusive toward their children (cf. Korbin 1981, 1987 for differing cultural standards of child abuse). The Abelam rarely if ever strike their own children. Withholding food is a much more common punishment, often accompanied by a matter-of-fact statement of cause and effect: "Well, you didn't do your share of the work, so you don't get your share of the food."

However, just as many American families sustain a level of physical child "abuse" considered inappropriate by Abelam standards, most Abelam marriages sustain occasional physical punishment of wives that would be judged "abusive" by American standards. Such discipline of women by their male relatives is the focus of this chapter. I will provide an overview of Abelam family violence and then analyze a series of representative cases in the course of examining the nature, frequency, and social context of family violence against women in Abelam society.

Ethnographic Background

The Abelam are non-Austronesian speakers living in the foothills of the Prince Alexander Mountains in East Sepik Province, Papua New Guinea. They are a horticultural group, densely populating lowlands and subsisting mostly on yams, taro, sweet potatoes, and sago supplemented by pork, small game, and various garden products. The focus of this study is the Samukundi dialect group, comprising about 10,000 of the roughly 60,000 Abelam. The Samukundi inhabit the northernmost part of Abelam territory, extending well into the Prince Alexander Mountains. Neligum village, the research site, is in the extreme north of Samukundi territory. Neligum has experienced the population explosion characteristic of the entire Abelam tribe since contact; its population has more than doubled in the twenty-five years (1974–99) I worked there. Yet there is still adequate land in the virgin forest to the north. Thus Neligum has not experienced the severe land shortages and concomitant land disputes that plague other Abelam populations.

The Abelam are nominally patrilineal and patrilocal; more than 80 percent of married couples live near the husband's family. Marriages are generally contracted between partners in different sections of the same village or from neighboring villages, so women are never far from their natal homes. Another pattern relevant to the present discussion is the tendency of the Abelam to visit frequently with friends and relatives and to sleep where they visit. In a time-allocation study in which I visited people during the evening and nighttime hours (Scaglion 1986a), people were frequently not found sleeping at home. Thus, when family violence erupts or is expected, family members can avoid confrontations temporarily simply by visiting away from home for a few days.

The Case Sample

I began my research in Neligum in 1974, about a year after a local court was established at Maprik, the subdistrict headquarters. In this still-colonial period the introduced court was almost never used voluntarily by the Abelam, and with a few exceptions (Scaglion 1976) conflict management was carried on much as it had been since before European contact. Conducting a study of conflict management in Neligum, I remained in residence throughout calendar year 1975 and used the case method (Black and Metzger 1965; Epstein 1967; Frake 1969; Gulliver 1969) to collect a sixty-five-case sample of the conflict cases that occurred in that year. These cases were recorded in detail on specially designed forms and included relevant data concerning the relationships between litigants, a history of the dispute, the nature of previous disputes, and so forth. Taken together, these cases constitute the total of all incidents that the people themselves defined as "trouble cases." For the Abelam, trouble cases are incidents that cause sufficient disruption in village harmony to result in remedial action. For this analysis, it is important to realize that mild, disciplinary beating of wives by husbands is socially sanctioned and *not* considered "trouble." Thus, this sample underrepresents the actual incidence of what Americans might view as family violence. In all of the spouse abuse cases in this sample, at least some persons considered the beatings sufficiently severe, frequent, or unjustified to constitute abuse by Abelam standards.

In 1977, village courts were introduced into the area. This changed the basic process of conflict management by integrating traditional and introduced remedy agents (Scaglion 1979, 1985). Since then, more extensive exposure to Western social patterns, especially through schooling, has altered the nature of Abelam family life. Therefore, quantitative data on the frequency of various types of conflict presented here are from the sixty-five trouble cases recorded in 1975 (analyzed in Scaglion 1976). This sample of all the conflicts involving the 553 Neligum residents in that year illustrates fairly "traditional" patterns. Cases reported in this chapter are also taken from this sample. To assess more recent social changes at the conclusion of this chapter, I have relied on cases that I observed after 1975, either in village courts or in the village itself.

The Nature of Family Violence

The 1975 sample of sixty-five cases shows that what Westerners today consider family violence was not uncommon in traditional Abelam society. Fifteen of these cases (23.1 percent of all disputes) involve physical violence between immediate family members. These cases, broken down by structural relationship between disputants, are detailed in table 10.1.

In another sample of 101 cases collected during 1974–76, mainly memory cases from the precontact and early colonial era, 22 (21.8 percent) involve violence between immediate family members. These display much the same pattern as seen in table 10.1. In the category of spouse violence, the overwhelming number of 1975 cases involve male physical abuse of women (82 percent). The others involve attacks on husbands by armed wives, angered because of sexual jealousies. The physical violence against women is undoubtedly a long-standing pattern. I once noticed a three-inch-long scar on the back of my Abelam grandmother's head. When I asked her about it, she explained that she had been injured many years ago, when she was a newly married woman, before she had had children. This was "when people were still using the stone axes and knives." Her husband thought she had been seeing another man. When he accused her, she denied it. They quarreled, and he cut her with a bamboo knife. This incident closely resembles cases collected in 1975 (see below).

Spousal Violence

My impression is that for most Abelam couples the level of spousal violence is rather low. The husband might slap the wife mildly with an open hand or deliver a single blow with a piece of firewood on rather rare occasions, perhaps once every few years. Newly married couples usually experience a period of adjustment in which a mutually tolerable level of spousal violence is established. By mutually tolerable violence, I do not mean to suggest that women are always satisfied with their situations. However, most women regard a certain amount of physical violence as an unfortunate part of married life. When I interviewed women about past beatings, particularly if the

Table 10.1. The Nature of Abelam Family Violence

Relationship between Disputants	Number of Cases	Percentage
Spouses	11	64.7
Siblings	3	17.6
Close intergenerational	2	11.8
Co-wives	1	5.9
Totals	17[a]	100.0

Source: Based on Scaglion (1976).

a. Exceeds the number of individual cases (15) because some cases involved two types of violence.

beatings were very mild, women often said that they were extremely angry at the time but later realized that they had been wrong and so they could accept the situation without much bitterness. If the level of physical violence against a woman is sufficiently low and infrequent that she does not regard her husband as "abusive," I consider the violence "tolerable" to the couple. There are, however, a few men who seem unusually abusive by nature, particularly during their younger years. Their marriages tend to be short-lived, not surviving the adjustment period. There are also couples who seem to sustain a rather high, recurring level of violence throughout their married years that is not "mutually tolerable." The following three cases illustrate fairly typical patterns of spousal violence that cause trouble in the village.

A Newly Married Young Couple

Wiseke,[1] a young man of nineteen, went to a yam festival at a neighboring village on 22 August 1975. These festivals take place following nearly six months of ritual sexual abstinence, and a great deal of courtship and sexual behavior takes place during the late night hours. Wiseke had not told his relatively new (second) wife, Kurepak, aged twenty-one, that he was going. He stayed overnight, returning home late the next morning.

When he finally returned, Kurepak yelled at him. He became angry, beat her unconscious with his fists, and walked off. Her in-laws tended her and sent for her father, Sambisany. Her injuries were so severe that her father feared she would die. As he tended her, one of his classificatory fathers (the young woman's grandfather), having heard of the trouble, arrived on the scene. He was so angered at the extent of Kurepak's injuries that he borrowed a spear and set out in search of Wiseke, vowing to kill him. Wiseke had hidden himself well, though, and was not to be found.

Wiseke lay low for about a week, and Kurepak eventually recovered. Her father suggested that she divorce Wiseke, but she refused. He was an extremely good-looking young man, and she did not want to leave him. As a second wife, she knew that her leaving temporarily would be a bad strategy: it would give her co-wife a chance to "strengthen" her hold on him and to "poison his mind" against her. She determined to return to her husband.

Kurepak's father and family had been opposed to the marriage from the beginning. It seems that Sambisany had married Wiseke's aunt as a second wife, and shortly afterward his first wife, Kurepak's mother, had died. Sambisany suggested that sorcery by Wiseke's kin group had been the cause.

When he could not convince his daughter to leave Wiseke, Sambisany lectured her, saying, "I didn't want you to marry him in the first place but you wouldn't listen and went to live with him anyway. They killed your mother and now they'll kill you. Well, that's your affair but Wiseke hasn't paid bride-price yet. I'll send word to him to pay. Then if he wants to kill you it's his business." After this was done, Sambisany calmed his classificatory father. In any case, the woman's grandfather had ceased looking for Wiseke when it was obvious that she would recover.

Subsequent Developments This couple divorced a few years later. Wiseke has shown himself to be an incorrigible womanizer who has never settled down. He has had a number of wives and girlfriends and displayed a pattern of physical abuse of women that is definitely not socially approved. However, when his wives have been unwilling to leave him, their male relatives have given limited support.

A Middle-Aged Couple

Saatkwak, a forty-eight-year-old married man with three children, was having an affair with Leves, a fifty-year-old widow with one child. He began referring to her as his "second wife," although she did not live with him or cook for him. Since Abelam marriages often begin as rather de facto affairs, cohabitation and sharing food are commonly regarded as signs that a couple is actually married.

Manyge, a woman of forty-six who had been married to Saatkwak for many years, became angry that he was referring to Leves as a second wife, although she had previously been ignoring their affair. On Monday, 5 May 1975, she confronted him about it. She became angry and began scolding him in public. He became angry, picked up a piece of firewood, and hit her over the head with it. It was not the first time he had physically abused her. He hit her about the head several times as she attempted to protect herself with her arms, whereupon she ran away.

Later that afternoon she went to the hamlet of a big-man, Waama, the principal mediator for her and her husband's ceremonial group. Because he was busy, Waama asked Manyge to wait for another time to have the case heard. But she was still angry and wanted to press her case immediately. He suggested she go to see the local government councillor. She went, but the councillor was not home, and she determined to take the case to the local court. She lodged her complaint with the police, who told her to bring her husband in. She approached Waama again, and he helped her bring her husband to the police station later that week. By this time she had cooled down and refused to press charges.

When the three returned together to the village, Manyge became afraid of possible reprisals by her husband and ran away again. She stayed for a few days with a female friend who lived in a different ceremonial group within the same village. Then she went to stay with her brother in her neighboring natal village.

On 12 May, Saatkwak went to his brother-in-law's house to bring Manyge back. The brother did not seem to want to take sides in the dispute, and Manyge agreed to return to Neligum with her husband. Later that day, though, when Saatkwak left for another neighboring village to help carry ritual objects for a ceremony, Manyge returned to her brother's house.

On 17 May, Manyge voluntarily decided to return once again to her home. When she arrived, her husband was away attending a yam festival in a neighboring village. He arrived home very late and there was no incident that night. Nevertheless, Waama feared more trouble. Knowing this couple's history of marital problems and that the husband frequently struck the wife, the bigman suggested to several of the husband's male relatives that they keep an eye on him. If he became physically abusive (without cause) they were instructed to beat *him*.

Five months later the couple argued again, and Saatkwak struck Manyge in the face with his open hand. Waama was sent for to arbitrate. Manyge accused her husband of being involved with yet another woman, but this time apparently without good reason. After trying unsuccessfully to calm both parties, Waama left, telling them that he was sick of their behavior and that they should deal with their own problems.

Subsequent Developments This couple has continued to have problems over the years, but they are still together. The husband continues to beat or strike his wife frequently during their quarrels. By emic standards his actions are right on the borderline of abuse. Some people describe him as abusive; others feel that he is justified. Many people consider the wife to be hot-headed and feel that she often precipitates their fights.

Another Middle-Aged Couple

In the wave of cargo-cult beliefs immediately preceding independence, people became convinced that another country was coming to "boss" Papua New Guinea (Scaglion 1983). Awungele, a forty-eight-year-old married man, cut a great deal of bamboo to build a resthouse for the new "country." But after hearing a lot of conflicting stories about what would actually happen at independence, he thought better of it. Maknambinje, a woman of fifty who had married Wano, age fifty-two, after his first wife died, was having an affair with Awungele. Realizing that Awungele had much extra bamboo, she approached her own husband about building a cookhouse for her and mentioned that their neighbor, Awungele, had extra bamboo. The husband approached Awungele and they agreed to build the house together.

After the frame was erected, Wano and Maknambinje had a fight. Wano had frequently threatened his wife with a piece of firewood or a bush knife and had beaten her over relatively minor matters. On this particular occasion he slapped her across the side of the face and told her to build her own cookhouse. After this, Awungele finished the house alone. This angered the husband.

The case festered for a few months. Finally, it was discussed at a village meeting on 10 November 1975. Awungele denied knowing that the husband had refused to build the house. He claimed that he had had some spare time and just built the house himself. Public opinion seemed to run against him. Most people believed that Maknambinje had convinced her lover to complete the house after her husband had refused to help.

After Awungele told his side of the story, Wano said in the sarcastic style characteristic of such situations, "Ah, her husband is dead, and so you put up a cookhouse for her." Wano had previously tried to convince his wife to move to a different part of the village, since he suspected her affair with Awungele. Now, at the village meeting, he repeated his request that they move. She replied that she wished to remain in their present location until she died. He said, "Oh, I see, you two would like to marry. All right, you two can stay together and I'll leave."

Several of the big-men who were mediating the dispute said no, that wasn't right, a woman should go with her husband. After hearing all this, Awungele said he did not want to hear any more of this talk and denied having an affair with Maknambinje.

While no definite "orders" were given and no particular decisions reached, exhortations were made for the couple to stay together, and it was more or less understood that this would happen.

Subsequent Developments The couple resided in separate hamlets for a time, but eventually they came together again. Their problems were never really resolved, and the pattern of wife beating continued on a sporadic basis. The woman is now deceased.

The above cases demonstrate the usual patterns of Abelam family violence. In the first case, a young man seriously abused his wife. This is most

- ask men about the 'roles' of diff women a) mothers b) sisters c) wives/partners d) other women

common in the early years of marriage. If the husband does not moderate his beatings to a socially acceptable level, the wife usually leaves him, temporarily at first and then permanently as the marriage ultimately breaks up, as happened in this instance. In other cases, newly married spouses fight but get together again after a cooling-off period, and the level of violence progressively declines. Still other couples display recurring patterns of spouse abuse serious enough to cause trouble but tolerable enough for the marriage to remain intact. The above cases also show that sexual jealousies are common causes of family violence and that polygynous marriages can cause severe problems until adjustments are made.

When women are severely abused they are not always physically passive, as were the women in these cases. Some women use violence to defend themselves. Others attack their husbands with a weapon. Again, this sort of behavior is most common in the early stages of marriages when couples are making adjustments. Just as some men seem particularly prone to spouse abuse, some "hot-blooded" women (as they are called by the Abelam) seem particularly prone to turning weapons against their spouses. The following is a typical case. Sexual jealousy is again the ultimate cause.

A Wife Attacks Her Husband

Paal, a twenty-eight-year-old man, had two wives. He shot a wallaby on 19 September 1975 and hung it up in his house. His second wife, Sapasalik, a young woman to whom he had been married for only a few months, took it down and prepared to cook it. His first wife, Nyangilak, to whom he had been married for many years and with whom he had three children, did not approve of the second wife. She told her co-wife to leave the wallaby alone, that it belonged to her. The second wife said that she was hungry and that she intended to cook it. The two began to fight. They grabbed at one another's clothing and hair and slapped each other. The husband intervened, pulling the two apart, but did not take sides. The wallaby remained uncooked.

A few days later, on 22 September, Paal shot an opossum and gave it to his first wife to cook. When it was nearly ready to eat, he began to worry about a possible quarrel concerning its distribution, so he asked his second wife to help him cut some *pitpit* (wild sugarcane) in the bush. The second wife refused, saying that she wanted to stay and eat the opossum. When he grabbed her arm to pull her along with him, she slashed him with her machete, resulting in a deep cut along the side of his wrist.

The first wife then came to the husband's aid. She grabbed her co-wife's hair and pulled her to the ground. Then she began beating Sapasalik with her fists. A bystander, a neighbor and friend of the husband, pulled the two women apart and calmed everyone.

Subsequent Developments After a year or two of adjustment, this family seems to have solved its problems. Nyangilak appears to have accepted her co-wife and Paal has remained married to both women for the past twenty years. Sapasalik has had three children, and there has been little if any family violence in the past two decades.

Brother-Sister and Father-Daughter Violence

Cases of spouse abuse and retaliation are the most common types of Abelam family violence. However, brothers disciplining sisters and, less frequently, fathers or other close male relatives disciplining daughters is not uncommon. The above cases show that abused wives frequently seek shelter with their male relatives for a time, most frequently with their brothers. Brothers have a responsibility to provide a home for their sisters whenever they are in need. They also have an interest in their sisters' upbringing. Violence between brothers and sisters generally involves elder brothers beating their younger sisters. The cause might be sexual behavior with inappropriate persons or at inappropriate times, failing to do their share of work, failing to meet family obligations, or similar unseemly behavior. The following is a typical case.

A Brother and His Sisters

On Friday night, 27 November 1975, a dance was held at Bainyik, where there is a vocational school and an agricultural research station. November is well into the ceremonial yam-growing season, and taboos against all sexual activity are in effect. The Abelam believe that sex stunts the growth of ceremonial yams.

The next morning Gumde, a young man twenty-one years old but nevertheless the senior active male of his lineage, noticed that his two sisters, Jejemu and Yaave, had not returned home the night before. A few years previously, several young men from the village, including Gumde, had suspected their sisters of attending these dances, waited for them along the road after one such event, and beat them. They were concerned about possible sexual relationships and indirect pollution (Scaglion 1986b), which would damage their yam crop.

When Gumde went to his garden that morning, he saw Jejemu sitting in front of the garden house. When she saw him coming she ran away, hoping he had not noticed her. This confirmed his suspicions that she had attended the dance. He took a shortcut back to the main part of the village and caught her. He cut a switch and beat her with it, mostly trying to hit her buttocks. Then he slapped her several times with his open hand as he scolded her.

She ran into the house, crying, as he stood outside berating her: What did she think she was doing? This was yam season and he did not want her running around. He was sick of this sort of behavior. A small crowd began to gather, including a few of Jejemu's other male relatives, who supported Gumde.

After a while, Gumde left to cut timber in the bush. When he returned to the village that afternoon, he found the younger sister, Yaave, and the above scene was repeated. The two girls spent the rest of the afternoon sulking in the house.

Subsequent Developments Neither of these sisters has married over the years, which is unusual. They remain under their brother's protection, and he helps support them economically. (He also supports the older sister's two children. The younger sister has no children.) This demonstrates the vested interest brothers have in their sisters' activities. Sisters always have a home with their brothers, throughout life if they never marry.

I have never seen or heard of a level of physical violence in brother-sister cases that exceeds the levels of social tolerance. In a few instances there is social disapproval of the causes of these beatings, however. People sometimes feel that brothers are too strict or are mistaken in their suspicions. In such cases, sisters may feel that their punishments are unjust and may seek shelter with friends for a time, while community gossip or comments cause their brothers to rethink their own actions.

Just as sisters are sometimes dependent on their brothers, the reverse is also true. In later life, sisters feed their brothers whenever the brothers' wives are in the menstrual huts, particularly when they are living close by. When sisters have married into a nearby village, they look after their brothers whenever their brothers visit the "new" village for ritual occasions, which are fairly common. They may also look after their brothers' friends at these times.

In addition to these practical considerations of mutual support and interdependence between brothers and sisters, there is usually a great deal of love and respect in such relationships. These factors act in concert to keep violence at a low level. Nevertheless, it is a level that probably exceeds Western standards.

Because of the lifelong ties between brothers and sisters, brothers are the male relatives who most commonly discipline unmarried women. But not all young women have brothers, and many have brothers who are very young. In such cases, a father or the closest adult male relative will take responsibility for disciplining a woman. The following case involves an uncle who acted in lieu of a brother.

An Older Male Relative and a Young Female

Simon was a young man from a Sepik River culture linguistically related to the Abelam. He had come to visit friends in Neligum village and had stayed for some time. After about a month, he began a trial marriage with a young woman from the village. Neither he nor his hosts had asked the young woman's relatives for their permission. Furthermore, although he claimed to be single, discreet inquiries by a village elder with Sepik River connections revealed that Simon already had two wives. The discovery of this deception precipitated a conflict case in which it was decided that the young woman would break off the relationship and go back to live with her own family. While conventions of hospitality did not permit driving Simon out of the village, village elders were angry and some began to watch him closely.

A neighboring village was planning to hold a *singsing* (ceremony) to dedicate a new *haus tambaran* (ceremonial house) on 25 April 1975, and Simon decided to attend. That afternoon Nyayala, a forty-two-year-old man, overheard another young woman, Baambil, age seventeen, making plans to meet Simon secretly at the ceremony. Nyayala was the girl's *wau* (mother's brother). In fact, their relationship was especially close in that Nyayala and Baambil's father had married through sister exchange. Although Nyayala was angry, he said nothing. Since his brother-in-law (the girl's actual father) was away and the young woman had no brothers, he decided to handle the matter himself. He went to his brother's hamlet, which was located adjacent to a path along which the girl would have to travel in order to attend the ceremony. About 7:30 P.M. he saw Simon pass by on his way to the *singsing*, and about ten minutes later he saw Baambil approaching along the same route.

He called out to her, and, when she came close to him, he grabbed her arm. He then began to drag her through the center of the village back to her parents' house, periodically hitting her buttocks with a switch he had cut. The whole way he berated her: Hadn't she learned anything from the other girl's experience? She should stay home and help her parents. She shouldn't be running off all the time chasing after young men. While the beating was undoubtedly painful, the young woman seemed to be even more upset by the public humiliation; the next day she wore a cloth over her head to "hide her shame."

Subsequent Developments Soon after this incident, the young woman married a man from a neighboring village. The marriage seems to be a happy one, and the couple has remained together for many years. No further incidents of physical violence between the woman and her uncle have occurred.

Discussion

An understanding of Abelam attitudes toward brother-sister and father-daughter violence sheds light on cultural attitudes toward spousal violence. Abelam men believe that many women, and particularly young women, are inclined to be somewhat "lazy" and "wayward." Whereas children are not fully developed human beings and do not always understand the consequences of their actions, females who have had their first-menstruation ceremony are adults, according to the Abelam, and should act accordingly. When they do not, their actions reflect badly on their entire family. In such cases, a close male relative must take responsibility for protecting the family reputation by disciplining the woman.

In many traditional Abelam marriages, more common in the past than now, the husband is considerably older than the wife. This is particularly true when the woman is a second or third wife. In such cases, especially during the early stages of marriage, the husband acts more like a father or elder brother in disciplining his young wife. When spouses are more closely matched in age the logic is not so clear, but Abelam men nevertheless seem to feel that much of the responsibility for "necessary" discipline of a young woman falls to her husband after marriage. In principle, traditional Abelam women also subscribe to these notions.

Traditional Abelam women have a great deal of power in formulating cultural standards of physical abuse. If a man punishes his wife (or sister or daughter) sufficiently frequently or severely to be culturally defined as abusive, the village women can censure him by collectively withholding services. His own mother and sisters can and will refuse to cook for him, making the same sort of matter-of-fact statement of cause and effect that they use to discipline children: "Well, you beat your wife for no reason, so don't expect help from me." Male friends and relatives can also withhold support from a wife beater, and a battered woman can always seek shelter with friends or relatives. In this manner, cultural standards of acceptable family violence are collectively set. Abelam women acting in concert have enormous power here, for men depend on them for a variety of things because of the sexual division of labor and the complementarity of gender roles (Scaglion 1986b).

Of course, social change in Abelam society has been pronounced in the past two decades as most of the younger generation has received some schooling and has had considerable exposure to Western culture. Abelam family structure now approximates European patterns more closely than in the past, when polygynous marriages were more common. The first census of Neligum village that I have been able to locate is from 1957. It shows that 11.8 percent of all marriages were polygynous. My own data from Upper Neligum show that 10.0 percent of all marriages in 1975 were polygynous, compared with only 4.8 percent in 1987. Thus, the creation of new polygynous unions, once a considerable cause of sexual jealousy, is declining, and spouses tend to be closer in age. Still, adultery or suspected adultery remains the major cause of contemporary domestic strife.

My intuitive opinion is that the frequency of spousal violence has increased in recent years. Young women are now much more likely to strike their husbands over matters (other than sexual jealousies) that traditionally they would have accepted or over new forms of behavior of which they do not approve. Indeed, I witnessed two such incidents during a recent field trip. Both occurred in relatively new marriages. One involved a wife who was angry because her husband was playing cards rather than tending to domestic duties; the other involved an argument over bride-price. In the bride-price case, the husband retaliated by also hitting the wife; in the card-playing case he did not. Nevertheless, twenty years ago it would have been rare for a woman to strike her husband first.

The Abelam have become a much more mobile population in the past twenty years. Once there was little access to vehicular transportation, and people remained close to home due to fears of tribal warfare and sorcery. Today, young men and women travel considerable distances for school, work, or recreation. In a small face-to-face society, sexual encounters are difficult to hide and suspicions are usually well grounded. In contemporary Abelam society, however, young married people are often suspicious of spousal adultery, frequently without proof. Whereas a guilty wife, recognizing fault, would be likely to accept a mild beating or severe tongue-lashing, an unjustly accused wife is more likely to return like for like, escalating the severity of spousal violence. In new-style marriages today, women are more likely to engage in both offensive and defensive physical violence against husbands.

Now, as in the past, Abelam marriages seem to be characterized by a fairly low level of violence after the initial adjustment period of several years. In contrast to the changing nature of spousal violence patterns, there has not been much change in the nature or relatively low level of brother-sister violence. However, I would still argue that all forms of family violence against women discussed in this chapter continue to be sustained at levels that would be considered abusive by American standards. The Abelam regard a certain level of physical violence against women as culturally acceptable. Nevertheless, Abelam women who feel that they are being physically abused can always seek shelter in their natal homes or with friends, where they receive both physical and moral support. These are options not always open to their American counterparts.

NOTES

Fieldwork in the Abelam area has been supported at various times by the Faculty Research Grants Committee, Central Research Development Fund, and the Department of Anthropology at the University of Pittsburgh; the Center for Studies of Crime and Delinquency, the National Institute of Mental Health; and the Justice Department and Law Reform Commission of Papua New Guinea. All support is gratefully acknowledged. An earlier version of this chapter appeared in *Pacific Studies* 13:3 (July 1990): 189–204. I am grateful to the journal for permission to use it in this volume.

I owe a special debt of gratitude to Ali Pomponio for help with this chapter. Not only did she provide many insightful comments during its production, but she graciously agreed to present it for me when I was unable to attend the session on domestic violence, for which it was originally prepared, at the 1989 Association for Social Anthropology in Oceania meeting. I absolve her of any blame for its contents, however, as I am sure she would have constructed it differently. I would also like to thank Dorothy Counts and the other contributors to this volume for helpful suggestions. Among my Abelam informants, Donna Jambiuwi deserves special mention for our many discussions on Abelam family violence.

1. This name is a pseudonym, as are all the names of Abelam disputants mentioned in this chapter. The pseudonyms used are all names of bird species in the Abelam language. These are commonly used as personal names. All quotations are from my field notes unless otherwise indicated.

REFERENCES CITED

Black, M., and D. Metzger. 1965. "Ethnographic Description and the Study of Law." *American Anthropologist* 67:141–65.

Epstein, A. L. 1967. "The Case Method in the Field of Law." In *The Craft of Social Anthropology.* Ed. A. L. Epstein. 153–80. London: Tavistock.

Frake, C. O. 1969. "Struck by Speech: The Yakan Concept of Litigation." In *Law in Culture and Society.* Ed. L. Nader. 147–67. Chicago: Aldine.

Gulliver, P. H. 1969. "Introduction to Case Studies of Law in Non-Western Societies." In *Law in Culture and Society.* Ed. L. Nader. 11–23. Chicago: Aldine.

Korbin, Jill. 1987. "Child Maltreatment in Cross-Cultural Perspective: Vulnerable

Children and Circumstances." In *Child Abuse and Neglect: Biosocial Dimensions.* Ed. R. J. Gelles and J. Lancaster. 31–55. New York: Aldine de Gruyter.

———, ed. 1981. *Child Abuse and Neglect: Cross-Cultural Perspectives.* Berkeley: University of California Press.

Scaglion, Richard. 1976. "Seasonal Patterns in Western Abelam Conflict Management Practices." Ph.D. diss., Department of Anthropology, University of Pittsburgh.

———. 1979. "Formal and Informal Operations of a Village Court in Maprik." *Melanesian Law Journal* 7:116–29.

———. 1983. "The 'Coming' of Independence in Papua New Guinea: An Abelam View." *Journal of the Polynesian Society* 92:463–86.

———. 1985. "Kiaps as Kings: Abelam Legal Change in Historical Perspective." In *History and Ethnohistory in Papua New Guinea.* Ed. D. Gewertz and E. L. Schieffelin. 77–99. Oceania Monograph No. 28. Sydney: Oceania Publications.

———. 1986a. "The Importance of Nighttime Observations in Time Allocation Studies." *American Anthropologist* 13:537–45.

———. 1986b. "Sexual Segregation and Ritual Pollution in Abelam Society." In *Self, Sex, and Gender in Cross-Cultural Fieldwork.* Ed. Tony Larry Whitehead and Mary Ellen Conaway. 151–63. Urbana: University of Illinois Press.

ELEVEN

Preventing Violence against Women: A Central American Case

Virginia Kerns

> It was after dark when Juliana came to get me. "Come quickly," she said. "Thomas is beating my mother." We crossed the yard to Juliana's house, and I could see her grandmother sitting on the steps with her arms folded, a look of subdued anger in her eyes. "No-good man," she murmured. An elderly neighbor, Petrona, stood nearby with another woman, a good friend of Juliana's mother. Petrona called out, "Don't beat your wife, Thomas. Her mother is here." Then both women shook their heads with dismay and Petrona motioned for me to look inside the house. Juliana's mother was leaning against the doorway, her face streaked with tears, while her husband sat on the floor cradling his head in his arms and moaning softly. "Don't cry, *núguchun* [mother]," I heard him say to her. "Don't cry."

> Earlier that day, Juliana's mother had complained to me that her husband spent too much money drinking rum with other men. There was never enough money for food, she protested, adding that she might leave him and go look for work at a citrus plantation in central Belize. "I don't have to beg him for one cent," she said. "I can get some money myself. My mother will take the children. She's old, you know, but Juliana is twelve now and she can help a lot with the other children." She paused, then added, "And if Thomas refuses to leave this house, I'll get some medicine [*árani*] and then he *must go.*"[1]

To explain these words and the event fully—to place them in cultural context and also in relation to the personal histories of the principals—would require not just this chapter but a book in itself. The cultural "gestalt" of marital conflict and violence is complex.[2] Even some rather straightforward questions are difficult to answer briefly at the outset. Why did Juliana say that "Thomas" was beating her mother? What did Thomas mean by calling his wife *núguchun*? Why did Petrona tell him that his wife's mother was there?

Who summoned the three women, and why did they stand outside the house watching? What kind of "medicine" did Juliana's mother intend to get? And why did she want Thomas to leave the house if she was planning to leave it herself? I will return to these questions at the end of this chapter, when the answers may be more meaningful, having been given a context.

This case of wife beating was one of two that I witnessed during a year of fieldwork in a Garífuna (Black Carib) community in Belize, Central America. I was also told of three other episodes that occurred during that year and about several that had taken place in the recent past or in different communities. These cases, which both women and men brought to my attention, provide some empirical and ethnographic detail about wife beating: the incidence, triggering events, types of intervention, levels of violence and severity of abuse or injury, and the outcome. By "outcome" I mean whether the abused woman leaves her husband temporarily, permanently, or stays in the relationship.

A central question in many studies of domestic violence in the United States concerns outcome: Why *do* some women stay in chronically violent marital relationships? The term "battered wife syndrome" is now used to define "a symptom complex occurring as a result of violence in which a woman has at any time received deliberate, severe, and repeated (more than three times) physical abuse from her husband, with the minimal injury of severe bruising."[3] Research conducted in other countries and a variety of cultural settings suggests that wife battering is not restricted to the United States or to the industrialized West.[4] But neither is it universal. As other chapters in this book illustrate, there are places where physical violence between husband and wife is very rare and others where wife battering is all too common. The Garífuna represent an intermediate case, one that initially seems anomalous: a culture in which incidents of spouse abuse are not highly unusual yet wife battering is practically unknown. Contrary to what might be expected, the overall frequency of conflict does not predict severity of abuse.[5]

I have the agreeable task, in other words, of trying to explain why Garífuna women in Belize *do not* stay in relationships with men who try to harm them and why instances of serious injury are very rare. To do this, I will focus on the cultural context of marital violence: specifically, on the culturally prescribed means of prevention and intervention, on sanctions and sanctuary. For the most part it is women who prevent—or, at the least, limit—male violence against women. I never learned of a case in which a woman had been severely beaten, to the point of drawing blood or breaking a bone, even when her husband tried to use a weapon. The worst reported case involved a man who hit his wife on several occasions; she left him each time and finally for good after being badly bruised. People spoke of more violent encounters between *former* spouses or "friends" (lovers who had never lived together). I was told of two different instances in which a young woman stabbed a man, not fatally, for having left her. It was especially unfortunate, people said, that each was a case of mistaken identity.

Men, Women, and Violence

The Garífuna are an Afro-Indian population whose settlements, some fifty towns and villages, lie along the Caribbean coast of Central America, from Belize to Nicaragua. They comprise about 10 percent of the population of Belize, and a smaller proportion of the population in the other countries. Several books have been written about various aspects of their culture and complex history;[6] three of them contain some mention of spouse abuse. One ethnographer notes that a woman who is unfaithful "is severely beaten" by her husband; another remarks that a woman who often quarrels with her spouse and who actually hits him will not easily find another man if she separates; a third states that an abused woman may seek sanctuary in her mother's house.[7]

No one ever told me that a man has the "right" to beat his wife under certain circumstances. Rather, wife beating is regarded as an unfortunate reality. Men and women agree that a man whose wife is unfaithful is entitled merely to leave her; but, they add, such restraint is unusual. Most view the use of physical force between adults as dangerous, wrong, and all too frequent an occurrence. They say that only parents, particularly mothers, can legitimately use force, and that it should be restricted to disciplining young children. A mother has the "right" to "lash" her child for disobedience.[8] She usually does so in public, while other children and adults watch; and the presence of these others compounds the child's fear with deep shame. Years later men and women can recall lashings that were memorably severe. It is surely not coincidental that an ancestor who appears in a dream, complaining of neglect and asking for ritual attention, may threaten to lash the dreamer unless a particular ritual is held.

Violence, as perceived by the Garífuna, often has a supernatural dimension. (By violence, I refer to any act of threatening, attempting, or actually causing bodily pain, injury, or death.) The agents of violence are thought to include a variety of spirits as well as other men and women.[9] Moreover, people can cause injury by using visible, ordinary means (their fists or weapons) or by resorting to supernatural methods (sorcery).[10]

Initially, I wondered if violence were mainly a matter of talk. I noticed that men and women tell—and retell—dramatic stories about disputes that took place many years ago and ended in violence: a fight, say, and later a death attributed to sorcery. Recent conflicts, including those between spouses, are also topics of daily talk. And it is not at all uncommon to hear someone air a grievance against another person and then threaten to "beat that bitch" or "beat that no-good man" (these words may come from either a man or a woman). In most cases, such threats are warnings, intended to serve notice and to protect one's interests. For example, a woman in her thirties who realized that her husband had a female admirer called out to the younger woman as she was passing by (one time too many that day): "I've got a switch here, and if I see you again I'm going to lash you. Then kick you. Then beat you. Then pay for you" (i.e., pay a court fine for assault). A young man who thought he'd been cheated by an older one "sent a message" (through an intermediary) that he was going to get a job so that he could buy a machete and "cut that thief."

Such threats rarely lead to physical assault. Usually the two parties simply avoid each other for some time. If one does confront the other, typically in a very public place, other people gather to listen and watch. As long as the conflict is limited to words, no one intervenes; but physical fighting between men, especially with weapons (a bottle, a stick, or, more seriously, a machete), causes immediate concern. Inevitably, one of the onlookers runs off to summon the combatants' kinswomen, preferably older ones, who will try to persuade the men to stop. I heard some stories about fighting between women (specifically, sexual rivals) but without weapons. There was no mention of any serious injury resulting or of other people intervening; usually, spectators simply gathered to listen and watch.

Cases of male-female conflict often, but not always, involve spouses or lovers (either current or former). Many people voice their reluctance to intervene in marital disputes, citing the adage, "Husband and wife is nobody's business." But if a quarrel escalates and a man strikes his wife, other women usually do intervene.

Wife Beating: Some Specifics

The proximate causes of wife beating are similar to those identified in research carried out in the United States. The triggering events include arguments about money (or the man's unemployment or drinking, both of which contribute to the shortage of money) and sexual jealousy or suspected infidelity.[11] In each of the five cases I witnessed or was told about, the man had been drinking before he abused his wife, and three of the men suspected that their wives were having affairs. The incidence of marital violence may also be similar. (This is, of course, mere supposition, since my figures come from a year's observation of one community, while estimates of frequency in the United States are commonly based on random samples and national surveys.) At any rate, the five cases that occurred in one Garífuna community in one year involved 8 percent of the coresidential couples. In the United States, from 5 to 7 percent of intact couples admit to kicking or more serious acts of violence in a given year.[12] (A limited survey on marital violence that was carried out in several countries, including Belize and the United States, also suggests that the frequencies may be similar.[13]) As in the United States, marital violence is more common among younger couples than older ones.[14] The average age of the Garífuna men who assaulted their wives was thirty-nine (the range was thirty-two to fifty years); the wives' average age was thirty-two (the range, twenty-three to forty-six years). Each of the couples was married, had one or more dependent children, and lived in a nuclear family household. (There are about as many extended family households, but younger couples tend to live in the nuclear family type. Slightly more than half the couples in the community are married, although coresidence without marriage is socially acceptable.)

In each of the five cases, other women intervened in some way. Usually they simply stood by as witnesses, shaming the man by their presence and asking him to stop. In the most serious case (discussed below), they helped the abused woman to escape, at some personal risk. She was the only one of the five women who left her husband permanently, returning to her mother's house in another community about forty miles away. Two women whose husbands hit them went away for several weeks and stayed with sisters who lived in a distant urban area. (Their mothers were no longer living.) Eventually, each of them returned, and there were no further incidents in the next year.

The other two women did not leave. By community consensus, neither was seriously injured (they were pushed and fell down); and each had initiated the physical violence, trying to hurt her husband and not simply to defend herself. One had knocked her husband down when he threatened to hit her. The other, Juliana's mother, as it happened, had thrown a bottle at her husband, grazing his cheek.

Significantly, none of the four couples who reconciled had a history of marital violence. A fifth woman, Francisca, left her husband permanently after several days of escalating conflict, in the course of which he had first slapped her, later kicked her, and eventually attacked her with a machete. The events, which I witnessed, are worth recounting in some detail. They provide a "worst case" example of wife beating and help to explain why chronic, severe abuse, or wife battering, was virtually unknown in Garífuna villages in Belize at the time of my fieldwork.

Wife Beating: A Case

Francisca and Matthew had married the year before, shortly after the birth of their son. They lived in her community at first but moved to Matthew's when he found work at a nearby banana plantation. The fact that Francisca had no close relatives there and that Matthew was widely known to have a violent temper (particularly when he drank) were later cited by many women as the reasons why she should never have agreed to follow her husband.

The first months were uneventful. Francisca often complained of loneliness and made two brief trips to visit her mother. On the second trip, she left her son with her mother, who promised to keep him for just a few weeks and then bring him back. Francisca returned alone to Matthew's community, where in a matter of days rumors began to circulate that she was having an affair with a younger man.[15] Eventually the rumors reached Matthew, who confronted his wife almost immediately and, in the course of an argument, slapped her. Her repeated denials finally had some effect, but it was short-lived. Several days later, after he had spent the morning drinking with friends, Matthew brought home a chicken and demanded that Francisca clean and cook it. When she refused, he kicked her. She ran out of the house and sought refuge at a neighbor's. The woman, who knew Matthew's reputation and was afraid of him, listened nervously to Francisca's complaints but then reminded her that it is a wife's duty to cook for her husband. She offered some onion, black pepper, and "ricardo" (*achiote,* Spanish) to use for seasoning. Francisca finally returned to the empty house, ingredients in hand, where she prepared the meal and left it on the table.

Later that day, during the afternoon lull, Francisca was sitting in the yard, talking to her neighbor and some other women, when someone called her name. Turning, the women saw Matthew approaching with a glint in his eye and, worse, a machete in his hand. Before Francisca could get to her feet, Matthew had grasped the machete by its blade and begun beating her with the handle. He was clearly drunk and unsteady on his feet, and finally she managed to pull away. All the other women had scattered, and now she faced a dilemma: Where could she find sanctuary? She had no close relatives in the community.

She fled, running past a dozen houses until finally she saw one with the door standing open. She darted inside, bolting the door behind her. The startled owner, a woman in her forties, reluctantly agreed to let Francisca hide for a few hours in another room; then, after locking the house, she went to speak to a neighbor. The two women set off on the pretext of running an errand, but in fact they wanted to learn Matthew's whereabouts. "I don't want her to stay in my house," the one said, fearing for her own safety. "Matthew is a bad, bad man." "We're all women," the other replied, "and it could happen to any of us."

During the next few days, Francisca hid in several different houses. Matthew was said to be looking for her; so was his mother, but apparently she felt genuine concern for Francisca. It seems that Matthew's mother had asked him what he had done to his wife, and when he told her, she got angry and said that "Francisca's mother wouldn't like that at all." Everyone agreed that Francisca's mother had the "right" to protect her daughter. Unfortunately, Francisca's mother lived forty miles away, and the journey could take two days.

Finally, the three women who had hidden Francisca made a plan to help her escape and return to her own community. Juliana's mother was one of these women, and she persuaded her younger brother, Raymond, to escort Francisca from the village in the middle of the night. He did so reluctantly, complaining that Matthew would probably suspect him of being Francisca's "friend" (lover) and might try to harm him.

As for Francisca, she swore never to live with Matthew again. Upon returning to her mother's house, she consulted a well-known "obeah man" (a specialist in sorcery) for "medicine" (*árani*) to keep her husband away. She sprinkled the special powder that he gave her along the perimeter of her mother's yard, where it would act as an invisible but powerful barrier to her husband. If Matthew crossed it, the obeah man said, he would sicken and then die. No one else would be affected by the substance.

Within a week, reports of this reached Matthew, who swore that he would "cut" Francisca (with a machete) someday. In the meantime, he made no attempt to see her. The three women and the man who had directly helped Francisca—none of them near relatives of hers—continued to worry about their personal safety should Matthew learn of their role in helping her escape. After all, they said, they had no real right to help her and had done so only because they feared for her life.

Why Women Leave

Wife battering is virtually unknown in Garífuna communities because women leave abusive men. To explain why they leave, and to do so with brevity, it is useful to begin with a contrasting and more familiar case. Research carried out in the United States suggests that a constellation of factors make it likely that some women will stay in chronically violent relationships. Although these studies often include psychological profiles of battered women—an attempt to explain in psychological terms why they stay with abusive men—I want to emphasize instead that many of the motivating factors are *culturally* based. I can identify at least ten:

1. the reluctance to "break up the family" ("the family" meaning a nuclear family household);
2. economic dependence and a lack of alternative means of support;
3. the fear of stigma if the abuse is known;
4. social isolation and domestic privacy, which make it unlikely that people outside the household see the violence;
5. the absence of intervention or ineffective intervention (traditionally by male police officers, who were often said to identify with the husband);
6. the lack of accessible and reliable sanctuary;
7. a legal system that defines marital violence as less serious than violence between strangers;
8. a criminal justice system that does not effectively control violent men (e.g., by failure to enforce restraining orders);
9. social attitudes of acceptance or tolerance toward marital violence (and a historical tradition in which "laws of chastisement" permitted husbands to use physical force against their wives); and
10. structural inequality between men and women, with women taught to accept a position of social inferiority and subordination.

This summary is by no means exhaustive. It does, however, provide a striking contrast to the conditions in which Garífuna women live in rural Belize. Some of the most important cultural differences have to do with patterns of marriage and postmarital residence, family structure, and conceptions of gender. As I will try to show, these probably help to limit the incidence of wife beating. They also provide women with the means to protect themselves from chronic abuse, primarily by making it rather easy for them to leave marital relationships and to enter new ones or to remain single. When a couple separates, the man and woman are each free to form a new union, whether or not they were legally married. Divorce is unnecessary and extremely rare.[16]

Although local endogamy (marriage within one's community) is not required, it is both preferred and the common practice. In three villages where I collected detailed census data, slightly more than half (57 percent) of the couples who lived together were married; and 85 percent of all the unions, legal or otherwise, were endogamous. Of the remainder, unions involving men and women from different locales, 7 percent of the couples lived in the woman's community of birth and just 2 percent in the man's. (Francisca was one of only four women who had agreed to live in the husband's community.) Finally, 6 percent of the couples were nonnatives.

A consequence of this pattern of marriage and postmarital residence is that the vast majority of women and men in these communities (92 percent and 87 percent, respectively, of those with spouses) live near their own relatives. Women say that the chance of financial hardship and physical abuse increases when they live far away from kin, especially their mothers and sisters. A mother has the recognized right to offer her daughter sanctuary, and people often told me that even a very angry man would hesitate to force his way into his mother-in-law's house.

Few women actually seek sanctuary, however, because in most cases intervention is effective. While people prefer to let spouses settle their differences by themselves, if a man begins to hit his wife, someone always alerts older kinswomen and neighbors. These women usually need do nothing more than make known their presence as witnesses to the act. This is said to shame the man, who knows he has no right to beat his wife. In only one case that I was told of did the man, who "had no shame," continue to hit his wife until another woman and man, both neighbors, restrained him.

Intervention is inevitable because the women's kin are usually nearby and have the right (and duty) to intervene and because marital violence is no secret.[17] Domestic privacy simply does not exist. Houses are not very large or substantial, and daily life is spent outside, usually in public view. Moreover, these are small communities where people know each other well, watch each other closely, and talk freely about what they see (or suspect).

In other words, everyone *does* know what goes on behind closed doors, and people inevitably criticize a man who beats his wife. More to the point, they do not encourage her to stay with him in order to "keep the family together" or to avoid the stigma of separation or economic hardship. Physical abuse is considered a legitimate reason to leave a relationship, and the expectation is that a woman will separate rather than endure mistreatment. Women do not consider themselves weak, helpless, or inferior to men, nor do men generally speak of women in these terms. There is one notable exception: many men do say that their *wives* should defer to them. Most women, in contrast, deny that this is a "rule" and say that ideally a marital relationship is one between equals who respect each other.[18] Perhaps this differing expectation of husbands and wives is a source of conflict in itself.[19]

Their allegiance to different extended families also creates some tension between spouses. These families center not on the marital but the mother-child relationship.[20] As a result, while marital separation may cause a "broken household," it does not usually result in a "broken family." Beyond these considerations, even financial need does not compel most women to stay with abusive husbands. A woman can usually count on her mother, siblings, or other close relatives to provide temporary shelter and food until she finds paid work or forms another union.

It sometimes happens that such a woman owns the house where she lives with her husband.[21] In that case, she must convince him to leave, and for this purpose she has a strong weapon at her disposal: sorcery. While sorcery is a double-edged sword, which can be used for one's benefit or otherwise, it usually seems to act as an equalizing force in women's dealings with men who try to harm them. Thus, Juliana's mother, who owned the house where she lived with her husband, Thomas, vowed to use sorcery to make him leave. In a sense, this would be her version of an eviction order. Likewise, Francisca had no need to obtain a restraining order to keep Matthew away from her mother's house; she simply paid an obeah man for protective "medicine"—a supernatural restraining order, as it were.

To return to the question raised at the outset, and to give it a summary answer, wife battering, resulting in serious injury, is practically unknown because women do not stay with men who abuse them. This is not simply a personal decision but clearly a cultural matter. These women have the means to leave and no compelling reason to stay. Most have learned to think of themselves as autonomous adults, and they reject the idea that their husbands "rule" them. The men who disagree, and who expect deference and compliance from their wives, may well be the ones who resort to physical force. The use of violence against women to enforce male dominance is well known from many other cultures, where it is an accepted and pervasive fact of social life. But in Garífuna communities, it is not sanctioned, nor is it tolerated by women.

The cases of wife beating that I witnessed help to illuminate some cultural factors that limit the severity (if not the overall frequency) of abuse and lead women to leave violent men. Taking an ethnographic approach to marital violence—examining actual cases in some detail and with knowledge of the cultural context—is also useful in another way. It points up the complex, *cultural* relationship among easily measured variables such as frequency and severity of abuse. A high overall frequency of marital violence may correlate with a high rate of injury in one cultural setting (e.g., where intervention is absent or ineffective) but not in another.[22] Understanding the findings of cross-national survey research, and explaining the variation, clearly requires detailed knowledge of the cultural context in which wife beating and wife battering occur.

An Explication and Epilogue

When Juliana came to get me, she said that Thomas was beating her mother. This was the first time I had heard her call him by any name other than terms meaning "father." I had assumed that he was her biological father until, after many months, she casually mentioned that he was in fact her stepfather. When I then asked why she referred to him as *núguchin* (father), she said simply, "He is my father because he feeds me." Calling him by name that night was not only a sign of disrespect but something of a renunciation.

I have referred to her mother throughout by teknonym, as "Juliana's mother." Like many adults with children, she was as commonly called by her teknonym (*túguchun* Juliana, "mother of Juliana") as by her given name or nickname. Most women bear children, and their primary social identity is as mothers (not as wives). The cultural value placed on motherhood is notably strong, and mother-child ties are central and enduring. When a man calls his daughter, his wife, or another woman by the term *núguchun* (my mother), he says it with tenderness. So it was when Thomas used this word as he tried to make up with his wife, after they had fought about his drinking.

Petrona had earlier called out to Thomas that his wife's mother was watching him, and she said this in order to shame him. Of all the witnesses, his mother-in-law's presence had the strongest effect. (Again, many people told me that a man is especially ashamed to treat his wife roughly in front of her mother, whose presence is said usually to make him stop.) The other two women later told me that they had come immediately when Juliana summoned them but with a deep sense of dread: after all, she was calling them to a scene of violence, and they feared for their own safety. It was testimony to their feelings of kinship and friendship that they responded so quickly.

As it turned out, Juliana's mother either settled her differences with her husband or decided to ignore them. The next few years of their relationship were reportedly rather tranquil. Her fears about Matthew, however, were realized when her younger brother, Raymond, died suddenly, less than a year after helping Francisca escape. His death came at the age of twenty-eight, without warning or apparent cause, in the middle of one night as he slept. It was widely believed that Matthew had poisoned him.

NOTES

This chapter is based primarily on ethnographic research that was carried out between 1973 and 1981 and included eighteen months of fieldwork in Belize. I am grateful to the Fulbright-Hays Commission, the Wenner-Gren Foundation, and the University of Illinois for funding my work. A more recent experience, serving as a board member of a community shelter for battered women, gave me the opportunity to learn about wife beating and wife battering in a second cultural setting and helped to provide the basis for comparing "here" and "there." I learned a great deal from the staff members of the shelter. The views expressed in this chapter are, however, solely my own.

1. All names are pseudonyms, but in every other respect the cases reported in this chapter are factual. Quotations are from my field notes unless otherwise indicated.

2. In their review of research on wife beating, Brienes and Gordon (1983:512) write that too often "questions turn upon specific acts, blows, pushes, weapons, rather than the gestalt of the conflict." This may be due to the fact that so much of the research has been carried out using survey techniques that are better suited to enumerating acts of violence than to understanding the "gestalt."

3. This definition appears in American College of Obstetricians and Gynecologists (1989:1), citing Parker and Schumacher (1977). The title of ACOG's Technical Bulletin No. 124 is *The Battered Woman.* As a member of the ACOG has pointed out, the fact that this problem has been "selected as the subject of a Technical Bulletin is quite significant." The bulletin is circulated to the many thousands of members of the ACOG and represents the "standard of care" (Jon H. Baker, M.D., personal communication 1989).

Brown's definition of wife battering differs in that it emphasizes severity of injury without specifying frequency: "wife battering . . . is something extraordinary, possibly resulting in severe injury, incapacitation, or even death" (this volume). It is, of course, very difficult to determine frequency in most ethnographic accounts. (See her discussion, in this volume, of problems with the literature.)

Finally, the term "battered women" is sometimes used very generally to refer to all those who have experienced any form of "physically injurious behavior" at the hands of a current or former male partner (Margolin et al. 1988:93). Such a definition makes no distinction as to frequency or severity of violence.

4. In northern Sri Lanka, for example, a researcher questioned and medically examined sixty battered women referred to him by the police over a three-year period. The majority suffered from head injuries, and 62 percent had been attacked with a weapon. Each of the women had been assaulted on at least three different occasions (Saravanapavananthan 1982). Also see Levinson (1988:443), who reports that "wife beating incidents resulting in death or permanent injury" occur in nearly half of the ninety societies in his cross-cultural sample.

5. By "overall frequency of conflict" I refer to all episodes occurring among couples in a community or population during a given period of time. In contrast, perhaps the frequency of abuse *between* a husband and wife does predict severity of injury, as violence may well escalate.

6. See Coelho (1981), Gonzalez (1969, 1988), Gullick (1976), Kerns (1983), Staiano (1986), and Taylor (1951).

7. See Taylor (1951:96), Gonzalez (1969:78), and Kerns (1997:110), respectively. In this chapter, I use the terms "husband," "wife," and "spouse" without any distinc-

tion as to the legal status of the relationship (see Kerns 1997:113 on language and terminology).

8. Presumably, fathers have this right as well, but I never saw a man use physical force to discipline his child. (My informants spoke of mothers as the primary disciplinarians of children.) The right to strike one's child is not reciprocal. For an adult to strike a parent is considered one of the worst moral transgressions, "a sin against God," as many put it (Kerns 1997:106).

9. For detailed descriptions of these spirits, see Staiano (1986:115–26) and Taylor (1951).

10. For a detailed discussion of sorcery, see Gonzalez (1970); see also Kerns (1997) and Staiano (1986).

11. According to Okun (1986:50), conflicts about financial problems and sexual jealousy are the most common triggering events leading to wife abuse in the United States. Straus et al. (1980:157) identify the five major issues of conflict as housekeeping, sex, social matters, money, and children.

12. For statistics on wife beating in the United States, see Okun (1986:39); see also Straus et al. (1980:32–33) and Gelles and Straus (1988:104).

13. Survey data for Belize were collected for Steinmetz (1981) by a research assistant who administered a questionnaire to students, presumably in an urban area. The respondents were 231 adolescents, 37 of whom were Garífuna (identified in the article as "Carib," the name by which they were then generally known in Belize). The students answered questions about episodes of violence between their parents. Acccording to the results, marital violence is more frequent among the Garífuna and Creoles than among Spanish-speaking Belizeans. The date of the survey is not given, but comparable data were collected for Steinmetz in several other countries from the mid- to late 1970s.

14. Straus et al. (1980:142) conclude that in the United States "younger couples are more violent" and that violence decreases with age.

15. She was twenty-three; the suspected lover was eighteen. Such rumors are common in Garífuna communities and are obviously very difficult to verify; young women are the usual subjects, although older women are sometimes suspected of having affairs as well (see Kerns 1992).

16. Decisions to establish and to end marital relationships are essentially individual matters, subject to minimal regulation. Legally married couples who separate rarely obtain a divorce but commonly form other unions (see Kerns 1997:114–15).

17. See Erchak (1984), Gibbs (1984), and Levinson (1985) on the importance of intervention and the absence of domestic privacy in many cultures. Beatrice Whiting is quoted in Gelles and Straus (1988:28) on communal residence as a preventive factor in domestic violence (see also Whiting and Whiting 1975:190).

18. The male informants who expressed this view—that women should defer to their husbands—used a highly global statement, "Men should rule women." Asked to explain, they spoke of a wife's deference as an ideal (Kerns 1997:92). Coelho (1955:86) notes that "the position of the woman in the family is in no way to be con-

ceived as subordinate, the principle involved being one of partnership under equal terms, not of one person commanding and the other obeying."

19. According to Finkelhor (1983:19), domestic violence is not only the abuse of power but sometimes a response to the perceived lack or loss of power.

20. For a full discussion of gender roles and family structure, see Kerns (1997:89–104, 120–46).

21. In one community, for example, more than 40 percent of the houses are owned by women (Kerns 1997:124). Some of these women are separated or widowed, but many reside with husbands.

22. See Steinmetz (1981), for example, whose preliminary figures from six countries show striking differences in the relationship of three variables: percentage of spouses using violence, frequency of marital violence, and severity of abuse.

REFERENCES CITED

American College of Obstetricians and Gynecologists. 1989. *The Battered Woman.* Technical Bulletin Number 124. Washington, D.C.

Brienes, Wini, and Linda Gordon. 1983. "The New Scholarship on Family Violence." *Signs* 8 (3): 490–503.

Coelho, Ruy Galvao de Andrade. 1955. "The Black Carib of Honduras: A Study in Acculturation." Ph.D. diss., Northwestern University.

———. 1981. *Los Negros Caribes de Honduras.* Tegucigalpa, Honduras: Editorial Guaymuras.

Erchak, Gerald M. 1984. "Cultural Anthropology and Spouse Abuse." *Current Anthropology* 25:331–32.

Finkelhor, David. 1983. "Common Features of Family Abuse." In *The Dark Side of Families: Current Family Violence Research.* Ed. David Finkelhor, Richard J. Gelles, Gerald T. Hotaling, and Murray A. Straus. 17–28. Beverly Hills, Calif.: Sage.

Gelles, Richard J., and Murray A. Straus. 1988. *Intimate Violence.* New York: Simon and Schuster.

Gibbs, James L. 1984. "On Cultural Anthropology and Spouse Abuse." *Current Anthropology* 25:533.

Gonzalez, Nancie L. 1969. *Black Carib Household Structure.* Seattle: University of Washington Press.

———. 1970. "Obeah and Other Witchcraft among the Black Caribs." In *Systems of North American Witchcraft and Sorcery.* Ed. Deward E. Walker. 93–109. Anthropological Monographs No. 1. Moscow: University of Idaho.

———. 1988. *Sojourners of the Caribbean: Ethnogenesis and Ethnohistory of the Garífuna.* Urbana: University of Illinois Press.

Gullick, C. J. M. R. 1976. *Exiled from St. Vincent: The Development of Black Carib Culture in Central America up to 1945.* Malta: Progress Press.

Kerns, Virginia. 1992. "Female Control of Sexuality: Garífuna Women at Middle Age." In *In Her Prime: New Views of Middle-Aged Women.* 2d ed. Ed. Virginia Kerns and Judith K. Brown. 95–111. Urbana: University of Illinois Press.

———. 1997. *Women and the Ancestors: Black Carib Kinship and Ritual.* 2d ed. Urbana: University of Illinois Press.

Levinson, David. 1985. "On Wife-Beating and Intervention." *Current Anthropology* 26:665–66.

———. 1988. "Family Violence in Cross-Cultural Perspective." In *Handbook of Family Violence.* Ed. Vincent B. Van Hasselt, Randall L. Morrison, Alan S. Bellack, and Michel Hersen. 435–55. New York: Plenum Press.

Margolin, Gayla, Linda G. Sibner, and Lisa Gleberman. 1988. "Wife Battering." In *Handbook of Family Violence.* Ed. Vincent B. Van Hasselt, Randall L. Morrison, Alan S. Bellack, and Michel Hersen. 89–117. New York: Plenum Press.

Okun, Lewis. 1986. *Woman Abuse: Facts Replacing Myths.* Albany: SUNY Press.

Parker, Barbara, and Dale N. Schumacher. 1977. "The Battered Wife Syndrome and Violence in the Nuclear Family of Origin: A Controlled Pilot Study." *American Journal of Public Health* 67:760–61.

Saravanapavananthan, N. 1982. "Wife Battering: A Study of Sixty Cases." *Forensic Science International* 20 (2): 163–66.

Staiano, Kathryn Vance. 1986. *Interpreting Signs of Illness: A Case Study in Medical Semiotics.* New York: Mouton de Gruyter.

Steinmetz, Suzanne K. 1981. "A Cross-Cultural Comparison of Marital Abuse." *Journal of Sociology and Social Welfare* 8 (2): 404–14.

Straus, Murray A., Richard J. Gelles, and Suzanne K. Steinmetz. 1980. *Behind Closed Doors: Violence in the American Family.* Garden City, N.Y.: Anchor/Doubleday.

Taylor, Douglas M. 1951. *The Black Carib of British Honduras.* Viking Fund Publications in Anthropology No. 17. New York: Wenner-Gren.

Whiting, John W. M., and Beatrice B. Whiting. 1975. "Aloofness and Intimacy of Husbands and Wives: A Cross-Cultural Study." *Ethos* 3 (2): 183–207.

TWELVE

Men's Rights/Women's Wrongs: Domestic Violence in Ecuador

Lauris McKee

In some traditional Andean communities, wife beating is a tacitly accepted outlet for male frustration and hostility. In towns and villages of rural Ecuador, younger men generally figure in reports of wife beating; if it occurs among older couples, one certainly hears less about it.

Awareness of potential husbandly violence is universal in the Andean community of Las Flores, whose customary practices are central to this study; mothers commonly warn daughters planning to marry that, sooner or later, their husbands will beat them. "That," they say, "is how men are" (*así son!*). That men assault women is not only within the range of possible marital comportment but figures in cultural expectations to the extent that one may view this kind of maltreatment as part of social structure. Furthermore, in Las Flores, no clear relationship exists between ethnicity and wife beating. Spouse abuse is reported in *blanco, mestizo,* and indigenous households.[1]

Despite fear-inspiring social expectations, the available evidence indicates that wife beating actually occurs in a minority of marriages in Las Flores and in other rural Ecuadorian locales. Part of the problem is that, with a few notable exceptions (Sanchez-Parga 1997; Stølen 1987; Bolton and Bolton 1975), this aspect of family relations is little documented in Andean ethnographic literature. The Boltons' fascinating research (using family interviews and recorded lawsuits) documents a high incidence of conjugal quarrels and wife-beating episodes in Incawatana, Peru. Still, no broad-scale statistical study of its frequency in Andean communities has been encountered. The lack of information can be attributed partially to the difficulty of collecting systematic evidence. As wife beating generally takes place behind closed doors, it is unusual to witness an incident or to be able to substantiate it.

Certainly, the brutality of some episodes of domestic violence guarantees its salience in women's minds, and gossip underscores it as a continuing latent threat. Accounts of wives maimed or beaten to death assure that women remain painfully aware that violence is a potential course of action open to husbands in any marital altercation.

The argument advanced here does not turn on the frequency of wife beating but rather on its institutionalization and the structural role it plays in supporting and perpetuating women's subordination and male dominance. I also examine an institution (a land-inheritance custom) that, paradoxically, may either mitigate or motivate wife-beating episodes. In the first case, it can result in awarding young wives (at least) an illusion of equality due to their economic contribution to the conjugal estate. In the second case, because this custom challenges an otherwise unambiguous male dominance, it may lead a man to dominate his wife through compensatory and violent displays of his "masculine" character.

The data for this chapter are based on a total of eleven cases that came to my attention (eight of which are drawn from an ethnographically studied, randomly selected sample of fifty-two families).[2] One episode took place in the street; I witnessed it together with a crowd of villagers. In four cases I saw the bruises and cuts that evidenced women's abuse on the day after the beating. Five other incidents were retrospectively recounted, including a case in which an informant had beaten his first wife to death several years before my fieldwork began. The informant (now remarried) had served seven years in prison for the crime.

The Village Setting

Las Flores is located in Tungurahua Province in the central Andean highlands and is comprised of some 276 households. The majority of the population is *mestizo* (although they are self-labeled as "whites"), and there is an indigenous minority.

The community is small, agrarian, and strongly familistic. It is sited in an arid valley made productive by a network of irrigation canals. Major cash crops are grains (wheat and barley); citrus fruits, particularly tangerines; and avocados, which are sold in the markets of Ambato and Quito. There also are several small factories that produce fruit-flavored liquor (*pisco*). The majority of village families own at least one small plot of land, although some are forced to rent or to sharecrop. The poorest villagers work as day laborers (*peones*). Although education is increasing career alternatives, the value placed on land ownership and the status it confers remains central in Floreño society. Ethnicity—whether one is labeled by others as *blanco* (white) or indigenous (Native South American)—also is significant in determining one's place in the social hierarchy, but land ownership or notable wealth can override ethnicity.

Gender Concepts and Wife Beating: The Synergy of Hispanic and Indigenous Ideology

Floreños, together with most rural Andeans, share a worldview that strongly supports the maintenance of male authority (but see Bourque and Warren 1981). Although women's control of household enterprises and their entrepreneurial activities act as important countervailing factors, patriarchal control still implicitly justifies the "disciplining" of wives and children.

Village men have a *collective* interest in the perpetuation of the gender hierarchy thus established, and individual behavior, particularly of young men, is monitored by the male community. If a man feels his domestic authority is compromised, his marital situation soon becomes a subject of village talk. If the "problem" persists, ridicule or insults from a coterie of male villagers who consider themselves hypermasculine, as well as a man's own reading of his gender role, may prod him into beating his wife.

The norm of investing an authority in males that has the potential to be violently pursued is often viewed as derived from a circum-Mediterranean ethos emphasizing honor and shame (Peristiany 1966; Pitt-Rivers 1954, 1977) that was imported to the New World in the sixteenth century by Hispanic invaders. This ethos predicates male honor on female chastity. According to Pitt-Rivers, "men claim authority over their wives, daughters and sisters, requiring of them moral qualities which they do not expect of themselves—after all, a man cannot afford to have too fine a moral conscience or he would not be able to meet his obligations to his family in the struggle for existence" (1977:79). Though the patterns of justification vary somewhat with class and ethnicity, men are responsible for protecting "their" women's chastity, and violation of it by another man is the ultimate insult whose redress may require the death of the violated woman (Taggart 1990).

Among the *mestizos* and *blancos* of Las Flores, male superiority is phrased traditionally in terms of *machismo,* a version of the Hispanic model of a dominant masculinity. Gillin's (1965:509) definition is one view of this trait: "The cultural concept involves sexual prowess, action-orientation (including verbal action) . . . but a real *macho* is one who is sure of himself, cognizant of his own inner worth, and willing to bet everything on such self-confidence."

But is self-confidence "face-work" (in the sense of Goffman's term), and thus superficial? Or is it intrinsic to male character (an essential male trait, or a purposively socialized stance)? Whatever the case may be, in coping with the harsh economic conditions of life in the rural Andes, an inner sense of worth is hard won for *both* sexes. Gilmore takes a different view of the Hispanic male ideal and states that *machismo* "spawns a zero-sum contest cosmology in which sexuality becomes a struggle of weakened men against more powerful women. . . . its motives lie in the emotion of a compensatory assertive sexuality, its expression an eroticized politics—an impulse to dominate, to conquer, and to ward off threats to masculine narcissism. *Machismo is nothing if not aggressive—if only in defense of a wounded pride*" (1987:19, emphasis added).

Compare this to various writers' interpretations of the indigenous (Native South American) ideal of male superiority. It encodes the notion that masculinity carries certain rights and powers but does not enshrine the particular constellation of qualities attributed to *machismo*. Although investigators have pointed to the notably aggressive behavior of some Quéchua and Aymara speakers (e.g., Bolton and Bolton 1975; Carter 1977; Sanchez-Parga 1997), indigenous social structure is described as relatively more egalitarian (Allen 1988; Belote 1978; Bourque and Warren 1981; Isbell 1978),[3] and traditional cosmology emphasizes duality and sex-complementarity. But complementarity in Andean usage always implies asymmetry and hierarchy. In Inca culture, the oppositional concepts older/younger, higher/lower, male/female, and so on, awarded a conceptually higher status to the first term in these pairs. Complementarity was used to represent and regulate the relationships between entities such as sectors of a community, based on their spatial location (e.g., Cuzco, the Inca capital, was divided into higher [*hanan*] and lower [*hurin*] sections) or the relationships obtaining between two interacting persons or groups of people. The right to ritual deference or respect was awarded to the privileged member of the dyad. Thus, things masculine had relatively higher status/value than things feminine.

Certainly, wife beating occurs in many indigenous households, and aggression against women is often seen as a masculine right (Bolton and Bolton 1975; Carter 1977; Deborah Caro, personal communication 1987; Linda Belote, personal communication 1984). Indigenous wives are reputed to "give as good as they get." This perception may be based on public observations of women defending themselves against men who are not their kin, but the data on domestic violence fail to document a strong, expected female response against husbandly violence other than abandonment. Belote observed a *hempla* ("example"; "morality play") in Saraguro, Ecuador, in which St. Joseph beat the Virgin Mary into the ground (literally, by pounding her into a prepared hole), for the reason, said informants, that "she deserved it."[4]

Olivia Harris, who studied an indigenous group in the Lake Titicaca re gion, notes: "In Laymi representation, for all the egalitarian sexual ideology, with its complementary division of labor, for all the organization of sexuality around a principle of balanced reciprocity, there are also phallocentric elements. In particular these coalesce around imagery of power and strength. A person who has performed some action out of the ordinary is said to have a big penis" (1980:80). Carter (1977) notes that inebriated Bolivian Aymara shout, "I am a man!"—which, depending on the context, can be taken as a general assertion of power, a challenge, or an insult.

Mestizo Gender Ideals

In table 12.1, the list of masculine and feminine traits collected from a sample of *mestizo* informants in Las Flores displays the semantic contours of gender ideals. The duality of ideal gender constructs is evidenced in the expressive qualities ascribed to each sex,[5] but it is important to reiterate that these are ideal representations: actual behavior—the realm of practice—is influenced by, but not isomorphic with, the actions and attitudes encoded in the trait list.

The trait list stresses the aggressive aspect of male behavior and the expressive-submissive aspect of female behavior, although only men cite women's role as workers. Women's trait list is longer for *both* sexes. Relative to men, they include more adjectives for their own gender that connote sub-

Table 12.1. Gender Ideals

Males		Females	
Ideal	Traits	Ideal	Traits
Men's View	Women's View	Men's View	Women's View
Strong	Strong	Good	Good
Bravo	Good	Tranquil	Tranquil
Honorable	*Bravo*	Unselfish	Sociable
Exigente	*Receloso*	Agreeable	Accessible
Rebellious	*Exigente*	Good-Worker	Unselfish
	Rebellious	Serious	Loving
	Understanding	Cheerful	Polite
	Responsible		Agreeable
			Docile
			Humble
			Humanitarian

Notes: The sample included twenty male and thirty-four female informants. The data were collected in 1975–76. Terms are arranged in an order reflecting frequency of mention. For example, the trait "humanitarian" was mentioned only by ten women and no men. Rough glosses of the Spanish terms are: *bravo* (angry, challenging, rude); *exigente* (insistent, demanding), *receloso* (mistrustful, suspicious).

missiveness (e.g., humble, docile, polite). This is significant given that the culturally expected responses to a husband's violent behavior are to pacify and cajole him, never to respond aggressively.

Women share a perception of men that contradicts and softens the *macho* persona, although these qualities stand in opposition (e.g., good/*bravo*, responsible/rebellious, and understanding/*receloso*). The notion of a dual masculine nature may indicate that men comport themselves differently in the home setting than when they are in the public view, or it simply may demonstrate that women view their men sympathetically and lovingly, overlooking the contradictions inherent in the culture's construction of masculinity.

Table 12.2 is a modification of table 12.1. It overrides frequency hierarchies and displays only consensus traits—the gender ideals both men and women ascribe to their own or the other sex. The polar construction of *shared* (consensus) gender ideals is evident here, as is an essentialist view of the sexes. A physically-active/hostile-defensive masculinity is juxtaposed with a passive/accessible-supportive femininity. The cultural script for intersex behavior that can lead to wife beating seems clearly written in this opposition.

The shared perception of male traits in table 12.2 reflects an agonistic symbology: a pattern of initiative and response gauged to protect men from the predations of others in the social world beyond the family (Walter 1981: 173), where dealings with persons who are neither consanguineal, affinal, or ritual kin (people who at least theoretically are obligated to treat one justly) are portrayed as fraught with deceit and the possibility of ending in financial ruin.[6] Extended into the domestic sphere, however, agonistic responses may pattern a man's treatment of his wife if he believes his dominance is besieged.

Consensus traits for women reflect their ideal family roles as wives and mothers and have little to do with expectations of their comportment in business relations. The adjectives connote a cheerful, accepting passivity that sets the tone for women's responses (even) to abusive husbands. But it is important to note that the clustering of traits around polar expressive styles emphasizes certain arenas of women's agency while ignoring others. Women's trait list describes their view of their behavior in the *home*, whereas men's trait list

Table 12.2. Consensus Traits (Shared Gender Ideals)

Males	Females
Strong	Good
Bravo	Tranquil
Exigente	Unselfish
Rebellious	Agreeable

relates to their behavior in the *extra-domestic world.* Women take an agonistic stance in their business dealings, whose tone can vary from cold-eyed demanding, to matter-of-fact bargaining, to a kind of good-humored aggressiveness. The point is, aggressivity is part of the normative conduct of women engaged in economic transactions with non-kin, although it goes unmentioned as an ideal trait. In defending their own and their family's interests, rural highland women are verbally aggressive and forceful (McKee 1997), and seasoned market women can back up verbal threats with physical ones.[7] So why do they put up with the behavior of an abusive husband?

Role compartmentalization and the lack of role transitivity in this respect are remarkable. Women's level-headed assessment of advantages and disadvantages evidenced in market exchanges is proscribed and elicits heavy social sanctions if exercised in conjugal conflicts. Cultural rules place married women in a no-win position. Ordinarily, young women say, they do not fight back or even remonstrate with husbands for maltreating them or for failing to take responsibility for the support of their children. Instead, the accepted tactic is to recruit relatives, compadres, or friends to counsel their husbands or to appeal to a man's fatherly love, suggesting that witnessing his violence makes his children ill with fright-sickness (*susto, espanto;* Rubel et al. 1984).

Although women deplore their personal experiences of masculine aggression and their submission to (a sometimes irrational) male authority, they generally share the worldview that justifies these stances as necessary to defend family interests against a predatory, exploitive world. This is, in fact, a realistic assessment, based on experience and underwritten by history. Spanish exploitation of the rural Ecuadorian labor force (Moreno Yanez 1977) was notorious and, since the late nineteenth century, rural workers have been subject to the oppression of their own wealthy elites.

It is not surprising, then, that traits communicating that a man is not to be trifled with are privileged over traits that trumpet expertise or steadfastness in work. Neither sex makes reference to men as workers, although women do list "responsibility" as an ideal.[8] Also absent from the list is the sexual component of the male "character," although its salience is evidenced in customs of socialization thought to ensure its expressions (McKee 1980) and in women's frequently expressed expectations that husbands will be unfaithful. (Advice given by an older to a younger woman who complained that her husband humiliated her by boasting of his many girlfriends was to reply "Mejor! Mejor! Haga lo que quiera; a mi no me importa!" (loosely glossed as "Good! Good! Do what you want; it doesn't matter to me!").

Equally surprising is men's omission of traits describing the softer side of masculine nature. Most men are loving and tender with their young children, although drunken men who beat their wives may turn their rage on their children as well.

The power of cultural opinion in securing conformity to gender ideals was seen in an incident involving one of my neighbors who joined her husband in assaulting two drunken men who began to vandalize their small bar after being stopped from playing the jukebox at top volume at two o'clock in the morning. My neighbor was a muscular woman who butchered hogs and roasted them whole, selling their meat in the weekly market. During the fracas, she picked up one of the drunks and threw him into the street. Having been awakened at 2:00 A.M. by the music and the noise, I heartily applauded her actions, but village commentary viewed them with universal disapproval. Both women and men were outraged and insisted that she had disgraced her husband by "acting like a man" and aggressively laying hands on the vandals. These social attitudes, strongly expressed, prevent women from responding to violence with violence (although occasionally the rules are broken, as in the case above) and from retaliating, most especially against abusive husbands.

It is clear that consensual gender traits correspond imperfectly and intermittently to reality and to a degree are situation-specific. Nevertheless, their "imagery of the extreme" in constructing gendered behavior provides the symbols each sex uses to interpret and evaluate the actions of the other in the crucible of conjugal relationships.

Factors Militating against Wife Beating

Institutionalizing oppositional traits as discussed above could, in theory, lead to untrammeled domestic violence. However, there are beliefs inherent in ethnopsychology that mitigate and moderate the expression of *any* aggression in the home. Unhappiness and especially frustration are pathogenic, producing the illness *pena* (Pedersen and Coloma 1983). There is a strong conviction that dissension, whether experienced or witnessed, also produces illness, which in extreme cases can be fatal. Children are especially susceptible to these illnesses, and contentious parents bear the guilt for causing their children's sickness.

Additionally, the institution of godparenthood (*compadrazgo*) establishes a means of mediating domestic disputes by recruiting trusted ritual kin who (usually) are not parents of the disputants. Marriage-godparents (*padrinos*) are specially charged with intervening in conjugal quarrels and helping to resolve them before they escalate to violence. *Padrinos* are pledged to be impartial in their judgments, and the offending party is "punished" by having his or her back whipped. Often *padrinos* determine that blame is mutual and whip both the husband and wife, exacting promises of reform. The presence of a formal means of mediating domestic conflicts indicates the cultural significance of domestic dissension.

Economic Asymmetry in the Marital Dyad and the Importance of Land Ownership

The oppositional construction of gender in Floreño discourse and in the unwritten rules of conduct is of consequence given the presence of a custom that has the potential to cause conflict in the initial years of a marriage. I refer to an inheritance custom practiced specifically in Las Flores that challenges young men's authority and dominance in the home. Drawing on informants' perceptions and reasoning concerning individual episodes of domestic violence, I argue that a specific contributing factor to spouse abuse is that when young couples marry, the dominance culturally demanded of husbands is ineluctably compromised due to the wives' status as landowners.

Many Floreñas become owners of small plots of land at the time of marriage. Land ownership confers a certain status in the village, in that it potentially provides the route to independence and subsistence security. Women as owners of real property have a relative superordination—not in terms of ideology, but in terms of economic resources. This is evidenced by the respect displayed for unmarried women who own significant amounts of land.

This custom has historical depth in many Andean communities. Silverblatt, in writing of post-Conquest Peru, states that "both parents were asked for their consent to a marriage of their offspring, and brides often received a portion of their inheritance at marriage. . . . By Andean custom (which is still practiced today), a woman maintains independent rights over all goods, including lands, that she might inherit. The concept of joint or common property did not (and does not) exist" (1980:155, 163).

Throughout the Andes, land is a highly valued, scarce good. Families try to provide their children with sufficient land for subsistence by the custom of partible inheritance. In other Andean communities, partition can mean that children of *both* sexes are given property prior to or at the time of marriage, which establishes their economic independence (Beals 1966; Caro 1983, 1985; Flores-Ochoa 1979; Skar 1979).[9] The pattern is different in Las Flores in that customary *scheduling* of land transfer from parents to children varies with *sex*.

Women are given the opportunity to claim their portion of their family's lands at the time of marriage, whereas men's inheritance usually is postponed until the demise of both parents. Although negotiation is possible, in poorer families this signifies that women relinquish all further claims on the parental estate.

Early inheritance by a family's daughters can advantage sons in that women may settle for smaller or less-productive plots due to their parents' continuing need for land. When the family's complete holdings are finally passed to the sons and unmarried daughters, the land they divide may be better in quality (or, if the family prospered, there may be more land to divide).

However partition is carried out, in a montane environment, a completely equitable distribution of land among offspring is virtually impossible. Families try to obtain small plots of land in several ecological zones where altitudinal variations and access to irrigation determine the kinds of cultigens that may be grown. Perceived disparities in the quality or quantity of land bequeathed to children lead to predictable (almost ubiquitous) conflicts among heirs that often end up in the courts.[10]

When a Floreña marries, which occurs between the ages of sixteen and twenty-three for the majority of women, she generally has the choice of taking her filial share of her parents' land or waiting until their death to inherit. Unless their families are unusually well off, women choose the first option. The result is that a wife's inherited land often constitutes the sole real property claimed by the newly married pair (although the law supports a husband's right to control property the couple purchases after marriage [Romoleroux de Morales 1975]).

Important to the argument here is that the land a woman inherits remains in her control and does not become the common property of the conjugal society. (Ecuadorian law awards legatees sole title to legacies acquired prior to or during marriage [Código Civil 1980: Art. 158].) Nevertheless, the land is a benefit to a woman's husband.[11] Couples usually work together in cultivating the land, and its produce *is* viewed as conjugal property (Luzuriaga 1980). In the normal case, when a woman dies, her land is divided among her children, who also eventually receive the lands of their deceased fathers.

Young men's *postponed* inheritance renders them economically vulnerable and is problematic for several reasons, a few of which are stated here. First, the attrition of family resources may result in little or nothing to inherit. Agricultural catastrophes are frequent in the highlands: untimely frost, drought, insect plagues, and landslides are perennial problems, and excess rainfall—for example, during the El Niño cycles of 1982–1983 and 1997–1998—rots crops and often forces impoverished farm families to sell their lands and migrate to cities.

Second, lawsuits among siblings dissatisfied with their legacies can delay men's actual possession of lands for years (Beals 1966). Third, land quality varies, and partition necessarily disadvantages some of the heirs. Waters (1988) shows a strong correlation between ownership of low-quality land and incidence of outmigration and wage employment.[12] Fourth, disinheritance of offspring is not uncommon. Preterition is a legal right and occurs when children offend or neglect parents.

Thus, men's inheritance is riskier. Claims to land are contingent on maintaining good relations with parents and can be used as leverage to induce sons to contribute their energies to parental enterprises. The point is that the scheduling of inheritance by sex serves a variety of cultural purposes but disadvantages young men in that the productive yield of a wife's land often is the sole source of equity available to the newly married pair. A proverb expresses the economic risk that marriage poses for men: "Él que se casa pide costal y taza para la plaza" (loosely glossed as, "The man who marries asks to be beggared [to sit with a cup and sack in the plaza]").

Floreño inheritance customs thus create a situation wherein young wives, as land owners, marry men who depend on that land for subsistence but cannot claim ownership rights. In colloquial terms, a wife is "one-up" on her husband. If, as noted earlier, asymmetry in the status of the pair becomes an emotional issue, men perceive their authority as compromised.

Other customs mitigate these circumstances, particularly if parent-offspring relationships are amiable. It is customary for newlyweds to reside with either her parents or his for a few years.[13] Such couples live rent free and pay only for the food they consume, although they render labor and other forms of assistance to the household. This arrangement permits newlyweds to save money for the purchase or rental of their own land parcels and/or to establish themselves in their own home, for neolocal residence is preferred in Las Flores, as in many Andean locales (Lambert 1977).

Also, a perceived social deficit can be defrayed in nonmaterial ways if other sorts of "capital" are available to a man (Bourdieu 1986). For example, a good deal of social credit is awarded a man whose character, in the opinion of his wife and his neighbors, is exemplary. If a man exerts his best efforts to meet family and work obligations and treats compadres, kin, and neighbors with respect and fairness, then his economic failures are largely overlooked as the misfortunes of a worthy man, and his wife counts herself lucky to have a "good," "understanding," and "responsible" husband.

Conversely, irresponsible husbands (often heavy drinkers) who place their own pleasure above family needs accumulate a social debit of ill-will and contempt in both the domestic and public spheres. Even so, such a man may escape public derision if he is economically solvent or successful; but in his home, if his economic contributions do not defray the emotional costs of neglect and irresponsibility toward his family, then the probability of wife beating increases.

Initial economic asymmetry usually is short-lived, as husbands' families sometimes lend them plots of land to work. Men can find employment for wages that are relatively higher than those earned by women performing the same work (McKee 1997; cf. Lobo 1986:46), and saving their wages during the "grace period" of coresidence with parents facilitates eventual economic independence.

The rarer case is when, after a protracted period of time, a husband has not or cannot achieve independence. Or else a wife's business successes augment her initial economic contribution to the family, thus increasing the number of benefits that accrue to the union. If the status disparity between spouses increases and a wife is completely financially independent, then her husband's authority over her is challenged. As a result, he may beat her in order to invoke his masculinity through a display of anger and strength.

Young couples' capacities as adults are on trial before the village "jury." The judgment of women's worth turns on their chastity and their devotion to their children; the judgment of men's worth is more complex and turns either on the degree of self-possession and self-control they display (a dominance over their own impulses) or on an agonistic stance and display of *machismo* (a dominance over others).

Discussion

How cultural gender constructs interact with another institution—inheritance customs—and how this interaction may result in wife beating is the focus of this chapter. But in exploring a single male motive—a felt sense of being relatively subordinate in the marital relationship—I do *not* discount the importance of other factors implicated in wife abuse. These include such disparate reasons as sexual jealousy, male frustration/anger over women's fertility (either the lack of it, as Stølen [1987] reports, or the expression of it in a new pregnancy), revenge, explicit legal validation of husbands' right to "discipline" wives (Okun 1986; Pagelow 1981), beliefs that beatings (due to jealousy) are a way of expressing love, alcohol-aided disinhibition of hostile feelings, and so on. Rather, I have sought to examine the operation of a single covert motive for wife abuse: the response of some men to their wives' superiority in resource control, given the unambiguous cultural emphasis on male authority and dominance.[14]

Skar (1979:449, 454), who worked with an indigenous agrarian group, emphasizes their sex-egalitarianism but observes: "The basic attitude to individual ownership coupled with economic inter-dependence, marks the relationship between the sexes as one of mutual respect and competition. . . . The competition between spouses arises from the fact that each keeps a careful eye on the productive capacities of individually owned resources. There is a constant measuring-up between the two adult household members to see that the other half is providing a fair share" (see also Harrison 1989).

I speculate that women's control of resources, including wives' accumulation of high social credit (Bourdieu 1986), is a factor that is operative in various other motives that have been implicated in domestic violence. Of equal importance is the degree of cultural support violence receives as a tactic for establishing male dominance.

If, in the opinion of other men, a man's dominance is threatened, does the fact that he beats his wife elevate or reestablish his dominance? Based on my data, I would have to answer yes: at least in the opinion of the most *machista* villagers, a beating is a display of dominance. When a married woman is too successful and exercises economic power, she threatens not only her husband but those village men whose own role security is tenuous. Jibes and jokes during drinking bouts can inspire a man's rage against his wife. Beating her reaffirms his dominant status.

I must immediately qualify these statements and note that those village men whose role identity is secure and who are the most respected by their fellows are never involved in these behaviors. They disapprove of wife beating and do not attempt to subvert new marital relationships.

Women generally look unfavorably on men who beat their wives but claim to understand the motives precipitating violence. The most traditional (and oldest) of my informants expressed sympathy for wives but always blamed them, assuring me that violence could have been averted had the women played a conventional wifely role. Failure to be a good cook, lack of attention to husbands due to their own work, or keeping an untidy house were some of the "failures" cited.

To a degree, both sexes excuse wife beaters (though not men's violence toward *others*) *if* they are drunk. In my data, for all cases of wife beating observed or reported, the men were inebriated and generally claimed amnesia on the morning after. Drunkenness "excuses" a man's behavior, as he is believed to be bereft of judgment (*juicio*).

Men's extramarital affairs, as counterposed to women's chastity, are another area of tension in marriages. There are faithful husbands and devoted fathers in Las Flores, but there are also members of the male community, whether married or single, who seem to take on themselves the vocation of involving young married men in extramarital affairs. They arrange young men's encounters with attractive women, often quite openly. At fiestas where there is dancing, one or two older men will drag a young man away from his wife to dance with an unmarried woman or with women whose sexual availability is the subject of community gossip. In fact, male infidelity is common and is expected by most wives.

Certainly, it appears that conjugal solidarity, in some obscure manner, threatens male solidarity. Whereas public demonstrations of affection between lovers, such as holding hands or walking arm-in-arm, are accepted to a degree, any such open display of affection between husbands and wives is proscribed. The solidarity of a significant sector of the male community often seems to depend on the subversion of marital closeness. Strong marital alliances, or women's domestic equality and/or economic success, are perceived as vitiating the male alliance and the ideology of dominance necessary to maintain the sex hierarchy.

Conclusion

The argument advanced in this chapter turns primarily on a conflict experienced by many young married couples in Las Flores: namely, the disjunction between the cultural constructions of gender—the idealized versions of masculinity and femininity, which unambiguously award dominance in the family to men—and the economic advantage given to women who bring inherited lands with them into marriage, whereas their husbands remain landless until the death of their parents. Domestic violence spawned by male resentment or uncomfortable awareness of dependency is at issue here. This is not to deny that there are numerous other tensions and factors implicated in incidents of domestic violence but merely to examine one of these factors with the attention it calls for.

NOTES

The material for this chapter was collected during fieldwork in 1975–76 and further substantiated during research in 1982–84. I am grateful to the National Institute of Mental Health (ADAMHA), which supported the first research period. I also thank the National Science Foundation for its support of more recent fieldwork and the International Population Program at Cornell University, which offered indispensable administrative and moral support. Insightful and valued comments on drafts of the original essay were given by Enrique Mayer, Ralph Bolton, Cheryl Pomeroy, Laurence Moore, and James Taggart. They, and the agencies who supported me, bear no responsibility for the ideas and conclusions expressed here, which barring scholarly indebtedness rest entirely on my shoulders. I wish to express my enduring admiration and affection for my Ecuadorian friends, especially to the women who have taught me so much and offered me their patience and kindness. Quotations are from my field notes unless otherwise indicated.

1. Native South Americans in Ecuador use the term *Runa* in self-reference. Ecuadorians consider "Indian" a pejorative term and substitute the euphemism *indígenes* when referring to *Runas*. Most *mestizos* (persons of mixed Hispanic and indigenous descent) use *blanco* self-referentially (cf. Stutzman 1981).

2. The sample of families was originally collected for a study of socialization processes.

3. Egalitarianism may vary among groups, however. See Villavicencio (1973:131), who writes of the Otavaleños of Ecuador and states that "within the family social and economic authority rest with the father, shared in a certain way with the mother, who finds herself submitting to the dispositions of her husband" (my translation).

4. The prevalence of wife beating needs much more documentation. At present, we have only bits of information. Levinson (1983), testing cross-culturally the hypothesis that the presence of physical punishment in childhood correlates with high levels of wife beating among adults, found wife beating common among the Aymara, although children were punished infrequently. An incident of wife beating is recounted by an indigenous victim in the ethnographic film *Andean Women* (distributed by Documentary Educational Resources, 101 Morse St., Watertown, ME), and Lobo (1986:15) states that wife beating and sneak-thievery are the most recurrent crimes in a Lima *barriada* whose residents include indigenous immigrants from the highlands. Bolton and Bolton (1975) recorded an extremely high incidence of Qolla family violence. Beals (1966) gives us counterevidence for the indigenous community of Nayón, Ecuador, where he heard of only one incident—a report, he says, that was hotly denied by the victim.

5. Gender ideals were first explored in Las Flores during the course of my first fieldwork and investigated further in other sites in 1982–84, where descriptions of behavioral traits ideal for each sex were collected and compiled.

6. This notion also affects one's contacts with evil supernatural forces. Demonstrating that one is *bravo/a* discourages attacks by *mal aire* (evil air), a common folk illness. Persons who are successful folk-healers (*curanderos* or *curanderas*) usually are characterized as *bravo/a* (McKee 1987).

7. The great majority of market vendors (both *comerciantes* and *feriantes*) and small shopkeepers are women. In commercial dealings, or in social intercourse with nonkin, women actively seek the advantage (a stance necessary to a good bargainer and expected by both customer and vendor). But they are most admired if they can drive a hard bargain with cheerfulness and good humor, for joking reduces tension and ill-will generated in competitive market exchanges (Sahlins 1972).

8. The norms of conjugal exchange are phrased, at their broadest, as the general needs of wives and husbands. In answering these needs, a husband's primary duty

is to contribute his earnings to his family (and not to waste money on gambling and drinking). A wife's primary charge is to be frugal and to augment family income through agricultural work or business enterprises; however, she must not do this at the expense of caring for her children. Mutually held expectations include adequate provision of food, whether from the fields or the cooking fire, concern for a partner's health and well-being, and proper performance of the myriad activities essential to an economically viable household. Husbands exact sexual fidelity from wives; wives hope for the same from husbands but are aware of peer pressure to involve men in casual affairs.

9. Caro (1983, 1985) notes that the herders of Ulla Ulla, Bolivia, give animals to children at significant stages in the life-cycle so that at marriage both husband and wife own herds (see also Flores-Ochoa 1979) and continue to retain ownership of their original animals and all offspring. In Nayón, Ecuador, parents who were able to afford it give land to both sons and daughters at marriage. From Beals's sample of families, one can calculate that 54 percent of men ($N = 24$) married wives who owned land and 47 percent of women ($N = 19$) married husbands who owned land (1966:213–17 and passim).

10. The location of plots is a particular source of concern, for economic viability requires cultivation of land distributed across different altitudinal levels (Bastien 1978; Brush 1977a; Mayer 1974; Murra 1975; Pomeroy 1988; Waters 1988).

11. Village endogamy helps reaggregate lands broken up by generations of partition. Often, multiple marriages are contracted over time between two families (brother-sister exchange is a preferred, if now rare, marriage form). Wealthier Floreño families restrict dispersion of family lands by seeking unions between first cousins, although these are proscribed in both sacred and secular law. This custom apparently was common to all social levels in the recent past, for it is found in almost one-third of marriages in the second ascending generation in my genealogical data. Brownrigg (1971) found cousin marriages among an indigenous group in the southern province of Cañar, but both Beals (1966) and Parsons (1945) report them as rare in the northern Ecuadorian communities where they worked. In Peru, Brush (1977b) finds cousin marriages in Bolívar Province, whereas marriages between kin closer than the fifth degree of relationship are regarded as incestuous in other Peruvian communities (Isbell 1978; Bolton 1973a).

12. Weiss (1985) points to relationships among population growth, farmland shortages, and increased urban migration in Ecuador.

13. Patrilocal postmarital residence is supposedly normative, though in my sample of ninety-two families there were fourteen paternal stem families and eight maternal stem families. Neolocal residence is the ideal, usually achieved after three to five years. There were forty-seven nuclear families in the sample, and the balance of families were classed as matrifocal, patrifocal, or collateral.

14. See also Sanchez-Parga (1997:29), who advances the hypothesis that domestic violence arises due to men's attempt to compensate for their dependence on wives by exercising dominance.

REFERENCES CITED

Allen, Catherine. 1988. *The Hold Life Has.* Washington, D.C.: Smithsonian Institution Press.

Bastien, Joseph. 1978. *Mountain of the Condor: Metaphor and Ritual in an Andean Ayllu.* New York: West Publishers.

Beals, Ralph. 1966. *A Community in Transition: Nayón, Ecuador.* Latin American Studies Vol. 2. Los Angeles: University of California Press.

Belote, Linda. 1978. "Prejudice and Pride: Indian-White Relations in Saraguro, Ecuador." Ph.D. diss., University of Illinois at Urbana-Champaign.

Bolton, Ralph. 1973a. "Tawanku: Intercouple Bonds in a Qolla Village (Peru)." *Anthropos* 68 (1–2): 145–55.

———. 1973b. "Aggression and Hypoglycemia among the Qolla: A Study in Psychobiological Anthropology." *Ethnology* 12 (3): 227–57.

Bolton, Ralph, and Charlene Bolton. 1975. *Conflictos en la Familia Andina: Un Estudio Antropológico entre los Campesinos Qolla.* Cuzco, Peru: Centro de Estudios Andinos.

Bourdieu, Pierre. 1986. *Outline of a Theory of Practice.* Cambridge: Cambridge University Press.

Bourque, Susan, and Kay Warren. 1981. *Women of the Andes: Patriarchy and Social Change in Two Peruvian Towns.* Ann Arbor: University of Michigan Press.

Brownrigg, Leslie. 1971. "Cañari Kinship Variations." Paper read at the 70th Annual Meeting of the American Anthropological Association, New York.

Brush, Stephen. 1977a. *Mountain, Field, and Family: The Economy and Human Ecology of an Andean Valley.* Philadelphia: University of Pennsylvania Press.

———. 1977b. "Kinship and Land Use in a Northern Sierra Community." In *Andean Kinship and Marriage.* Ed. Ralph Bolton and Enrique Mayer. 136–52. Special Publication No. 7. Washington, D.C.: American Anthropological Association.

Caro, Deborah. 1983. "Land Tenure and Women's Status among Herders in Ulla Ulla, Bolivia." Paper read at the 82nd Annual Meeting of the American Anthropological Association, Chicago, Illinois.

———. 1985. "'Those Who Divide Us': Resistance and Change among Pastoral Ayllus in Ulla Ulla, Bolivia." Ph.D. diss., Johns Hopkins University.

Carter, William. 1977. "Trial Marriage in the Andes?" In *Andean Kinship and Marriage.* Ed. Ralph Bolton and Enrique Mayer. 177–216. Special Publication No. 7. Washington, D.C.: American Anthropological Association.

Código Civil. 1980. 7th ed. Quito, Ecuador: Corporación de Estudios y Publicaciones.

Flores-Ochoa, Jorge. 1979. *Pastoralists of the Andes: The Alpaca Herders of Paratia.* Philadelphia: ISHI.

Gillin, John. 1965. "Ethos Components in Modern Latin American Culture." In *Contemporary Cultures and Societies of Latin America.* Ed. Dwight Heath and Richard Adams. 503–17. New York: Random House.

Gilmore, David. 1987. *Aggression and Community.* New Haven, Conn.: Yale University Press.

Goffman, Erving. 1967. *Interaction Ritual.* New York: Doubleday.

Harris, Olivia. 1980. "The Power of Signs: Gender, Culture, and the World in the Bolivian Andes." In *Nature, Culture, and Gender.* Ed. Carol MacCormack and Marilyn Strathern. 70–94. New York: Cambridge University Press.

Harrison, Regina. 1989. *Signs, Songs, and Memory in the Andes.* Austin: University of Texas Press.

Isbell, Billie Jean. 1978. *To Defend Ourselves: Ecology and Ritual in an Andean Village.* Austin: University of Texas Press.

Lambert, Bernd. 1977. "Bilaterality in the Andes." In *Andean Kinship and Marriage.* Ed. Ralph Bolton and Enrique Mayer. 1–27. Special Publication No. 7. Washington, D.C.: American Anthropological Association.

Levinson, David. 1983. "Physical Punishment of Children and Wife-Beating in Cross-Cultural Perspective." In *International Perspectives on Family Violence.* Ed. Richard Gelles and C. Cornell. 73–77. Lexington, Mass.: D.C. Heath.

Lobo, Susan. 1986. *A House of My Own: Social Organization in the Squatter Settlements of Lima, Peru.* Tucson: University of Arizona Press.

Luzuriaga, Carlos. 1980. "Situación de la mujer en el Ecuador: Comentarios derivados de una revisión de la literatura." Internal document. Misión USAID en el Ecuador.

Mayer, Enrique. 1974. "Las Reglas del Juego en la Reciprocidad Andina." In *Reciprocidad e Intercambio en los Andes Peruanos.* Ed. Giorgio Alberti and Enrique Mayer. 37–65. Lima: Instituto de Estudios Peruanos.

McKee, Lauris. 1980. "Ideals and Actualities: Socialization of Gender in an Ecuadorian Village." Ph.D. diss., Cornell University.

———. 1987. "Ethnomedical Treatment of Children's Diarrheal Illnesses." In *Cross-Cultural Perspectives on Women and Health Care.* Ed. Ruthbeth Finerman and Werner Wilbert. 1147–55. Special issue of *Social Science and Medicine* 25 (10).

———. 1997. "Women's Work in Rural Ecuador: Multiple Resource Strategies and the Gendered Division of Labor." In *Women and Economic Change: Andean Perspectives.* Ed. Ann Miles and Hans Buechler. 13–30. Washington, D.C.: Society for Latin American Anthropology, American Anthropological Association.

Moreno Yanez, Segundo. 1977. *Sublevaciones Indígenas en la Audiencia de Quito: Desde comienzos del siglo XVIII hasta finales de la colonia.* Quito: Ponfifícia Universidad Católica.

Murra, John V. 1975. *Formaciones económicas y políticas del mundo andino.* Lima, Peru: Instituto de Estudios Peruanos.

Okun, Lewis. 1986. *Woman Abuse: Facts Replacing Myths.* Albany: SUNY Press.

Pagelow, Mildred. 1981. *Woman-Battering: Victims and Their Experiences.* Beverly Hills, Calif.: Sage.

Parsons, Elsie Clews. 1945. *Peguche: A Study of Andean Indians.* Chicago: University of Chicago Press.

Pedersen, Duncan, and Carlos Coloma. 1983. "Traditional Medicine in Ecuador: The Structure of the Non-Formal Health Systems." *Social Science and Medicine* 17 (1983): 1249–55.

Peristiany, J. G. 1966. "Honor and Shame in a Cypriot Highland Village." In *Honor and Shame: The Values of Mediterranean Society.* Ed. J. G. Peristiany. 173–90. Chicago: University of Chicago Press.

Pitt-Rivers, J. T. 1954. *The People of the Sierra.* Chicago: University of Chicago Press.

———. 1977. *The Fate of Schechem.* Cambridge: Cambridge University Press.

Pomeroy, Cheryl. 1988. "Fincas familiares multizonales en la vertiente occidental de los Andes Ecuatorianas." In *Nuevas investigaciones antropológicas Ecuatorianas.* Ed. Lauris McKee and Silvia Argüello. 125–51. Quito, Eucador: Abya Yala.

Romoleroux de Morales, Ketty. 1975. *Situación jurídica y social de la mujer en el Ecuador.* Guayaquil, Ecuador: Universidad de Guayaquil.

Rubel, Arthur, Carl O'Nell, and Roland Collado-Ardon. 1984. *Susto: A Folk Illness.* Berkeley: University of California Press.

Sahlins, Marshall. 1972. *Stone Age Economics.* Chicago: Aldine-Atherton.

Sanchez-Parga, José. 1997. *Antropo-Lógicas Andinas.* Quito, Ecuador: Abya Yala.

Silverblatt, Irene. 1980. "'The Universe Has Turned Inside Out . . . There Is No Justice for Us Here': Andean Women under Spanish Rule." In *Women and Colonization: Anthropological Perspectives.* Ed. Mona Etienne and Eleanor Leacock. 149–85. South Hadley, Mass.: Bergin and Garvey.

———. 1987. *Sun, Moon, and Witches: Gender Ideologies and Class in Inca and Colonial Peru.* Princeton, N.J.: Princeton University Press.

Skar, Sarah Lund. 1979. "The Use of the Public-Private Framework in the Analysis of Egalitarian Societies: The Case of a Quéchua Community in Highland Peru." *Women's Studies International Quarterly* 2 (4): 449–60.

Stølen, Kristi. 1987. *A media voz: Relaciones de género en la Sierra Ecuatoriana.* Quito, Ecuador: CEPLAES.

Stutzman, Ronald. 1980. "El Mestizaje: An All-Inclusive Ideology of Exclusion." In *Cultural Transformations and Ethnicity in Modern Ecuador.* Ed. Norman E. Whitten, Jr. 45–94. Urbana: University of Illinois Press.

Taggart, James. 1990. *Enchanted Maidens: Gender Relations in Spanish Folktales of Courtship and Marriage.* Princeton, N.J.: Princeton University Press.

Villavicencio Rivadenéira, Gladys. 1973. *Relaciones Interétnicas en Otavalo.* México City: Instituto Indigenista Interamericano.

Walter, Lynn. 1981. "Social Strategies and the Fiesta Complex in an Otavaleño Community." *American Ethnologist* 8:172–85.

Waters, William. 1988. "La Propiedad de la Tierra y la Forma de Producción: Estructura y Transformaciones en Cantón Salcedo, Ecuador." In *Nuevas investigaciones antropológicas Ecuatorianas.* Ed. Lauris McKee and Silvia Argüello. 89–123. Quito, Ecuador: Abya Yala.

Weiss, Wendy. 1985. "The Social Organization of Property and Work: A Study of Migrants from the Rural Ecuadorian Sierra." *American Ethnologist* 12:468–88.

Zuidema, Thomas. 1977. "The Inca Kinship System: A New Theoretical View." In *Andean Kinship and Marriage.* Ed. Ralph Bolton and Enrique Mayer. 240–92. Special Publication No. 7. Washington, D.C.: American Anthropological Association.

THIRTEEN

Like Teeth Biting Tongue: The Proscription and Practice of Spouse Abuse in Mayotte

Michael Lambek

Lela ndraiky hify fanyekitry. Teeth and tongue live happily side by side most of the time, but occasionally the tongue gets bitten. Villagers in Mayotte say people are like this too. In a characteristic spatial idiom for social intimacy, they say even people who are in the same place (*mahala raiky*) occasionally fight with each other. Fighting among intimates is wrong and stupid, it is a means of hurting oneself, the proverb seems to say, but it happens. This chapter is about why spouse abuse is wrong in Mayotte and how it sometimes happens.

Unlike what is described for many of the societies in this volume, spouse abuse in Mayotte is strongly frowned on and appears to happen relatively infrequently. Since it is harder to demonstrate an absence than to report a presence, it is critical to begin with the grounds on which my claims are based. My evidence and analysis are not based on surveys or statistics but rather on a case study approach (Werbner 1984). I conducted participant-observation fieldwork in a pair of neighboring villages in Mayotte over the course of ten years, from 1975 to 1985. This includes about eighteen months in residence in these communities.[1] During this time I never directly witnessed an incident of wife beating. However, without systematically questioning people about the subject, I heard about six distinct cases, and I rely extensively on what people said about them. One of these incidents took place several years before my first visit to Mayotte and another occurred among people I did not know who were living in a distant village. There were undoubtedly more cases than those I encountered, since a woman who submits to physical abuse may be ashamed of it and may keep quiet for as long as she wishes to maintain the marriage. Still, the number of such additional cases was probably low since the dense settlement pattern makes privacy difficult to maintain, most abused wives would retaliate loudly, and I had access to a good deal of local gossip. Moreover, the number of incidents can be contrasted with the much higher rates of violence between people of the same sex; I observed and heard about many more physical fights between pairs of men or pairs of women.

Starting from the cases of spouse abuse themselves, I try to elucidate the local view of why domestic violence is wrong. I attempt to provide a context for understanding the meaning of spouse abuse for people in Mayotte, arguing in terms of local moral precepts. A shorter section at the end of the chapter shifts to the level of behavioral and material factors that may affect the incidence of abuse.

First, however, I should say a few words about the general social context. Mayotte is an island, some 275 kilometers square, located in the Comoro Archipelago of the western Indian Ocean, approximately halfway between Madagascar and Tanzania. I worked in a pair of neighboring and closely related villages with populations of about 425 and 150 persons respectively in 1975 and 50 percent more than that a decade later. I cannot say how typical these villages are with regard to the issues at hand. Most of the residents are native speakers of Kibushy, a northern dialect of Malagasy; it is possibly of significance that of the six cases of abuse I know about, three of the violent men were speakers of Shimaore, a Bantu language and the language of the indigenous majority on Mayotte. Although the origins of the first Malagasy speakers on Mayotte are unknown, the ancestors of those among whom I lived arrived for the most part during the nineteenth century either as immigrants from northern and northwestern Madagascar or as indentured laborers from East Africa. (The latter group have lost their original language[s].) Mayotte has been under French control since 1841, but for most of this century prior to 1975 it has suffered, if that is the word, a good deal of neglect from the metropole. Enforced labor on European-owned plantations declined radically at the turn of the century, and in 1975 wage labor was a sporadic activity on the part of most men. Most labor was directed to subsistence cultivation on family-owned plots (the use rights to which were often lent freely to other villagers or kin), to fishing in the rich lagoon, and to cash cropping, primarily of ylang ylang. The distilled oil of ylang ylang flowers is a basic element in the French perfume industry, and its production during the 1970s provided a relatively good return. By 1985 the situation had changed; male wage labor, often in construction, had become much more important, and access to land was significantly restricted. In all periods, however, the production strategy of an ordinary household was marked by its diversification.

Inheritance is bilateral in Mayotte, and most women share property rights with their siblings and sometimes with their spouses. Karen Sacks's title *Sisters and Wives* is an apposite characterization of the statuses of women in

Mayotte. The conjugal pair forms the key unit of subsistence production in the village, though specific conjugal pairs are far less durable and often less solidary than the deeper ties among siblings. Most important for the present discussion is the fact that virtually all women own their own homes, and these homes are usually located in their natal villages, close to kin. When marriages are village-exogamous it is usually, but not always, the husband who moves.

The people of Mayotte are practicing Muslims, but relations between the sexes hardly correspond to the Western stereotypes of Islam. Women are not segregated to any significant extent from men and do not wear veils; nowadays they have a good deal of say in the choice of their first marriage partner and full say thereafter, can terminate a marriage virtually at will, and are frequently public political and ceremonial actors. Motherhood is not the only "career" open to them (Lambek 1988, 1992). However, their privileges and opportunities are not so great as those of men, especially in the spheres of wage labor, cash crop production, and Islamic ritual. Clitoridectomy is not practiced; the one severe obligation placed on a woman, that she be a virgin at her first marriage, can be interpreted in a partially positive light as a mark and source of a woman's personal autonomy (Lambek 1983). In effect, defloration is the last moment, not the first, in which other adults have control over her body, and these are her parents, not her husband. If a bride is found not to be a virgin, the only way the groom can retaliate (which he probably won't) is to walk out. If anyone has the right to beat the bride for her lapse, and such an outcome is by no means inevitable, it is her father, and then for the last time. Finally, a highly relevant aspect of Islam is the prohibition of alcohol. What drinking there is among villagers is largely restricted to palm wine consumed by young men; in the ordinary drinker it does not produce threatening behavior.

While I have not actually witnessed a violent incident, knowing local women as I do I cannot imagine that it would be entirely one-sided. The culture in general is characterized by a high degree of verbal assertiveness and oral aggression, often couched in jokes, although the behavior between husbands and wives is fairly circumspect. If anything, women (of all ages) appear more aggressive than men, although of course there are many exceptions to this generalization from both sexes. Young children in particular are often the objects of verbal aggression. At the same time, physical strength and violence are not idealized, and actual violence makes people uneasy. Assertive behavior expresses an ethos of equality, not domination. In the boxing game (*mrenge*) sometimes practiced by boys, the sparring partners should be evenly matched and are pulled apart the instant they make contact; it always seemed to me that there was more action in the exclamations of the spectators than in the ring itself.[2] A good deal of "violent" behavior (as well as sanctions against violence) is also carried out indirectly through sorcery or sorcery projection and harnessing divine justice and retribution, although accusations are rarely made openly.

Spouses and Siblings

The first case of spouse abuse came to my attention when I saw a friend of mine, Ali, a man in his thirties who was the village imam and local intellectual, chasing Zainaba, one of his adult sisters, through the village; he was shouting at her to leave the community. The story is as follows. On the evening of a Muslim feast day, an ex-husband of Zainaba had arrived at her home in order to visit his children. Zainaba's current husband, Kolo, who was drunk at the time, became enraged and tried to beat Zainaba. Zainaba's brothers and nephews came running to her defense, fending off Kolo, a large, strong man, with sticks. The next day, after consultation with the village elders, Zainaba's relatives announced that they wanted Kolo to leave the village. Zainaba and her siblings were members of the village by rights of inheritance and descent from a founder (as well as by residence and participation), whereas Kolo was an outsider, resident only as a result of his recent marriage. The relatives had both the right and the power to force Kolo to leave, and public opinion was firmly on their side. They said that they found Kolo's behavior intolerable and were fed up with the domestic quarreling; this was not the first incident, and they feared future violence.[3]

They were even ready, they threatened, to take the case to the civil authorities (*sirkal*), an outcome that from everyone's point of view was undesirable and a strategy of last resort. This was a clear-cut and solidary reaction on the part of an abused wife's kin toward her spouse. It illustrates that domestic violence is unacceptable and that it is not entirely a "private" matter, that the wife's kin will intervene and that they are prepared to render the whole thing "public," whether at the level of the village or the state. What was particularly troublesome to Zainaba's kin was that while their strategy toward Kolo was unambiguous, their obligations vis-à-vis Zainaba herself were not. Zainaba did not wish to separate from her husband, and her kin did not have the right to force her to do so. Hence, they were presenting her with the unpalatable option of leaving with Kolo, a situation that might put her at an increased risk of violence. The family had never liked Kolo; Zainaba had married him against their express warnings and advice. They were angry with her for helping to maintain a situation of domestic quarreling and hurt, that after so much mistreatment Zainaba stood opposed to them rather than to

Kolo, claiming that she loved him and wanted to stay with him. Thus Ali had become infuriated with Zainaba and had chased her around the village, screaming at her to leave because she had created and perpetuated a situation of dispute and emotional turmoil with her natal kin (she had "made her mother cry") and because, by rejecting their authority, she was forcing her kin to make a decision whose likely effect made them feel uneasy. As a cooler member of the family expressed it, they would rather lose a daughter (if they had to) than retain this son-in-law.

Kolo left the village three days later, but only after threatening Ali. (Somewhat to my surpise, Ali dismissed the threat, claiming to be much more powerful than Kolo. This confidence came from the sense that the forces of divine justice are much stronger than any attacks, directly physical or by means of sorcery, that Kolo could instigate.) Zainaba stayed behind out of fear of her mother and brothers (her father was dead). A week later Zainaba's mother received a letter from the leading Islamic cleric on the island interceding on Kolo's behalf and asking the village to readmit him. Zainaba's mother was furious at this intervention over a matter she thought was none of the cleric's business. Two days later Kolo appeared with money to give the family in order to effect a reconciliation. Zainaba's kin flatly refused—they said later that Kolo had acquired the money by stealing a cow—and so Kolo left a second time. This time, however, Zainaba went with him. Ali said he didn't mind seeing her go since she never listened to her kin anymore; when people don't listen to the advice of their kin, things always go badly for them. Moreover, he said, Kolo was Zainaba's eighth husband, indicating that she didn't know her own mind—besides which eight is always a bad number. Ali added that he could easily do medicine to make Zainaba fall out of love with Kolo and thus choose to stay home, but he wouldn't because he was so angry with her. In his view, Zainaba just liked to cause trouble, and by this point he felt she deserved whatever treatment she would get.

Some weeks after this Zainaba returned home alone, made her peace with her mother, and subsequently married husband number nine. The next time I remember seeing Kolo was ten years later when he started a fight at a spirit possession healing ritual and had to be forcibly evicted by the patient's husband and brothers. He was drunk, capitulated easily, and looked a good deal the worse for wear.

Zainaba's story sets the episode of physical spouse abuse in the wider contexts of fear, violence, anger, and morality, and it counterposes the legitimate rights and permanent interests of consanguineal kin with the weaker and different bonds of affinity. Consanguines are responsible for one another's welfare and exert a strong moral influence on behavior. Consanguineal kin are supposed to guarantee the autonomy of the individual, who in turn must show proper respect. Zainaba's family had expected her to listen to them. It was her consistent rejection of their concern that frustrated and angered them. The emotions that were raised had as much to do with "sibling abuse" (in both directions, perhaps) as with Kolo's violence per se. Most of all, the story is about transgressing—again in two directions—the correct limits of autonomy. Kolo had no right to abuse Zainaba, and Zainaba had no justification to be so independent from her family as to let herself be victimized by him.

Marital separation (which functions as de facto divorce) is easy and common in Mayotte and not necessarily viewed negatively. A divorced woman often keeps custody of the children and in no case need lose contact with them. As adults, Kolo and Zainaba could readily have broken off the marriage and should have done so. As Ali said, when you no longer love a woman, you leave, you don't start beating her. Zainaba could also have asked Kolo to go. After the fight, she had the freedom to leave with her husband or stay at home without him, but out of common sense and acknowledgment of her kin's legitimate concern, she should have chosen to stay. (Of course, from her point of view, which is not represented here, she may have had good reason to escape the domination of her kin.)

Aside from the violence, the case illustrates more general dilemmas faced by everyone of both sexes in Mayotte: whether the "love" and attention one shows one's spouse, and the dependence on them one allows oneself to feel, should match that which one shows or feels for one's kin, and what should be the correct course of action when these are in competition. In cases without violence the proper course of action, or the one in the best interests of the actor, is not always so easily discernible. Some married couples pride themselves on the length of their union and state that they see themselves as a unity (*ulu araiky*). But, in general, the perspective is different from what we would expect in North America.[4] Thus, I have heard women berate their sisters for being loyal to a husband and not changing spouses frequently. From the actor's point of view, emotional investment in the marital relationship may not appear to be particularly secure.

Moral Authority and Corporal Autonomy

Zainaba's story also demonstrates that violence is not universally frowned on, nor is fear absent from kin relationships. In general, the more solidary the relationship (in descending order, children to their parents, between siblings, between neighbors), the less justifiable the violence. Yet it is precisely in the relationships that are supposed to be the most solidary that transgression of the norms of behavior will give rise to the strongest emotions. Ali's behavior toward his sister was frowned on (while nonviolent, Ali was viewed as someone too quick to anger; people feared his temper), yet it was understood. Beating a spouse is not understood; or, rather, it can only be understood in a way that unacceptably devalues the victim.

The issue can best be explored through another case. Sua was discussing with me some reservations about her current marriage to a rather passive man younger than herself. She mentioned that her eldest son had expressed the desire to return to his father, from whom she had been separated. Her ex-husband was a vigorous, jovial, and well-respected man, and so I was rather taken aback at her categorical refusal to consider the union. She then confided that during their first marriage he used to hit her. They had been residing virilocally in a community about two hours by foot from her natal village. Rumors of the abuse reached her parents, who questioned her closely on her visits home, but she always denied it, saying that people were just gossips and that if it were true she would have left him. In a sense, as long as she wished to stay with the man her discretion vis-à-vis her parents was more appropriate than Zainaba's loud quarreling. However, the reason for her silence was a good deal more straightforward: she felt humiliated by her situation. Her resentment toward her husband grew, and she hit back and eventually left him. Her explanation was simple: "He treated me like a child."[5]

Another story makes the same point from a happier direction. One evening a small group of men were chatting in the center of the village. One of them recounted how his goat had died that day. It had been taken into the bush to feed but was tethered on such a steep slope that it strangled itself on its own cord. With humorous resignation the man said, "If it had been one of my children who had been so careless with the animals I would have beaten him, but what could I do—it was my wife!"

Spouse abuse is illegitimate in Mayotte precisely because spouses ought not to be in a moral relationship to each other of parent to child. A husband should not beat his wife and a wife should not put up with it if he does. The perpetrator of such violence is in the wrong, but the victim is also partly in the wrong if she doesn't put a stop to it. If she submits, she is acting like a child, and if she is going to act like a child, then she should do so only in relation to her parents and siblings and not in her relation to her husband, since only the former can be assumed to have her best interests at heart. Returning to the first case for a moment, we can now see more clearly how, by allowing herself to be treated like a child by her husband, Zainaba was rejecting her kinship position vis-à-vis her true parents.[6]

The prohibition of spouse abuse cannot be put down simply to the abhorrence of violence per se. One might say, following Margaret Mead on culture and temperament, that a violent individual like Kolo is a misfit in a society like Mayotte. This is true to some extent, but I think one has to look more carefully. The issue is not only the presence or absence of violence or the simple positive or negative evaluation placed on it but the means and directions in which it is channeled and more or less appropriately utilized—that is, its meaning in various contexts. Ali chased Zainaba around the village and threatened her in the context of a relationship of siblingship and a situation of legitimate concern and hurt feelings where such behavior, while incorrect, was not gratuitous. He was, in a sense, berating her "for her own good," something a husband is viewed as having neither the right nor necessarily the interest to do. Ali would have drawn greater censure and, incidentally, made a good deal more of a fool of himself had he been chasing his wife. His behavior had meaningful reference to the channels of deep emotion and moral authority.[7] Likewise, Ali was confident in his ability to harness morally positive mystical violence in order to protect himself from Kolo.

Direct physical violence[8] is acceptable in Mayotte in only two kinds of relationships, and even then it is subject to a series of constraints. The first is the relationship of adversaries or rivals, people of equivalent status generally competing for a sexual partner. The second relationship, which is unidirectional, is that of parents over their children. (The term *parents* is broadly defined here and may, in certain circumstances, include siblings.) In both these kinds of relationships the level of acceptable violence is limited. Bystanders will usually step in to break up the conflict, especially if the antagonists seem unequally matched; if their statuses are such (e.g., elders) that the violence embarrasses the audience; if the fight threatens to have wider repercussions; or if one of the parties seems likely to get badly hurt. While a fight between young women or men using no weapons might be allowed to run its course and might even be watched with enjoyment by some, most other violence is stopped quickly. Children receive an occasional cuff or deliberate single hit with a switch from a parent or Koranic teacher,[9] but anything of longer duration, especially if the adult seems out of control, will be stopped by others. For example, I have seen neighbors intervene only moments after a mother erupted in rage and began hitting her daughter, aged perhaps eight, for forgetting to fetch firewood. The mother was admonished that one strike was enough. Parents who resort to violence that is excessive or deemed by others to be illegitimate will be criticized by kin or spoken about behind their backs by others.

In essence, one of the key differences between childhood and adulthood in Mayotte is the autonomy that adults have over their own bodies. Children can be threatened with beatings and sometimes receive them from caretakers. According to one male informant it is even permissible for a brother to beat an older sister if he perceives she is doing wrong; significantly, this informant's example came up in a discussion of the control of a girl's premarital sexuality. Otherwise, it is a grave wrong for a person of junior status, younger in years or in generation, to hit someone of senior status, especially a parent. An incident in which a youth hit his father was much commented on in shocked tones, and the perpetrator of such an act must actively seek his or her parent's pardon or else suffer the effects of a curse. Here it is not so much the physical act per se that is objected to but the statement it encodes. Hitting a parent reverses the proper direction of authority.

Unlike adults, children can be ordered to do things. Children also suffer corporal violence in the ritual sphere: boys are circumcised, girls are deflowered by their husbands (an act often discreetly supervised by their grandmothers), and children of both sexes must undergo, prior to circumcision or defloration, an inhalation of smoke said to be far more painful than either procedure. The only occasion on which an adult would be smoked is during the course of what local practitioners consider an extreme treatment of last resort to remove a dangerous spirit that has caused a prolonged psychotic break; the aim of the treatment is precisely to enable the patient to regain control over his or her own body. In all other circumstances an adult's body is inviolate. A dying adult is shielded behind a curtain from onlookers, and the appearance of corporal autonomy is maintained to the degree that a corpse is never unclothed, even while it is being cleansed and the last traces from the digestive tract removed.

Adultery and the Violence between Rivals

The corporal autonomy of adults is also reflected in sexual mores. Adultery is quite common; yet while injured spouses respond with hurt and anger, they cannot, in the strict sense of the term, punish each other for adultery since neither of them is under the sexual control of the other. If a husband is angry about his wife's sexual exploits (and some men are complaisant), his aggression is more appropriately directed toward his wife's lover. An angry husband may react in one of three ways: he can leave his wife, he can reduce the amount of material support he provides, or he can fight with the interloper, either physically or by means of sorcery.[10] But the person most likely to retaliate is the wife or girlfriend (or, in certain situations, even the ex-wife) of the woman's lover.

In other words, where adultery or the suspicion of adultery leads to violence, it is most likely and most appropriately to occur between the parties of the same sex. A man or woman may attempt to beat up the spouse's lover. When a woman suspects her husband of unfaithfulness, before making an accusation she ought to follow him to the other woman's house in order to verify her suspicions and catch the couple in the act. She will then walk in on them, in a cultural scenario known as *mangka vamba,* raise a ruckus, pull her husband away or walk off with his clothes, and perhaps start a brawl with the other woman. Brawls between women may also take place in public and sometimes escalate to include kinswomen of the major protagonists, although it is felt that senior women should not participate. These fights may be rough; I know of cases where the loser has required medical attention. Fights between men are probably less frequent but they may, on occasion, be more violent.[11] One senior man of the village is said in his youth to have lain in wait for his wife's lover with an ax and to have spent some time in prison for wounding him. The level of his violence was directly related to the fact that the interloper was his own classificatory older brother and hence a "parental" figure, precisely the sort of person who should have protected his interests.

This case indicates clearly that the primary injury and hence the retribution is conceived to take place between members of the same sex (though village gossip also said that the wife had treated her husband very badly). Adults have relative autonomy regarding their own sexual behavior; what they do not have the right to do is trespass on the partners of others. Marriage is a relationship where one partner has rights *to* but not *in* the other partner.[12] Husbands and wives can do as they please vis-à-vis each other (more or less; marriage partners ought to treat each other with respect) but those outside the marriage cannot.

In sum, rivals have, in a sense, the right to fight each other. To be beaten by a rival is not to submit to a claim of moral authority because none is intended. Between rivals, fighting is a demonstration of equality. But between spouses, quite apart from the physical abuse itself, it is the assertion of the perpetrator, manifest in the husband's act, of an illegitimate claim to authority over the victim, which is (or should be) much resented by the wife and by her kin.

Factors Contributing to Domestic Violence

The fact that spouse abuse is conceptually, morally, and emotionally wrong undoubtedly keeps the incidence down but of course does not prevent its occurrence. One might expect the incidence of violence to rise where the plausibility of the cultural view is less well supported by social and material factors. For example, in the past, when the age discrepancy between spouses was often much greater, the husband might more readily have attempted to take on a "parental" role of authority toward his wife. Today, when women's access to the means of production becomes indirect as the wives of wage earners, wives do in fact take on a dependent relationship to their husbands (Sacks 1979) and the cultural conceptions might be weakened as a result. Moreover, in the course of such a process of change, structural factors are likely to raise the tensions between marriage partners—for example, by generating contradictory expectations or by placing an absolute strain on the household budget. Domestic violence might follow; the cultural perspective presented above could only account for why it might still be less than in some other societies undergoing similar structural changes. This kind of argument could be used to account for differential ratios of violence in different sectors of the population or within the same community over time.

My data do not allow me to make that general argument, but I can say something about the kinds of contexts in which violence is more likely to occur in a given rural community where the cultural view presented above remains in operation. Two sets of factors are relevant here, those that weaken the informal social control against violence and those that increase the tensions between spouses. Relevant to both is the residence pattern. Where spouses come from different villages and are residing virilocally, it may be somewhat easier for abuse to be carried out than in the more common uxorilocal situation. Also significant is the pattern of seasonal residence in the fields. Many households spend the agricultural season or periods of it in relatively isolated dwellings, quite unlike the densely packed villages. On one occasion, when a middle-aged couple returned after a sojourn in the bush, the wife issued a complaint of physical abuse against her husband, asking a senior man to mediate between the couple and to propose a form of compensation for the wife. Incidentally, this shows that it is not only a woman's kin who guarantee her safety; in the absence of kin, a woman can represent herself.

The reason for this couple's quarrel brings up the most common issue around which marital conflict forms, namely, polygyny. Polygyny is an issue because of the sexual/emotional jealousy and sense of loss it sometimes entails and because of its relevance to debate about the proper ways to spend the household's resources. The wife is in a subordinate situation because Islam permits polygyny and because she has far less control over household earnings than her husband. Polygyny here is an overt manifestation of an Islamic model of sex roles and conjugal relations that differs from that described earlier and has been only partially accepted by the community—and then more by men than by women. Despite the fact that polygyny is permissible and may, in some situations, be readily accepted, it is often viewed by the first wife as a breach of faith and a disruption, not to say destruction, of common domestic projects.[13] When removed from the level of threat to practice, it renders inequality direct, specific, and explicit. Hence, I do not think it is unfair to say that in Mayotte, though not necessarily in all societies in which the institution is found, polygyny is itself a form of spouse abuse. Whether that is a valid interpretation or not, women faced with polygyny may respond with outright hostility or passive resistance that in turn may sorely try the husband's patience (especially, we might speculate, if he is already feeling guilty or harassed with trying to support two households). The potential for domestic violence rises.[14]

A third factor that increases the level of violence has to do with individual predisposition to violent behavior. The husband in the first case described in this chapter was simply a highly aggressive person. The social factors that might contribute to the etiology of violent dispositions in Mayotte are beyond the scope of this chapter, but the existence of "people who like to hit" (*ulu mitia mamanggu*) is recognized in Mayotte. Violent individuals are referred to as *ratsy fangahy* (of bad disposition or personality). Spouses of such people are victims simply because they are within reach and not because of anything intrinsic to the social constitution of marriage.

A final question to ask relates to the factors that discourage an abused woman from leaving her husband and hence perpetuate the conditions that lead to violence. In Mayotte this can be summed up descriptively, to borrow Sacks's (1979) formula, by saying that for some reason sisterhood is outweighed by wifehood, whether this be due to virilocal residence, infatuation, or lack or absence of kin. A potent factor for some women is the fear of poverty. Most women own their houses and household goods and are able to depend on their kin group membership for access to subsistence land, but these things are not sufficient. For the daily necessities that only money can buy—for example, kerosene, soap, salt, clothing—most women rely on their husbands. Some, though by no means all, women find it embarrassing and inconvenient to have to rely on lovers. Husbands have come to be in increasingly short supply, and brothers are less reliable since men too have greater expenses and are shifting their investment away from both women and the wider kin group (Solway 1990). In particular, older women and women with many children may have difficulty finding a new husband, though this should immediately be qualified by adding that many of them do and that other women have built alternate bases of support and may not even be interested in remarrying (Lambek 1992).

Conclusion

The preceding argument has demonstrated why spouse abuse is wrong in Mayotte. I have tried to show that the relationship between spouses is conceptualized at a basic level as one in which violence is inappropriate. In the local view this is not just because violence itself is bad but because the very constitution of the marital relationship precludes it. It is not that women are the weaker sex and must be protected or cherished but that marriage is a relationship between complementary (but not identical or equivalent) adults who should treat each other with consideration and respect (*ishima*). Perhaps a wife owes her husband respect in a wider range of domains and contexts than the reverse, but this does not change the basic point. Marriage need not be a relationship of great emotional dependency or intensity; the esteem in which one holds one's partner need not be grounded in emotional depths and need not be maintained in the face of evidence that suggests the spouse is not worthy of it. In theory, letting go of a spouse should be an easy matter; in practice, people recognize that this frequently is not the case. So violence is inappropriate because marital partners are supposed to form a solitary unit composed of complements rather than equivalents in which the husband does not have "parental" authority over the wife and because this unit need not give rise to the sort of violent passions that in other kinds of cultures might be idealized or naturalized. I would suspect that this general view, or something like it, is characteristic of Malagasy speakers throughout Madagascar. A quick and informal oral survey among a number of colleagues with experience in various parts of the island suggests that domestic violence is frowned on everywhere.

I have demonstrated some of the reasons why spouse abuse is viewed as wrong in Mayotte and have also suggested the conditons under which such moral considerations may be undermined or in which women become vulnerable despite them. These conditions, such as social isolation or economic dependency, may be relevant for the analysis of spouse abuse in any society. But what is more important, I think, is to demonstrate that the presence of a strong disapproval of marital violence can and does work reasonably effectively to control it. Hence, recourse to biological arguments is unwarranted. Rather, the next step is to show how a position such as that taken against marital violence in Mayotte fits into the larger system of gender, marriage, power, and prestige. A suggestive beginning for such an approach may be found in the attempt of Collier and Rosaldo (1981) to account for the links among marriage systems, gender constructs, and political processes. They attempt to identify the links among such factors as spouse abuse, peer violence, and the cultural emphasis on women's sexuality rather than motherhood. Although this chapter is not the place to develop a model of social relations in Mayotte along the lines they suggest, it is clear that the autonomy of women and men, their rights over their respective bodies, the respect in which they should hold each other, and their interests in protecting themselves from rivals are interconnected and are linked to basic social and political processes.

NOTES

Field research was conducted with the financial assistance of the Social Sciences and Humanities Research Council of Canada, the National Science Foundation, the National Geographic Society, and the University of Toronto. I thank Judith Brown for encouraging me to write this essay and all the editors for their patience and helpful suggestions with revisions. Jacqueline Solway has contributed substantially to the argument; her perception of the relationship between the sexes in Mayotte has been invaluable to me. The following individuals have also kindly commented on their experience of spouse abuse elsewhere in Madagascar: Georges Heurtebize, Susan Kus, Victor Raharijaona, and Lesley Sharpe. None of them necessarily shares my conclusions. Quotations are from my field notes unless otherwise indicated. The chapter remains substantially unrevised from the 1992 version; hence, the "ethnographic present" is now out of date.

1. Data from fieldwork subsequent to 1985 has not been incorporated into this chapter. Social change in Mayotte has been enormous, but its impact on the incidence of spouse abuse remains unanalyzed.

2. I should note that this discussion pertains to the villages in which I lived. An initial residence in town provoked quite a different experience. There, one of my most vivid memories is of children (of mixed sex) playing a game in which the "victim" buries his head in his arms and has to guess who is rapping him hard on the skull with his knuckles.

3. Even before this incident I had considered Kolo to be potentially violent. He had been one of the very few people to act in a gratuitously unpleasant and even threatening manner toward me, and I was relieved to discover that the community shared my view of him.

4. Nor is this perspective similar to the African cases described by Sacks (1979). Not only are wives less subordinate in Mayotte but, as Jacqueline Solway has pointed out to me in our discussions of this topic, the sister/wife contrast in Mayotte is paralleled by a similar duality of status for men. However, in the patrilineal societies analyzed by Sacks, there is no such symmetry; the status of brother is dominant and that of husband is largely absorbed into it.

5. It is a curious fact that the man who beat Sua had also been previously married

to Zainaba. For a while Zainaba and Sua were even co-wives, and it may be that Zainaba has been a victim in more than one of her marriages. Her marriage with this man ended quite differently from Sua's: he discovered she was having an affair and sent her home.

6. Furthermore, in letting her kin become aware of her position and yet not allowing them to help, she was treating them without due consideration and indicating to them that she didn't fully know her own mind—hence, she was demonstrating her childlike condition.

7. Had he actually hit his adult sister it might have been a different story.

8. The question of legitimacy of various forms of "mystical" violence (e.g., "sorcery" and retributive prayer) is complex and cannot be treated here (but see Lambek 1993). It should be emphasized that the corpus of violence as it is understood in Mayotte includes much more than direct physical beating.

9. The threat of violence is a major pedagogical tool in the primary Koranic classes.

10. When a man commits adultery, his wife can throw him out, demand money from him, or fight the other woman. The fact that a woman can request financial recompense from a husband while a husband can retaliate against a wayward wife by withdrawing financial support indicates the underlying sexual economy. As culturally defined, sex is a woman's resource, while cash is a man's. One man justified the attack on a wife's lover in the following terms: The man has gone to great expense, he has built his wife a house (this is not all that common in practice but the subsequent disloyalty on the part of the wife is a common story), he buys her new clothes all the time, he supplies her with food . . . and then she takes a lover. Yet this justifies his action against the other man rather than the wife! Adultery shows just how tenuous men's power is; the only thing that makes a woman dependent on an individual man is her sense of obligation and justice—and, of course, loyalty is precisely the trait that Mayotte men fear women lack. To a degree the system encourages such disloyalty on the part of women; as long as women are defined as the proper object of men's expenditures, a woman can play the field to considerable material advantage (Ottino 1964).

11. The greater occurence of violence between women may be a reflection of the fact that they have fewer means of controlling the sexual exploits of their husbands than the reverse or that they feel they have more to lose by a spouse's infidelity. It is also a product of the fact that women consider themselves responsible for minding the taboos (*mitana fady*). When a woman trespasses on another's territory, it is both a violation of expectation and a direct insult. That this is not simply a product of competition over spouses is indicated by the fact that a woman may feel insulted by a kinswoman's sexual relations with or marriage to a man from whom she has already long since been separated herself, even when there have been several intervening marriages on both sides.

12. This follows Robert Murphy's dictum that "when a man gets married, he thinks that he is marrying a woman, but a bit of reflection on his altered status reveals that he has entered into a state of antimarriage with all women. By defining a tie to one

woman, he has defined a status toward all other women" (1980:215). Of course, the same holds true in reverse for a woman.

13. It is not only the first wife who may experience a breach of faith. Sometimes it is the second wife who discovers only after her marriage that the union she has engaged in is in fact polygynous.

14. For a means of indirect ("mystical") and sometimes effective retaliation on the part of wives, see Lambek (1980). For such retaliation by the wife's mother, see Lambek (1990).

REFERENCES CITED

Collier, Jane F., and Michelle Z. Rosaldo. 1981. "Politics and Gender in Simple Societies." In *Sexual Meanings: The Cultural Construction of Gender and Sexuality.* Ed. Sherry B. Ortner and Harriet Whitehead. 275–329. New York: Cambridge University Press.

Lambek, Michael. 1980. "Spirits and Spouses: Possession as a System of Communication among the Malagasy Speakers of Mayotte." *American Ethnologist* 7:318–31.

———. 1983. "Virgin Marriage and the Autonomy of Women in Mayotte." *Signs* 9 (2): 264–81.

———. 1988. "Graceful Exits: Spirit Possession as Personal Performance in Mayotte." *Culture* 8 (1): 59–69.

———. 1990. "The Practice of Islamic Experts in a Village on Mayotte." *Journal of Religion in Africa* 20 (1): 20–40.

———. 1992. "Motherhood and Other Careers in Mayotte (Comoro Islands)." In *In Her Prime: New Views of Middle-Aged Women.* 2d ed. Ed. Virginia Kerns and Judith K. Brown. 77–92. Urbana: University of Illinois Press.

———. 1993. *Knowledge and Practice in Mayotte: Local Discourses of Islam, Sorcery, and Spirit Possession.* Toronto: University of Toronto Press.

Murphy, Robert. 1980 [1971]. *The Dialectics of Social Life.* New York: Columbia University Press.

Ottino, Paul. 1964. "La Crise du système familial et matrimonial des Sakalava de Nosy Be." *Civilisation Malgache* 1:225–48.

Sacks, Karen. 1979. *Sisters and Wives: The Past and Future of Sexual Equality.* Westport, Conn.: Greenwood.

Solway, Jacqueline S. 1990. "Affines and Spouses, Friends and Lovers: The Passing of Polygyny in Botswana." *Journal of Anthropological Research* 46 (1): 41–66.

Werbner, Richard P. 1984. "The Manchester School in South-Central Africa." *Annual Review of Anthropology* 13:157–85.

FOURTEEN

Wife Beating in India: Variations on a Theme

Barbara Diane Miller

A drum, a peasant, a Sudra [laborer], an animal, a woman—all of these are fit to be beaten.

—Tulsidas, *The Ramcharitmanas* (sixteenth century)

Given newspaper coverage in the West and in India about bride-burning murders and especially the case of a young Rajasthani widow who immolated herself on her husband's funeral pyre in 1987, India looms large as a society in which wives do not fare well. On a global scale, important measures of female status such as longevity, literacy, and labor participation all place India in the lowest ranges. Less recognized is the fact that almost everything about female status in India varies, sometimes dramatically, by region, class or caste, and life-cycle stage.[1]

This chapter addresses a particular feature of intrahousehold relationships: the physical abuse—beating or battering—of a spouse, usually the wife by the husband in the overwhelming majority of cases cross-culturally.[2] A central issue in intrahousehold violence is dominance: who hits whom is not a random matter. Throughout the world, children do not generally beat adults, aged people do not beat the physically fit, and women do not beat men. These broad statements reflect general truths about power differentials in society and in the household. The perspective I adopt here is that wife beating in India is caused, both indirectly and directly, by male dominance.

Male dominance encompasses a complex system of female devaluation and disfranchisement in much of India that puts women at a disadvantage in terms of low intrahousehold status and restricted bargaining power, a limited range of alternate life courses (outside marriage), and few escape routes from violent situations. This approach is similar to one adopted for Western society by Straus (1980) but places more emphasis on patriarchy as the key factor underlying the whole system, with socially contextualized variation throughout the country. Thus, I contend that wife beating can be added to the list of features of "the male supremacist complex" defined more than two decades ago by Divale and Harris (1976).[3]

Within the vast generalization that India is a male-dominated society and that spouse abuse there is more likely to mean wife abuse than husband abuse, I seek to discover degrees of variation. Does wife beating or battering seem more prevalent in regions, classes, and at life-cycle stages where female status is the lowest—for instance, the northern plains area, propertied groups, and young brides?[4] What other social variables are related to the risk of being beaten, to averting risk, or to escaping from a risk-prone context?

A range of factors are involved, all related in one way or another to the nature and degree of a woman's dependence on her marital household. Dependency can be economic—a woman may or may not earn enough money to support herself and her children without her husband and his family. Dependence may also be kinship-regulated—a woman in her marital family may or may not live far from her natal family, divorce may or may not be an acceptable option, and remarriage may or may not be a locally accepted practice. Other factors such as a woman's literacy may be important in her ability to attain some control over her domestic situation. Less amenable to cultural analysis are other factors such as a woman's degree of self-esteem, which may prompt her to leave an intolerable situation and find assistance from the few organizations and shelters that exist to help abused women in India.

Some of these independent variables have been analyzed in the Indian context, and they can provide a framework within which to examine patterns of wife beating and wife battering. Unfortunately, studies of the dependent variable are rare.[5] At this point in our knowledge, I can do only two things: first, describe the social framework within which wife abuse exists; and second, present some provocative case material gleaned from a variety of secondary sources. The evidence gathered so far does not in any way provide a "data set" by which hypotheses can be tested. We cannot learn if frequency or type of abuse is higher or lower in certain regions or classes or particular life-cycle stages. Rather, the evidence provides a bare beginning for understanding some of the social contexts of wife beating in India that may be usefully compared with the other material presented in this book.

The Framework

In the next few pages I will present a summary of a model of how to study social variation in women's status in Indian society that I have been designing and refining over the past two decades. This model is necessarily simplified due to space constraints. I collapse several important subvariables into three supervariables: region, class/caste, and life-cycle stage.

Regional differences in female status are strong in India. In the northern plains region, women appear to have the lowest intrahousehold status in all of India, whereas their status is higher in southern India and in the Himalayan zone in the far north (Berreman 1987; Dyson and Moore 1983; Miller 1981). Indicators of status on which this generalization is based include: juvenile sex ratios, labor participation rates, and literacy. Women in the northern plains tend to have lower labor force participation rates than elsewhere in India. Thus, insofar as income earning may be an enhancement of intrahousehold power, northern women are more deprived of this possible source of strength.[6] Generally, women in northern areas are less literate than elsewhere in India, and insofar as literacy may be empowering, women are relatively deprived of this source of strength. Kinship regulations in northern India are also important limiting factors for women's autonomy: village exogamy is the rule in the northern plains (I use the shorthand term "North" for this region) and marriage distances are long, whereas village endogamy is frequent in the South. Furthermore, hypergamy (marriage of a woman with a man whose family has higher socioeconomic standing than her natal family) in the North means that wife-givers have lower status than wife-takers, while isogamy in the South provides equality between both families. The bride and groom are strangers in the North but often acquainted with each other in the South as co-villagers or even cross-cousins. This list of socially constructed disadvantages for a bride in the North compared to the South could be expanded, but those elements mentioned provide an adequate, though overgeneralized, background. Class/caste differences are less amenable to generalization than are regional differences. I have suggested previously that upper-class/caste females have lower relative status to males in their class/caste than do women of lower social strata (Miller 1981). Several measures, including juvenile sex ratios and labor participation rates, indicate that the intrahousehold status of upper-strata females in the North is the lowest in all of India. Intrahousehold male dominance in the lower strata appears to be countered by the fact the women tend to work outside the home for wages and thus gain some economic independence from their husbands. Extended households are more characteristic of propertied, upper-strata groups and may be a context for greater control of females in a patrilineal setting.[7] The absence of a mother-in-law in nuclear households can be seen as a potentially liberating factor for a wife. Poverty, of course, is more prevalent in the lower strata and may provide unknown levels of stress, prompting violence by males. Alcohol abuse by males may be more prevalent in the lower social strata, though I know of no study documenting this possibility.

Life-cycle changes in female status in India are significant (Vatuk 1992). Generally, for adult women especially in the North the lowest point is the early years of marriage. At this time, the woman has to adapt to a new household situation, has not yet borne children (most especially prized sons), has the hardest chores to do, and has the least to eat. The presence of a mother-in-law, who seeks to maintain close ties with her son almost in competition with the new bride, is generally a negative factor for the in-marrying girl. With the bearing of children, especially sons, the domestic power of the wife improves. In later years, as a female head of household with an aging husband or as a widow with sons, she may well assume the preeminent position in the household. Wife battering then logically appears most likely for a young wife in an extended household with no children or no sons. This life-cycle pattern iterates to an extent with those of region and class since both patrilineal extended households (Frenzen and Miller 1986; Kolenda 1967) and extreme son preference are more prevalent in the northern plains region than elsewhere in India (Dyson and Moore 1983; Miller 1981).

This broad framework applies more directly to the rural population. The urban elite—and its particular pattern in the North of bride-burning murders—may require a somewhat different approach, one that is beyond the scope of this chapter. As with any model, this one does not provide answers but rather is meant as a guide in the consideration of the available evidence on wife beating.

The Evidence

The examples presented here are gleaned from a variety of sources—primarily ethnographies and articles in journals and magazines, with novels as supporting material. This "dataset" constitutes an "opportunistic sample" of sources rather than an exhaustive overview, but it nevertheless offers some useful insights.

Region

A limited collection of secondary evidence cannot reveal much about regional frequencies, but no all-India survey data on wife beating are obtainable as an alternate source of information. So far, I have cases from all over India and elsewhere in South Asia attesting to a very widespread pattern indeed.

A number of authors report that wife beating is characteristic of several households in the villages in which they have worked: in the Punjab (Horowitz and Kishwar 1984), Uttar Pradesh (Ahmed-Ghosh 1987), West Bengal (Rohner and Chaki-Sircar 1988), Karnataka (Beals 1980; Dhruvarajan 1989), Andhra Pradesh (Mies 1982), Tamil Nadu (Gough 1981), and Kerala (Gulati 1981). These cases come from states all over India, both northern and southern. Further research of the secondary literature is needed to determine patterns of more frequent reporting for some regions than others; at present, the "sample" is too limited.

A newspaper survey reveals that (presumably for urban, literate respondents) 99 percent of Pakistani women working at home and 77 percent of women working outside the home have been beaten by their husbands (International Women's Tribune Center 1985). In Sri Lanka, an anthropologist reports that wife beating was "universal" in a village studied in the 1950s (Obeyesekere 1963). In northwestern Bangladesh, a village woman told researchers, "Here in the village the men work all day ploughing with cows. So they think they should treat their women like cows too, shouting at them and beating them" (Hartmann and Boyce 1984:81).

It is doubtful that any region of South Asia is clearly characterized by the absence of wife beating. Rather, the salient question concerns possible regional variation in degree and frequency, and it is for these measures that we lack information.

Class/Caste

References to wife beating among both higher and lower social strata are found in the literature but say nothing about comparative frequency or degree. Rohner and Chaki-Sircar (1988) document wife beating among both high-caste and untouchable groups in a West Bengal village in eastern India. Gough (1981) notes that in Kumbapettai village, Tamil Nadu, almost all households in the 1950s were known to have had instances of wife beating. Mies (1982:78, 134) provides comments from some Kapu (high-caste) women in Andhra Pradesh, in South India, that in the past women were beaten for talking with men other than their husbands and not hiding from their elders, but now they are beaten for wanting to go to a friend's home to make lace. One of five case studies of poor working women in Kerala, South India, mentions wife beatings (Gulati 1981:104).

A number of reports in the 1980s indicate that "bride burnings" generally involved middle- and upper-class households in large northern cities (Kishwar and Vanita 1984:224–33; Palriwala 1985) and in southern cities as well

(Krishnakumari and Geetha 1983). In most cases, a young bride is continually harassed, particularly by her husband and mother-in-law, to bring more gifts from her natal family to her marital household even after the dowry has been paid. When harassment fails, the bride characteristically is murdered by dousing her with kerosene and then setting her on fire. In this way, it can be claimed by her in-laws that she died in a cooking accident. Widowed, the young man is then free to marry again and bring in another bride with her dowry and subsequent gifts. Reports of such cases often mention physical abuse of the bride prior to her murder. For example, here is the story of Kanchan, a twenty-four-year-old stenographer who lived in Delhi:

> On 29 June, she went straight to her parents' house in Malviya Nagar and told them she felt unsafe because her husband and in-laws were persistently demanding money for a scooter, and were ill-treating her. Her husband came at night and forced her to return with him. When she reached home, she was beaten by her husband in the presence of her brother who was also insulted and turned out when he protested. He went to the police station and complained he feared his sister's life was in danger. The police refused to intervene in "family affairs." In the middle of the night, Kanchan's parents were informed that she had been badly burnt and admitted to Lohia hospital. They rushed there but she was already dead. (Kishwar and Vanita 1984:224)

We do not know how often such beatings, followed by fatal fire "accidents," occur in India. While most evidence locates bride-burning deaths in families of the urban, upper, and middle classes, the possibility exists that such deaths also occur in other contexts.

Women's Income

Women who work outside the home and earn an income are beaten as well as those who do not. Urban victims of beating and murder for dowry demands are often in the labor force (Kishwar and Vanita 1984:224–33). Poor working women are also victims (Gulati 1981:104). One particularly revealing case concerns a Tamil woman migrant to Delhi who worked as a domestic servant: "Devaki was beaten frequently by her husband for years when he was sitting idle at home, entirely dependent on her wages for survival. She tolerated this until his death a year ago" (Rani and Kaul 1986:8).

Thus, earning an income is not always a sufficient guarantee that a woman will either be able to use her financial strength to bargain for better treatment in the home or to leave an abusive husband. But the uninvestigated possibility exists that there may be a greater propensity for income-earning women to cope with an abusive situation by leaving than for non-income-earning women.

Household Structure

Examples of wife beating can be found for nuclear as well as extended households. Having in-laws on the scene does not appear to protect a woman from being beaten; rather, it often seems to exacerbate wife abuse. Beatings associated with in-law instigation are associated with the extreme bride-burning cases mentioned above, as well as village cases. For instance, Rohner and Chaki-Sircar (1988) found in a West Bengal village that there were at least eleven high-caste homes where wives have been beaten by their husbands, "often" at the instigation of their mothers-in-law. The association of wife beating in extended households with behavioral control is vividly portrayed in a Punjabi novel mentioned by Kakar (1987): a husband beat his wife because she would not lower her gaze in front of him, and she steadfastly refused to do so even when his parents also insisted that she should.

Still, the presence of a mother-in-law is not a necessary ingredient for wife beating, as women in nuclear households are also beaten. Cases include the Tamil domestic maid mentioned above (Rani and Kaul 1986) and Devaki, the poor construction worker described by Gulati (1981).

Dowry, Alcohol, and Sex

This congeries of topics includes factors that often appear as proximate causes for wife beating in the literature. Dowry demands by a woman's in-laws are the most frequently mentioned reason for her ill treatment. Such references are common for urban as well as village-based bride-burning cases. Gulati (1981:104) links dowry demands with the frequent quarrels between Devaki, the construction worker, and her husband that generally resulted "in Devaki getting a few blows."

Alcohol consumption by husbands is commonly associated with wife beating in the literature on India.[8] Horowitz and Kishwar (1984) report that alcohol abuse is routine in the Punjabi village they studied and that inebriated husbands tend to beat their wives. The story of Malarkodi, a Bombay slum-dwelling woman, is particularly stark:

> She had been badly beaten up and killed by her drunken husband. He also kicked her in the vagina. This caused internal bleeding which killed her. We

> soon came to know the whole story. Some time ago, Malarkodi had run off to Madras with a former boyfriend. Her husband went and brought her back, promising to behave well. But after that, he continued to remind her of her elopement. He used to drink and beat her up. . . . But this Sunday the routine took a fatal turn. She died. . . . When we went to the police inspector of Tilak Nagar to demand Malarkodi's dead body, he said, "Why are you taking up this issue? She was an immoral woman. Otherwise, no sane husband would do this." (Kishwar and Vanita 1984:215)

A husband's demands for sex with his wife are also related to wife beating. Kakar (1987) mentions that interviews with rural women who have migrated to Delhi reveal that the women submit to intercourse for fear of being beaten. A study of sexual behavior in Kumaon, a mountainous area of northern India, found a common pattern of a husband beating his wife as part of sexual activity (Kapur 1987:46–47). This report is confusing because men assert that beatings are a sign of love and therefore not part of casual extramarital sex but only sex with one's wife. When asked about the association between love and beatings, the wives did not seem convinced that the two were related.

Ways Out

For the woman who does not wish to endure a domestic situation in which she is vulnerable to beatings, only two options exist: getting her husband to stop beating her or else leaving him. Various possibilities exist to empower a woman to do either of these, but as mentioned above, most of these are not options for northern women, particularly northern upper-strata women.

Support from a woman's natal kin might be thought to be an important option for all Indian women, but such is not the case. In northern India, a woman's natal family may be many miles away and she is not allowed to travel alone. If she wants to go home, someone from her natal family must come and fetch her. Her natal family's power to influence her treatment is also limited by the fact that its status is generally lower than that of her husband's, due to hypergamy. A much stronger position is afforded a bride in South India due to the proximity of her natal kin and their equality with her marital family.

Divorce is an option limited mainly to lower-class women or to women in elite, Westernized, urban families. In the rural areas, high-caste women would be seriously stigmatized if they were to seek divorces, and their options after divorce are narrow as well: they must either return to their natal families or fend for themselves.

Suicide appears to be the ultimate way out, resorted to by unknown numbers of women every year because of unhappiness in their marital homes (for comparative information on women's suicide in Papua New Guinea, see Counts 1987). The highest rates of suicide among women in several Asian countries occur in the very late teens and early twenties, a point in the life cycle when the stresses of marriage may be at their worst (Headley 1983; Miller and Kearney 1987).

There are a few cases in the literature of women who threaten to fight back. A low-caste West Bengali woman left her abusive husband and went to her parents' home. When her husband came to fetch her, she yelled at him to go away: "If you come again, I'll throw stones at you and break your head" (Rohner and Chaki-Sircar 1988:51). A woman working as a cashew nut processor in Sri Lanka had a husband who physically assaulted her from the beginning of their marriage (Casinader et al. 1987:318). She sent him away but allowed him to return twice. His behavior improved, she says, because she had threatened to strike back if he assaulted her again. A scene in a Punjabi novel mentioned by Kakar (1987) depicts a poor Sikh family in which the husband drinks heavily. His wife quarrels with him about it, and such quarrels often end in violence. But she tries to "give as good as she gets," though his superior strength usually makes him the victor.

One ethnographic report of a wife actually striking her husband is described by Nanda (1986:46) from her research on the *hijras* (male transvestites). The wife in the couple, a *hijra,* was a prostitute married to one of her former patrons who wished that she would discontinue her earlier work. She tells him, "Don't put any restrictions on me," and comments, "If he gives me too much back talk, I give him good whacks." It is telling that this rare case of a wife hitting a husband involves a man in the role of wife.

If a woman is lucky enough to bear several healthy sons and thereby secure her intrahousehold position, and as she ages and gains control of household decision making, her chances of being beaten are likely to decline. Age therefore brings some freedom from physical abuse (see Brown 1982 on the status of older women cross-culturally).

Psychological Hints

A study of the psychological status of women in India, particularly rural women, is urgently needed. We may expect low self-esteem among girls brought up in cultures where sons are clearly favored.[9] Likewise, low self-esteem might be expected among women socialized to serve others first, knowing that one is the lowest priority in terms of the most basic welfare expenditures on food and health care. Even in homes where daughters are treated as well as sons, they must eventually realign with another household group after marriage, something most men in India never have to do.

It is not surprising, given the literature indicating women's strong internalization of inferiority, that some women feel they deserve to be beaten. One ethnographer reports that some women say they are beaten because they have done something wrong (Ahmed-Ghosh 1987). A study by the women's group Saheli (Research Center on Women's Studies 1986:12) of four battered urban women found that the women accepted their beatings as part of their subservient role. Obviously, not all women accept being beaten. Some try to avoid abuse through acceptable options like visits to their natal home, some threaten to hit back, and others opt out of the situation entirely through suicide.

Conclusion

Wife beating is one part of the wider system of male dominance that pervades much of India and as such cannot be understood fully apart from it. This chapter proposes a framework for looking at variations in wife beating and reviews some of the evidence available from disparate sources. No systematic study of wife beating in India has been done, and only a very few case studies undertaken by women's organizations exist. The topic is not an easy one on which to conduct fieldwork, but it is important that such abuse becomes a topic of research attention. Without careful research, it is difficult to judge the extent of the problem or which areas and subpopulations are most at risk. Socially focused studies are needed to help determine how one might best devise targeted programs to subvert or circumvent social structures that place women at risk of being beaten—sometimes to death—as a matter of daily routine.

NOTES

This chapter was prepared with the support of the National Science Foundation during a year at the University of California researching gender discrimination in India. Discussions with Deborah Balk of the Graduate Group in Demography and Gerald Berreman of the Department of Anthropology at UC-Berkeley were helpful. Judith Brown's communications about wife beating and approaches to its study enhanced my thinking on the subject. Joyce Dietrich of the South Asia Program at Cornell University typed the manuscript. Quotations are from my field notes unless otherwise indicated.

1. Close examination of household-by-household differences within a single village reveal variation at that level too. But this chapter considers broader patterns within which individual-level data vary.

2. Definitional problems abound (see, e.g., the discussion in Campbell 1985). Since the data on physical abuse of wives in India are so poor, one cannot even attempt to discriminate between forms of abuse, such as beating compared to battering.

3. Divale and Harris (1976) consider tribal societies in their analysis, not peasant or industrialized societies in which male supremacist complexes also exist.

4. This model, which states that higher-class females have poorer intrahousehold status than lower-class females depends on within-class male-female comparisons. Anyone comparing the overall welfare of a rich Jat woman with a poor Chamar woman might be able to claim that the Jat woman is better off. But my approach compares, for example, Jat men with Jat women and Chamar men with Chamar women.

5. One could write an entire essay on the methodological problems that would be entailed in a field study of wife beating.

6. Schlegel and Barry (1986) have analyzed data from 181 nonindustrialized societies. They demonstrate that "women's productive activities have effects on the value accorded to females and the freedom they have to control their own persons" (1986:143). They found a lower incidence of rape where women make a substantial contribution to subsistence.

7. An interesting comparison could be made between the treatment of wives in patrilineal and matrilineal extended households. It may be that in the latter any abusive behavior toward women would be meted out by brothers on sisters.

8. An association between alcohol abuse and spouse abuse, based on an analysis of African data, is proposed by Erchak (1984).

9. Kakar (1978) offers important observations about the treatment of daughters and their self-esteem in India.

REFERENCES CITED

Ahmed-Ghosh, Huma. 1987. "Changes in the Status of North Indian Women: A Case Study of Palitpur Village." Women in International Development Working Paper No. 141. East Lansing: Michigan State University, Office of Women in International Development.

Beals, Alan R. 1980. *Gopalpur: A South Indian Village.* New York: Holt, Rinehart and Winston.

Berreman, Gerald. 1987. "Sanskritization as Female Oppression." Paper presented at Wenner-Gren International Symposium No. 103: The Anthropology of Gender Hierarchies. Mijas, Spain.

Brown, Judith K. 1982. "Cross-Cultural Perspectives on Middle-Aged Women." *Current Anthropology* 23:143–56.

Campbell, Jacquelyn C. 1985. "Beating of Wives: A Cross-Cultural Perspective." *Victimology* 10:174–85.

Casinader, Rex A., Sepalika Fernando, and Karuna Gamage. 1987. "Women's Issues and Men's Roles: Sri Lankan Village Experience." In *Geography of Gender in the Third World.* Ed. Janet H. Momsen and Janet Townsend. 309–22. London: Hutchinson.

Counts, Dorothy. 1987. "Female Suicide and Wife Abuse." *Suicide* 17:194–204.

Divale, William Tulio, and Marvin Harris. 1976. "Population, Warfare, and the Male Supremacist Complex." *American Anthropologist* 78:521–38.

Dhruvarajan, Vanaja. 1989. *Hindu Women and the Power of Ideology.* Granby, Mass.: Bergin and Garvey.

Dyson, Tim, and Mick Moore. 1983. "Gender Relations, Female Autonomy, and Demographic Behavior: Regional Contrasts within India." *Population and Development Review* 9 (1): 35–60.

Erchak, Gerald M. 1984. "Cultural Anthropology and Spouse Abuse." *Cultural Anthropology* 25 (3): 331–32.

Frenzen, Paul D., and Barbara Diane Miller. 1986. "Regional Patterns of Household Complexity in India." Paper presented at the annual meeting of the Population Association of America. Chicago.

Gough, Kathleen. 1981. *Rural Society in Southeast India.* New York: Cambridge University Press.

Gulati, Leela. 1981. *Profiles in Female Poverty: A Study of Poor Working Women in Kerala.* Delhi: Hindustan Publishing Co.

Hartmann, Betsy, and James Boyce. 1984. *A Quiet Violence: View from a Bangaladesh Village.* London: Zed Press.

Headley, Lee A., ed. 1983. *Suicide in Asia and the Near East.* Berkeley: University of California Press.

Horowitz, Berny, and Madhu Kishwar. 1984. "Family Life: The Unequal Deal." In *In Search of Answers: Indian Women's Voices from Manushi.* Ed. Madhu Kishwar and Ruth Vanita. 69–103. London: Zed Press.

International Women's Tribune Center. 1985. Newsletter #32. Quoted in *WID Bulletin* (January 1987): 13. East Lansing: Michigan State University, Office of Women in International Development.

Kakar, Sudhir. 1978. *The Inner World: A Psycho-analytic Study of Childhood and Society in India.* New York: Oxford University Press.

———. 1987. "Eros and Oneiros in Indian Fiction." De Vos Memorial Lecture. Department of Anthropology, University of California at Berkeley.

Kapur, Tribhuwan. 1987. *Sexual Life of the Kumaonis: A New Approach to Sexuality.* New Delhi: Vikas Publishing.

Kishwar, Madhu, and Ruth Vanita. 1984. Section titled "Family Violence." In *In Search of Answers: Indian Women's Voices from Manushi.* Ed. Madhu Kishwar and Ruth Vanita. 203–41. London: Zed Press.

Kolenda, Pauline M. 1967. "Regional Differences in Indian Family Structure." In *Regions and Regionalism in Indian Family Structure: An Exploratory Study.* Ed. Robert I. Crane. 147–226. Durham, N.C.: Duke University Program in Comparative Studies on Southern Asia.

Krishnakumari, N. S., and A. S. Geetha. 1983. *A Report on the Problem of Dowry in Bangalor City.* New Delhi: Joint Women's Programme, CISRS.

Mies, Maria. 1982. *The Lace Makers of Narsapur: Indian Housewives Produce for the World Market.* London: Zed Press.

Miller, Barbara D. 1981. *The Endangered Sex: Neglect of Female Children in Rural North India.* Ithaca, N.Y.: Cornell University Press.

Miller, Barbara Diane, and Robert N. Kearney. 1987. "Women's Suicide in Sri Lanka." In *Women and Health: Cross-Cultural Perspectives.* Ed. Patricia Whelan. 110–23. South Hadley, Mass.: Bergin and Garvey.

Nanda, Serena. 1986. "The Hijras of India: Cultural and Individual Dimensions of an Institutionalized Third Gender Role." In *Anthropology and Homosexual Behavior.* Ed. Evelyn Blackwood. 35–54. New York: Haworth Press.

Obeyesekere, Gananath. 1963. "Pregnancy Cravings (*Dola Duka*) in Relation to Social Structure and Personality in a Sinhalese Village." *American Anthropologist* 65:323–42.

Palriwala, Rajni. 1985. "Women Are Not for Burning: The Anti-Dowry Movement in Delhi." Paper presented at Wenner-Gren International Symposium No. 99: Anthropological Perspectives on Women's Collective Action: An Assessment of the Decade, 1975–1985. Mijas, Spain.

Rani, Prabha, and Poonam Kaul. 1986. "For Two Meals a Day: A Report on Tamil Domestic Maids." *Manushi* 35:2–9.

Research Center on Women's Studies. 1986. *RCWS Newsletter* [Bombay] 7 (3–4).

Rohner, Ronald, and Manjusri Chaki-Sircar. 1988. *Mothers and Children in a Bengali Village.* Hanover, N.H.: University Press of New England.

Schlegel, Alice, and Herbert Barry III. 1986. "The Cultural Consequences of Female Contribution to Subsistence." *American Anthropologist* 88:142–50.

Straus, Murray A. 1980. "Sexual Inequality and Wife Beating." In *The Social Causes of Husband-Wife Violence.* Ed. Murray A. Straus and Gerald T. Hotaling. 86–93. Minneapolis: University of Minnesota Press.

Vatuk, Sylvia. 1992. "Sexuality and the Middle-Aged Women in South Asia." In *In Her Prime: New Views of Middle-Aged Women.* 2d ed. Ed. Virginia Kerns and Judith K. Brown. 155–70. Urbana: University of Illinois Press.

FIFTEEN

Wife Abuse among Indo-Fijians

Shireen Lateef

Shanti was a thirty-year-old accounts clerk who was married with four children aged between ten and two. Shanti lived with her husband and his family. Her mother-in-law and sister-in-law disliked her, ill-treated her and made her perform the bulk of the household chores even though she was in full-time paid employment while they were not. Shanti's mother-in-law consistently complained to her husband that she was lazy, disobedient and disrespectful. The complaints led to arguments between Shanti, her mother-in-law, sister-in-law and husband, often resulting in Shanti being beaten by her husband.

Shanti's husband also hit her for reasons besides her mother-in-law's complaint. Sometimes when Shanti expressed her desire to live away from her in-laws or asked her husband when they would get their own house, arguments ensued leading eventually to her being given at least a few slaps. On other occasions she received beatings because her husband was suspicious and jealous, accusing her of fraternizing with other males.

In June 1986, a couple of days after some bad floods when their house was flooded out, Shanti attempted suicide by drinking paraquat (pesticide). While in the hospital she told her friend and work colleague that life had become too unbearable and cleaning up after the floods was the last straw. She said, "You know what they're like at home." Shanti died three days later.[1]

Suicide was Shanti's solution to a life that she perceived to be unbearable and from which there was no other escape. Admittedly, suicide is an extreme and atypical response to the physical abuse to which many Indo-Fijian wives are subjected. A more typical response would be to accept violence as the inevitable fate of being a wife and to bear it in silence.

Physical violence is taken for granted as part of being a wife in the Indo-Fijian society. This is not to imply that all Indo-Fijian wives are subjected to constant physical violence. Rather, it suggests that violence is experienced by many Indo-Fijian wives at least occasionally and is accepted by the community as part of a woman's life. Varying degrees of violence are imposed on wives, and their control by the occasional use of the *danda* (stick) is seldom questioned by either males or females.

The threat and use of physical violence against wives is a powerful and effective mechanism for ensuring the maintenance and reproduction of traditional gender relations among Indo-Fijians. However, blatant, overt control of wives through the use of violence is not always necessary since wives control their own behavior, especially in the face of a powerful and influential familial ideology that stresses the need for female submission to male control. Violence is used as a supplementary mechanism of social control to assert and consolidate male dominance and female subordination within the family.

For Shanti, suicide was the solution for a complex set of problems, not the least of which was physical violence that she encountered in her life as an Indo-Fijian woman. It is within this wider context of an Indo-Fijian woman's life in Suva that I wish to discuss how wife abuse grows out of and supports Indo-Fijian culture.

The Setting

The Fiji Islands are situated in the southwest Pacific and have a total land area of approximately 7,022 square miles. Fiji acquired independence from the British in 1970. Of a total population of approximately 700,000, Indo-Fijians constitute 50.5 percent and indigenous Fijians 42.4 percent, with the remainder being other Pacific Islanders, Europeans, and Chinese.

The vast majority of Indo-Fijians are the direct descendants of indentured laborers taken to Fiji by the British to work in the sugarcane plantations between the years 1879 and 1916. After serving periods of indenture ranging from five to ten years, the majority became free settlers, while only a small minority returned to India (Lal 1983).

What passes in Fiji today as Indo-Fijian culture is a syncretic form of Indian culture that was derived from the hegemonic influence of North Indian culture (Jayawardena 1968:438, 1980:431). Little difference exists between Indo-Fijian Hindus and Muslims in family organization, rules and regulations governing women's behavior, and generally in the social relations of gender.[2] Hence, the term *Indo-Fijian* is used to refer to both Hindus and Muslims. The women of my study come from different class backgrounds and include Hindus and Muslims. Few participate in paid employment and those who do tend to be in traditional "pink-collar" occupations such as typists, sales assistants, and clerks.

Gender Relations and the Roles and Status of Wives

Wife abuse among Indo-Fijians must be located and analyzed in the wider context of gender relations within the family in order to explain and understand the nature, reasons, experience, and acceptance of this violence. What follows is an analysis of gender relations among Indo-Fijians with particular emphasis on the ideal roles and status of wives in order to provide the backdrop for a discussion of wife abuse.

The patriarchal, patrilineal, and patrivirilocal North Indian family pattern and ideology have generally established hegemonic influence among Indo-Fijians. The essential characteristics of the North Indian family are: male dominance and female subordination, males as the economic providers with females as the economic dependents, spatial and social confinement of women, male inheritance of family property, and females as reproducers of the male lineage and repositories of family honor (*izzat*) (Kishwar 1984; Mies 1980; Gupta 1976; Jeffery 1979).

Any analysis of gender relations and the status of women in the family among Indo-Fijians requires reference to the ideology of *purdah*[3] and to the family and material structure of the household. *Purdah* in the sense of complete veiling and seclusion of women is absent in Fiji, although it is undeniably present in its more subtle manifestations. No clear-cut distinctions between Hindu and Muslim forms of *purdah* as identified by Papanek (1973) and Jacobson and Wadley (1982) are discernible. *Purdah* as it is practiced among Indo-Fijians is a synthesis of the numerous variations shared by Hindu and Muslim communities in South Asia (Vatuk 1982).

The essential elements of *purdah* are the segregation of the sexes, the sexual protection of women, and the maintenance of family honor. It is this ideology that leads to the creation of separate spheres of existence for males and females: men belong to the public realm of economics and politics, women to the private domestic realm with their spatial movements restricted. Hence, women's role is largely confined to marriage, the performance of household chores, bearing and rearing children, and caring for menfolk. These separate spheres of existence result in women being denied access to the labor market; consequently, they are rendered economically dependent on males. The ideology of *purdah* also sets the parameters for the deferential relations between males and females and provides the guidelines for female behavior and demeanor. Since women are perceived as both sexually vulnerable and sexually impulsive, their sexual protection and control is of utmost importance; the honor of the entire family rests in the purity of its women.

Purdah ideology is integrally related to and supports a familial ideology that vests ultimate authority in the father or, in his absence, the eldest male in the household. Females and younger males are subject to the control of the male head to whom deference is given. This ideology of male supremacy in the family is reflected in the greater importance of male over female children. Male children are viewed as assets, since they will become the future economic providers and ensure the continuance of the patriline. Female children are viewed as economic and social liabilities, since they are economically dependent and pose a potential threat to the reputation of the family until husbands are found for them (Kishwar 1984; Mies 1980; Gupta 1976). Marriage is necessary and inevitable for women. Arranged marriage is the preferred and dominant form because of the limits on spatial mobility and social interactions and the strict segregation of the sexes.

The wifely role is preeminent in Hinduism and the Hindu law books; the *Dharma Sastras* (Rules of Right Conduct) provide concrete and explicit guidelines for women's roles as wives (Jacobson and Wadley 1977:20). The laws of Manu stress that women must always be controlled by men: daughters by fathers, wives by husbands, and widows by sons. In addition, husbands must be revered as gods despite their failings (Mies 1980:43). Kapadia reports that a woman's "only concern in life was to see that all her services needed by her husband were properly performed by her, the satisfaction of her husband being her sole joy in life" (1955:169). Blind worship of husbands is referred to as *pativrata* (one who worships her lord) and is "considered the highest ideal of womanhood in Hinduism" (Mies 1980:44). The lengths to which a wife must go in her duty to serve her husband is a constant theme in Muslim and Hindu sacred texts, popular literature and films, and folk and oral traditions, "often created and propagated by women" (Jacobson and Wadley 1977:125).

A recurring theme at Indo-Fijian weddings is the misfortune of the bride (i.e., the hardships and difficulties she will encounter in her conjugal home at the hands of her husband, mother-in-law, and sisters-in-law). Traditionally, a woman's wedding is a sad occasion for her; it is when she leaves the caring and protected environment of her natal family to take up residence in the strange, unknown, and sometimes cruel environment of her conjugal family. Many of the wedding rituals, particularly those performed by women, acknowledge and stress the future submissive and subordinate role of wives, the hardships imposed by tyrannical mothers-in-law, and the need for women to passively submit to these controls without struggle.

Similarly in Islam, marriage is encouraged and required of women in order to control their sexuality and enable them to realize their most important roles: wife, child rearer, and homemaker. Unmarried males and females pose a threat to the social order of Islam, since humans are believed to inherently possess animalistic sexual urges that need to be regulated and controlled (Minai 1981:12). The institution of marriage is recommended as the legitimate outlet for human sexual instinct and for the propagation of the human race (Maududi 1979:93).

Childbearing and child rearing are women's prime and unique roles in society, and it is through these activities that women make a contribution to society. Furthermore, a woman's natural function in life is to provide for the man "a place of peace and comfort" (Maududi 1979:138). In the Hadith (sayings of the Prophet), "women are assigned the position of fertile fields where men can sow seeds and watch them grow" (Ferdows and Ferdows 1983:57).

Since marriage in Islam is a civil contract, divorce is permissible, while in Hinduism marriage is a religious sacrament and divorce is therefore not permissible. However, Muslim women need the consent of husbands to obtain a divorce, whereas men need no such consent from their wives. Despite legal provisions for separation and divorce, marriage is ideally insoluble and permanent and divorce is considered abhorrent and is definitely discouraged among Hindus and Muslims in Fiji. Familial ideology not only discourages divorce but extols the suffering and sacrifice of women for the benefit of the family. A woman's salvation lies in uncomplaining service to her husband and children irrespective of the husband's bad character, his failure to provide adequate economic support, or his maltreatment of her. Total devotion, respect, obedience, and service to husbands is viewed as the true function of wives (Jacobson and Wadley 1977:124).

The privileged position of males within the family is reflected in the specified code of conduct regulating male/female interactions within the family. Respect, deference, and distance are the essential features of this code of conduct, supported by the ideology of *purdah*. Interactions between husbands and wives clearly reflect male dominance within the household. Respectful wives do not "answer back" or argue and generally maintain silence when anger and aggression are directed at them.

This familial ideology of female obedience, service, and subservience to men is further reinforced by the higher status of married women over unmarried women, women with children over childless women, women with sons over those without sons, and older women over younger women. As women get older, bear children, marry off their children, and become grandmothers, the relationship between a husband and wife becomes more egalitarian. Older women have more control over their own spatial movements, social interactions, behavior, and household decisions and often wield considerable power over younger women (Brown 1982, 1992).

The ideological support for patriarchy and patrilineality is reflected in the veneration of the mother. It is in the service and devotion to her children that a woman is honored and able to acquire social status and some degree of power (Basham 1974). While ultimate authority rests with males, in many instances older women are the ones who actually exercise this authority on behalf of the family. Senior women have a positive stake in their households and actively work to protect and reproduce the patriarchal, patrilocal family.

The Nature of Marital Violence

The vast majority of my informants have either been subjected to or threatened with violence at some time in their lives. This is not to claim that all women are equally threatened by or subjected to physical violence throughout their lives. Older women—that is, women with adult married children—are rarely if ever subjected to physical violence. However, violence pervades the lives of young married women and, occasionally, older women who have yet to consolidate their positions in the household.

The form and extent of physical violence imposed on wives extends from a slap, push, kick, or shove to solid punches. The most common and consistently used form of violence is slapping the face. Wives are also often pushed against walls, their heads are slammed against walls, and objects are thrown at them. The following case studies illustrate some of the reasons, context, and nature of violence imposed on Indo-Fijian wives.

Case Study 1: Sarita

Sarita is twenty-seven years old, married, with a four-year-old son, and working as a high school teacher. Her husband runs a small business, and the family rents a house in one of Suva's affluent suburbs. They have a live-in domestic worker who performs most of the household chores except cooking.

Sarita met her husband while she was attending the university in Suva, and hers is a "love marriage." While at the university she lived on campus because her parents live in another town. Prior to marriage she lived with her husband for one year; they decided to marry when she became pregnant. Her husband's parents were not happy about the marriage. In their opinion Sarita did not come from a "good" family and her character was "questionable" since she had lived with their son before marriage. Conflict continues to exist between Sarita and her in-laws.

Sarita and her husband often socialize with other young couples, attend Western-style parties, and frequent nightclubs and restaurants. Unlike many other Indo-Fijian women, Sarita drinks alcohol and sometimes smokes cigarettes, has an informal relationship with her husband, and interacts with him as an equal.

Sarita's husband beat her before their marriage, once they began living together. In later years the beatings became more frequent. On two occasions Sarita left her husband and stayed with a girlfriend; her husband harassed her and "begged" her to return. Each time he promised never to hit her again, so for her "son's sake" she returned to live with him.

According to Sarita, the main precipitating factor in the violence is that she "ask[s] him too many questions or criticize[s] his parents." However, when he is beating her other reasons also emerge, such as the fact that he does not want her to smoke or he suspects she is having an affair with his cousin. On other occasions he hits her because he does not want her to go out with her female friends at night, which Sarita occasionally does. On one occasion he beat Sarita because she complained that his mother was spreading rumors about her. While beating her he said, "You talk too much nowadays."

On another occasion Sarita discovered some love letters from a woman her husband had visited during an overseas trip. She confronted him and demanded to know who this woman was and whether she was the reason their phone bill was so high. When he refused to answer, Sarita kept screaming and demanding an answer. At this point he started hitting her, saying that his mother was right, that Sarita "had trapped him into marriage by getting pregnant." He punched her so hard that she fell against the door and hit her head. He then picked her up, threw her across the room, and started kicking her. Bear in mind that Sarita's husband is a big man almost twice her size.

Case Study 2: Rina

Rina is thirty years of age, married, with two small children, and working in a professional occupation. Her husband is a bank clerk, and they live with his parents and his unmarried, twenty-five-year-old sister.

Rina is originally from India, and her marriage was arranged. Since her family does not reside in Fiji, she feels isolated and without support. Her husband beats her, seldom takes her out, and taunts her. When she entered paid employment approximately three years prior to my interview with her, he took her earnings and gave her nothing. Her colleagues at work encouraged her to open her own bank account and not to give her earnings to her husband. Rina followed their advice and told her husband she wished to leave him and return to India with their children. Her husband responded by hiding her passport and informing her that he would never give his consent to take their children out of the country.

Rina's husband beats her for a variety of reasons. Sometimes he beats her when he is drunk and sometimes because his mother complains that Rina does not do any work and is argumentative and disrespectful. According to Rina, her mother-in-law mistreats her, makes her do all the cleaning and cooking for the entire household, and makes up stories about her. Occasionally Rina's husband beats her because she confronts him about love letters from other women or because he is generally dissatisfied with her.

The arguments usually commence when he comes home drunk and demands that Rina serve him dinner. Invariably he is dissatisfied with the dinner and starts abusing her. In response, Rina comments on his drunkenness, he slaps her, and both of them engage in verbal abuse. Then he starts beating her for her lack of respect, for opening her own bank account, and for arguing with his mother. Some of Rina's work colleagues have verified that she is beaten by her husband and that she often comes to work with bruises on her face, arms, and legs.

While he is beating her, Rina's husband often taunts her by saying, "What are you going to do? Where are you going to go? You have nowhere to go, no one wants you, even your family don't want you. You think you can save your money and go back to India—well, you can't."

These cases illustrate the reasons for which wives are beaten by husbands, which can be generally classified as suspected infidelity, insolence, not demonstrating the required deference toward husbands and mothers-in law, and not adequately performing wifely duties. Violence is used by husbands to demonstrate their anger and frustration, to keep women in their place, and, most important, to assert and display their power and dominant status in the household. The oft-quoted threat "*bahuth baath niklii ek jhapar de ga*" ("if you talk too much I'll give you a slap") frequently becomes a reality.

It is noteworthy that the same words and sentences are used by men as threats to control both wives and children. Often even the husband's tone in speaking to his wife is remarkably similar to that used by females and males when speaking to children. By contrast, wives respond to their husbands as they would to their fathers, by speaking in quiet, gentle tones that demonstrate their deference.

The precipitating factors for wife abuse are generally varied and confused. Complaints of mothers-in-law, as in Shanti's and Rina's cases, combined with alcohol consumption and general discontent with a wife's behavior can result in a man beating his wife. The initial trigger is often something trivial; if the wife answers back, the husband feels he is being provoked and all his dissatisfactions—including complaints from his mother about his wife's behavior—will emerge. However, neither mothers-in-law nor alcohol are sufficient explanations for wife abuse since wives are also beaten when husbands are sober and without encouragement from mothers-in-law. A more adequate explanation rests in the fundamental inequality between husbands and wives, an inequality that gives husbands the power and privilege to beat their wives.

The majority of my informants explained that they complied with and did not resist restrictions placed on them because they feared physical violence by their husbands. For example, many women are critical of their husbands' excessive consumption of liquor yet seldom openly communicate their disapproval because they fear being beaten. Even the threat of violence is a powerful mechanism for keeping wives within the guidelines of proper conduct. Comments such as "My husband would kill me," "My husband will cut my arms and legs off," or "I don't wish to be kicked and beaten" are common from wives even though not necessarily meant to be taken literally.

Despite the threat of violence combined with a powerful ideology demanding compliance, women are not necessarily passive or "pathetic" victims of an insidious system. Women are fully aware of their inferior position, the privileged position of their husbands, and the injustices of the social system. They are quick to articulate their grievances and express discontent to any sympathetic and willing listeners. Compliance coexists with resentment, discontent, and instances of insubordination. Women sometimes engage secretly in rule-breaking behavior; for example, some wives have affairs. The instances of misbehavior and the various strategies women employ to create more space for themselves indicate that women do not simply inherit the culture and accept it. Rather, they reconstruct and recreate it through their everyday interactions.

In many cases, women repeatedly engage in the same behavior that they were beaten for in the past, as in Sarita's and Shanti's cases. Sarita argues with her husband even while she is being beaten, and sometimes she deliberately taunts her husband with comments that exacerbate his anger. Wives like these are asserting their right to argue with their husbands and are refusing to accept total male control even at the risk of being beaten.

Tensions of Modernization

The growth of the Fijian economy, particularly during the 1970s, generated increased employment opportunities for women and greater prospects for a higher standard of living. Dual income families became more attractive and working women were sought as marriage partners. To reap the benefits of women's paid employment, ideological readjustments were made whereby women are permitted to engage in certain types of paid employment not markedly inconsistent with the requirements of *purdah*. Occupations in which interactions with unrelated males are minimal, no night work is entailed, and women can be supervised are considered acceptable.[4] Hence, some 14 percent of urban Indo-Fijian women are engaged in paid employment (Fiji Bureau of Statistics 1986).

Women's increased participation in paid employment and education, combined with increasing Western modernist influences, has meant that traditional familial ideology is slowly being undermined. Especially among the young middle classes, husband/wife relationships in many ways resemble Western nuclear families. For example, interactions are more informal and relaxed, women are not as constrained spatially and socially, husbands and wives spend their leisure time together, and couples espouse a belief in egalitarian "partnering" relationships.

The "modern" Westernized Indo-Fijian woman, often with tertiary education and in paid employment, is increasingly asserting and exercising her rights in this kind of relationship. Economically independent women like Sarita assume they have a right to confront their husbands, demand answers, and argue with them. By contrast, the "modern" Indo-Fijian male (like Sarita's husband), by resorting to violence, demonstrates a reluctance to totally surrender ultimate power and control. Younger Westernized women view this use of physical violence by males as unacceptable and as an important symbol of women's subordinate status and position in the family and community. Women like Sarita question the right of their husbands to subject them to violence and are humiliated and angered by it.

Yet even among these women small doses of violence are tolerated and explained away. They accept the right of males to "slap" them occasionally as a consequence of the enduring traditional ideologies that remain influential although declining in importance. The competing and conflicting ideologies are a source of confusion in gender relations and of tension and conflict in these "modern" families.

The problem of coexisting conflicting and competing ideologies is not easily resolved. The old order does not simply disappear to be replaced by a new order. Instead, a more complex situation emerges with elements of both orders coexisting. In these instances, physical violence is used as a supplementary mechanism of control, and ideology plays a crucial role in women's acceptance of the use of physical violence by men.

Wife Abuse: Recommended, Accepted, and Sanctioned

The vast majority of men and women accept, seldom question, and even positively sanction men's right to control "their" women by the occasional slap, punch, or push. The community views a wife's overstepping the boundaries of proper conduct as sufficient justification for the imposition of physical violence. An abused women who "talks too much" or who aggravates her husband or his kin is given little sympathy, since such behavior is considered a form of provocation (Chowning 1985; Bradley 1985). Wife beating is the right and prerogative of husbands and the fate of wives if wives are to be kept in line and properly controlled. On many occasions I heard women recommend a few good slaps to bring certain women back into line. Men often remark that women whose husbands treat them too easily have become spoiled, or they comment, "His wife should be given a few kicks," or "If she were my wife, I'd give her a good beating."

Men who do not beat their wives, especially if their wives are perceived to be "deviant" in some way, are ridiculed by both men and women. In one case a man whose wife ran away with another man was ridiculed for being "weak" and "pathetic." The story goes that "even when he went and brought his wife back, he didn't give her a beating! But her brother gave her a good beating" since she had shamed not only her conjugal family but also her natal family.

Women regard men who do not occasionally slap their wives as being "under the wife's thumb." The English phrase "petticoat government" is used among middle-class men and women and refers to relationships in which the wife is assumed to be dominant because the male never subjects her to any violence. Another common phrase used by males and females to describe relationships in which wives are not kept under strict control is "*uu to apan aurat ke muur pe charhai ke rakhis*" ("he has allowed his wife to sit on top of his head").

Yet, extreme cases of physical violence (e.g., where the victim requires medical attention) are not condoned. While wife beating is acceptable, wife battering is discouraged and frowned on. On numerous occasions I heard women and men criticize husbands who beat their wives on a weekly basis, those who beat pregnant women, or those who caused their wives serious injury. Even mothers who may have initially incited their sons to beat their wives sometimes intervene to stop their sons from crossing the boundaries of acceptable violence, with comments such as, "Don't hit her too much," or "There's no need to keep hitting her," or "She's learned her lesson." At the same time, these phrases imply that a little hitting is acceptable.

Women's acquiescence and contribution to their own subordination demonstrate the power and persuasiveness of traditional gender ideologies. It could be argued that they have fully internalized these ideologies, since women are part of the system that continually reinforces the status quo. But while ideological subordination of women is an important factor in explaining why women accept and even encourage male violence, it can only provide a partial explanation. Whenever women get the chance, they "cheat" the system by harboring resentment, expressing discontent, and engaging in acts of insubordination, even when it results in violence. Their willingness to break the rules is evidence that their ideological subordination is neither thorough nor complete (Jeffery 1979).

Explanations based on the ideological subordination of women also fail to take account of the fact that women are not just pathetic victims of an overwhelming system and may have a positive stake in maintaining the status quo. Senior women of the household, for example, enjoy the respect of younger members (male and female) and wield considerable power and authority over younger women, especially daughters-in-law. Sons have a particularly close relationship with their mothers and show immense respect and affection for them. In fact, as sons grow older they are likely to intervene and protect their mothers from any violence imposed by their fathers. Usually a husband stops hitting his wife when their sons are old enough to protect her.

At this later period of the life cycle a woman reaps the benefits of having endured the hardships of being a young wife and daughter-in-law in a strange and sometimes hostile environment; in turn, she is likely to impose similar hardships on other women (Brown 1982, 1992). Her suffering, patience, and conformity as a young woman are rewarded when her sons bring home wives for her to supervise and control. As a senior woman her loyalties and interests are invested in the households of her sons. As such, she actively works to protect the reputation and honor of her family and to reproduce the status quo.

Such a system creates divisions between women in the household rather than generating solidarity against men. The divergent interests of women partially explain why women encourage or recommend physical violence against other women, especially their female affines. Stereotypical images of tyrannical mothers-in-law, wicked sisters-in-law, and oppressed daughters-in-law in the popular culture of Hindi films reflect the competition and conflict among mothers-in-law and daughters-in-law, among the wives of brothers, and among sisters-in-law. Mothers compete with wives for their sons' affections. Wives of brothers compete for their mothers-in-law's support and patronage and for a greater share of the household resources for themselves and their children. Sisters compete with their brothers' wives for affection. These conflicts are structural barriers that prevent women from realizing their common interests and from taking joint action against either males or the system.

At another level the system that oppresses women also cares for them and protects them from the harsh realities of the outside world. Increasing unemployment, lack of job opportunities, and the absence of an adequate state welfare system mean that women, especially those not in paid employment, are dependent on the family-based household for their livelihood. It is no wonder that young and old women have a positive stake in ensuring the survival of the traditional household. The economic support provided by the males of the family is a powerful mechanism ensuring that women will conform and actively work to perpetuate the system. Without this financial support women could easily be rendered destitute.

Against this background, the nonconformity and insubordination of younger, economically independent modern wives makes sense, for unlike older and more traditional wives, they do not have a positive stake in maintaining the status quo since they are not economically dependent on males for their livelihood. Because they are members of modern, Westernized nuclear families, their sons will set up separate households and are therefore unlikely to bring wives for them to control and supervise in the future. Furthermore, modern younger women living in nuclear households can afford to espouse a general aversion to male violence against women since they are not subjected to the same degree of tension, conflict, and competition that is suffered by women living in traditional family-based households. The costs of insubordination for young modern wives are not as great as for the more traditional wives since they do not have a similar investment in sustaining the system. No rewards for patience and conformity await them in the future.

Abused Wives: What Options?

The powerlessness of wives becomes glaringly obvious when we search for options available to victims of violence. In short, the vast majority of wives have few options but to endure the violence, wait for seniority, and hope to be reborn as males in their next life.[5]

The taunts of husbands like Rina's are generally true. The majority of women have nowhere to go since they are economically dependent on their husbands and their families prefer that they remain married. Such women are locked into violent relationships because of an ideology that stresses the permanence of marriage and a lack of alternatives. This explains why economically dependent wives are hesitant to confront their husbands and to fight back.

Returning to her family of origin is seldom a viable option for an abused woman. Her parents may have died or become economically dependent on their sons. Although brothers traditionally have the responsibility for maintaining sisters and their children if their husbands divorce them, in reality, economic pressures and family tensions make this unlikely. Occasionally, however, women do return to their natal homes if their marriages are exceptionally violent and no children are involved. In one instance a woman without children who needed hospital treatment on numerous occasions and became very ill was finally taken back by her financially independent parents. More often than not, however, parents will attempt to talk a violent son-in-law (sometimes through his parents) out of such behavior and will coax their daughter into perservering with the marriage. Marriage is meant to be permanent, and women's suffering within marriage is taken for granted.

Even modern, Westernized working wives who are not totally dependent on their husbands are hesitant to leave violent marriages. As is the case with Sarita, they leave their husbands for short periods but almost invariably return, only to be subjected to violence again. On her income alone, Sarita's son was likely to be denied the opportunities he could otherwise have. Although fathers are generally required to continue providing support for their children after divorce, support orders are difficult to enforce in Fiji, as they are in many other countries. Divorce for women like Sarita could also mean the risk of losing custody of their children.

Because divorce in Fiji, except after a five-year period of separation, can only be obtained through claiming fault by one party, the potential exists for women to be seriously disadvantaged. If women are proven to be at fault—as in failing to fulfill marital obligations—they could be denied maintenance or custody of their children. Hence, fear of losing their children and concern about their own welfare are among the main reasons women are reluctant to leave violent husbands.

There are other reasons as well. Young modern women claim they cannot contemplate divorce because it would bring shame on their natal families, they would be the targets of gossip and rumor, and they would receive little support from their families. This lack of support is evident in the greater proportion of Indo-Fijian females, as compared with ethnic Fijian women, who receive welfare support, statistics confirmed by officers of both welfare groups. The majority of women receiving welfare whom I spoke with claimed they had been deserted, thrown out, or maltreated by their husbands and in-laws and that their own families either did not want them or could not afford to take them back. The fate of many divorced Indo-Fijian women who end up as destitutes requiring welfare and food handouts from charities acts as a powerful deterrent to divorce. At the same time it keeps women submissive and tolerant even of violent marriages.

For some women, like Shanti, the absence of viable alternatives when their patience and tolerance is finally exhausted leaves them only one option: suicide. By committing suicide they communicate to their families, friends, and acquaintainces the suffering they have endured and their lack of alternatives. They also may attract some sympathy. Suicide by Indo-Fijian women appears primarily to be an escape from an intolerable life.

A disturbing 203 cases of suicide by Indo-Fijian women were recorded by the Fiji Bureau of Statistics between the years 1977 and 1982 compared with 25 suicides among indigenous Fijian females. Indo-Fijian women who commit suicide are mainly under the age of thirty, an age that coincides with the period in their life when they are likely to have the least power and control (Haynes 1984). Haynes found that the major precipitating factors for female suicides (where families chose to provide reasons) were marital and family (in-laws) conflict (1984:435). The choice of suicide as a solution by so many Indo-Fijian women is an indictment of the insidious system under which they are forced to live their rather precarious lives.

Conclusion

The threat and use of physical violence is a powerful mechanism by which husbands exercise and assert power and control over wives. While the enduring influence and persuasiveness of familial ideology ensures female submission with little male intervention, the occasional use and persistent threat of violence consolidates male dominance and female subordination within the family. The presence of violence as part of the taken-for-granted world of being female is indicative of the status of women in Indo-Fijian society.

NOTES

The research for this chapter was undertaken as part of a wider study on gender relations among Indo-Fijians in Suva. The data were gathered between 1983 and 1987. No reference is made to the May 1987 military coup in Fiji as the data were gathered prior to the coup. Much gratitude is owed to Dorothy Counts for her encouragement, insightful comments, and suggestions on an earlier draft of this essay. Thanks are also due to Ruth Walker for her typing. An earlier version of this chapter dealing with domestic violence in general appeared as "Rule by the 'Danda': Domestic Violence amongst Indo-Fijians" in *Pacific Studies* 13:3 (July 1990): 43–62. I am grateful for permission from the journal to use that material here. Quotations are from my field notes unless otherwise indicated.

1. This chapter is dedicated to the memory of Shanti, who was a gentle and unassuming woman. She was not just another one of my informants but a friend of the family and someone I had known for nearly ten years.

2. This is not to imply that no divisions exist or that Indo-Fijians constitute a homogenous group. On the contrary, divisions between Hindu/Muslim, North Indian/South Indian, urban/rural, and rich/poor all exist. Hinduism and Islam are practiced with great fervor, and marriage is endogamous by religion.

3. *Purdah* literally means "curtain," although in common usage it refers to the various modes of secluding women either by confining them to an enclosed space or by veiling them, the strict segregation of the sexes, the "symbolic sheltering" (Papanek 1973) of women, and a moral code of conduct (Jeffery 1979; Vatuk 1982). *Purdah* is practiced throughout North India in Hindu and Muslim communities (Jacobson and Wadley 1977; Jeffery 1979; Papanek 1973; Sharma 1980), although distinctions between Hindu and Muslim patterns are known to exist. The ideology and numerous manifestations of *purdah* are deeply ingrained in the South Asian sociocultural system and have been retained (albeit in a modified form) among Indo-Fijians. *Purdah* can be viewed as the major organizing principle for the controls on women's sexuality, spatial movements, social interactions, behavior, demeanor, and the sexual division of labor. For a more detailed discussion of *purdah* ideology, see Lateef (1992).

4. For more details on appropriate and inappropriate occupations, see Lateef (1986).

5. When I asked women the question "What do you hope to return as in your next life?" virtually all replied "Male."

REFERENCES CITED

Basham, Arthur L. 1974. *The Wonder That Was India.* London: Fontana.

Bradley, S. C. 1985. "Attitudes and Practices Relating to Marital Violence among the

Tolai of East New Britain." In *Domestic Violence in Papua New Guinea.* Ed. Susan Toft. 32–71. Papua New Guinea Law Reform Monograph No. 3. Boroko.

Brown, Judith K. 1982. "Cross-Cultural Perspectives on Middle-Aged Women." *Current Anthropology* 23:143–56.

———. 1992. "Lives of Middle-Aged Women." In *In Her Prime: A New View of Middle-Aged Women.* 2d ed. Ed. Virginia Kerns and Judith K. Brown. 17–30. Urbana: University of Illinois Press.

Chowning, Ann. 1985. "Kove Women and Violence: The Context of Wife Beating in a West New Britain Society." In *Domestic Violence in Papua New Guinea.* Ed. Susan Toft. 72–91. Papua New Guinea Law Reform Monograph No. 3. Boroko.

Ferdows, Adele K., and Amir H. Ferdows. 1983. "Women in Shi' i Fiqh: Images through the Hadith." In *Women and Revolution in Iran.* Ed. G. Nashat. 55–68. Boulder, Colo.: Westview Press.

Fiji Bureau of Statistics. 1986. *Report of the Census of the Population.* Suva: Government Printer.

Gupta, A. R. 1976. *Women in Hindu Society.* New Delhi: Jyotsna Prakashan.

Haynes, Ruth. 1984. "Suicide in Fiji: A Preliminary Study." *British Journal of Psychiatry* 145:433–38.

Jacobson, Doranne, and Susan Wadley. 1977. *Women in India: Two Perspectives.* Columbia, Mo.: South Asia Books.

Jayawardena, Chandra. 1968. "Migration and Social Change: A Survey of Indian Communities Overseas." *Geographical Review* 58:426–42.

———. 1980. "Culture and Ethnicity in Guyana and Fiji." *Man* 15 (3): 430–50.

Jeffery, Patricia. 1979. *Frogs in a Well: Indian Women in Purdah.* London: Zed Press.

Kapadia, Kanailal M. 1955. *Marriage and Family in India.* London: Oxford University Press.

Kishwar, Madhu. 1984. "Some Aspects of Bondage." In *In Search of Answers: Indian Women's Voices from Manushi.* Ed. Madhu Kishwar and Ruth Vanita. 230–41. London: Zed Press.

Lal, Brij. 1983. *The Girmitiyas: The Origins of the Fiji Indians.* Canberra: Australian National University Press.

Lateef, Shireen. 1986. "Because They Have Nice Uniforms: The Career Aspirations of Schoolgirls in Suva, Fiji." In *Development in the Pacific: What Women Say.* 45–47. Canberra: Australian Council for Overseas Aid.

———. 1990. "Rule by the 'Danda': Domestic Violence amongst Indo-Fijians." *Pacific Studies* 13 (3): 43–62.

Maududi, Sajed A. 1979. *Purdah and the Status of Women in Islam.* 4th ed. Lahore, Pakistan: Islamic Publications.

Mies, Maria. 1980. *Indian Women and Patriarchy: Conflicts and Dilemmas of Students and Working Women.* Trans. Sarah K. Sarkar. New Delhi: Concept Publishing Co.

Minai, Naila. 1981. *Women in Islam: Traditions and Transition in the Middle East.* New York: Seaview Books.

Papanek, Hanna. 1973. "Purdah: Separate Worlds and Symbolic Shelter." *Comparative Studies in Society and History* 15:289–325.

Sharma, Ursula. 1980. *Women, Work, and Property in North-West India.* London: Tavistock.

Vatuk, Sylvia. 1982. "Purdah Revisited: A Comparison of Hindu and Muslim Interpretations of the Current Meaning of Purdah in South Asia." In *Separate Worlds: Studies of Purdah in South Asia.* Ed. Hanna Papanek and Gail Minnault. 54–78. Delhi: Chanakya Publishing.

SIXTEEN

Wife Abuse and the Political System: A Middle Eastern Case Study

Mary Elaine Hegland

> *If a wife goes bad, said the mullah in explaining the Arabic of Surah 4, verse 34 of the Qor'an, or if there is a difference between husband and wife, first he should scold her and speak with her. If that did not work, he should become* ghar *with her—stop interacting with her. If that did not work, he should administer corporal punishment—but there should be no resulting marks on her body—it should not turn black and blue.*

Although wife abuse is common in Iran, it is a subject that has received almost no attention from scholars and little has been written on it. The purpose of this chapter is to examine the problem in Iran, to show the connection between wife beating and the Iranian political system, and to raise questions for further research. The data on which this analysis is based come from my own research as well as from published sources. The two case histories of wife abuse presented exemplify social process in a political system characterized by arbitrariness and the need to dominate. The degree to which a woman could be abused depended on political skill, that is, the power relationships and resources that people were able to muster in their continuous effort to control others and to avoid being manipulated themselves.

The Research

My data are from my 1978–79 field research in the village of Aliabad in southwestern Iran and other periods spent in Iran between 1966 and 1978 and from my interviews in the United States between 1987 and 1990 with mainly middle-aged Iranian women who had received some of their education in America as well as their mothers and aunts visiting from Iran. During my research in Iran between June 1978 and December 1979 I did not interview my informants specifically about wife beating, but my interviews in the United States did focus on the topic.[1] The time frame for most of the events

I describe here is June 1978 to December 1979, although I also recount incidents that happened within the memory of informants. As it is not possible to ascertain current conditions in Iran, I use the past tense in my discussion.

The Village Political System and Wife Abuse

In 1978 and 1979 Aliabad was a large village of some three thousand people located half an hour by bus from the outskirts of the city of Shiraz, capital of the province of Fars in southwestern Iran. Local political factions battled for control over agricultural land and the powerful position of headman for the absentee landlord. Because there was only a weak centralized government before the oil boom of the 1960s and 1970s, local factions had to rely on the strength of their fighting men for political power. During the relative anarchy of the revolutionary period between 1978 and 1980, local police control declined and competition between local factions in Aliabad resumed. (For further discussion of the political system of Aliabad, see Hooglund [Hegland] 1982.)

In the local political system, young men were valued as fighters while women were valued as reproducers and as the means of creating or solidifying relations with other groups through marriage. Women's work and hospitality were invaluable, and their role was central in producing support for their kin in the local system, where repetitive and intense social interaction was required to maintain political alliances. (For further discussion of the roles of women in the Aliabad political system see Hegland 1986b.)

Although devalued as persons, women were valued as resources (Vieille 1979). If men could control women, they could utilize their labor, so important in the political process. Women were also valuable as a means of demonstrating control and authority. The protection of dependents of both sexes and their submission and obedience effectively signaled to other political actors the dominance and political strength of a political leader and his faction.[2]

In this fluctuating, authoritarian village political system, men demonstrated their political superiority by intimidating others. To make others—enemies, followers, and dependents—afraid of them, they engaged in acts of violence. It was incumbent on those in authority to instill "respect"—or, more accurately, fear—in those for whom they were responsible in order to extract the required compliance and correct behavior. Children and women were chastised in order to force them to live up to the expectations of the system. According to Erika Friedl, who has conducted research on women's issues and child rearing in Iran, "The beating of children is an educational device. In my village research site, children have to be beaten to keep them on the right path and if a woman misbehaves, she has to be beaten for the same reason. Beating is a teaching device, but it's also a means of dealing with subordination and dissent" (personal communication 1989).

In order to carry on their political and economic struggles, the older generation needed to control the younger generation. Young men were needed for their labor and their fighting abilities. In addition to the political work a young man might carry out for his father, sons were a main source of money, work, and other resources for many older couples. Young women were needed for their labor power and for their reproductive capacities.

Parents obtained a wife for their son, but they often sought to minimize the contact and affection between the couple, fearing that the wife would compete for the resources produced by him. By physically abusing his wife the son served the purposes of the older generation and the kin group as a whole.

In Aliabad, people were the most important resource. Control over property was not secure; rather, one needed people and their connections to get and keep control over land and other resources. Women were a means of gathering people and connections and were, therefore, valuable and carefully controlled. Often women learned the political importance of controlling people and sought to build their own power by influencing others.[3]

The treatment of a young bride was sufficient to quell any thoughts of independence. Generally, she improved her situation and gained power by fulfilling her duties and producing children. Whereas a younger woman was kept in line through force and intimidation, an older woman developed a stake in her husband's family and kinship group. Because of her children, she was willing to do whatever she could to support the interests of her husband's family. She gained power in proportion to her effectiveness in working for the family and keeping family members under control. Young women and young men learned that the best way to gain power and a more comfortable life was to manipulate the system, to build up a power base, to become the people who controlled and intimidated others. From being a weak and subservient bride herself, a woman often turned into a mother-in-law who tightly controlled and even aided in the abuse of new daughters-in-law (Brown 1982, 1992; Mernissi 1987; Rassam 1980). Older women exchanged their services as controllers of young women for acceptance and status in their husbands' family. A woman wanted her husband's and the community's approval that would result from good management of her daughter-in-law. She also wanted to retain the devotion of her son rather than lose it to her daughter in-law.

Marriage, Kinship, and the Expectations of Women

"When I was born, the minute they told my mother it was a girl she began to cry bitterly. She refused to feed me for three days. She was ashamed in front of her family-in-law. But my aunts were happy and showing the baby to everyone. Then my aunts tried to tell her—you should be ashamed, she's a lovely baby, you should be happy—so she gave up and fed me. She thought it was shameful for an important man to have a daughter." These words of an urban friend illustrate the lesson learned by girls at an early age: that they are valued less than boys. Girls were not expected to promote their own interests but to be available to others for service. They were raised to be homebound, obedient, and extremely concerned about their reputations.

A number of factors put the wife into a subservient and dependent position in relation to her husband. Girls were usually relatively young at marriage—ten to twelve was not unusual (Guppy 1988:44; Haeri 1983:242, 243). An age difference of ten or more years between bride and groom was typical. The bride usually had a lower level of education than the groom. Most girls were removed from school at puberty and were therefore unable to obtain an education that might enable them to support themselves.[4] Young women were carefully guarded, married young, and then subdued as new wives. Therefore, they generally bowed to the wishes of the older generation in forming a contract between families.

The requirement of virginity on the part of the bride caused girls to be sheltered, isolated, and inexperienced in dealing with others outside of a small group of family, kin, and neighbors. Traditionally, Iranian women were not allowed to make decisions concerning their own lives (Farmanfarmaian 1976).[5] Every effort was made to keep women in a position of economic dependence and therefore unable to leave the control of fathers, husbands, or brothers.

If a woman were to work, the male in charge of her would be considered unable to support her, a shameful state of affairs. Although girls from less economically comfortable families worked in the local carpet shop, they were taken out before marriage.[6] Only some twelve adult women out of a village of about three thousand did any work for money outside of the home. All except one of these women were single, widowed, or the wives of men who could not support them.

Village women were isolated from contact with outsiders and encapsulated in a watchful group of female guardians composed of affines, relatives, and neighbors (Friedl 1983:222). Such isolation restricted their access to potentially helpful connections and to the examples set by more independent women. They had little or no perception of alternatives.

Women were supposed to stay at home as much as possible, turning to close neighbors and relatives for companionship. Women, especially those who were younger and politically more valuable, could only leave the village in the company of relatives. After extracting a promise of secrecy, one village woman told me of her friendship with a city woman whom she visited periodically and who helped her out with little gifts. This type of friendship was unusual.

Men were raised to be aggressive, to devalue women and their activities, to use violence to get what they wanted, and to demonstrate the power and strength required for political survival. Men were expected to keep control over their womenfolk; failure to do so meant a loss of standing for the entire family. Many men were willing to use corporal punishment to extract obedience and maintain control, and they received social support when doing so.[7]

Most women were not able to get away from abuse. For women, beatings emphasized their position of subservience and dependence; they must tolerate abuse and learn to live with the situation. Some did not take wife beating very seriously. Others might counsel patience, saying that this is what women have to live with. People were not eager to intervene. Abuse kept wives relatively cowed and acquiescent. Forcible defloration on the wedding night, subsequent intercourse forced on the bride by the groom, the eventual submission of wives to unwanted sexual intercourse, and beatings were all acts of dominance from the male point of view and acts of submission from the female point of view. These were repeated reminders to women of their positions of relative powerlessness and the necessity of obedience to their husbands and to others in authority over them.

A woman generally had to come to terms with a violent relationship without external help. Rarely would she be able to divorce and support herself. Separation was possible only if her father or brother were willing to take on the economic burden and the embarrassment of sheltering her. Separation and divorce were shameful; and, as she was no longer a virgin, a divorcée would enter a second marriage with even less leverage than she had enjoyed in her first.

The requirement that women must protect the reputation, the *qaybat,* of the family generally served to keep them quiet about any abuse. They were reluctant to talk to others about how their husbands treated them. Ziba, in the case study discussed below, denied the abuse when her mother asked her about it.[8] The repeated invasions of their persons, the attacks against their bodies, which they felt forced to tolerate, and the stories of the beatings and forced sexual relations endured by other women formed for wives a bleak image of their lives and the relative hopelessness of changing their situation.

The Iranian kinship system is bilateral, with a couple generally maintaining ties with both sides of the family. Village endogamy was the rule. The association between a young woman and her own family was usually close. Shortly after marriage a bride was expected to visit her parents' home for a few days.

A wife was not to complain of mistreatment from her husband. Her husband was expected to maintain complete authority over her, and her father had no right to interfere. However, during her marriage a woman maintained her connection with her natal family and usually visited often at their home. Since the relationship continued, her father and brother were assumed to still care for her and to be concerned about her welfare. It did not speak well of a man's position and power if his daughter or sister were consistently mistreated and others in the community were aware of it. Should it come to the attention of her father that her husband was beating her excessively, her father might provide a refuge for her. He would not take any action against the husband, however, for the husband had full authority to treat his wife as he wished. Moreover, parents wanted their daughters to marry and fathers did not wish to become involved in controversy over their daughter's treatment.

The result of these contradictory ideas was ambivalence about responsibility for married women. This ambivalence lent itself to manipulation and negotiation between a woman's husband and her male relatives. The outcome of the negotiations depended on the relative power of the husband versus the father or brother.

Wife abuse, then, was a result of the hierarchical and violent nature of the political system and, in turn, served to perpetuate it. Beatings intimidated the bride and kept her reproductive powers and labor under the control of her husband and his family. Abuse effectively taught young women that the best way to beat the system was to join it and become manipulators and abusers—often through their sons. Wife abuse became one more arena for men to demonstrate or jockey for political power.

Wife Beating in Iran

Iranian men beat their wives and sisters when the women threatened to step outside the parameters of the hierarchical, authoritarian system. When wives disobeyed husbands or talked back to them, when they did not immediately and cheerfully perform the labor required of them, when they were not sufficiently submissive and sympathetic to in-laws, then they were punished.

Correct behavior was not enough; correct *affect* also was owed to superiors. Brothers were in charge of sisters and were responsible for their correct behavior toward other males as well as their obedience to superiors—including themselves. Beatings reminded women of their role and their duties and of their relatively defenseless position in the social system.

Wife beating was common in Iran. Almost every Iranian I questioned in the United States had stories of abuse to relate. According to a city woman who had visited a number of villages and was on close terms with a number of village women who came to work for her as maids, "Among villagers, wife beating is very, very common; they do it all the time. In my country it is common among poor people. Naneh Kayvan (her maid and close friend from a village) said all villagers beat up their wives" (personal communication 1989).

Ethnographic short stories (actual occurrences written in short story form) support these observations. In Friedl's book we read of a brother who beat his sister for greeting her cousin in public and of another brother who beat his sister for talking back (1989:48, 132). Husbands beat their wives because they are disobedient, insubordinate, or bad tempered; because they talk back or complain about the husband's mother and sister; as a result of complaints from the husband's sister; to reprimand about adultery; or because the husband felt upset and frustrated (Friedl 1989:50, 55, 64, 69, 84, 94, 95, 226). There are some who argue that wife beating does not occur in urban areas or among well-educated peoples (e.g., Bauer 1985:173). There is, however, evidence that it occurs in towns and cities as well as villages and is common among all classes.[9]

Wife Beating in Aliabad

Wife beating was not discussed openly in Aliabad. On one occasion I was present when a young woman wept softly as she told her older neighbor about abuse from her husband. When I was living in a second courtyard, a young woman told me about some episodes of physical abuse from her husband and that she had wept in frustration and repeatedly hit her head against the wall. In thinking about his upcoming wedding, a friend revealed the fear that he too might come to beat his wife since his father beat his mother.

Two cases that came to my attention resulted in separation. First is the case of Ziba, who told me about her problems with her husband when I visited her father's home during her stay there. From this story it can be seen how Ziba cleverly obtained what she wanted from living up to the expectations of a "passive" and obedient daughter. In the second case, Goltaj's relatives told me about her situation with her husband. In both cases the relative political power of the protagonists was related to the outcome of their conflict over the wife abuse.

Ziba

I was married two years ago. . . . When I went, I had earrings, bracelets, and other jewelry. My husband's sister took them from me. She said, "The price of gold is going up—let me sell them for you and give you the money"—and then she never gave me the money. My mother-in-law took the money that was given to me at the time of my wedding. When the baby was born she took the money that was given to me at this time too.

My husband is twenty-two; he works at the gravel factory. When they get extra money from their shares and he buys me a lamb so I get meat, my mother-in-law is jealous. She's jealous of anything I get. I haven't had a new *chador* [veil] or anything else since I was married—my mother-in-law won't allow it. She won't allow her son to visit my parents. She says, "What do you want to do there?"

When I wash the baby's clothes, she asks me, "Why are you constantly washing the baby's clothes?" If I'm washing clothes and the baby is lying in the sun, she won't pick her up—even though the baby is her son's child. She complains to her son, "Look, she comes and washes clothes in the *hoze* [small courtyard pool]." Where *should* I wash them?

At first he believed his mother, but then he came to realize it was his mother's fault. He gets 3,500 tomans a month.[10] Someone who gets this salary should have his own rooms by now, should have a home. But his father buys and sells animals. His father says to him, "Lend me some money; I want to buy an animal"—and then doesn't give the money back.

He used to come home from the factory and would laugh and joke with me a couple of hours, I swear! But then they said bad things about me. They said, "Your wife is no good." Then he would come home and go over to their room. I would wait without eating dinner—I felt it was better to eat together—and then when he came back at midnight, he said his mother had pressured him into eating dinner there. They said bad things about me so that he would come home from the factory and stay over there until bedtime and even then when he came home he wouldn't talk to me, as they had told him not to. What sort of a life is this? A person is alone all the time and then even in the evening alone, going to sleep alone to wake up in the morning and be alone.

I never told my mother how it was for me. When the neighbors told her, and she asked me about it, I'd say they were lying.

Then on that day, the father came home shouting and swearing and said the shepherd had taken the animals to drink and two of his lambs had fallen in the water and drowned. They told me and I didn't say anything. He kept on shouting and going on.

When he came home, they told him that two of the lambs had died and I wasn't sorry about it, I didn't take it hard. He beat me from eight at night and continued to beat me until twelve midnight. At twelve o'clock I fell asleep without being aware of anything, not even the thought of my father and mother.

When I woke up I was ill, and I kept vomiting—I hadn't eaten dinner or lunch the day before. They took me to my father's and my parents took me to the hospital. My husband stayed with me the first two days in the hospital. All of the doctors and nurses came to ask me how I got bruises all over my face and body. I said I fell down a stairs—they doubted it. His mother and father scolded him because he stayed with me. They kept telling him to get a divorce. He said to them, "I haven't gotten tired of this wife, I want my wife, I want this wife."

When I got out of the hospital, I came to stay with my parents. His parents kept encouraging him to get a divorce. At first, at night he ate supper here at my parents' house and then went there to sleep. But his parents scolded him. He wanted to move to another home, but they wouldn't let him, so he stopped going home after work. He wanted to move in with his mother's brother on the other side of the highway. His uncle had told me, "I know what my sister's like—come and live with us." So he took a pickup truck to his parents' house to get his stuff. They wouldn't let him take it. Then they fought with the uncle who then fought with my husband, saying, "Why are your parents like this?" Finally, the aunt came over to my parent's house to get me to come back. They want me back now so that their son will come back. But I wouldn't go, and then the aunt fought with them.

I won't go until my husband comes back. I will only go if my father tells me to go. They won't let me have any of my clothes and things. Finally my parents told him, "She doesn't have any clothes; she has to wear her sister's clothes," so he got me a blouse and a couple of loose house pants, but no shoes. Now I'm waiting to see what my husband and my father will say. Now I'm in my father's house. I'll do whatever he says.

It's because of his parents. Whenever he beat me, it was the parents who ordered him to do it. He always swore his parents ordered him to do it. He was always sorry afterwards. He would realize his parents were wrong. I used to work so hard. I swept my mother-in-law's house and did so much.

In July 1979 I had gone over to the home of Ziba's parents to interview her father, who had been head of the peasants in the village. Ziba's mother said something about marrying with strangers—her son-in-law was from the upper section of the village and not a relative. The people up there were rougher, the mother felt. The fact that there were no respected elders in that neighborhood was also a problem, according to Ziba's mother. Although Ziba herself blamed her in-laws, her mother felt Ziba's husband was also at fault.

"Ziba and the baby have been here for forty days—and he has never asked about his daughter. Some people just don't care about their children."

Sometime later, as I was hurrying through a village alleyway, I heard a call; Ziba had seen me and urged me to come up and see her new home. She was pleased with her modest, second-story room. Now that she and her husband were away from the influence of his parents, she indicated, things were much better. In spite of abuse, not all women were entirely cowed. Ziba managed to get a home for herself and her husband away from his parents, against their will. The same political system in which women were used as a means of forming alliances between families also allowed them to use their intermediate position to gain their own aims.

Ziba's in-laws felt threatened when their son spent so much enjoyable time with his wife, and they tried to turn him against Ziba. Probably, they feared loss of control over his salary. Knowing that people who spend time and eat together develop mutual feelings of closeness and obligation, his parents tried to limit the time their son spent with Ziba and increase the time he spent with them. They also told him to beat her.

Ziba did not tell her parents about the abuse and, in fact, denied it when they questioned her. However, her husband's parents became frightened when Ziba was badly injured and took her home to her father, who was politically more powerful than her father-in-law. As a proper young woman, Ziba behaved passively, saying, "I'm in my father's house. I'll do whatever he says." Ziba's success in the competition over her husband was due to her father's eminence in the village. Her battering gave Ziba the publicity to obtain her father's support for the couple's move to their own home. His father-in-law's respected position in the village community also helped the young man (who did not wish to lose his wife) to stand up to his parents.

Goltaj The second case study involves Goltaj and her husband, Mehdi, who often physically abused her and, being dissatisfied with her, had several times sent her back to her father's home. Mehdi was about twenty-four years old and worked as a policeman or guard in the nearby city. When he wanted his wife back, he would send his mother to fetch her. One time, Goltaj's brother Cyrus would not hand her over to Mehdi's mother, saying that Mehdi himself must come after her, along with several of his male kin. Cyrus insisted that they needed to talk the matter over. Mehdi refused to come. On the evening of 8 December 1978, Mehdi attacked and stabbed Cyrus in the side, seriously wounding him. The attack occurred during the religious self-flagellation procession of mourning for the martyrdom of Imam Hosein. Mehdi said his attack was prompted by loyalty to the shah, as he was a monarchist and Cyrus was a village leader supporting the revolutionary forces but the entire village knew that Mehdi was furious over Cyrus's refusal to return Goltaj to him.

Crowds of visitors, anxious to show their support for Cyrus against Mehdi, came to see Cyrus in the hospital. The incident brought about a shift in village opinion from pro-shah—or at least accommodating to the shah's regime—to pro-Khomeini and pro-revolution. If this is how shah supporters behaved, villagers felt, the shah and his followers should be ousted.

Cyrus gradually recovered from his wound. On 11 February 1979, during the hubbub of the day the government fell, several people beat up Mehdi. He was taken to the nearby city; when he returned, he went to Cyrus's courtyard and called out for Cyrus's uncle (also Cyrus's stepfather and Goltaj's father).[11] When Mehdi came to the door, he and the men who were with him beat the older man about the head with large sticks. The uncle was taken to the hospital. In a vengeful mood, a crowd attacked the shop belonging to Mehdi's mother's brother, pulling down the roof, taking goods and candy, and tearing up the *chadors* from Mecca.

On 14 February the whole clan met at Cyrus's home to decide on a course of action. They discussed their options with a great deal of shouting and anger. They should kill Mehdi, some men felt, because they had to show people they were not weak. Some people probably already thought they were weak since Mehdi had almost killed Cyrus and they had done nothing about it, these men argued. They couldn't let Mehdi get away with *two* near killings. "The sooner Goltaj's divorce goes through, the better," one relative confided. "The conflict will continue until then."

No further violence occurred; rather, Cyrus's clan pursued the matter through the court system. Later in the summer, Cyrus's new bride commented on the case:

> Goltaj is sixteen. She was fourteen when she got married. Cyrus was against her marrying Mehdi—boys are together in the alleyways, so they know each other better. But his father said to him, "So, are *you* going to support her then?" She has been living with her father for about a year now. They get 600 tomans every month from the husband for her and the child's expenses. It would be better if she got the divorce; then they could get the money from the bride price and so on. Sometimes her husband says he'll give her a divorce, sometimes not. His family tell him, "Divorce her. She's no good; you can't get along with her."
>
> Now they're waiting for a hearing in court to see what will happen. If she didn't have the little girl it would be all right; she could get married again. But it's rare for a divorced woman with children to remarry—her new hus-

> band wouldn't accept the children. Usually children stay with the mother in case of divorce, although sometimes a boy will himself say that he wants to go and stay with his father. Girls always stay with the mother. (Goltaj's sister-in-law, bride of Cyrus, 17 July 1979)

In October 1979 I learned from Mehdi's sister that Mehdi had gone to claim his daughter and that the little girl was now with Mehdi's mother, who lived with him and cared for the child. According to Mehdi's sister, Mehdi and Goltaj were going to get a divorce.[12]

Both of these cases reveal the determination of parents to keep control over their sons and to avoid losing them to their daughters-in-law. Ziba was in competition with her husband's parents over her husband and the resources he provided. A widow, such as Mehdi's mother, often felt especially dependent on her son and thus vulnerable to her loss of influence over him.[13]

The case of Goltaj illustrates one important reason why women will not complain of ill treatment or leave their abusing husbands: if they do, their children are generally lost to them. When Mehdi reclaimed his baby daughter, no one stopped him because everyone recognized his right to his child.

The husband likewise had the right to mistreat his wife. Goltaj's relatives did not mobilize to protect her or to seek revenge on Mehdi for beating her.[14] It was only when Cyrus was injured that his kinsmen took action. Injury to a male was not tolerated.

Cyrus was a popular young man in the village, and he had a larger kinship group than Mehdi did. Although Cyrus had stronger backing in the village, Mehdi had counted on the intervention of forces outside the village: he believed he had the power of Iranian government forces behind him. He was convinced that, if necessary, local gendarmes and other government bodies such as the court system would back him in his violence against Cyrus.

Up until that point, the rural police had protected pro-shah individuals in the village. However, Mehdi's stabbing of Cyrus took place in the midst of the revolution when the balance of power was in flux. Villagers sensed the decline in the power of the pro-shah forces. Their analysis of political conditions, together with their outrage at the stabbing of Cyrus, led the majority of villagers to swing their support to Cyrus and the pro-Khomeini revolutionary forces. The Pahlavi's government fell about two months later, on 11 February 1979. Mehdi lacked support either within or outside the village, whereas Cyrus was connected to the new government. Goltaj did not go back to her husband's home for more abuse but stayed with her brother and father. Mehdi was furious at Cyrus for providing a refuge for Goltaj but could do nothing about it.

Conclusion

The men in Aliabad were pressured by the authoritarian political system int obeying their elders in exchange for receiving valuable resources—such a wives. In turn, the men abused their wives, cowing them and usually leavin them with the feeling that they had few alternatives but to submit to thei husbands. Men's labor was thus put to use in the political system. Womer through bitter experience, learned how to survive and gain some degree c power in the system. As they grew older, they sought to gain power by ma nipulating other people. Among their more precious resources were thei sons.

Wives were valued for their labor and reproductive capacity. Howeve their in-laws felt they must be controlled and distanced from their husbands A wife often felt it was in her own interests to leave her in-law's home, an she would try to persuade her husband to move. Parents who relied on th income and labor of their son considered it to be in their best interest for thei daughter-in-law to be abused, cowed, helpless, and submissive rather than part of a decision-making husband-wife team.

In the authoritarian, hierarchical village political system, wife abuse wa just one way in which inferiors were connected to superiors. Sons who wer dominated by their elders in turn subjugated their wives. Older women wh had suffered under an earlier generation in their husbands' families in turr tyrannized their daughters-in-law.

In Aliabad, such relationships were not necessarily static but rested on th difference in power between persons—a balance of power that might chang at any time. Young brides might develop resources and power bases in thei husbands' home. Women might accrue power over their lifetime and eventually be surrounded by loving children; they might also find themselve caring for helpless and socially isolated elderly husbands who had previousl abused them. Over generations, women in general might have more acces to resources such as education and jobs and be less susceptible to abuse from their husbands. Sons working in the new jobs available as a result of the oil boom were less dependent on their fathers and less subject to the wishes o the older generation.

A father or brother, because of his attachment to an abused daughter or sister and out of concern for his own reputation, might provide refuge for her. This was true especially if he were in a more powerful political position than the abusive husband. However, if the husband were politically powerful, the abuse would be less likely to come to public attention. The relative power of in-laws might change over time because of political shifts at the local or national level. Such changes would affect sanctions on abuse and the sanctuary available to an abused wife. The latter depended on the views of the community and the relative power of those abusing her versus those seeking to protect her. In Aliabad, abused wives were subject to the vicissitudes of the political system. Men with greater political power not only could abuse their wives with greater impunity but could more readily protect sisters and daughters from abuse.

The case of Ziba shows how an apparently helpless abused wife was able to use abuse by her husband, her obedience to social expectations, and the higher status of her father to gain her own ends: a home for herself and her husband separate from her in-laws. In the hierarchical, fluctuating political system of an Iranian village, wife abuse could become an issue in political competition among male in-laws. The ability to abuse a woman or to protect a woman from abuse changed with the fluctuating political power of the protagonists.

NOTES

The name of the village and all names of persons have been changed in order to protect privacy. Quotations are from my field notes unless otherwise indicated. For research and writing funding I am grateful to the Social Science Research Council and the American Council of Learned Societies; the Anthropology Department and the Southwest Asian and North Africa Program of the State University of New York at Binghamton; the Educational Foundation of the American Association of University Women; the Center for Near Eastern and North African Studies of the University of Michigan, Ann Arbor; the National Endowment for the Humanities; Franklin and Marshall College; and Santa Clara University. My deep gratitude goes to those women who shared with me the often distressing stories of mistreatment and especially to some of my close friends who revealed painful memories in hopes of helping to bring about positive change. Generous assistance and constructive criticism have been provided by Akbar Aghajanian, Erika Friedl, Patricia Higgins, Anne Marie Ominski, Nancy Lindisfarne, the editors of this volume, and others whose names are best not mentioned.

1. One of the reasons for the dearth of social science material on wife beating and battering is likely the reluctance of researchers to tackle these sensitive topics.

2. See also Papanek (1973, 1979, 1984), Sharma (1980), Sanday (1981), and Vieille (1979).

3. For a discussion of women's labor and its political importance, as well as women's activities in politics, see Hegland (1986b, 1991). For a discussion of political system and process, see Hooglund [Hegland] (1982) and Hegland (1986a).

4. Although the fiancé of one young woman, the daughter of an enlightened

schoolteacher, gave his approval for her to attend the university, her future father-in-law rejected her plans to have a career. "My son is perfectly capable of supporting her," was his outraged comment.

5. In a dramatic illustration of this point, Friedl relates the words of a woman who resisted her marriage: "I was about ten or eleven then, before I even had my first period, but I had grown quite a bit and no longer was so weak and skinny. I cried and screamed and kicked and scratched and bit like a cornered cat, but they just beat me up, my mother and my father did. My sister cried with me. My father's brother, when he came to sign the marriage contract, even clobbered me with his rifle butt until I said yes" (1989:185, 186; see also Guppy 1988:32, 40, 43, 56, 156).

6. Many men elsewhere in Iran also did not wish their wives to work. Farmanfarmaian states, "In Iran we have discovered that many divorces and family disputes result from the wife's desire to work and the husband's refusal to give consent" (1976:28, 29). See also Guppy (1988:30) and Friedl (1981).

7. Fathi reports on a father who supported his son-in-law's beating of his daughter and, in fact, urged him to use a chain for flogging her (1985:155). Not all Iranians share these attitudes or feel that wife beating is acceptable. One urban Iranian woman told me, "My father thinks anyone who beats his wife is out of his mind."

8. Friedl relates an aunt's comments about her niece: "I myself have seen her with a black eye, her veil drawn half across her face. 'The cow hit me,' she said. The cow indeed" (1989:94).

9. Although one urban informant felt wife beating was not common among the educated, stating that "the educated don't beat up their wives unless they get very mean and aggressive," other indications are to the contrary. During the course of conducting research in Iran in the summer of 1989, Friedl asked an Iranian social scientist and his wife about wife beating: "At first they said it was a class thing. The lower classes do it more. Then they looked at each other and one would say, 'So and so beats his wife,' and the other said, 'And so and so in such and such a department does it,' until between the two of them they came up with a whole list of wife beating cases in the academic community" (personal communication 1989).

Educated Iranian friends living in the United States told me of the physical abuse of their relatively well educated female relatives in Iran and of their own physical abuse and that of their friends in the United States. According to Friedl (personal communication 1989), wife abuse appears to be increasing in Iran. After the revolution, the responsibility for controlling and punishing women was shared by larger circles of men. Groups of men calling themselves "Whippers of Naked Women" roamed the city to chastise improperly covered women. Revolutionary guards, of course, feel themselves responsible for the correct behavior and appearance of all women. On these matters see Friedl (1989:85, 86) and Hegland (1982:500, 1983:188). With government required *hejab* (modesty), the state has also taken on itself the functions of monitoring and controlling women. Wife abuse also appears to be common, at least in some areas, elsewhere in the Middle East. See Sawsan el-Messiri (1979:538), Nayra Atiya (1982), Nawal El Saadawi (1983), and Wedad Zenie-Ziegler (1988).

10. In the late 1970s there were about 7.5 tomans to the dollar.

11. It was not uncommon for a man to marry his brother's widow.

12. Both cases have characteristics similar to those found by researchers in wife abuse in the United States and elsewhere. See Campbell (1985), Levinson (1988), Masumura (1979), Walker (1979, 1984), and Yllo and Bograd (1988).

13. Other stories told of great control by mothers-in-law, such as a mother-in-law sleeping between her son and his wife. See also Ghalem (1984) and Friedl (1989:94).

Upper- and middle-class women, as well as village women, have marital problems because of interference by their in-laws. In his analysis of 285 cases, an Iranian psychiatrist found marital problems causing difficulty for 40 percent of the women. The leading marital issue among these women was the "woman's struggle to free herself from in-law interference" (Bagheri 1981:47).

14. In cross-cultural research on wife abuse, Masumura found that "in most societies, wife abuse, whether homicidal or not, does not call forth revenge by the wife's kin" (1979:55). Vieille has likewise found Iranian village women to be devalued (1979).

REFERENCES CITED

Atiya, Nayra. 1982. *Khul-Khaal: Five Egyptian Women Tell Their Stories.* Syracuse, N.Y.: Syracuse University Press.

Bagheri, Abbas S. 1981. "Precipitating Factors of Neurotic Reactions in Middle- and Upper Middle-Class Persian Women (Iran)." *International Journal of Social Psychiatry* 27:47–51.

Bauer, Janet. 1985. "Demographic Change, Women, and the Family in a Migrant Neighborhood of Teheran." In *Women and the Family in Iran.* Ed. Asghar Fathi. 158–86. Leiden: E. J. Brill.

Brown, Judith K. 1982. "Cross-Cultural Perspectives on Middle-Aged Women." *Current Anthropology* 23:143–56.

———. 1992. "Lives of Middle-Aged Women." In *In Her Prime: New Views of Middle-Aged Women.* 2d ed. Ed. Virginia Kerns and Judith K. Brown. 17–30. Urbana: University of Illinois Press.

Campbell, Jacquelyn C. 1985. "Beating of Wives: A Cross-Cultural Perspective." *Victimology* 10:174–85.

el-Messiri, Sawsan. 1979. "Self-Images of Traditional Urban Women in Cairo." In *Women in the Muslim World.* Ed. Lois Beck and Nikki Keddie. 522–40. Cambridge, Mass.: Harvard University Press.

El Saadawi, Nawal. 1983. *Woman at Point Zero.* London: Zed Books.

Farmanfarmaian, Khodadad. 1976. "Women and Decision Making: With Special Reference to Iran and Other Developing Countries." *Labour and Society* 1:25–32.

Fathi, Asghar. 1985. "Social Integration in the Traditional Urban Family." In *Women and the Family in Iran.* Ed. Asghar Fathi. 151–57. Leiden: E. J. Brill.

Friedl, Erika. 1981. "Women and the Division of Labor in an Iranian Village." *Middle East Research and Information Project Reports* 95:12–18.

———. 1983. "State Ideology and Village Women." In *Women and Revolution in Iran* Ed. Guity Nashat. 217–30. Boulder, Colo.: Westview Press.

———. 1989. *Women of Deh Koh: Lives in an Iranian Village.* Washington, D.C. Smithsonian Institution Press.

Ghalem, Ali. 1984. *A Wife for My Son.* Chicago: Banner Press.

Guppy, Shusha. 1988. *The Blindfold Horse: Memories of a Persian Childhood.* Boston Beacon Press.

Haeri, Shahla. 1983. "The Institution of Mut'a Marriage in Iran: A Formal and Historical Perspective." In *Women and Revolution in Iran.* Ed. Guity Nashat. 231–52 Boulder, Colo.: Westview Press.

Hegland, Mary Elaine. 1982. "'Traditional' Iranian Women: How They Cope." *Middle East Journal* 36:483–501.

———. 1983. "Aliabad Women: Revolution as Religious Activity." In *Women and Revolution in Iran.* Ed. Guity Nashat. 171–94. Boulder, Colo.: Westview Press.

———. 1986a. "Imam Khomaini's Village: Recruitment to Revolution." Ph.D. diss Department of Anthropology, State University of New York at Binghamton.

———. 1986b. "Political Roles of Iranian Village Women." *Middle East Research and Information Project Reports* 138:14–19, 46.

———. 1991. "Political Roles of Aliabad Women: The Public/Private Dichotomy Transcended." In *Women in Middle Eastern History: Shifting Boundaries in Sex and Gender.* Ed. Nikki R. Keddie and Beth Baron. 215–30. New Haven, Conn.: Yale University Press.

Hooglund [Hegland], Mary. 1982. "Religious Ritual and Political Struggle in an Iranian Village." *Middle East Research and Information Project Reports* 102:10–17, 23

Levinson, David. 1988. "Family Violence in Cross-Cultural Perspective." In *Handbook of Family Violence.* Ed. Vincent B. Van Hasselt, Randall L. Morrison, Alan S Bellack, and Michel Hersen. 435–55. New York: Plenum Press.

Masumura, Wilfred T. 1979. "Wife Abuse and Other Forms of Aggression." *Victimology: An International Journal* 4:46–59.

Mernissi, Fatima. 1987. *Beyond the Veil: Male-Female Dynamics in Modern Muslim Society.* Bloomington: Indiana University Press.

Papanek, Hanna. 1973. "Purdah: Separate Worlds and Symbolic Shelter." *Comparative Studies in Society and History* 15:289–325.

———. 1979. "Family Status Production: The 'Work' and 'Non-Work' of Women." *Signs* 4:775–81.

———. 1984. "False Specialization and the Purdah of Scholarship: A Review Article." *Journal of Asian Studies* 44:127–48.

Rassam, Amal. 1980. "Women and Domestic Power in Morocco." *International Journal of Middle East Studies* 12:171–79.

Sanday, Peggy Reeves. 1981. "The Socio-Cultural Context of Rape: A Cross-Cultural Study." *Journal of Social Issues* 37:5–27.

Sharma, Ursula. 1980. *Women, Work, and Property in North-West India.* London: Tavistock.

Vieille, Paul. 1979. "Iranian Women in Family Alliance and Sexual Politics." In *Women in the Muslim World.* Ed. Lois Beck and Nikki Keddie. 451–72. Cambridge, Mass.: Harvard University Press.

Walker, Lenore E. 1979. *The Battered Woman.* New York: Harper and Row.

———. 1984. *The Battered Woman Syndrome.* New York: Springer.

Yllo, Kersti, and Michele Bograd, eds. 1988. *Feminist Perspectives on Wife Abuse.* Newbury Park, Calif.: Sage.

Zenie-Ziegler, Wedad. 1988. *In Search of Shadows: Conversations with Egyptian Women.* London: Zed Books.

SEVENTEEN

Wife Abuse in the Context of Development and Change: A Case from Taiwan

Rita S. Gallin

References to both verbal and physical wife abuse are scattered through th literature on China. Most consist of a sentence or two noting that abuse doe occur, but rarely are specific incidents or the related dynamics discusse (Cohen 1976:199; Lang 1946:201; Yang 1945:55). This chapter both support and challenges the tradition by discussing, first, the general phenomenon a well as a specific case of wife beating and, second, the reasons that underli such abuse in a Taiwanese rural community.

This chapter is based on data collected in Hsin Hsing, a village that ha changed over the period of study (1957–82) from an economic system base almost purely on agriculture to one founded predominantly on off-far employment.[1] I begin by describing life in the traditional Chinese family an the socioeconomic transformation of the village; then I discuss wife abus in the village, concluding with comments on the cause of violence in th hierarchically structured family.

The Traditional Chinese Family

The "economic family," the *jia,* is the basic socioeconomic unit in China Such a family can take one of three forms: conjugal, stem, or joint. The conjugal family consists of a husband, wife, and their unmarried children; th joint family adds two or more married sons and their wives and children t this core group. The stem family—which lies on a continuum between th conjugal and joint family types—includes parents, their unmarried offspring and one married son with his wife and children.

China's patrilineal kinship structure recognizes only male children as descent group members with rights to the family's property.[2] In the past, and to a large extent today, residence was patrilocal; when a woman married, she left her natal home to live as a member of her husband's family, severing her formal ties with her father's household. Parents considered daughters a liability—as household members who drained family resources when they were children and who withdrew their assets of domestic labor and earning power when they married. Sons, by contrast, steadily contributed to the family's economic security during its growth and expansion and provided a source of support in old age. Parents therefore strongly preferred male children.

Members of the older generation also strongly favored arranged marriages. Marriage brought a new member into the household, joined two people in order to produce children, and established an alliance between families. The needs of the family therefore took precedence over the desires of the individual in the selection of a mate. When parents arranged marriages, they attempted to recruit women who would be compliant, capable workers who were able to produce heirs for the group and who came from families willing to forge bonds of cooperation and obligation.

Traditionally, then, an authoritarian hierarchy based on gender, generation, and age dominated life within the family. The oldest male had the highest status, and women's status, although it increased with age and the birth of sons, was lower than that of any man. The roots anchoring this hierarchy were the mores of the "three obediences," which required a woman to defer to father, husband, and sons, and the norms of piety (*xiao*), which obligated offspring to repay parents for nurturing them. Both principles served as forms of social control, perpetuating the family, the subordination of women to men, and the domination of the young by the old.

Development in Hsin Hsing Village

Hsin Hsing is a nucleated village approximately 125 miles southwest of Taiwan's major city, Taipei, and located beside a road that runs between two market towns. Its people, like most in the area, are Hokkien (Minnan) speakers whose ancestors emigrated from Fujian, China, several hundred years ago.

The registered population of the village in 1958 was 609 people grouped into ninety-nine economic families. Conjugal families predominated, accounting for 66 percent of village families (56 percent of the population). By contrast, only 5 percent of village families (10 percent of the population) were of the joint type, while the remaining 29 percent of families (35 percent of the population) lived in stem families.

During the 1950s, no significant industries or job opportunities existed locally, and land was the primary means of production. Almost all families were agriculturalists, deriving most of their livelihood from two crops of rice, marketable vegetables grown in a third crop, and, in some cases, from farm labor hired out for wages. Men who worked outside the home in the fields dominated the public domain. Women managed the house and children, raised poultry, contributed to farm production by weeding fields and drying rice, and, in their "spare time," wove fiber hats at home to supplement the family income.

As in most of Taiwan, the structure of marriage in Hsin Hsing during the 1950s was framed by Chinese tradition (Freedman 1979:290; B. Gallin 1966: 204–13). Yet, because Hsin Hsing was a village undergoing change, tradition had been modified so that a young woman and man were allowed to have some part in the decision about the desirability of their marriage. A brief meeting was arranged during which the couple could see each other, and each was asked for an opinion about the tentatively chosen mate. Given the brevity of the meeting, the young couple could not really evaluate each other, except perhaps by appearance, and if they were at all filial they were not likely to reject their parents' choices. Consequently, after this initial meeting the young couple had no further contact with each other until their marriage.

Given this traditionalism, one might ask how the villagers responded to the transformation of Hsin Hsing's economic system in the 1970s, when labor-intensive factories, service shops, retail stores, and construction outfits burgeoned in the area. During this period, seven small satellite factories, three artisan workshops, and twenty-six shops and small businesses were established in the village (Gallin and Gallin 1982).

A comparison of the village population in 1979 with the population in 1958 suggests one change. By 1979 only 383 people lived in Hsin Hsing, although the villagers considered the population to include 543 people in seventy-three households. Further, conjugal families no longer predominated in the village; only 45 percent of families (30 percent of the population) were of this simple type. Fully 18 percent of families (34 percent of the population) were of the joint type, while the remaining 39 percent of families (36 percent of the population) were of the stem type.

Further examination of the data suggests another way in which the villagers responded to economic change. By 1979, 85 percent of resident families' incomes derived from off-farm employment, and almost half of the villagers sixteen years of age or older no longer identified farming as either their primary or their secondary activity. Nevertheless, the movement of villagers off the land was not limited only to men. In 1979, one-half of the married women and four-fifths of the single women in the village worked for remuneration (R. Gallin 1984a).

The wage employment of single women and men, not surprisingly, was accompanied by modifications in the way marriages were arranged. Parents' monopoly on mate selection disappeared, although the maintenance of family continuity required that parents still be involved in negotiations. Once negotiations between families were completed, dating in the Western sense usually occurred. Consequently, women and men frequently married each other after having already developed an emotional commitment.

Wife Beating in Hsin Hsing

The cruelty of a Chinese mother-in-law toward her daughter-in-law is common knowledge, and during the 1950s an older woman's treatment of a younger woman in Hsin Hsing was no different.[3] In 1982, women frequently spoke of the bitterness of their early years of marriage, when they were saddled with work under the close supervision and scrutiny of their mothers-in-law. Many described the capricious ways in which the older woman exercised authority by cursing, harassing, and even beating them on occasion.[4]

Such tyranny by a mother-in-law has been explained in terms of the need to break a newcomer into the ways of the home (Baker 1979:43). A young woman had to be socialized and integrated into the household, and in the division of labor this task fell to her mother-in-law. To enforce obedience, and perhaps to retaliate for her own lifelong subjugation, an older woman might well resort to physical abuse of a daughter-in-law with whom she was dissatisfied.

Ten women I spoke with reported that men also had beaten their wives to keep them in line. These men had acted as agents of their mothers, who had demanded they bend their wives to the older women's will. One might ask why an older woman would find it necessary to impose her authority through her son. Enforcing compliance was considered to be the mother-in-law's prerogative; a daughter-in-law did not have sufficient power as an individual to defy her mother-in-law or disobey her commands.

The explanation for a mother-in-law's abrogation of authority to her son must therefore lie elsewhere. In Hsin Hsing, the reason for the transfer of authority most likely was rivalry for the affections of the son. An older woman had first come as a stranger to her husband's family and the birth of her son had improved her status within it and guaranteed her old-age insurance. She had spent years nurturing her relationship with her son and tying him firmly to her (Wolf 1972:32–41). She saw the young wife as a competitor for claims on her son, someone who would deprive her of her son's loyalty and support.

Older women had witnessed cases in which, despite the mother's stratagems to protect the filial bond between her son and herself, a real compatibility or unity of interest had developed between the husband and wife, so that the husband had listened to his wife's views and had accepted her advice. From the perspective of the mother, such an alliance represented a powerful and significant threat to her relations with her son, because the younger woman could use her husband to remove the older woman from the family. To counter this threat, then, the mother-in-law enlisted her son as an ally in the abuse of his wife. Because he had been taught that the goal of marriage was the continuation of the family, and because he had close emotional ties with his mother, the man sacrificed his personal feelings toward his wife and beat her. The effect was that his acquiescence to his mother's demand reaffirmed and strengthened his solidarity with her, while his wife's resentment toward him for the beating negated and weakened his solidarity with her. Also, the invigoration of filial ties and erosion of marital bonds contributed to the family's longevity and the older woman's future economic and social security.

Undoubtedly, the ability of a mother-in-law to work her will so successfully reflected a young brides's lack of recourse. The husband was expected to, and as we saw did, side with his mother in dealings with his wife. Her neighbors were reluctant to interfere; "husband-wife violence . . . [was] regarded as something 'to shut the door and listen to'" (Harrell 1982:128). Nor could her father and brothers be counted on to intervene on her behalf (Levy 1949:188; Wolf 1975:124).

The inaction of her relatives was due in part to the fact that they did not see her that often: marriage was usually village exogamous; people were poor; transportation facilities were not well developed; and visiting primarily revolved around village-based religious events. Thus, unless the abuse of a woman was extreme, her natal family probably was not aware that she had been beaten until long after the incident had occurred.[5] However, their inaction was also due in part to the fact that most affines were unwilling to jeopardize a meaningful and utilitarian relationship; ties of affinity served as an important foundation for economic activities and were a source of support supplementing that which derived from patrilineal kin (B. Gallin 1966:165–81; Gallin and Gallin 1985). It was therefore not in the family's interest to support a female relative who "belonged" to a unit from which it hoped to elicit assistance.

An abused wife had but two alternatives available to relieve her misery: she could endure it and look to the time when she would assume the role of the wife of the head of the house; or she could escape it by committing suicide. I have no firsthand knowledge that any woman from Hsin Hsing chose this alternative, but Margery Wolf has pointed out that "for peasant women suicide was . . . and still is . . . a socially acceptable solution to a variety of problems that offer no other solution" (1975:112).

Given this situation, did the pattern of wife abuse and the reasons that underlie it change with the transformation of the village's economy? One way to begin to answer this question is to look at the way brides were integrated into the households of their husbands in the 1970s. We saw above that in the 1950s young women had few resources with which to contend the authority of their mothers-in-law. By contrast, in the 1970s young brides were not as helpless in dealing with their mothers-in-law as the older women had been with theirs, because they brought decided emotional and economic advantages to the relationship (R. Gallin 1984b, 1986).

First, the mutual affection that a young couple developed during the betrothal period represented in marriage a serious challenge to the mother-son bond on which an older woman depended to subjugate her daughter-in-law. Second, the value of a young woman's *sai-khia* (private money)—which represented a sizable portion of the seed money for the conjugal family a woman and her husband would eventually establish and which he would head—outweighed the resources a man's mother had at her command.[6] An older woman, then, was no longer assured of the loyalty and support of her son in confrontations with his wife.

Perhaps for this reason a mother-in-law undertook with moderation the integration of a new bride into the household. Although older women frequently complained about their daughters-in-law's failings, they tended to avoid direct confrontations with them. It was better to side-step an issue than pit a son's ties to his mother against those to his wife, since at best a son might remain neutral and withdraw from the fray, but at worst he might defend his wife.

Ironically, the material resources that allowed young women to negotiate the new role relationship with their mothers-in-law precipitated the 1979 beating described below. The couple involved in the incident had been married about seven years, and the husband drank and gambled heavily. Although he and his wife were members of a joint family, the woman knew that division of the large unit was inevitable and that, when it occurred, she would not be able to depend on her husband, certainly not as a stable source of support for their conjugal family.

It was therefore in her interest to guard her *sai-khia*—to invest and cultivate it for future use. Consequently, when her husband demanded that she give him her private money she refused. Unable to extract the money from her through verbal abuse, he resorted to physical abuse and beat her. Despite this beating, the young woman remained uncowed. She had very practical reasons not to give up her *sai-khia:* the future prosperity of her family and more important, the future prosperity of her two sons—which would determine the nature of her life in old age—depended on this money.

Like her counterparts in the 1950s, the young woman had little recours to escape her husband's abuse. Divorce was not really a viable option; customary law required that sons remain with their father when a marriage wa dissolved, and without sons a woman would have no one to take responsibility for her in her old age. Her father and brothers also were unlikely to offe protection or a haven to which she could retreat. The increasing importanc of affinal ties in the world of a cash economy meant they would place thei family's interests before her needs.

Indeed, her natal family did not intercede on her behalf to demand tha her husband stop his abuse. Rather, recognizing the importance and delicac of affinal ties, her father acted as his son-in-law's agent and also beat her. To reinforce his own family's security, her father forced her to give her *sai-khia*—her bulwark against her future insecurity—to her husband.

Summary and Conclusion

To summarize, during the 1950s wife abuse was triggered by a mother's fear that her son's wife would alienate him from her and would relegate her to an old age fraught with insecurity and loneliness. By contrast, in 1979 the abuse was provoked by a young woman's fear that her husband would squander her *sai-khia* and therefore jeopardize her chance to enjoy a secure old age. On face value, it would appear that in the absence of a well-developed social security system women's attempts to ensure the support of others in their old age underlie wife abuse in Hsin Hsing.

This explanation masks the fundamental cause of wife abuse in the village and constitutes victim blaming. The perceived coalition of a young woman with her husband and the refusal of a wife to relinquish her private money were not the causes of wife beating, though they provided significant excuses for it. In the cases described, young women were considered to have stepped outside the bounds of the cultural definition of femininity by challenging the traditional authority of both the older women and the man. Therefore, to strengthen and sustain the hierarchical structure of subordination within the family, beating young women was believed to be justified. The abuse of women in Hsin Hsing, in short, was motivated by the need of the older women and the men to reaffirm their control over the women who, by cultural definition, were their subordinates.

NOTES

Research on which this chapter is based was carried out in collaboration with Bernard Gallin, whose insights have helped me immeasurably. We acknowledge with thanks the organizations that provided financial assistance over the years and made our field trips to Taiwan possible. Specifically, funding was provided by a Foreign Area Training Fellowship, Fulbright-Hays Research Grants, the Asian Studies Center of Michigan State University, the Midwest Universities Consortium for International Activities, the Social Science Research Council, and the Pacific Cultural Foundation. Quotations are from my field notes unless otherwise indicated.

1. The research covers the period from 1957 to 1982. The first field trip, in 1957–58, involved a seventeen-month residence in the village of Hsin Hsing. This was followed by two separate studies, in 1965–66 and 1969–70, of outmigrants from the area. The most recent research spanned two months in 1977, six months in 1979, and one month in 1982. During these visits we collected data using both anthropological and sociological techniques, including participant observation, in-depth interviews, surveys, censuses, and collection of official statistics contained in the local family, land, school, and economic records.

2. Laws in both Taiwan and the People's Republic of China have attempted to alter this traditional pattern of inheritance by providing women with institutionalized access to the property of their families of origin. However, women seldom claim their inheritance; rather, they accept their dowries as their patrimony.

3. Wife abuse was never a focus of the research, and we did not interview villagers directly about the phenomenon. Interviews with approximately three hundred people as well as our own observations suggest that mothers-in-law in Hsin Hsing treated their daughters-in-law harshly and that the relationship between older and younger women in the family was an unhappy one.

4. During the summer of 1982 I interviewed twenty-five women aged forty-seven and older about changes in family life. In comparing their early years of marriage with those of their daughters-in-law, only one woman reported that she had been treated well by her mother-in-law; the remaining twenty-four reported that their mothers-in-law had been cruel to them. Of these twenty-four women, fully half said the older women "beat" them, although only about six qualified their reports by indicating that their skin became "black and blue" as a result. Unfortunately, I did not pursue the subject in the interviews, and I do not know how frequently the beatings occurred.

5. I use the term "extreme" to describe cases of wife abuse in which a woman required medical treatment after she was beaten. No Hsin Hsing woman described such an occurrence, but Wolf (1975) speaks to the issue.

6. Cash and jewelry are given to a young woman as part of her dowry, the amount varying with the economic condition of her natal family. In contrast to the other items a woman takes with her to her husband's home at marriage, this cash and jewelry is

considered to belong to her and not to the family as a whole. Taiwanese call this "private property" a woman's *sai-khia.* On family division, a woman's *sai-khia* is merged with the property inherited by her husband, and she loses control of her private fund. The practice of *sai-khia* was recognized in Hsin Hsing during the 1950s but was not prevalent because of the poverty of the local people.

REFERENCES CITED

Baker, Hugh D. R. 1979. *Chinese Family and Kinship.* New York: Columbia University Press.

Cohen, Myron. 1976. *House United House Divided.* New York: Columbia University Press.

Freedman, Maurice. 1979. "Ritual Aspects of Chinese Kinship and Marriage." In *The Study of Chinese Society: Essays by Maurice Freedman.* Ed. G. William Skinner. 273–95. Stanford, Calif.: Stanford University Press.

Gallin, Bernard. 1966. *Hsin Hsing, Taiwan: A Chinese Village in Change.* Berkeley: University of California Press.

Gallin, Bernard, and Rita S. Gallin. 1982. "Socioeconomic Life in Rural Taiwan: Twenty Years of Development and Change." *Modern China* 8 (2): 205–46.

———. 1985. "Matrilateral and Affinal Relationships in Changing Chinese Society." In *The Chinese Family and Its Ritual Behavior.* Ed. Hsieh Jin-chang and Chuang Ying-Chang. 101–16. Taipei, Taiwan: Institute of Ethnology, Academia Sinica.

Gallin, Rita S. 1984a. "The Entry of Chinese Women into the Rural Labor Force: A Case Study from Taiwan." *Signs* 9 (3): 383–98.

———. 1984b. "Women, Family, and the Political Economy of Taiwan." *Journal of Peasant Studies* 12 (1): 76–92.

———. 1986. "Mothers-in-Law and Daughters-in-Law: Intergenerational Relations within the Chinese Family in Taiwan." *Journal of Cross-Cultural Gerontology* 1 (1): 31–49.

Harrell, Stevan. 1982. *Ploughshare Village.* Seattle: University of Washington Press.

Lang, Olga. 1946. *Chinese Family and Society.* New Haven, Conn.: Yale University Press.

Levy, Marion J., Jr. 1949. *The Family Revolution in Modern China.* Cambridge, Mass.: Harvard University Press.

Wolf, Margery. 1972. *Women and the Family in Rural Taiwan.* Stanford, Calif.: Stanford University Press.

———. 1975. "Women and Suicide in China." In *Women and Chinese Society.* Ed. Margery Wolf and Roxane Witke. 111–41. Stanford, Calif.: Stanford University Press.

Yang, Martin. 1945. *A Chinese Village: Taitou Shantung Province.* New York: Columbia University Press.

EIGHTEEN

Sanctions and Sanctuary: Wife Battering within Cultural Contexts

Jacquelyn C. Campbell

This volume presents evidence from fifteen cultures and also from primates demonstrating the range of wife beating and the context in which it escalates to wife battering or is circumscribed. In this chapter I will review explanatory theories for wife beating from the Western social sciences and then use the evidence from this volume to support or challenge these theories. This sample of cultures is obviously too small to give definitive validation or refutation of any theory, but it has the advantage of presenting less complex cultures than those usually studied in wife abuse research. Consequently, there is the opportunity to examine cultural variables less confounded by other societal influences. Unfortunately, cultural influences on wife battering have been omitted from much of the literature of Western social sciences (Lockhart 1987; Torres 1987), although the situation is improving (e.g., Heise et al. 1994; O'Keefe 1994; Wessel and Campbell 1997; Sorenson and Telles 1991; Williams 1989; Richie 1993; Asbury 1993; Gondolf et al. 1988; Hampton and Gelles 1994; Richie 1996; Sorenson 1996; Gaffney et al. 1997). This volume adds important information that can inform the selection of cultural influences to be operationalized in future research. Finally, the knowledge gained from this cultural-perspective review will be synthesized to summarize the additional information and suggest ways it can be used to help prevent or at least limit wife beating in all cultures.

In an earlier essay (Campbell 1985), I argued that evidence from other cultures used to explain wife beating was often problematic if it relied on secondary sources based on evidence contributed by primarily male anthropologists using primarily male informants. The evidence in this volume is primary data collected by anthropologists, a majority of whom are female, using direct observations and female as well as male informants. Thus, the evidence here can be presumed to be less androcentric than that usually reported and in fact may be considered gynocentric. It can therefore be expected to shed a different light on what facilitates or discourages wife beating.

Wife Battering versus Wife Beating

Despite attempts to do so (Gondolf 1988; Levinson 1989; Snyder and Fruchtman 1981), it has been difficult to identify typologies of assault against female partners that hold up in more than one sample. For instance, Levinson (1989) identifies three types of wife beating according to cultural sanctions: (1) for adultery only, (2) "for cause" (culturally agreed on reasons such as failure to properly enact the female role), and (3) at will. However, his cross-cultural data provide little support for this division in terms of differentiation by severity, frequency, or degree of outside intervention. Part of the problem may be the data sources as outlined above and part may be the complexities of wife beating.[1] For instance, in the United States, all three types could be said to apply depending on the informant queried. The same can be seen in some of the less-multifaceted cultures described in the previous chapters.

In this volume we attempt to discriminate between wife beating and wife battering (originally differentiated in Counts 1990; see also table 18.1 for definitions). Wife beating can be described as at least an ambivalently condoned, most often occasional (although sometimes frequent), and most often not seriously or permanently injurious act of physical aggression against at least some of the female partners in a culture. As such, this practice is close to universal in terms of occurrence by group (not individual) in humans and animals, thereby making it difficult to determine culturally specific causative factors. Instead, it is more useful to concentrate on what within a society facilitates the escalation of wife beating to wife battering or keeps it within the range of wife beating. This is not to say that we find wife beating (or husband beating) acceptable but that we want to concentrate on what is theoretically and practically promising.

Table 18.1. Definitions

Wife beating	At least ambivalently condoned; most often occasional (although sometimes frequent); most often not a seriously or permanently injurious act of physical aggression against at least some of the female partners in a culture.
Wife battering	Ongoing and severe acts of physical violence within a context of coercive control not seen as usual by others in that society.
Mutual or bilateral couple violence	Either partner equally likely to begin physically assaultive exchanges; no pattern of coercive control of one partner by the other.

In this chapter I propose that individual psychological factors within a context of cultural tolerance (if not acceptance; Greenblat 1985) may be most predictive of the occurrence of wife beating (a particular man hitting a woman occasionally and not seriously throughout the course of a relationship), while cultural, political, and economic factors at the societal level can control or facilitate that individual's acts of violence toward his spouse becoming and remaining frequently repeated and severe. This pattern of escalation is the usual case according to evidence from the Straus and Gelles (1990) U.S. national sample and other data (e.g., Jacobson et al. 1996). It is a pattern also found in other cultures, as noted by several authors in this volume (especially McDowell, Kerns, and Miller).

The differentiation between wife beating and wife battering is useful in terms of distinguishing the latter from the more generalized "spouse abuse" or "domestic violence." In some cultures, including those of North America, women also commit acts of violence against male partners. Without separating acts of self-defense and mutual combat from those unilaterally initiated, North American empirical data can be interpreted as demonstrating close to equal numbers of acts of violence toward male partners as those directed toward females (for data related to the ongoing debate see Bachman and Saltzman 1995; Fagan and Browne 1994; Dobash et al. 1992; Saunders 1988; Steinmetz and Lucca 1988). The assumption in this chapter is that violence between intimate partners anywhere could be and sometimes (although far less frequently) is husband beating or bilateral beating rather than wife beating, depending on the gender of the initiator(s).

According to Levinson's (1989) sample of small-scale societies, husband beating occurs cross-culturally only where there is also wife beating. Male partner beating occurs in a majority of households in only 6.7 percent of cultures (compared with wife beating in all or a majority of households in 48.7 percent of the sample) and occurs at all in 26.9 percent of societies (versus 84.5 percent for wife beating). These data do not rule out the possibility that all of the violence by women is in the context of a bilaterally violent relationship or in self-defense. It certainly supports that the majority of violence against intimate partners is against women.

Degrees of Beating and Battering Represented

The data presented in this volume resemble Levinson's data. Although the societies featured here are by no means a random sampling, they were not systematically selected because of relative presence or absence of beating. The editors tried to include a variety of points along a continuum of intimat partner violence, and representation from a number of geographic areas anc a range of societal development were equally strong inclusion considerations Our sample contains six societies with high degrees of wife beating (Ira India, Taiwan, Indo-Fijian, Bun, and Kaliai), five with less-frequent and ubiq uitous beatings (Aboriginal, Abelam, Ecuadorian Indians, !Kung, and Uje lang), three with infrequent beatings (Garífuna, Nagovisi, and Mayotte), anc one society, the Wape, with almost no cases (see table 18.2).

In two of the cultures (Bun and Aboriginal) there is also a high degree o mutual violence. Since in both societies wife beating also takes place amon the same couples and little evidence exists of a more one-sided, otherwis controlling husband battering in either society, I will use the term *mutual* o *bilateral violence* to describe these exchanges. Even though the female ma use weapons to fight when her mate is using "only" hands and fee (McDowell), this needs to be interpreted in the context of the usual dimor phisms (male size and strength advantages) and male socialization to us hands and feet as instruments of aggression. Thus, female use of weapon in response to male fists may appear to be an increase in violence and thereb make her the more aggressive, but her weapon tactic usually only evens the exchange. The two mutually violent cultures are not particularly similar otherwise, with the Bun exhibiting more wife beating (and battering) than the Aboriginal. Thus, there is at least the possibility that this mutual violence is

Table 18.2. Frequency and Ubiquity of Wife Beating, Wife Battering, and Mutual Violence in Fifteen Societies

Society	Chapter No.	Wife Beating	Wife Battering	Mutual Violence
Iran	16	3	3	0
India	14	3	3	0
Indo-Fijian	15	3	3	0
Taiwanese	17	3	2	0
Bun	6	3	2	2
Kaliai	5	3	1–2	0
Abelam	10	2–3	1–2	1
Aborigine	3	2	1	3
Ecuadorian	12	2	1	0
!Kung	4	2	1	0
Ujelang	9	2	1	1
Garífuna	11	1	0	0
Nagovisi	8	1	0	0
Mayotte	13	1	0	0
Wape	7	0	0	0

Key: 3 = high frequency and ubiquity; 2 = medium frequency and ubiquity; 1 = low frequency and ubiquity; 0 = essentially none a differentially influenced, although related, phenomenon than either beating or battering. This is a possibility taken into account only marginally in Western social science research.

Using Levinson's (1989) and other cross-cultural data (e.g., Heise et al. 1994; Carroll 1980; Masamura 1979; Wessel and Campbell 1997), as well as studies from Westernized cultures (e.g., Campbell 1989; Dobash and Dobash 1979; Saunders 1988), we contend that battering, in contrast to partner beating and mutual violence, is a phenomenon almost exclusively directed toward women and includes other kinds of coercive control as well as ongoing and severe acts of violence not seen as usual by others in the society (Campbell and Humphreys 1993). Wife battering is what is meant in most Western social science research on violence against female partners, but there are studies that include acts of wife beating, and most do not differentiate the two. For instance, Straus and Gelles (1990) differentiate severe and minor violence but base the distinction solely on the seriousness of the violent tactic rather than on outcomes such as degree of injury. Parker and Schumacher (1977) separate the battered woman's syndrome victim from the "violence syndrome averter," but they do so in terms of the woman's behavioral responses to violence from the male partner, rather than the degree and context of the violence used against her. Finally, Michael Johnson (1995) advances a differentiation between "common couple violence" (occasional, more likely to be mutual, usually minor) and "patriarchal terrorism" (male perpetrated, escalating, with the motivation of control) that is quite similar to the beating and battering differentiation. His typology is based on observations about North American domestic violence surveys and other scholarship and helps to explain many of the controversies and inconsistencies that have arisen in the last decade of Western social science research in the field.

Based on the evidence in this volume, there is definitely a correlation between wife beating and wife battering in a society. However, while wife battering is horrifyingly frequent in Iran and India, it is not as ubiquitous in the other four cultures where wife beating abounds. Hopefully, theory can help us understand the differences among these groups as well as what facilitates relative partner nonviolence in the remaining societies. Some of those societies are actually normatively accepting of wife beating but have very little (Ecuadorian Indians, Aboriginal, Ujelang) or virtually no (Garífuna) battering.

Although we believe we are contributing to theory in order to suggest means of decreasing the physical, emotional, and societal damages of wife battering, we do not believe it is possible to identify simple linear causative factors easily remedied. As with most human behavior, the use of violence is complex, with an interplay of individual, contextual, and societal forces.

Explanatory Theories

Western social sciences have used a variety of theories to explain the occurrence of wife beating, and many schemes have been used for their classification. For this volume, we have divided the theories into the broad categories of psychological and sociological/cultural and concentrate on the latter as more appropriate for examination with anthropological evidence (Brown this volume). Various forms of stress and trauma, social learning, and exchange theory have received the most empirical support and attention in psychology, although it is recognized that each has societal components as well as explanations within the individual psyche (Van Hasselt et al. 1988). Psychoanalytic and neuropsychological reasons for wife beating have also been explored but are less well accepted, partly because of the victim-blaming and perpetrator-excusing logical extensions of these perspectives (Yllo and Bograd 1988) and partly because of a lack of consistent empirical support (for representative reviews see Hanrahan et al. 1993; Johnson 1996; Tolman and Bennett 1990; and Crowell and Burgess 1996). Sociobiological (or evolutionary psychological) theory has been used in connection with homicide of women (Daly and Wilson 1988; Dearwater et al. 1998; Wilson et al. 1995; Wingood and DiClemente 1997), which can be conceptualized as the far end of the continuum of wife beating (Campbell 1992). This framework has been discussed by Draper (this volume). In this chapter I will concentrate on reviewing the theories, especially feminist, resource, subculture of violence, and systems theories, which use wider societal perspectives. The societal factors used in social learning and exchange theories will also be examined.

Feminist Explanatory Theory

The use of this theory to explain wife battering was originally most fully explicated by Rebecca and Russell Dobash (1979) in their exemplar text *Violence against Wives.* The basic premise is that wife battering is allowed and encouraged by patriarchal societal organizations that mandate women's dominance by men, by force if necessary. Feminist perspectives include wife battering with other forms of violence against women (rather than other forms of "family violence") as measures that keep women dominated in patriarchal societies (Daly 1979; Hanmer and Maynard 1985; Radford and Russell 1992). The historical precedents for wife battering have been used as supporting evidence (e.g., Davidson 1978; Pleck 1987), as has research using measurement of societal patriarchal structures correlated with rates of violence against women (Baron and Straus 1987; Yllo 1984) and studies examining individual batterers in North America and elsewhere (Berenson et al. 1992; Stewart and Cecutti 1993; Haj-Yahia 1997).

However, both cross-cultural and individual person studies make clear that there is not a simple linear correlation between female status in a society or in a couple and rates of wife assault (Campbell 1985; Levinson 1989; Straus and Gelles 1990; Yllo 1984). In fact, there may be a curvilinear relationship, with wife battering relatively low in societies where women's status is the lowest, since there are other norms that effectively control women (Campbell 1985). Women's status and power are complex variables with many different manifestations (Whiting 1965; Collier 1974). Where women's status is most in flux and in contention would be where battering could be expected to be highest; and where there is the most equality, rates would be expected to be low. In fact, Gartner et al. (1990) found that perceived challenges to male dominance place women at especially high risk for homicide from their spouses.

Studies of the relationship between women's status or power and wife assault have been confounded by various measures of both variables. For instance, Levinson (1989) found family-status variables (economic, decision making, and divorce restrictions) more predictive of wife beating than societal-level variables (control of premarital sexual behavior, place of residence, property inheritance). An important exception was female economic work groups, which were predictive of the absence of wife beating (not differentiated from wife battering). Similarly, while economic dependence of women and male decision-making norms within couples are associated with wife battering in the United States (Kalmuss and Straus 1990; Straus and Gelles 1990), individual male attitudes toward women and sex-role stereotypes do not consistently differentiate abusive men from others (Stark 1990; Dutton 1995; Hotaling and Sugarman 1986; Tolman and Bennett 1990).

In the data compiled for this volume, we do not find full support for feminist theory, but we find support for some of the premises and important implications for theory modification. In the feminist view, male sexual jealousy is seen as an expression of a socialized view of women as the property of men and is accompanied by other aspects of male controlling behavior (e.g., economic coercion, social isolation). This better explains the range of male sexual jealousy found in our data than parental certainty concerns from evolutionary psychology, which could be expected to be universal. We can see a general pattern of strong male sexual jealousy in the societies with serious wife battering (e.g., Iran, India, Indo-Fijian) and very little jealousy among the Wape, Garífuna, Nagovisi, and Mayotte, the four societies with almost no wife battering and far less beating of wives. The cultures between the extremes show more variation.

Other expressions of the premise of male ownership of women can be identified as: (1) female chastity before marriage as critical to the value of a woman (Iran, Indo-Fijian), (2) dowry payments (India),[2] (3) forced sex in marriage (Iran), and (4) physical punishment by other male kin (Bun).[3] However, the Ecuadorian Indians present an interesting exception to the pattern, with female chastity and other aspects of male control the ideal (but considerable female autonomy the reality) and woman battering kept relatively low. Obviously, there are other aspects of the status of women and relative presence of patriarchal norms that affect physical violence.

The role of mothers-in-law in the battering of wives as seen in Iran, among the Indo-Fijians, and formerly in Taiwan seems counterintuitive to the feminist case. Yet Daly (1979) identifies the role of other women as "token torturers" in a variety of historical and current practices of violence against women (e.g., Chinese mothers as the footbinders and African village wise women used to circumcise young females), whereby women (usually older) are forced by patriarchal societies to inflict violence on other women in order to gain some modicum of personal power and to save the other women from being unacceptable in terms of the societal norms. In contrast, Brown (1982; Kerns and Brown 1992) offers a more complex and satisfying development of the role of middle-aged women cross-culturally. She presents evidence that an increase in power in middle age is universal for women and by no means always accompanied by her own use of violence. In Brown's review, the frequent mother and adult son bond is characterized more often by attachment than by dominance. As described in this volume, the magical powers exhibited by older Kaliai and Ujelang women are perceived in those cultures as a means of violence used against men at least as often as against other women.

Women having some sort of significant power in the culture outside of the home, either economic (!Kung, Wape, Garífuna, Aboriginal, Mayotte, and Ecuadorian Indian) or magical (Kaliai, Ujelang, and Garífuna), does seem to provide some protection against wife battering that is supportive of the feminist case. There is some negative evidence in Taiwan and among the Indo-Fijians, where societal development has afforded economic possibilities for wives but battering continues. However, it can be argued that the strong continuing ethic of females as property and the societal norms supporting the beating of wives in those cultures is so far overcoming any autonomy development in women.

The Ecuadorian Indians again offer an interesting contrast. Here the traditional economic power of women coupled with female decision-making authority in the home seems to protect women from the degree of battering that the otherwise machismo ethics and beating norms would seem to dictate. Yet the ideal for women is passivity, and women and men are perceived to have very different natures, with men destined to be dominant in marriage. The feminist model does not hold up as well with these people, who exhibit much of quintessential patriarchy yet relatively little battering.

The islanders of Mayotte also offer a culture at first glance at odds with the feminist model. The Mayotte are Muslims, which is generally thought of as a strictly patriarchal religion with strong beliefs in women as property and sanctions for the beating of wives for correction. Indeed, these villagers strongly proscribe premarital sexual activity, but women otherwise wield a comparatively substantial amount of political power and personal autonomy, even postmarital sexual autonomy. The ritual defloration of young girls by their husbands in this culture can be considered another instance of violence against women. However, the act is often monitored by grandmothers and perhaps consequently not experienced negatively, which the feminist viewpoint could interpret as an act of female solidarity protection. The contrast between the responses of Iranian and Mayotte brides to a similar act (in outcome, yet very different in quality) points out the fallacy of equating acts of "violence" toward women across cultures.

Wife beating on Mayotte is extremely infrequent and battering is unknown. Divorce is easy for women, and their kin will actively intervene if the violence appears to be getting out of hand. Violence between marital partners is negatively sanctioned among the people of Mayotte. All this is obviously in great contrast to Iran, although the basic religious premises are the same.

This combination of sanction and sanctuary is a powerful influence against wife beating becoming wife battering, as is discussed by Brown (this volume). In the feminist framework, these would be seen as concomitant with female power in the culture and antithetical to a strictly patriarchal society. When we examine the evidence in this volume, we do find a strong association between sanction against battering, sanctuary for those severely beaten, and low levels or absence of battering. Thus, all four of our battering-absent societies (Mayotte, Garífuna, Nagovisi, and Wape) have significant sanctions against battering, clearly demonstrated by active community and/or kin intervention when things get out of hand, and sanctuary for the woman if she is beaten. For the Nagovisi, the sanctuary takes the form of the man having to leave. The Wape may represent the model feminist case, where female groups provide the active community intervention against potential beating, presenting a compelling image of women surrounding a home where there is marital conflict until the wife joins them outside. Similarly, there is female solidarity of the Garífuna around violence against women, taking the form of the community women shaming the man. When seen in conjunction with

Levinson's (1989) correlations, this evidence suggests that female solidarity groups around any issue may be protective against wife battering, in addition to the negative sanction specifically against battering provided in our examples. This can be contrasted with the divisions among Taiwanese, Bun, and Indo-Fijian women.

In contrast to feminist theory, the majority of the cultures demonstrate differential sanctions between beating and battering (the former always more acceptable). For instance, on Mayotte and even more striking among the Garífuna, there is some acceptance of wife beating although none of battering. There is also kin intervention to prevent battering (not beating) based on ideas of male kin ownership of Mayotte and Kaliai women, thus combining a patriarchal premise with a sanction against battering. Community intervention among the Kaliai and the !Kung is when there is battering, not beating. Also nonsupportive of feminist theory as currently articulated is the contrast between the Aboriginal use of violence toward wives as an expression of anger, not dominance, as opposed to the clear dominance purpose of Ecuadorian Indian males, despite approximately equal levels of battering and beating in the two groups. In addition, the cultures with strong conventions of female passivity (Taiwan, Indo-Fijian, Ecuadorian Indian, Iran, and India) have different degrees of wife battering, and many Kaliai and Bun women, hardly passive, are being rather severely battered. An absence of female passivity as the ideal is associated more with an absence of mutual violence than with battering. All of these data are problematic in the feminist viewpoint as heretofore explicated.

As frequently stated by Dobash and Dobash (1979, 1998) and other feminist theorists, research attempting to support the "case against the patriarchy" can be no more simply operationalized or explicated than research investigating other theoretical premises. The stance taken is that individual couple data is meaningless without the societal context, including the historical context. Everyone can find examples of women who beat their male partners and/or women who have substantial power in a society where other women are beaten. This does not disprove the feminist explications for wife battering. In fact, the differentiation among mutual violence, battering, and beating as advanced herein may make feminist theory more explanatory for battering.

Resource or Status Inconsistency Theory

The basic premise of resource theory as applied to family violence by Goode (1971) is that the family is a power system like any other, and when a person does not have other resources, he or she will be more likely to use violence in order to maintain power. This proposition helps explain the correlation between poverty and wife battering that has been found consistently in North American research (Hotaling and Sugarman 1986, 1990; Bachman and Saltzman 1995). There has also been research support for the more specific operationalization of resource theory, namely, status inconsistency. In this conceptualization a husband who perceives that his status relative to his wife is inconsistent with the societal norms is more likely to use violence. Thus, the woman having more education or a better job than her male partner would be at risk for wife battering, especially if he strongly believes in male-dominance prerogatives (Allen and Straus 1980; Hornung et al. 1981; Stark 1990).

In cultures where rapidly changing mores and societal developments are decreasing traditional male resources, resource theory would predict an increase in wife beating. Yet among the Taiwanese and Indo-Fijians this does not seem to be happening. Although wife battering is relatively frequent and severe, it seems to be decreasing (if changing at all) as women define their roles differently and no longer sanction abuse. Changing relative status also does not seem to be increasing wife beating among the !Kung, and very low male resources characterize both the relatively violent Bun males and the totally nonviolent Wape. However, for individual men the theory perhaps does work. In some of the case descriptions in this volume, the wife was apparently being beaten more because of an individual challenge against a male role. This also fits with the notion of a curvilinear relationship between wife battering and female status.

Iran offers an interesting case in which the short-term Westernizing of society apparently decreased wife battering temporarily and then the return to a strictly interpreted patriarchal Muslim structure increased the abuse again (see Hegland, this volume). Thus societal sanctions were apparently stronger than individual status inconsistency, and increased relative power of women, even if temporary, seemed to accompany decreased violence against them.

Culture/Subculture of Violence

Theorists seeking to explain violence in a particular society have often looked to the cultural norms surrounding violent practices. Thus, various forms of violence (e.g., homicide and warfare) are often correlated in individual societies, and certain cultures are characterized as being generally violent. Both Masamura (1979) and Lester (1980) sought to correlate other indices of violence with wife beating in simple societies and found conflicting results.

Levinson (1989) found wife beating to be part of a pattern of violence within families and among acquaintances but different from aggression toward strangers.

A general culture of violence premise is most applicable in homogeneous small-scale societies rather than complex, multicultural nations such as the United States. The subculture of violence theory was originally developed by sociologists to explain differential rates of interpersonal violence (mainly homicide) among differing ethnic and income groups in the United States (Wolfgang and Ferracuti 1981). They used social learning theory to explain the transmission of norms supporting interpersonal violence within certain subcultures (mainly minority groups and the lower class), such as definitions of toughness, masculinity, and honor. In violent subcultures, these definitions include a willingness to use violence in delineated situations even when it otherwise would not be advantageous to do so.

Bowker (1983) extends the theoretical premise to wife beating, identifying some male subcultures that justify wife abuse by reinforcing norms of male dominance. Therefore, men who are most involved with a peer group supporting dominance by force would be most violent toward their female partners. Research by Carroll (1980) and Smith (1989) gives some support to Bowker's premises. Bowker's application and supporting research extend the concept of a wife-beating subculture beyond the lower class, better explaining the pattern of violence toward women in the United States. In addition, research suggesting that batterers who are violent only toward their wives can be differentiated (by social class as well as other factors) from wife abusers who are also violent with nonfamily members helped to integrate the general subculture of violence theory with Bowker's application (Gondolf 1988; Holtzworth-Munroe and Stuart 1994; Jacobson et al. 1996; Shields et al. 1988; Stark 1990).

The subculture of violence theory in general has been criticized on theoretical grounds and because of a lack of research support. For instance, it can be argued that when poverty is controlled, the differences in homicide rates among U.S. ethnic groups all but disappear (Hawkins 1986, 1993; Stark 1990). Bernard (1990) advances an integration of the subculture premises with cognitive aggression theories that has the potential of better explaining data and could be applied to wife abuse, but this application has not yet been undertaken.

Evidence from this volume's anthropological primary data related to cultural/subcultural theory centers on the degree of general violence in the society, the amount of active community intervention against wife beating and battering (signaling a general cultural norm against such violence), and the acceptance of definitions of masculinity (at least among some groups), which includes violence and/or dominance of women (see Hanrahan et al. 1993 for further explanation of the integration of these variables). In Iran we find a model case, where high levels of wife beating and battering accompany extreme general violence and warfare, no community intervention against violence toward wives, and masculinity definitions that include general aggression and dominance of women. The Wape represent the opposite extreme in all aspects.

All of the other cultures discussed here present an extremely mixed picture in terms of these variables. We find approximately similar high levels of both wife beating and wife battering among the Taiwanese, Indo-Fijians, Bun, and Kaliai but greatly disparate levels of general violence, present or historical warfare, and aggressive masculinity norms, which seem to vary together. Even though general aggressive masculinity norms have been thought generally to accompany dominance over women norms (e.g., Hanrahan et al. 1993), we find both the Taiwanese and Indo-Fijians having strong norms of male dominance accompanied by relative nonaggression in other spheres, while among the Ujelang we find the opposite juxtaposition. There also seems to be more active community interference against wife beating where masculinity norms do not strongly encourage dominance of women.

Thus, we find little support for the general culture of violence theory extended to wife beating and only marginal support for a subculture of violence notion. Ujelang young men appear to be very much young men described in Western sociological subculture of violence theory, but the majority of the examples here are more monocultural in nature. The differential norms regarding female dominance and aggression in general are somewhat congruent with the research that finds different typologies of batterers, obviously with different norms of masculine behavior. However, this does not necessarily support a subculture of violence theory extended to wife abuse. Instead, one might better advance a culture/subculture of violence against women theory that would have more in keeping with feminist perspectives than those used to explain general homicide. In fact, homicide epidemiologists are beginning to recognize the strikingly different dynamics between homicides in the United States involving women and the far more frequent and more frequently theoretically addressed killings among men (Campbell 1995; Mercy and Saltzman 1989; Radford and Russell 1992).

Systems Theory

The use of systems theory to explain wife abuse has been most completely articulated and tested by Murray Straus and his associates in an impressive body of research that spans the 1980s and 1990s. Straus incorporates the beating of wives within the category of "marital violence" that is seen as part of family violence. While recognizing that the most injurious violence in marriages is that against wives and that inequality in individual marriages and societal structures influences wife beating, Straus emphasizes other factors in the system as being equally or more important (Kalmuss and Straus 1990; Yllo and Straus 1990). Straus (1990) and Straus and Smith (1990) identify six major causes of family violence: stress (stressful life events), intrafamily conflict, male dominance in the family and society, cultural norms permitting family violence, family socialization for violence, and the pervasiveness of violence in the society. Systems theory also posits the presence of feedback mechanisms that serve to further encourage the phenomenon once it has begun (see Giles-Sims 1983 for a complete explication of the systems feedback mechanism applied to wife battering).

A cornerstone of family violence systems theory is the interrelationship between wife abuse and child abuse, a relationship that Straus (1990), in his national random survey, found most robust for those fathers who severely battered their wives. A feminist analysis might posit that this relationship is in fact reflective only of extremely controlling and violent men seeking to dominate all members of their families (Stark and Flitcraft 1988). However, Straus also ascertained that women who were beaten were more likely to abuse their children, although those who were severely battered were less likely to abuse their children than those who were moderately abused. In addition, Straus found increased physical punishment of parents in their childhood associated with increased rates of child abuse and marital violence in their family of procreation.

In the cultures described in this volume, there is only mixed association between violence toward children and the beating of wives. We find severe child physical punishment and/or other forms of family violence in the Iranian, Kaliai, and Bun cultures and slightly less but still noteworthy examples of the same among the Indo-Fijians and Taiwanese villagers, all cultures with at least moderate levels of wife beating and battering. Yet the Indian people, among whom wife beating is widespread, are extremely gentle toward their children, whereas the Wape and Ujelang use corporal punishment with their children, yet women in those societies are battered far less often. Similarly, Levinson (1989) did not find a clear relationship between violence toward children and violence toward wives. Generally, small-scale societies do not exhibit anything like the child abuse seen in Western, industrialized countries, and the systems model is therefore difficult to support in terms of the socialization for violence in families (McGehee 1985). However, in future work it may be useful to differentiate child beating from child battering as a way of sorting out the existing discrepancies. We also find the same mixed evidence around general societal violence as was reviewed in the previous section.

The evidence presented in this volume does not allow any estimation of individual family stress, but we certainly see several entire societies under extreme stress, in terms of massive systems change (Iran, Aboriginal, Mayotte, !Kung, Taiwanese, and, to a somewhat lesser extent, Kaliai and Indo-Fijian) and/or extreme poverty (Aboriginal and Wape). Yet the amount of wife battering varies considerably among these societies, and those for which we have longitudinal data show no particular increase in violence against female partners accompanying the social change.

In defense of systems theory, we have reviewed the primarily supportive evidence in our cultures linking male dominance and cultural norms to wife battering in the feminist section. We also find some clear evidence of societal feedback mechanisms that maintain and increase the beating of wives in the majority of cultures that exhibit moderate or frequent levels of the practice. However, these feedback mechanisms (such as the Iranian community encouragement of keeping a wife submissive and disapproval if she is not) would be interpreted in the feminist framework as a male dominance system maintenance mechanism.

Adding new insights to a systems approach are the negative feedback loops provided by some of the societies discussed here. For instance, the Ecuadorian Indians, recognizing the potential for wife beating (considered normative) to escalate to battering, assign compadres to each young couple. These persons are responsible for mediating conjugal quarrels. There is also a strong balance or reciprocity notion important in this society, but the ideal sum total (at least immediately after marriage) is for men to have more (behavior and goods) than women. We also see a balance ideal among the Bun, Ujelang, and Nagovisi. The latter peoples provide several nonviolent but serious strategies available for discord, somewhat similar to the evidence from Ecuador. This can be contrasted with the strict hierarchies considered normative for all relationships in Iran and India. Thus, balance ideals do not seem to protect against wife beating, but they, along with other societal remedies specifically aimed at decreasing marital conflict, may serve to keep wife battering in check, even where wife beating is relatively severe.

Social Learning Theory

Social learning theory has provided rather consistent evidence in the Western social sciences to explain at least some of family violence in general and wife abuse specifically. Battering husbands in the United States have more often than not come from homes where wife abuse and/or child abuse was practiced (Hotaling and Sugarman 1986; Straus and Gelles 1990; Stark 1990). Thus, the behavior was modeled, with reinforcement provided by the media and peers. The corollary from a less complex society would be childhood experiences of physical violence, exposure to the beating of one's mother, and reinforcement from an ideal of the warrior-type male. As previously noted, the contributors to this volume are unable to provide much evidence of violence toward children and have found relatively little support for a connection of male ideals of aggression with wife battering. However, wife-battering societies have apparently condoned violence against women over many generations. We do not have the data to look at individual families over time, but in small-scale societies with little isolation of nuclear families, it is certainly possible to easily learn behavior from others in the community. Social learning theory can be a corollary for all of the major theories thus far advanced as a mechanism by which individual batterers learn this behavior. Although contributors to this volume have found less support for this mechanism than has been advanced in psychosocial research, we cannot say it does not operate.

Exchange Theory

Gelles (1983) draws on existing behavioral exchange theory and criminology's social control theory to advance his exchange/social theory (usually referred to as exchange theory) of family violence. It is behavioral in origin, with the premise that human beings act in order to be rewarded and to avoid punishment. As applied to family violence, Gelles posits that family members will be violent toward each other if the benefits outweigh the costs. He points out the lack of inevitable negative sanctions against violent family members as a social control deficit, a premise that has been supported by research documenting batterers' perception of an absence of sanctions against such behavior in the United States (Carmody and Williams 1987). According to Gelles, the isolation and privacy of the U.S. nuclear family also adds to the ability of a family member to be violent without cost. Benefits of wife beating include increased power and control and an enhanced "tough guy" image.

Most of the cultures described in this volume have very little nuclear family isolation; in fact, only India and increasingly Taiwan even approximate the degree of family privacy found in the United States. Yet in Taiwan, wife battering is, if anything, decreasing as extended family living arrangements become less common. Furthermore, in the societies discussed here we see a wide range of violence against women all in relatively communal living situations.

In contrast, the notion of sanctions against wife battering does seem to be an important factor that fits in exchange theory. As frequently noted by the contributors to this volume, when there is very little privacy in small villages and when homes are anything but soundproof, it is much easier for community negative sanctions to be applied at the exact times they are needed. Few of the societies have formalized sanctions such as laws or criminal proceedings, but this is being tried by the Kaliai to curb wife beating, which is now being recognized as a problematic custom. The Wape have a unique system for sanctions—namely, their ancestors—but it obviously works very well in increasing the costs of violence. We also find some cultures (Ujelang, Ecuadorian Indian, and Mayotte) where community sanctions against battering seem to overcome individual proclivities for beating and dominance that well might escalate to abuse.

This evidence supporting exchange theory could also be used within a systems or feminist framework. The basic issue is whether or not one views human beings from a behaviorist viewpoint, an assumption not addressed by our data. The Wape also seem to argue against the notion that everyone would use violence if there were insufficient social controls.

Conclusions

The evidence from the small-scale societies presented in this volume does not fully support one of the theoretical models to the exclusion of the others but instead suggests that none of the Western social science theories explains all of the patterns of wife beating and battering that have been described. Thus, anthropological evidence has some important additions to make to the scholarly and practical formulations about the beating of wives. Specifically, the editors of this volume found only limited support for the cultural/subcultural, resource, and social learning theories as now articulated; were unable to evaluate the underlying premise of exchange theory; argued that systems theory, in order to work across cultures, needs either to separate wife and child abuse or differentiate between child beating and child battering; and postulated that feminist theory had considerable support but would need to differentiate among wife beating, wife battering, and mutual violence (and admit the latter exists) to be more explanatory.

This review has also helped to emphasize the importance of societal-level influences on violence, a premise that is important for policy and prevention initiatives. Individuals do not seem to vary much across cultures in terms of psychological imperatives; young adult and adolescent males seem to be struggling with defining their roles, with how to be a "real" man according to whatever norms their cultures or subcultures have established. For example, the young, married, male Ujelang who wishes he could enact an unmarried warrior role is similar to the young, married, working-class U.S. man who wishes he could be either a really tough guy or a very rich guy, both of which have significant power in this society. Each goes out to drink with his friends, many of whom are unmarried and project a sense of freedom, even though the unattached males have their own status problems. Each may go back home and attack his wife. We are not sure whether this individual act is because of a patriarchal, behavioral, ethnological or psychological (status inconsistency, low self-esteem, frustration) imperative, but it is in the society's response to the beating that we see differences. In the Ujelang village, the man will be chastised if he does more than hit once; in the United States, his actions usually will go unremarked and definitely unrebuked by any but his partner and will probably escalate. Among the Ujelang, there is community scrutiny and evaluation of both the husband's and the wife's action by political leaders. In both places we see the male blaming the female's behavior. Sexual jealousy and female role enactment proscriptions, whether issues of parental certainty or patriarchy, abound worldwide (although we see an exception among the Wape). However, community acceptance of these "excuses" occurs to varying degrees.

The idea of group solidarity is also very important among the Ujelang; thus, where we can add negative sanctions against battering to a sense of group honor based on nonviolence and decent treatment of women (as the Kaliai are attempting to establish), there is a chance that battering will be limited. It is also clear that options for women are necessary, including personal autonomy, economic opportunity, and the ability to form close linkages with other women. Actual female power, as well as community sanction, seems stronger than male dominance norms in decreasing the amount of battering otherwise expected among the Ujelang, Ecuadorian Indians, and Mayotte. It is useful if the cultural (or subcultural) definition of a "real" man excludes the idea of controlling women by force if necessary, but it is apparent that societal structures and anticipatory community mechanisms can overcome individual propensities to violence.

The calls from feminist and systems theory activists to change the societal structures that allow and facilitate battering are thus supported by the anthropological data presented here. Sanctuary for beaten women is a necessary cornerstone in all cultures and is provided by wife abuse shelters in most industrialized countries. In other countries, such as Nicaragua, there are female centers that address legal and employment issues for women but also provide opportunities for women to address battering collectively (Wessel and Campbell 1997). Much more needs to be done to provide similar sanctuary and opportunities in Iran and Taiwan. Since the data for this volume were collected, there have been increasing community-level initiatives in India that are extremely heartening (Kelkar 1994). There also need to be strong societal and international sanctions against wife beating and especially battering, though we have shown that small group realities can be stronger than official sanctions in either direction. Changing neighborhood- and community-level realities is also a more realistic strategy than changing the precepts of an ancient religion or the lineage, locality, and/or property exchanges associated with marriage.

The work reviewed here thus extends the premise of changing societal structures to a focus of action on the small community or neighborhood level. In the United States, the plight of battered women has been publicized nationally, resulting in laws and shelters and at least a moderate increase in the economic and political status of women. Although work in these arenas needs to continue, perhaps it is time to start applying sanctions at the neighborhood level. Let us make individual batterers known to their communities, their churches, their schools, and their job sites for public censure. Let us work toward forming community- and neighborhood-level groups of women, for economic solidarity and for solidarity against men who batter. When a woman is being beaten, her neighbors can call the police if they are made aware of the warning signs. In this way, we can mimic Wape women, the compadres of Ecuadorian Indians, the kin and community courts of the Nagovisi, the male friends and relatives in Abelam, and the !Kung neighbors. These are all widely divergent societies, yet they all have mechanisms to limit the harm from wife beating. By some measures, these cultures can be described as "primitive" or less "developed," but when it comes to the beating of wives, they have much to teach us.

NOTES

1. Levinson (1989), who thoughtfully counters this critique by controlling for the gender of the anthropologist, found that the basic relationship between his quantified measures of wife beating and other societal factors remain essentially the same. This strategy does not solve the issues of secondary data and gender of informants, but it increases the credibility of his work and other work using compiled anthropological data sets in terms of gender bias. It also strengthens the case for considering the findings in his volume in conjunction with the data presented here.

2. Without feminist analysis, as presented by Miller (this volume), the dowry murders in India may not seem related to male jealousy.

3. See Young (1989) for an excellent example of how the less-complex societal enforcement of chastity before marriage has been translated into complex societal terms. See also Collier and Rosaldo (1981) for a discussion of the correlates of bridewealth societies, including those with dowry payments, also briefly discussed by Lambek (this volume).

REFERENCES CITED

Allen, C. M., and Murray A. Straus. 1980. "Resources, Power, and Husband-Wife Violence." In *Social Causes of Husband-Wife Violence.* Ed. Murray A. Straus and Gerald T. Hotaling. 188–208. Minneapolis: University of Minnesota Press.

Asbury, Jo-Ellen. 1993. "Violence in Families of Color in the United States." In *Family Violence: Prevention and Treatment.* Ed. Robert L. Hampton, T. Gullotta, G. Adams, E. Potter, and R. Weissberg. 159–76. Newbury Park, Calif.: Sage.

Bachman, Ronet, and Linda Saltzman. 1995. *Violence against Women: Estimates from the Redesigned Survey.* Washington, D.C.: Department of Justice.

Baron, Larry, and Murray A. Straus. 1987. "Legitimate Violence, Violent Attitudes, and Rape: A Test of the Cultural Spillover Theory." *Annal of the New York Academy of Sciences* 528:79–100.

Berenson, Abbey, Norma Stiglich, Gregg Wilkinson, and Garland Anderson. 1992. "Prevalence of Physical and Sexual Assault in Pregnant Adolescents." *Journal of Adolescent Health* 12:466–69.

Bernard, Thomas J. 1990. "Angry Aggression among the 'Truly Disadvantaged.'" *Criminology* 28 (1): 73–96.

Bowker, Lee H. 1983. *Beating Wife-Beating.* Lexington, Mass.: Lexington Books.

Brown, Judith K. 1982. "Cross-Cultural Perspectives on Middle-Aged Women." *Current Anthropology* 23:143–56.

Campbell, Jacquelyn C. 1985. "Beating of Wives: A Cross-Cultural Perspective." *Victimology* 10:174–85.

———. 1989. "A Test of Two Explanatory Models of Women's Responses to Battering." *Nursing Research* 38:18–24.

———. 1992. "'If I Can't Have You, No One Can': Issues of Power and Control in the Homicide of Women." In *Femicide: The Politics of Woman Killing.* Ed. Jayne Radford and Diana E. Russell. 99–113. New York: Twayne.

———. 1995. *Assessing Dangerousness: Violence by Sexual Offenders, Batterers, and Child Abusers.* Newbury Park, Calif.: Sage.

Campbell, Jacquelyn C., and Janice Humphreys, eds. 1993. *Nursing Care of Survivors of Family Violence.* St. Louis: Mosby.

Carmody, Dianne C., and Kirk Williams. 1987. "Wife Assault and the Perceptions of Sanctions." *Violence and Victims* 2:25–38.

Carroll, James C. 1980. "Cultural-Consistency Theory of Family Violence in Mexican-American and Jewish-American Ethnic Groups." In *The Social Causes of Husband-Wife Violence.* Ed. Murray A. Straus and Gerald T. Hotaling. Minneapolis: University of Minnesota Press.

Collier, Jane F. 1974. "Women in Politics." In *Woman, Culture, and Society.* Ed. Michelle Z. Rosaldo and Louise Lamphere. 89–96. Stanford, Calif.: Stanford University Press.

Collier, Jane F., and Michelle Z. Rosaldo. 1981. "Politics and Gender in Simple Societies." In *Sexual Meanings: The Cultural Construction of Gender and Sexuality.* Ed. Sherry Ortner and Harriet Whitehead. 275–329. New York: Cambridge University Press.

Counts, Dorothy Ayers. 1990. "Introduction." In *Domestic Violence in Oceania.* Ed. Dorothy Ayers Counts. 1–6. Special issue of *Pacific Studies* 13 (3).

Crowell, Nancy, and Ann W. Burgess. 1996. *Understanding Violence against Women.* Washington, D.C.: National Academy Press.

Daly, Martin, and Margo Wilson. 1988. *Homicide.* New York: Aldine de Gruyter.

Daly, Mary. 1979. *Gyn/Ecology: The Metaethics of Radical Feminism.* Boston: Beacon Press.

Davidson, Terry. 1978. *Conjugal Crime: Understanding and Changing the Wife-Beating Problem.* New York: Hawthorn Books.

Dearwater, Stephen, et al. 1998. "Prevalence of Intimate Partner Abuse in Women Treated at Community Hospital Emergency Departments." *Journal of the American Medical Association* 280 (5): 433–38.

Dobash, Rebecca Emerson, and Russell Dobash. 1979. *Violence against Wives.* New York: Free Press.

———. 1998. *Rethinking Violence against Women.* Thousand Oaks, Calif.: Sage.

Dobash, Rebecca, Russell Dobash, Margo Wilson, and Martin Daly. 1992. "Cross-National Collaborative Group: The Changing Rate of Major Depression." *Journal of the American Medical Association* 268:3098–105.

Dutton, Donald G. 1995. *The Domestic Assault of Women.* Newton, Mass.: Allyn and Bacon.

Fagan, Jeffrey, and Angela Browne. 1994. "Violence between Spouses and Intimates: Physical Aggression between Women and Men in Intimate Relationships." In *Understanding and Preventing Violence: Social Influences.* Ed. Albert Reiss and Jeffrey Roth. 115–292. Washington, D.C.: National Academy Press.

Gaffney, K. F., E. Choi, Y. Kwanghyoung, G. B. Jones, C. Bowman, and N. N. Tavangar. 1997. "Stressful Events among Pregnant Salvadoran Women: A Cross-Cultural Comparison." *Journal of Obstetrical, Gynecological, and Neonatal Nursing* 26 (3): 303–10.

Gartner, Rosemary, K. Baker, and F.C. Pampel. 1990. "Gender Stratification and the Gender Gap in Homicide Victimization." *Social Problems* 37:593–612.

Gelles, Richard J. 1983. "An Exchange/Social Theory." In *The Dark Side of Families: Current Family Violence Research.* Ed. David Finkelhor, Richard J. Gelles, Gerald T. Hotaling, and Murray A. Straus. 151–65. Beverly Hills, Calif.: Sage.

Giles-Sims, Jean. 1983. *Wife-Battering: A Systems Theory Approach.* New York: Guilford Press.

Gondolf, Edward. 1988. "Who Are Those Guys? Toward a Behavioral Typology of Batterers." *Violence and Victims* 3 (3): 187–203.

Gondolf, Edward W., Ellen Fisher, and J. Richard McFerron. 1988. "Racial Differences among Shelter Residents: A Comparison of Anglo, Black, and Hispanic Battered Women." *Journal of Family Violence* 3 (1): 39–51.

Goode, William. 1971. "Force and Violence in the Family." *Journal of Marriage and the Family* 33:624–36.

Greenblat, Cathy. 1985. "Don't Hit Your Wife 'Unless': Preliminary Findings on Normative Support for the Use of Physical Force by Husbands." *Victimology* 10:221–41.

Haj-Yahia, Muhammad M. 1997. "Predicting Beliefs about Wife Beating among Engaged Arab Men in Israel." *Journal of Family Violence* 12 (4): 530–45.

Hampton, Robert L., and Richard J. Gelles. 1994. "Violence toward Black Women in a Nationally Representative Sample of Black Families." *Journal of Comparative Family Studies* 25 (1): 105–19.

Hanmer, Jalna, and Mary Maynard, eds. 1985. *Women, Violence, and Social Control.* Atlantic Highlands, N.J.: Humanities Press.

Hanrahan, Patricia, Jacquelyn Campbell, and Yvonne Ulrich. 1993. "Theories of Violence." In *Nursing Care of Survivors of Family Violence.* Ed. Jacquelyn C. Campbell and Janice Humphreys. 3–35. St. Louis: Mosby.

Hawkins, Darnell F. 1986. *Homicide among Black Americans.* Lanham, Md.: University Press of America.

———. 1993. "Inequality, Culture, and Interpersonal Violence." *Health Affairs* 12:80–95.

Heise, Lori L., Jacqueline Pitanguy, and Adrienne Germain. 1994. *Violence against Women: The Hidden Health Burden.* Washington, D.C.: World Bank.

Holtzworth-Munroe, Amy, and Gregory Stuart. 1994. "Typologies of Male Batterers: Three Subtypes and the Differences among Them." *Psychological Bulletin* 116 (3): 476–97.

Hornung, Carlton A., B. Claire McCullough, and Taichi Sugimoto. 1981. "Status Relationships in Marriage: Risk Factors in Spouse Abuse." *Journal of Marriage and the Family* 43 (3): 675–92.

Hotaling, Gerald, and David Sugarman. 1986. "An Analysis of Risk Markers in Husband to Wife Violence: The Current State of Knowledge." *Violence and Victims* 1:101–24.

———. 1990. "A Risk Marker Analysis of Assaulted Wives." *Journal of Family Violence* 5:1–3.

Jacobson, N. S., J. M. Gottman, E. Gortner, S. Berns, and J. W. Shortt. 1996. "Psychological Factors in the Longitudinal Course of Battering: When Do the Couples Split Up? When Does the Abuse Decrease?" *Violence and Victims* 11 (4): 371–92.

Johnson, Harriette C. 1996. "Violence and Biology: A Review of the Literature." *Families in Society: The Journal of Contemporary Human Services* 1:3–18.

Johnson, Michael P. 1995. "Patriarchal Terrorism and Common Couple Violence: Two Forms of Violence against Women." *Journal of Marriage and the Family* 57:283–94.

Kalmuss, Debra S., and Murray A. Straus. 1990. "Wife's Marital Dependency and Wife Abuse." In *Physical Violence in American Families.* Ed. Murray A. Straus and Richard Gelles. 369–82. New Brunswick, N.J.: Transaction Press.

Kelkar, Govind. 1994. "Stopping the Violence against Women: Fifteen Years of Activism in India." In *Freedom from Violence: Women's Strategies from Around the World.* Ed. Margaret Schuler. 75–99. Washington, D.C.: Women, Law and Development.

Kerns, Virginia, and Judith K. Brown, eds. 1992. *In Her Prime: New Views of Middle-Aged Women.* 2d ed. Urbana: University of Illinois Press.

Lester, David. 1980. "A Cross-Culture Study of Wife Abuse." *Aggressive Behavior* 6:361–64.

Levinson, David. 1989. *Family Violence in Cross-Cultural Perspectives.* Newbury Park, Calif.: Sage.

Lockhart, Lettie L. 1987. "A Re-examination of the Effects of Race and Social Class on the Incidence of Marital Violence: A Search for Reliable Differences." *Journal of Marriage and the Family* 49:603–10.

Masamura, Wilfred T. 1979. "Wife Abuse and Other Forms of Aggression." *Victimology* 2:479–85.

McGehee, Charles L. 1985. "Responses to Child Abuse in World Perspective." *Victimology* 10:140–63.

Mercy, James A., and Linda Saltzman. 1989. "Fatal Violence among Spouses in the United States, 1976–85." *American Journal of Public Health* 79:595–99.

O'Keefe, Maureen. 1994. "Racial/Ethnic Differences among Battered Women and Their Children." *Journal of Child and Family Studies* 3 (3): 282–305.

Parker, Barbara, and Dale N. Schumacher. 1977. "The Battered Wife Syndrome and Violence in the Nuclear Family of Origin: A Controlled Pilot Study." *American Journal of Public Health* 67:760–61.

Pleck, Elizabeth. 1987. *Domestic Tyranny: The Making of Social Policy against Family Violence from Colonial Times to the Present.* New York: Oxford University Press.

Radford, Jayne, and Diana E. Russell. 1992. *Femicide: The Politics of Woman Killing.* New York: Twayne.

Richie, Beth. 1993. *Wings of Gauze: Women of Color and the Experience of Health and Illness.* Detroit: Wayne State University Press.

———. 1996. *Compelled to Crime.* New York: Routledge.

Saunders, Daniel G. 1988. "Wife Abuse, Husband Abuse, or Mutual Combat? A Feminist Perspective on the Empirical Findings." In *Feminist Perspectives on Wife Abuse.* Ed. Kersti Yllo and Michele Bograd. 90–113. Newbury Park, Calif.: Sage.

Shields, Nancy, George J. McCall, and Christine R. Hanneke. 1988. "Patterns of Family and Nonfamily Violence: Violent Husbands and Violent Men." *Violence and Victims* 3 (2): 83–97.

Smith, Michael D. 1989. "Is There a Patriarchal Subculture of Wife Abusers?" Paper presented at the annual meeting of the American Criminological Society. San Francisco.

Snyder, D., and L. Fruchtman. 1981. "Differential Patterns of Wife Abuse: A Data-Based Typology." *Journal of Consulting and Clinical Psychology* 49:878–85.

Sorenson, Susan. 1996. "Violence against Women: Examining Ethnic Differences and Commonalities." *Evaluation Review* 20 (2): 123–45.

Sorenson, Susan, and C. Telles. 1991. "Self-Reports of Spousal Violence in a Mexican-American and Non-Hispanic White Population." *Violence and Victims* 6 (1): 3–15.

Stark, Evan. 1990. "Rethinking Homicide: Violence, Race, and the Politics of Gender." *International Journal of Health Services* 20:3–26.

Stark, Evan, and Ann Flitcraft. 1988. "Women and Children at Risk: A Feminist Perspective on Child Abuse." *International Journal of Health Services* 18:197–218.

Steinmetz, Suzanne K., and Joseph H. Lucca. 1988. "Husband Battering." In *Handbook of Family Violence.* Ed. Vincent Van Hasselt, Randall L. Morrison, Alan S. Bellack, and Michel Hersen. 233–46. New York: Plenum Press.

Stewart, D. E., and A. Cecutti. 1993. "Physical Abuse in Pregnancy." *Canadian Medical Association Journal* 149:1257–63.

Straus, Murray A. 1990. "Ordinary Violence, Child Abuse, and Wife-Beating: What Do They Have in Common?" In *Physical Violence in American Families.* Ed. Murray A. Straus and Richard Gelles. 403–23. New Brunswick, N.J.: Transaction Press.

Straus, Murray A., and Christine Smith. 1990. "Violence in Hispanic Families in the United States: Incidence Rates and Structural Interpretations." In *Physical Violence in American Families.* Ed. Murray A. Straus and Richard Gelles. 341–67. New Brunswick, N.J.: Transaction Press.

Straus, Murray A., and Richard Gelles, eds. 1990. *Physical Violence in American Families.* New Brunswick, N.J.: Transaction Press.

Tolman, Richard, and Larry Bennett. 1990. "A Review of Quantitative Research on Men Who Batter." *Journal of Interpersonal Violence* 5:87–118.

Torres, Sara. 1987. "Hispanic-American Battered Women: Why Consider Cultural Differences?" *Response* 10:20–21.

Van Hasselt, Vincent, Randall L. Morrison, Alan S. Bellack, and Michel Hersen, eds. 1988. *Handbook of Family Violence.* New York: Plenum Press.

Wessel, Lois, and Jacquelyn C. Campbell. 1997. "Providing Sanctuary for Battered Women: Nicaragua's Casas de la Mujer." *Issues in Mental Health Nursing* 18:455–76.

Whiting, Beatrice. 1965. "Sex Identity Conflict and Physical Violence: A Comparative Study." *American Anthropologist* 67:123–40.

Williams, Oliver. 1989. "Sexual Conquest and Patterns of Black-on-Black Violence: A Structural-Cultural Perspective." *Violence and Victims* 4:257–74.

Wilson, Margo, Holly Johnson, and Martin Daly. 1995. "Lethal and Non-Lethal Violence against Wives." *Canadian Journal of Criminology* 37:331–62.

Wingood, Gina, and Ralph DiClemente. 1997. "The Effects of an Abusive Primary Partner on the Condom Use and Sexual Negotiation Practices of African-American Women." *American Journal of Public Health* 87:1016–18.

Wolfgang, Marvin E., and Franco Ferracuti. 1981. *The Subculture of Violence*. Rpt., Beverly Hills, Calif.: Sage.

Yllo, Kersti. 1984. "The Status of Women, Marital Equality, and Violence against Wives." *Journal of Family Issues* 3:307–20.

Yllo, Kersti, and Michele Bograd, eds. 1988. *Feminist Perspectives on Wife Abuse.* Newbury Park, Calif.: Sage.

Yllo, Kersti, and Murray A. Straus. 1990. "Patriarchy and Violence against Wives: The Impact of Structural and Normative Factors." In *Physical Violence in American Families.* Ed. Murray A. Straus and Richard Gelles. 383–99. New Brunswick, N.J.: Transaction Press.

Young, Kathleen Z. 1989. "The Imperishable Virginity of Saint Maria Goretti." *Gender and Society* 3 (4): 474–82.

NINETEEN

"Women's Rights Are Human Rights": International Law and the Culture of Domestic Violence

Jean G. Zorn

What should women do if they believe that domestic violence is unlikely to stop so long as legal sanctions against it are ineffective or nonexistent? One answer is to work with and through governmental authorities and international organizations to create effective sanctions against wife beating and to promote enforcement by nation-states of laws that protect women from violence. This is what women have been doing over the past two decades, both within their own countries[1] and internationally.

In this chapter I will focus on the new international order that activist women are creating. First, I will briefly describe their heroic (and largely successful) efforts to broaden the scope of international law so that freedom from domestic violence has become recognized as a basic human right protected by international treaties and covenants.[2] In so doing, women are aware that they are trying to use law to change cultures. Then I will examine the relations of law and culture and discuss whether international law can or should be used to effect cultural change.

Overcoming International Law

Many legal barriers had to be overcome before freedom from domestic violence was recognized as a human right that nations are mandated by international law to protect. Nations, not people, were the only recognized parties under classical international law (the body of treaties, conventions, and customary agreements that constituted international law until the entry of postcolonial countries into the world of nations). Until the adoption by the United Nations General Assembly in 1948 of the Universal Declaration of Human Rights,[3] international law concerned itself only with the rights of countries as against one another and not with the rights of individuals or groups within those countries. The Universal Declaration of Human Rights gave individuals status under international law, declaring that individuals have rights that their governments ought not to inhibit. The Declaration made nation-states responsible for ensuring that people within their borders were not denied these rights.

However, the Declaration's utility for women was limited. First, its categorization of human rights encompassed only civil and political rights, the relations between people and their governments and the activities (such as speech, assembly, and voting) that take place in the public sphere. Although (at the insistence of Eleanor Roosevelt) it provided that women should be treated equally with men in the recognition of these rights, the Declaration was deficient in ignoring the private sphere, where most of the world's women spend most of their lives and where most injuries to them occur. The inattention to economic and social rights was not an oversight. Drafted primarily by men, the Declaration manifested the male perspective that matters concerning home and family are beyond the purview of law (Romany 1993).

Second, the Declaration, like all international law instruments at the time, was premised on the view that, even in the field of human rights, international law governs nations and does not apply directly to individuals. The Declaration prohibited certain acts done by countries against individuals, but it did not prohibit acts done by individuals against other individuals. Since wife beating is perpetrated on women by individuals, not by their countries, the Universal Declaration of Human Rights did not recognize it as the violation of a right. Under classical international law, women were subjected to a burden of double domesticity. Wrongs done to them went unrecognized by international law becaused they occurred in the domestic sphere (the home) and because they were not perpetrated on women by domestic law (the law of the nation-state).

Women activists have pointed out that, by ignoring women's needs and interests, the Declaration may have been actively harmful to women. By allowing governments (and individuals) to believe that they have done all that needs to be done for women when they have given women political rights, the Declaration may actually have done a disservice to women who continue to be denied education equal to that of men; to be forced into unwanted marriages; to have no rights over property; to have limited or no access to the kinds of employment that will give them economic security; and to suffer from wife beating, rape, sexual abuse, genital mutilation, and other forms of violence.

The Convention on the Elimination of All Forms of Discrimination against Women (CEDAW), adopted by the U.N. General Assembly in 1979 and opened for signature in 1980, attempted to remedy some of the Declaration's deficiencies, particularly with respect to women's individual rights. Recognizing that true equality is not a matter of civil and political access alone, it broadened the areas in which discrimination against women would constitute a violation of international law by providing, in article 3, that women should be guaranteed equality in the exercise of their human rights "in all fields, in particular in the political, social, economic and cultural fields." It brought violations of human rights by individuals within the purview of international law, at least indirectly, by making countries responsible for the actions of private parties. By ratifying the convention, countries agreed that they "condemn[ed] discrimination against women in all its forms" and would "pursue by all appropriate means without delay a policy of eliminating discrimination against women . . . by any person, organization or enterprise" (article 2).

But CEDAW is not a perfect instrument. Although article 2 requires countries to "modify or abolish existing laws, regulations, customs and practices which constitute discrimination against women," it does not explicitly state that wife beating or other forms of violence against women fall within this category. Also, the mandate to "pursue . . . without delay a policy of eliminating discrimination" is limited by the qualification that the pursuit need be only by "all appropriate means." This phrasing raises the obvious question: Appropriate for whom? If the means are those appropriate to the state, and if the rulers of that state argue that the elimination of domestic violence is inappropriate according to their circumstances, what recourse is there? Rebecca Cook (1994) argues persuasively that appropriateness is to be judged by international authorities and not by the miscreant nations, but nothing in the convention makes this clear, and the international authorities have little power to enforce this view.

CEDAW would be more effective if individuals who violate the human rights of women could be directly penalized for violating the convention, but CEDAW's only remedy for human rights violations perpetrated by individuals is to suggest that countries abolish those customs and practices that discriminate against women. Although it has moved beyond the absolute focus on countries that characterized classical international law, CEDAW is still bound by international law's state-centered vision. Nation-states were arbitrary constructs from their beginnings. The fractured territories created during and at the end of the colonial period starkly demonstrated the illusory nature of concepts like statehood and state sovereignty, and these concepts have become even more problematic in the postcolonial world. A number of commentators (e.g., Hom 1996; Knop 1993) argue persuasively that an emphasis on national boundaries, national sovereignty, or national character is not only misplaced but a diversion that limits effective change.

The rules of international law are difficult, if not impossible, to enforce. There are no courts with sure and certain jurisdiction over all nations concerning all matters, and no international police force charged with the enforcement of the rules of international law. No nation willingly gives up its powers to others, nor, short of war, can nations be forced to do so. Even those that have ratified treaties or conventions, thereby promising to abide by the document, do not always obey—and are not always penalized for their failure to do so. To the extent that international law is enforced at all, it is generally by persuasion, negotiation, and, if those means fail, war. The international law process is very similar to the legal processes in nonstate societies.

CEDAW has even less enforcement power built into it than do most treaties. Although it has been ratified by 135 countries (not including the United States), many ratified it with significant qualifications. It is administered by the Committee on the Elimination of Discrimination against Women, whose powers are limited to taking reports from parties to the convention about their attempts to meet its aspiration that discrimination against women be abolished and suggesting ways in which nations could more effectively meet this goal. While negative publicity arising from CEDAW reports may shame some governments into taking more aggressive action against domestic violence, many governments, especially those in countries where women have little political voice, may easily ignore the suggestions in these reports.

In the 1980s, women's groups (NGOs) began a worldwide campaign to make freedom from domestic and other forms of violence a universally recognized human right. In 1985, the final document of the Second United Nations Conference on Women, held in Nairobi, Kenya, affirmed that violence against women is a serious and widespread problem that deserves international attention. In response, in 1992 the Committee on the Elimination of Discrimination against Women issued guidelines to the nations that signed CEDAW, informing them that gender-based violence[4] constitutes discrimination and that "full implementation of the Convention requires States to take positive measures to eliminate all forms of violence against women" (1992:xx). Women's groups, determined to bring the issue to a forum that was not seen as organized primarily for and by women, prepared intensively for the Fifth World Conference on Human Rights, held in Vienna in 1993. There, "women presented delegates with almost 500,000 signatures from 128 countries demanding that they recognize violence as an abuse of women's rights. They also held an international tribunal, moderated by an esteemed panel of judges, where women presented well-documented and moving cases of gender-based abuse" (Heise 1995:1209). The Vienna Declaration and Programme of Action, adopted by the conference, included a section on women's rights, noting that they are part of human rights, and stated unequivocally that governments are responsible for enacting laws and policies to protect women from domestic and other forms of gender-based violence. The Declaration of the Fourth World Conference on Women, held in 1995 in Beijing, China, provides that "women's rights are human rights" (at para. 14). The Beijing Declaration makes it clear that among the human rights most necessary to women is the right to be free from violence.

International women's groups have succeeded in creating a new international legal order in which domestic violence is recognized as a wrong that governments should address with appropriate sanctions. But, as women themselves have recognized, this new order may conflict with the customs of many of the world's societies (Gunning 1992). Should international law impose itself on cultures that are in disagreement with it? If so, can it do it successfully?

Overcoming Culture

The government of the People's Republic of China has stated many times, especially in the past decade, that it considers human rights to be a matter between a government and its citizens and that it resents what it considers intrusions by other nations into its internal affairs (Hom 1992). China is not alone in this view. The governments of many non-Western countries have taken this position from time to time. They ground their arguments on sovereignty (the freedom of a country's goverment to act as it sees fit with regard to its own citizens and within its own borders), and on cultural relativity (that the list of rights contained in international treaties and conventions, such as the Universal Declaration of Human Rights and CEDAW, are the peculiar products of Western cultures, inapplicable—even antithetical—to the customs and conditions of non-Western cultures).

The argument by postcolonial nations that international human rights law may be culturally biased strikes a chord not only with anthropologists but also with the women who wish to include women's rights on the human rights agenda (Armstrong et al. 1993; Kaganas and Murray 1994). By promoting the interests of Western nations, classical international law promoted the interests of the people in power, who, for the most part, were and are men. Colonies and postcolonial nations suffered under the Western cultural hegemony of classical international law; so too have women, which is why women have worked to change international law so that it reflects their concerns. But women have also suffered under their own cultures, and their efforts to restate international law have been intended, quite overtly, to bring pressure on governments to eliminate customs that discriminate against women. Article 2 of CEDAW requires that governments modify or abolish not only governmental laws and regulations that discriminate against women but also "customs and practices" that do so. The next part of this chapter reviews the debates about whether international human rights law interferes with cultures—and whether it should interfere—and then asks whether, even if it should, it can.

Should/Does International Women's Human Rights Law Interfere with Culture?

If we define the culture of a society as the customary behaviors, values, and beliefs of the people within that social grouping, then, as the other chapters in this volume demonstrate, wife beating is part of the cultural fabric of many, if not all, societies. Not only do men in many of the societies described beat their wives from time to time, but most men (and many, if not most, women) in these societies believe that, so long as men do not cross the line (wherever that line may be) into battering, wife beating is socially acceptable, even expected. Men who do not physically chastise their wives are derided, and women who offend against male-centered norms are informed that their husbands should beat them more.

Some governments, pointing to the general acceptance in their societies of discrimination against women, argue that gender inequality is customary, an integral part of the culture, and as such should not be interfered with by international law. In lawyers' discourse, these arguments are framed as a debate about whether human rights are universal or relative—whether all governments must afford a common set of rights to their citizens, regardless of nationality, gender, or culture, or whether individual governments may tailor those rights to the conditions and circumstances of the nation. The Universal Declaration of Human Rights, like the U.S. Constitution, is a product of the universalist view that, above and beyond law or culture, there are certain inalienable civil and political rights that all governments must recognize and protect. However, relativists note that the Western powers used claims to the universality of certain rules and principles as justification for imposing Western laws and legal institutions on colonized peoples. Relativists see little difference between today's argument that the right to vote is universal and yesterday's declaration that colonial courts should recognize and apply only those customs that were not "repugnant to the general principles of humanity."[5] Both spring from the ethnocentric notion that Western laws are generally applicable, whereas customary norms are special and may even be immoral.

During the colonial period and in the early postcolonial years, most people who sympathized with the once-colonized nations also sympathized with their view that human rights are relative and may change from culture to culture. They noted that the very notion of human rights is a Western idea, predicated on individualism, on notions of personhood, self-interest, and bodily boundaries that are not necessarily shared by communal societies. They also noted that the supposedly universal rights were those that any well-fed, middle-class entrepreneur would want in relation to his or her democratic government, not those to which a subsistence gardener or underfed peasant might aspire. They were struck by the absence of the rights to food, shelter, and the protection of community and family; and they could not help but note that it was distinctly to the advantage of Western governments and multinational corporations that everyone be granted the rights that the West espoused—and no others.

The appeal of the relativist position lessens when the discussion moves from the right to vote or to assemble and focuses instead on the rights of women to be treated as equal to men in the social and economic spheres and to be free from violence. When governments argue that they cannot grant property rights to women or that they must adhere to laws that predicate citizenship on the father's nationality alone or that they will not impose sanctions on wife beating because to do so would be to interfere with time-honored custom, then activist women are divided. They are divided from one another, possibly from the women who live in traditional cultures, and certainly within themselves. They ask whether, as Western activist women, or even as third-world activist women, they ought to legislate for women in other cultural settings.[6] This question is especially difficult for women who are anthropologists, a discipline that is premised on cultural relativism and recognizes that one cannot alter one custom without causing unforeseeable effects across the culture as a whole.

However, ethnography can inform the legal argument by defining and describing custom more accurately and with more texture, as the chapters in this volume have done. When governments, which are, after all, composed primarily of men, use custom as their excuse for not recognizing women's rights, they tend not to define what they mean by custom. If wife beating occurs in almost every society in the world, if it is almost universal, then can it be said to be part of any society's unique culture? It is certainly not what sets that society apart from all others, that which gives the society its special character. One could argue that, even if international law should recognize cultural differences, universally applicable rules of international law may govern any behavior that is itself all but universal.[7]

Even if wife beating is not a worldwide phenomenon, one might still question whether it is a custom so integral to the cultural fabric of any nation that it must be maintained. Arguments for the preservation of the customs and cultures of Africa or the Pacific usually focus on those customs that have existed (in the words of many statutes) from time immemorial.[8] If wife beating is a phenomenon of more recent vintage, as some of the contributors to this volume suggest it may be, and particularly if it came into existence or into its present form only in the colonial or postcolonial era, then arguments for its preservation have less resonance.

A few years ago, I was privy to a discussion about domestic violence between a group of women from Papua New Guinea and a group of Native Americans.[9] The evening began with a showing of *Stap Easy,* a video in Melanesian pidgin that was produced by Papua New Guinea women's groups and tells the story of a Highlands woman who goes to her son's teacher, the family's pastor, and a clan elder (all of whom are men from Papua New Guinea) for help when her husband beats her. The elder counsels the husband that wife beating is a custom from the old days that must be given up. The Native American men, both of whom were Navajo, criticized the video vehemently. They agreed with its explicit message that domestic violence should be eradicated. They disagreed with its implicit message that wife beating was part of traditional culture, arguing that one of the many reasons for putting an end to domestic violence is that, like other contemporary disfunctions in community life, it is a product of colonialism.

I do not presume to know who, if anyone, was correct in this dispute. It may be that the Navajo men were correct about the sources of wife beating in Navajo culture and the Papua New Guinea women were correct about its sources in their cultures. It also may be possible that both the Navajo and the Papua New Guineans were reconceptualizing precolonial traditions and customs in ways that suit current needs. It is certainly true that both views serve the purpose of trying to end wife beating in their respective societies. For the Navajo, this aim may be best served by the argument that the activity is non-Navajo, that it was imposed by the colonizers or by the colonial experience. At the very least, this suggests that Navajo men wish to distance themselves and their culture from the practice and consequently are prepared to act against it.[10] In the Papua New Guinea context, where it is still generally believed that domestic violence is an integral part of traditional culture, it may be politically necessary to criticize tradition in order to change contemporary behavior.

Whatever the substantive merits of the dispute, embedded in the discussion were a number of important insights about culture and change. Those who argue for the relativist view of human rights are relative about rights but absolute about culture, which they say is eternally fixed and must be protected from any laws or actions that might try to alter it. If, however, cultures do adapt, then there is considerably less force in their argument. We know that cultures are complicated networks of mutually reinforcing customs that constantly evolve, interrelating with and adjusting to new trends in law, economics, politics, and other customs. It may be that the cultures of many societies are already changing in the direction of greater equality for, and less violence against, women (Armstrong et al. 1993).

Even where people still seem to be following the customs that characterized their group in precolonial times, the customs may have taken on meanings and functions very different from those they historically had. A custom that had one meaning or function in the social framework of a bygone era will have very different meanings and functions under other social conditions. A custom that once was integral to the culture may come to exist only as a formality, an old pattern fast slipping away, or as an essentially disfunctional response to unwelcome socioeconomic dislocations. For example, in precolonial times wife beating may had some social utility: it may have been a mark of a man's status as head of his household or lineage, or it may have been part of a network of mutually supporting customs that, taken together, were not entirely detrimental to women. In today's society, however, divorced from that network of other customs, wife beating may have taken on different, less useful meanings. It may be, like alcohol, merely a means for some men to vent the frustration caused by lack of, or confusion about, male status in a rapidly changing environment.

Since anthropologists deal with nonstate societies and with groups whose territories cross national boundaries, they are uniquely positioned to counter the notion that culture and the state are one—a notion that also seems to lurk at the heart of the relativist critique. When a government argues that it cannot legislate to prohibit violations of women's human rights on the grounds that the behavior is customary, it is suggesting that cultural and national boundaries are contiguous. However, just as customs change in form and meaning over time, so too in complex societies do they differ from class to class and area to area. In many Pacific societies, customs now vary not only from one indigenous group to another but from rural to urban, from wealthy to poor, from educated to noneducated—and from male to female. It may be that in every society there are groups whose customs still include wife beating and groups whose customs are nondiscriminatory. If international law must subordinate itself to custom, which group's customs should it recognize?

If the relativists, in their insistence that custom trumps international law, are referring to the customs recognized by the courts in postcolonial countries, then they are referring, in large part, to an oddly truncated and anachronistic set of customs. State courts have never dealt well with custom. They have never been certain what it is—whether it consists of behaviors or of beliefs about what behavior should be; whether it consists only of time-honored, precolonial practices or whether courts can recognize and apply changing customs (Zorn 1994–95). During the colonial period, state courts tended to adopt into state law only those customs that suited the interests of colonial authorities, most of which also sustained traditional male authority (Gordon 1991; Chanock 1994). In the process of being adopted by the courts, custom changes into customary law, into a rule that will be applied in the same way to all cases on the same topic that thereafter come before the court, regardless of the extent to which customs on the ground have changed. Customary law is not an accurate reflection of contemporary customs.

What all of this suggests, however, is not that international human rights law should in all circumstances override custom but that the question of what constitutes custom is still open for discussion. In this discussion, the voices of third- and fourth-world women cannot be ignored. They may tell us that it is ethnocentric merely to condemn wife beating, as female genital surgery has been condemned, without taking account of the context. Isabelle Gunning (1992) points out that, if one is to prohibit customs that do serve a social function, one has to be prepared to offer something in their place.

The debate over whether violence against women should be interdicted by international law is not amenable to easy solutions, which may explain why there are so many reservations to CEDAW. I have argued here that governmental defenses based on "custom" ought not to be unquestioningly accepted, but I do not mean to suggest that custom is not to be respected. It is one thing to question what people mean when they use "custom" as an excuse for acts of wanton cruelty. It is quite another to proceed arrogantly and ethnocentrically, as if customs and cultures do not exist.

Can International Law Change Culture?

The Convention on the Elimination of All Forms of Discrimination against Women was drafted with the express intent of changing those customs under which women face discriminatory or unequal treatment. Nations that are parties to the convention are held responsible not only for their own laws that discriminate against women but for their failure to legislate against discriminatory practices by private individuals, even if those practices are customary (articles 1–3). But given the uncertainties about whether governments, which have state law and broad enforcement powers at their disposal, can change culture, one must wonder whether international law can do so, given its severely limited enforcement mechanisms.

The easy answer is that law and culture change one another all the time. Law is, after all, a part, product, and shaper of culture. The model of the legal process postulated by classical liberalism posits a continuing evolutionary interaction between law and culture. Although state law does not reflect culture perfectly, it cannot exist if it is entirely inimical to the culture of which it is a part. At the same time laws, when enforced, do operate to change behavior. Over time, these behavioral alterations accumulate and solidify, eventually resulting in new sets of expectations, values, and beliefs, which in turn can result in further changes to the laws. For example, the laws enacted in the United States in the 1960s forbidding discrimination in employment and public accommodations may not have resulted in a perfectly egalitarian and nondiscriminatory society, but they have modified private behaviors and, to some extent, even beliefs.

This theory, however, is premised on the notion that law and culture begin with some measure of congruity. Laws imposed from outside the culture may create major alterations in the culture but not necessarily those that were expected. Colonized societies changed greatly, partly due to the imposed laws but not usually in the ways intended by the colonial authorities. For example, the Australian colonial administration believed that it was introducing democratic processes into the Highlands of Papua New Guinea, but what the Enga learned from this experience of colonial rule was that government is something to be manipulated to achieve one's own ends (Gordon and Meggitt 1985).

The last major outside intervention into postcolonial legal systems was the law and development movement. Lawyers and law professors from the United States descended on Africa in the early 1970s intent on producing democratic liberalism, due process, and the "rule of law" (Trubek and Galanter 1974). They succeeded in part in that significant aspects of traditional village governance were destroyed, but they did not succeed in replacing traditional structures with "modern" governments and legal institutions, as was their intent. Their intervention contributed to the breakdown of time-honored systems of social control and social cohesion, leaving no alternative theory or practice of good governance in their place. It is little wonder, then, that intrusions from the outside, particularly those supported by the Western powers, are met with disapproval by the governments and peoples of formerly colonized nations.

Social change does not occur merely because a new law is enacted; rather, there must be effective enforcement and other means, both within and outside governments, of supporting the new law. International initiatives will become local realities only to the extent that governments are willing to enact legislation that supports these initiatives and to implement that legislation. Moreover, even where new laws are enacted and enforced, they will become part of the fabric of the culture only if they are accompanied by the educational efforts of governmental and nongovernmental organizations. CEDAW does not call for any of the supportive measures—education, improved health care, access to employment opportunities—that would enable women to achieve economic independence, perhaps the surest way of freeing them from violence. International law is unlikely to modify culture in these matters without strong assistance from domestic law and domestic activity.

Conclusions and Afterthoughts

Activist women have made much progress in their endeavor to focus attention on gender-based violence and other aspects of discrimination against women. They have succeeded in changing the basic structures of international human rights law. Human rights are no longer seen as consisting solely of the political and civil relations between citizens and their governments. The definition of human rights has been broadened to include the social and economic spheres, and international law is not limited to relations among nations or even to laws enacted, or actions taken, by them. Rather, CEDAW protects women against their governments—and, at least indirectly, against the acts of private persons, such as spouses.

There is still much work to be done if this new international order is to result in social change. The norms and values that support and sustain domestic violence continue to permeate most cultures. It is therefore necessary to be culturally sensitive while simultaneously working to end domestic violence. One way to do so is to begin not from the law or from the custom but from human needs. The questions that sustain such an endeavor come more from anthropology than from law. Who are the women requiring the assistance that international and domestic laws ought to provide? What are their needs? Asking how CEDAW's aims can best be met in each cultural context is a very different question from asking whether these aims should be met at all.

APPENDIX: TREATIES, CONVENTIONS, AND OTHER INTERNATIONAL LEGAL DOCUMENTS

Universal Declaration of Human Rights, G.A. Res. 217A(III), U.N. GAOR, 3d Sess., U.N. Doc. A/810 (1948).

Convention on the Elimination of All Forms of Discrimination against Women (CEDAW), G.A. Res. 34/180, U.N. GAOR, 34th Sess., Suppl. No. 46, at 193, U.N. Doc. A/34/46 (1979). Opened for signature on March 1, 1980, 1249 U.N.T.S. 14. As of December 31, 1993, 130 countries had signed the convention.

Committee on the Elimination of Discrimination against Women, General Recommendation No. 19, 11th Sess., Agenda Item 7, U.N. Doc. CEDAW/C/1992/L.1/Add.15 (1992).

Vienna Declaration and Programme of Action, 1993 World Conference on Human Rights, U.N. Doc. A/Conf. 157/24 (1993), 32 I.L.M. 1661 (1993).

Declaration on the Elimination of Violence against Women, G.A. Res. 104, U.N. GAOR, 48th Sess., Agenda Item 111, U.N. Doc. A/RES/48/104 (1994).

Beijing Declaration and Programme of Action, Report of the Fourth World Conference on Women, Fourth World Conference on Women, Beijing, China, U.N. Doc. A/CONF.177/20 (1995).

NOTES

Special thanks are due to my colleagues Janet Calvo, Rhonda Copelon, and Kristen Booth Glen, who got me started; to Sharon Hom and Penelope Andrews, who kept me going; to Stephen Zorn and Heather Zorn, who made the first draft readable; and to the women of Papua New Guinea, exemplars for us all.

1. In Papua New Guinea, for example, a coalition of women's groups, supported by the Papua New Guinea Law Reform Commission, has created videos, posters, and pamphlets to increase women's awareness of the protections afforded them by current laws and to influence police and magistrates to enforce these laws against men who beat their wives. The women's groups have also been working to have tougher, more effective laws enacted (Law Reform Commission of Papua New Guinea 1986; Toft 1985).

2. For detailed accounts of women's struggle to gain recognition under international law of women's rights, I direct the reader to the list of references cited. Because I expect that some readers will want to pursue other issues raised in this chapter, I have also included a bibliography of recent articles not referenced here.

3. Citations to the declarations, conventions, and other international law documents discussed herein are included in the appendix.

4. Gender-based violence is defined in international law as any violence perpetrated on people because of their gender. It would include wife beating and wife battering, rape and sexual abuse, female infanticide, female genital mutilation, and forced pros-

titution. CEDAW does not expressly outlaw violence, but it does outlaw discrimination against women, and gender-based violence is considered discriminatory in that it happens only to women and only because they are women (Hom 1992; Cook 1994b).

5. This exclusionary phrase, which allowed judges of the colonial courts to impose imported laws on indigenous peoples while purporting to bring custom into the formal legal system, appears in the legislation of many Pacific and African colonies. It is still in the laws of some of them, even after independence.

6. The argument has been carried on most tellingly in relation to female genital surgeries (Gunning 1992).

7. I want to thank Janet Calvo in particular for this insight.

8. See, for example, the preindependence version of Papua New Guinea's Customs Recognition Act (called, until 1975, the Native Customs Recognition Act). The act permitted state courts to recognize as state law only those customs of indigenous Papua New Guineans that had existed "from time immemorial."

9. The discussion, which took place in Port Moresby, was part of a visit in July 1993 to Melanesia of five Native American tribal court judges, lawyers, and lay advocates who were studying Pacific customary law and customary courts. The Papua New Guineans who took part in the evening's discussion were representatives of women's groups who had been active in combating domestic violence. The Native American group consisted of three women (two from Pueblo villages and one Klingit) and two Navajo men. It was the men who engaged most vociferously in this discussion.

10. My thanks to Harriet Lyons for suggesting this interpretation of the Navajo position.

REFERENCES CITED

Armstrong, Alice, et al. 1993. "Uncovering Reality: Excavating Women's Rights in African Family Law." *International Journal of Law and Family* 7:314–69.

Chanock, Martin. 1991. "Law, State, and Culture: Thinking about Customary Law after Apartheid." *Acta Juridica* 1991:52–70.

Cook, Rebecca J. 1994. "State Responsibility for Violations of Women's Human Rights." *Harvard Human Rights Journal* 7:125–75.

Gordon, Robert J. 1991. "Vernacular Law and the Future of Human Rights in Namibia." *Acta Juridica* 1991:86–103.

Gordon, Robert J., and Mervyn Meggitt. 1985. *Law and Order in the New Guinea Highlands: Encounters with Enga.* Hanover, N.H.: University Press of New England.

Gunning, Isabelle R. 1992. "Arrogant Perception, World-Traveling, and Multi-Cultural Feminism: The Case of Female Genital Surgeries." *Columbia Human Rights Law Review* 23:189–248.

Heise, Lori L. 1995. "Violence against Women: Translating International Advocacy into Concrete Change." *American University Law Review* 44:1207–11.

Hom, Sharon K. 1992. "Female Infanticide in China: The Human Rights Specter and Thoughts towards (An)other Vision." *Columbia Human Rights Law Review* 23:249–314.

———. 1996. "Re-Positioning Human Rights Discourse on 'Asian' Perspectives." *Buffalo Journal of International Law* 3:209–34.

Kaganas, Felicity, and Christina Murray. 1994. "Law and Women's Rights in South Africa: An Overview." *Acta Juridica* 1994:1–38.

Knop, Karen. 1993. "Re/Statements: Feminism and State Sovereignty in International Law." *Transnational and Contemporary Problems* 3:293–344.

Law Reform Commission of Papua New Guinea. 1986. *Domestic Violence.* Law Reform Commission of Papua New Guinea Report No. 14. Port Moresby.

Romany, Celina. 1993 "Women as Aliens: A Feminist Critique of the Public/Private Distinction in International Human Rights Law." *Harvard Human Rights Journal* 6 (Spring): 37–125.

Toft, Susan, ed. 1985. *Domestic Violence in Papua New Guinea.* Papua New Guinea Law Reform Commission Monograph No. 3. Boroko.

Trubek, David, and Marc Galanter. 1974. "Scholars in Self-Estrangement: Some Reflections on the Crisis of Law and Development Studies in the United States." *Wisconsin Law Review* 1974:1062–102.

Zorn, Jean G. 1994–95. "Women, Custom, and State Law in Papua New Guinea." *Third World Legal Studies* 1994–95:169–205.

ADDITIONAL SOURCES

Andrews, Penelope. 1997. "Violence against Aboriginal Women in Australia: Possibilities for Redress within the International Human Rights Framework." *Albany Law Review* 60:917–41.

Bunch, Charlotte. 1995. "The Global Campaign for Women's Human Rights: Where Next After Vienna?" *St. John's Law Review* 69:171–78.

Charlesworth, Hilary,, Christine Chinkin, and Shelley Wright. 1991. "Feminist Approaches to International Law." *American Journal of International Law* 85:613–45.

Cook, Rebecca J., ed. 1994. *Human Rights International Perspectives.* Philadelphia: University of Pennsylvania Press.

Copelon, Rhonda. 1994a. "Surfacing Gender: Re-Engraving Crimes against Women in Humanitarian Law." *Hastings Women's Law Journal* 5:243–65.

———. 1994b. "Recognizing the Egregious in the Everyday: Domestic Violence as Torture." *Columbia Human Rights Law Review* 25:291–367.

Culliton, Katherine M. 1993. "Finding a Mechanism to Enforce Women's Right to State Protection from Domestic Violence in the Americas." *Harvard International Law Journal* 34:507–61.

Daly, Kathleen. 1994. *Putting Women First: Gender, Crime, and Punishment.* New Haven, Conn.: Yale University Press.

Defeis, Elizabeth. 1995. "Women's Human Rights in the Twenty-First Century." *Fordham International Law Journal* 18:1748–55.

Dietz, Elizabeth. 1996. "Violence against Women in the United States: An International Solution." *Arizona Journal of International and Comparative Law* 13:551–94.

Duclos, Nitya. 1990. "Lessons of Difference: Feminist Theory on Cultural Diversity." *Buffalo Law Review* 38:325–81.

Engle, Karen. 1992. "International Human Rights and Feminism: When Discourses Meet." *Michigan Journal of International Law* 13:517–610.

Gunning, Isabelle R. 1991. "Modernizing Customary International Law: The Challenge of Human Rights." *Virginia Journal of International Law* 31:211–47.

Hernandez-Truyol, Berta Esperanza. 1996. "Women's Rights as Human Rights: Rules, Realities, and the Role of Culture—A Formula for Reform." *Brooklyn Journal of International Law* 21:605–77.

Holt, Renee. 1991. "Women's Rights and International Law: The Struggle for Recognition and Enforcement." *Columbia Journal of Gender and Law* 1:117–41.

Jordan, Ann D. 1996. "Human Rights, Violence against Women, and Economic Development: The People's Republic of China Experience." *Columbia Journal of Gender and Law* 5:216–72.

Lewis, Hope. 1995. "Between *Irua* and 'Feminine Genital Mutilation': Feminist Human Rights Discourse and the Cultural Divide." *Harvard Human Rights Journal* 8:1–55.

Malone, Linda A. 1996. "Beyond Bosnia and *In Re Kasinga:* A Feminist Perspective on Recent Developments in Protecting Women from Sexual Violence." *Boston University International Law Journal* 14:319–40.

Mertus, Julie, and Pamela Goldberg. 1994. "A Perspective on Women and International Human Rights after the Vienna Declaration: The Inside/Outside Construct." *New York University Journal of International Law and Politics* 26:201–34.

Nhlapo, Thandabantu. 1994–95. "Indigenous Law and Gender in South Africa: Taking Human Rights and Cultural Diversity Seriously." *Third World Legal Studies* 1994–95:49–71.

Rao, Arati. 1995. "Women's Rights as Human Rights: Local Limits and International Standards." *Harvard Human Rights Journal* 8:277–83.

Sullivan, Donna J. 1994. "Women's Human Rights and the 1993 World Conference on Human Rights." *American Journal of International Law* 88:152–67.

Thomas, Dorothy Q., and Michele E. Beasley. 1995. "Domestic Violence as a Human Rights Issue." *Albany Law Review* 58:1119–47.

CONTRIBUTORS

JUDITH K. BROWN, a professor of anthropology at Oakland University, has published cross-cultural studies of initiation rites for girls, women's economic roles, and middle-aged women. She has been a postdoctoral fellow at the Bunting Institute and a visiting scholar at Stanford University, Bryn Mawr College, and Harvard University. She is the coeditor (with Virginia Kerns) of *In Her Prime: New Views of Middle-Aged Women* (2d ed., 1992) and (with Jeanette Dickerson-Putman) of *Women among Women: Anthropological Perspectives on Female Age Hierarchies* (1998).

VICTORIA K. BURBANK, an associate professor in the Department of Anthropology at the University of Western Australia, has undertaken fieldwork in Arnhem Land, Australia, for various periods of time between 1977 and 1997. Her publications include *Aboriginal Adolescence: Maidenhood in an Australian Community* (1988) and *Fighting Women: Anger and Aggression in Aboriginal Australia* (1994).

JACQUELYN C. CAMPBELL is the Anna D. Wolfe Endowed Professor and associate dean for doctoral education programs and research at Johns Hopkins University School of Nursing, with a joint appointment in the School of Hygiene and Public Health. She is the author or coauthor of more than eighty publications on battering and has recently edited two collections on the subject, *Assessing the Risk of Dangerousness: Potential for Further Violence of Sexual Offenders, Batterers, and Child Abusers* (1995) and *Empowering Survivors of Abuse: Health Care for Battered Women and Their Children* (1998).

LAURENCE MARSHALL CARUCCI, a professor of anthropology in the Department of Sociology and Anthropology at Montana State University, has conducted field research on ritual, aging, gender, kinship and social organization, drugs, food, and World War II among the people of Enewetak, Ujelang, Majuro, and Kwajalein Atolls in the Republic of the Marshall Islands. His publications include *Nuclear Nativity:*

Rituals of Renewal and Empowerment in the Marshall Islands (1997) and *In Anxious Anticipation of the Uneven Fruits of Kwajalein Atoll* (1997).

DOROTHY AYERS COUNTS, a professor of anthropology at the University of Waterloo, has conducted research in West New Britain Province, Papua New Guinea, since 1966. Among her publications are *Middlemen and Brokers in Oceanis* (1982), coedited with William Rodman, and *Aging and Its Transformations: Moving toward Death in Pacific Societies* (1992 [1985]), coedited with David R. Counts. She has also published numerous journal articles and book chapters on mythology, cargo belief and activity, political and economic change, aging and dying, domestic violence, and female suicide.

CHARLES B. CRAWFORD, a professor of psychology at Simon Fraser University, conducts research on the reproductive suppression model of anorexic behavior in women. He is the coeditor (with Dennis Krebs) of *Handbook of Evolutionary Psychology: Ideas, Issues, and Applications* (1998).

PATRICIA DRAPER is a professor of anthropology at the University of Nebraska whose research interests include hunter gatherers, African ethnography, and cross-cultural studies of aging and adult development. Her most recent publications include chapters in two edited collections, *In Balancing Acts: Women and the Process of Social Change* (1992) and *The Evolving Female* (1997).

RITA S. GALLIN, an associate professor of sociology at Michigan State University, has published extensively on economic development and social change in Taiwan in journals and edited volumes. She is the founding editor of *The Women and International Development Annual,* published by Westview Press.

MARY ELAINE HEGLAND teaches social-cultural anthropology, with an emphasis on Middle Eastern and women's studies, at Santa Clara University. She conducted field research on religion, ritual, and revolution in an Iranian village during 1978 and 1979 and currently is working on research projects with Iranian women in the United States. She has published articles in such journals as *Political and Legal Anthropology Review, SIGNS,* and the *American Ethnologist* and contributed essays to *Mixed Blessings: Gender and Religious Fundamentalism Cross-Culturally* (1997) and *Women and Revolution: Global Expressions* (1998), among other collections.

VIRGINIA KERNS, an associate professor and chairperson of the Department of Anthropology at the College of William and Mary, is the author of *Women and the Ancestors: Black Carib Kinship and Ritual* (1983), the coeditor (with Judith K. Brown) of *In Her Prime: New Views of Middle-Aged Women* (2d ed., 1992), and a former associate editor of the *American Ethnologist.* She serves on the board of directors of the Williamsburg (Virginia) Task Force on Battered Women/Sexual Assault.

MICHAEL LAMBEK is a professor of anthropology at the University of Toronto. He is the coeditor (with Paul Antze) of *Tense Past: Cultural Essays in Trauma and Memory* (1996) and (with Andrew Strathern) of *Bodies and Persons: Comparative Perspectives from Africa and Melanesia* (1998) and the author of *Human Spirits: A Cultural Account of Trance in Mayotte* (1981) and *Knowledge and Practice in Mayotte: Local Discourses of Islam, Sorcery, and Spirit Possession* (1993), as well as numerous articles on various aspects of gender, personhood, ritual, and knowledge.

SHIREEN LATEEF, an Indo-Fijian anthropologist, taught at the School of Early Childhood Studies at the University of Melbourne. She earned a Ph.D. degree from Monash University in Victoria, Australia, following field research among Indo-Fijian women in Suva, Fiji. Her publications include a chapter in *Development in the Pacific: What Women Say* (1986).

DAVID LEVINSON, a cultural anthropologist and, since 1995, coprincipal in Berkshire Reference Works, Great Barrington, Massachusetts, was affiliated with the Human Relations Area Files for twenty-one years. He is the editor of the *Encyclopedia of Marriage and Family* (1995), the *Encyclopedia of World Cultures* (1990–95; CD-ROM, 1998), and the *Encyclopedia of Human Emotion* (1999), as well as Human Experience Series for ABC-Clio (1994–98). His research interests are in human relations and social issues.

HARRIET D. LYONS is an associate professor in the Department of Anthropology and Classical Studies at the University of Waterloo and also teaches in the Women's Studies Program. She has published many articles on the history of sexuality and the study of mass communications in Nigeria, some in collaboration with her husband, Andrew Lyons.

NANCY MCDOWELL, who taught anthropology at Franklin and Marshall College for many years, is a professor of anthropology at Beloit College. She conducted field research in Bun, Papua New Guinea, in 1972–73, 1977, and 1981. Her publications include *Reproductive Decision-Making and the Value of Children in Rural Papua New Guinea* (1987) and *The Mundugumor: From the Field Notes of Margaret Mead and Reo Fortune* (1991).

LAURIS MCKEE, Associate Professor Emerita at Franklin and Marshall College, has conducted field research on gender issues, sex differentials in socialization, and ethnomedical beliefs and practices in the Andean region of Ecuador since 1975. Her publications include the edited volume *Child Survival and Sex Differentials in the Treatment of Children* (1984) and essays in *Portraits of Culture* (1994) and *Women and Economic Change: Andean Perspectives* (1997). *Evil Wind, Evil Air,* one of her five video documentaries on Ecuadorian ethnomedicine, won an Award for Excellence from the Society for Visual Anthropology.

BARBARA DIANE MILLER, an associate professor of anthropology and international affairs at George Washington University, has long studied women's status in India. Her publications include *The Endangered Sex: Neglect of Female Children in Rural North India* (2d ed., 1997); two edited collections, *Sex and Gender Hierarchies* (1993) and *Hair: Its Power and Meaning in Asian Cultures* (1998); and *Cultural Anthropology* (1999), a textbook.

WILLIAM E. MITCHELL, Professor Emeritus of Anthropology at the University of Vermont, has conducted fieldwork among the Lujere, Iatmul, and Wape peoples of Papua New Guinea, the Chinese and Jews of New York City, and child patients at a mental institution. His research interests center on problems of family and kinship, psychological anthropology, exchange theory, and ethnotherapy. His publications include *The Bamboo Fire: Fieldwork with the New Guinea Wape* (1987); *Clowning as Critical Practice: Performance Humor in the South Pacific* (1992), an edited collection; and *Magical Curing* (videocassette, 1988), an ethnographic film about the Wape of Papua New Guinea.

JILL NASH, a professor and chairperson of the Department of Anthropology at the State University College at Buffalo, New York, is the author of *Matriliny and Modernisation: The Nagovisi of South Bougainville* (1974) as well as numerous articles on the Nagovisi of North Solomons Province, Papua New Guinea. Her major research interests are Melanesia, gender, and kinship.

RICHARD SCAGLION, a professor of anthropology at the University of Pittsburgh who specializes in law and conflict studies, was the director of customary law development for the Law Reform Commission of Papua New Guinea. His publications include the edited collections *Homicide Compensation in Papua New Guinea: Problems and Prospects* (1981), *Customary Law in Papua New Guinea: A Melanesian View* (1983), and *Customary Law and Legal Development in Papua New Guinea* (1987).

KAREN KELJO TRACY, an associate professor of psychology at Marygrove College, conducts research on cultural diversity, including the cultures of disabilities, and the application of evolutionary theory to aesthetic appreciation. Her publications include a chapter in *Consumers as Providers in Psychiatric Rehabilitation* (1997).

JEAN G. ZORN is a professor of law at the City University of New York Law School. Her major research interests are in the customary law of Papua New Guinea and the relations between customary law and state legal systems.

INDEX

Typeset in 10.5/13 Minion
with Minion display
Designed by Paula Newcomb
Composed by Jim Proefrock
at the University of Illinois Press
Manufactured by Versa Press, Inc.

University of Illinois Press
1325 South Oak Street
Champaign, IL 61820-6903
www.press.uillinois.edu